Grammar in use

Intermediate

with answers

SECOND EDITION

D1157276

Raymond Murphy

with William R. Smalzer

CAMBRIDGE UNIVERSITY PRESS
Cambridge, New York, Melbourne, Madrid, Cape Town, Singapore, São Paulo, Delhi

Cambridge University Press
32 Avenue of the Americas, New York, NY 10013–2473, USA

www.cambridge.org
Information on this title: www.cambridge.org/9780521528764

First published 1989
Second edition 2000
22nd printing 2008

Printed in Hong Kong, China, by Golden Cup Printing Company Limited

A catalog record for this book is available from the British Library

Library of Congress Cataloging in Publication data available

ISBN 978-0-521-62598-2 pack consisting of student's book with answers and audio CD
ISBN 978-0-521-62598-5 pack consisting of student's book without answers and audio CD
ISBN 978-0-521-52876-4 student's book with answers/Korea
ISBN 978-0-521-79720-7 workbook with answers
ISBN 978-0-521-79719-1 workbook without answers

Book design: Adventure House, NYC
Layout: Kate Winter
Illustrations: Randy Jones and Susann Ferris Jones

오디오 카세트 별도 판매 (목차에 표시된 오디오 부분)

Contents

If you are not sure which units you need to study, use the STUDY GUIDE on page 294.

If you are not sure which units you need to study,
use the **STUDY GUIDE** on page 294.

**If you are not sure which units you need to study,
use the STUDY GUIDE on page 294.**

**If you are not sure which units you need to study,
use the STUDY GUIDE on page 294.**

To the Student

This book is for students who want help with North American English grammar. It is written for you to use without a teacher. The book will be useful for you if you are not sure of the answers to questions like these:

- What is the difference between *I did* and *I have done?*
- When do we use *will* for the future?
- What is the structure after *I wish?*
- When do we say *used to do* and when do we say *used to doing?*
- When do we use *the?*
- What is the difference between *like* and *as?*

These and many other points of English grammar are explained in the book and there are exercises on each point.

Level

The book is intended mainly for intermediate students (students who have already studied the basic grammar of English). It concentrates on structures which intermediate students want to use but which often cause difficulty. Advanced students who have problems with grammar will also find the book useful. The book is *not* suitable for beginning learners.

How the book is organized

There are 133 units in the book. Each unit concentrates on a particular point of grammar. Some problems (for example, the present perfect or the use of *the*) are covered in more than one unit. For a list of units, see the *Contents* at the beginning of the book.

Each unit consists of two facing pages. On the left there are explanations and examples; on the right there are exercises. At the back of the book there is an *Answer Key* for you to check your answers to the exercises (page 302).

There are also six *Appendices* at the back of the book (pages 268–276). These include irregular verbs, summaries of verb forms, spelling and British English.

Finally, there is a detailed *Index* at the very end of the book (page 334).

How to use the book

The units are not in order of difficulty, so it is not intended that you work through the book from beginning to end. Every learner has different problems and you should use this book to help you with the grammar that *you* find difficult. It is suggested that you work in this way:

- Use the *Contents* or *Index* to find which unit deals with the point you are interested in.
- If you are not sure which units you need to study, use the *Study Guide* on page 294.
- Study the explanation and examples on the left-hand page of the unit you have chosen.
- Do the exercises on the right-hand page.
- Check your answers in the *Answer Key*.
- If your answers are not correct, study the left-hand page again to see what went wrong.

You can, of course, use the book simply as a reference book without doing the exercises.

Additional Exercises

At the back of the book there are *Additional Exercises* (pages 277–293). These exercises bring together some of the grammar points from a number of different units. For example, Exercise 14 brings together grammar points from Units 25–31. You can use these exercises for extra practice after you have studied and practiced the grammar in the units concerned.

Audio CD

An audio CD is available for use with this book. It contains recordings of example sentences from carefully selected units in the book. These units are marked with this symbol 🎧 in the *Contents*. It is suggested that you use the CD to listen to the grammatical structures taught in these units, recorded in natural-sounding speech.

To the Teacher

Grammar in Use Intermediate was written as a self-study grammar book but teachers may also find it useful as additional course material in cases where further work on grammar is necessary.

The book will probably be most useful at middle- and upper-intermediate levels (where all or nearly all of the material will be relevant), and can serve both as a basis for revision and as a means for practicing new structures. It will also be useful for some more advanced students who have problems with grammar and need a book for reference and practice. The book is not intended to be used by beginning learners.

The units are organized in grammatical categories (*Present and past, Articles and nouns, Prepositions*, etc.). They are not ordered according to level of difficulty, so the book should not be worked through from beginning to end. It should be used selectively and flexibly in accordance with the grammar syllabus being used and the difficulties students are having.

The book can be used for immediate consolidation or for later revision or remedial work. It might be used by the whole class or by individual students needing extra help. The left-hand pages (explanations and examples) are written for the student to use individually but they may, of course, be used by the teacher as a source of ideas and information on which to base a lesson. The student then has the left-hand page as a record of what has been taught and can refer to it in the future. The exercises can be done individually, in class or as homework. Alternatively (and additionally), individual students can be directed to study certain units of the book by themselves if they have particular difficulties not shared by other students in their class. The forms presented in *Grammar in Use* are those which are most used and generally accepted in standard spoken North American English. Some native speakers may regard some of these usages as "incorrect," for example the use of *who* as an object pronoun, or the use of *they* to mean "he or she." In this book, such usages are treated as standard.

This new edition of *Grammar in Use* contains a set of *Additional Exercises* (pages 277–293). These exercises provide "mixed" practice by bringing together grammar points from a number of different units.

A classroom edition of *Grammar in Use* is also available. It contains no answer key and some teachers might therefore prefer it for use with their students.

Grammar in Use Intermediate Second Edition

While this is a completely new edition of *Grammar in Use*, the general structure and character of the original book remain the same. The main changes from the original are:

- There are new units on compound nouns (Unit 77), *there* and *it* (Unit 81), *each* and *every* (Unit 88) and *by* (Unit 124).

- Some units have been redesigned, for example Unit 71 (*school* or *the school*) and Unit 92 on relative clauses.

- Some of the material has been reorganized. For example, Units 3–4 (present continuous and simple present) and Units 66–67 (countable and uncountable nouns) correspond to single units in the original edition. The material in Units 128–132 (verb + preposition) has been completely rearranged.

- Some of the units have been reordered and nearly all units have a different number from the original edition. A few units have been moved to different parts of the book. For example, Unit 33 (*had better* and *it's time* . . .) is the new rewritten version of the original Unit 62.

- On the left-hand pages, many of the explanations have been rewritten and many of the examples have been changed.

- Many of the original exercises have been either modified or completely replaced with new exercises.

- The Second Edition is available both with and without answers at the back of the book.

- In the edition with answers there is a new *Study Guide* to help students decide which units to study.

- There are two new appendices on future forms and British English. The other appendices have been revised.

- There is a new section of *Additional Exercises* at the back of the book (see page 277).

- There is a new Audio CD included with this edition, affixed to the inside back cover of the book. It contains recordings of example sentences.

Grammar *in use*

Intermediate

with answers

Present Continuous (*I am doing*)

a. 연속적인, 계속적인, 끊어지않는 ; [문법] 진행형의

: 현재 진행형

A

Study this example situation:

Ann is in her car. She is on her way to work.
She **is driving** to work.

This means: she is driving now, at the time of
speaking. The action is not finished.

Am/is/are -ing is the *present continuous*:

I	**am** (= I'm)	driving
he/she/it	**is** (= he's, etc.)	working
we/you/they	**are** (= we're, etc.)	doing, etc.

B

~을 한창 하는 중에

I am doing something = I'm in the middle of doing something; I've started doing it and I
haven't finished yet. Often the action is happening at the time of speaking:

- ■ Please don't make so much noise. **I'm working.** (*not* I work)
- ■ "Where's Lauren?" "She's **taking** a bath." (*not* She takes a bath)
- ■ Let's go out now. It **isn't raining** anymore. (*not* It doesn't rain)
- ■ (*at a party*) Hello, Lisa. **Are** you **enjoying** the party? (*not* Do you enjoy)
- ■ I'm tired. **I'm going** to bed now. Good night!

But the action is **not** **necessarily** happening at the time of speaking. For example:

반드시 ~은 아니다 [부분부정]
ad. 반드시

Tom and Ann are talking. Tom says:

지금, 현재

I'm reading an interesting book at the moment.
I'll lend it to you when I've finished it.

Tom is not reading the book at the time of speaking.
He means that he has started it but has not finished it yet.
He is in the middle of reading it.

Here are some more examples:

- ■ Maria wants to work in Italy, so she **is studying** Italian. (but perhaps she isn't studying
  Italian exactly at the time of speaking)
- ■ Some friends of mine **are building** their own house.

C

We use the present continuous when we talk about things happening in a period around now
(for example, **today / this week / tonight**, etc.):

- ■ "You're **working** hard today." "Yes, I have a lot to do." (*not* You work hard today)
- ■ "Is Sarah **working** this week?" "No, she's on vacation."

We use the present continuous when we talk about changes happening now or around now:

- ■ The population of the world **is rising** very fast. (*not* rises)
- ■ Is your English **getting** better? (*not* Does your English get better?)

Exercises

1.1 Complete the sentences using one of the following verbs in the correct form.

~~come~~ ~~get~~ happen ~~look~~ ~~make~~ ~~start~~ ~~stay~~ try ~~work~~

1. "You *'re working* hard today." "Yes, I have a lot to do."
2. I *'m looking* for Christine. Do you know where she is?
3. It *'s getting* dark. Should I turn on the light?
4. They don't have anywhere to live at the moment. They *'re staying* with friends until they find a place.
5. "Ann! Let's go!" "OK, I *'m coming* ."
6. Do you have an umbrella? It *'s starting* to rain.
7. You *'re making* a lot of noise. Could you please be quieter? I *'m trying* to concentrate.
8. Why are all these people here? What *'s happening* ?

1.2 Use the words in parentheses to complete the questions.

1. "*Is Brad working* this week?" "No, he's on vacation." (Brad / work)
2. Why *are you looking* at me like that? What's the matter? (you / look)
3. "Jenny is a student at the university." "Is she? What *'s she studying* ?" (she / study)
4. *Is anybody listening* to the radio, or can I turn it off? (anybody / listen)
5. How is your English? *Is it getting* better? (it / get)

1.3 Put the verb into the correct form. Sometimes you need the negative (*I'm not doing*, etc.).

1. I'm tired. I *'m going* (go) to bed now. Good night!
2. We can go out now. It *isn't raining* (rain) anymore.
3. Laura phoned me last night. She's on vacation in France. She *'s having* (have) a great time and doesn't want to come back.
4. I want to lose weight, so this week I *'m not eating* (eat) lunch.
5. Angela has just started evening classes. She *'s studying* (study) German.
6. I think Dave and Amy had an argument. They *aren't speaking* (speak) to each other.

1.4 Read this conversation between Brian and Sarah. Put the verbs into the correct form.

Sarah: Brian! I haven't seen you in ages. What (1) *are you doing* (you / do) these days?
Brian: I (2) *'m training* (train) to be a police officer.
Sarah: Really? What's it like? (3) *Are you enjoying* (you / enjoy) it?
Brian: It's all right. How about you?
Sarah: Well, actually, I (4) *'m not working* (not / work) right now.
   I (5) *'m trying* (try) to find a job, but it's not easy. But I'm pretty busy.
   I (6) *'m painting* (paint) my apartment.
Brian: (7) *Are you doing* (you / do) it alone?
Sarah: No, some friends of mine (8) *are helping* (help) me.

1.5 Complete the sentences using one of these verbs: change fall get increase ~~rise~~
You don't have to use all the verbs, and you can use a verb more than once.

1. The population of the world *is rising* very fast.
2. Robert is still sick, but he *'s getting* better slowly.
3. The world *is changing* . Things never stay the same.
4. The cost of living *is rising / increasing* . Every year things are more expensive.
5. The economic situation is already very bad, and it *is getting* worse.

3

Simple Present (*I do*)

Study this example situation:

Alex is a bus driver, but now he is in bed asleep. So:
He is not driving a bus. (He is asleep.)
but He **drives** a bus. (He is a bus driver.)
drive(s)/work(s)/do(es), etc., is the *simple present.*

I/we/you/they	**drive/work/do**, etc.
he/she/it	**drives/works/does**, etc.

We use the simple present to talk about things in general. We use it to say that something happens all the time or repeatedly or that something is true in general. It is not important whether the action is happening at the time of speaking:

- Nurses **take** care of patients in hospitals.
- I usually **leave** for work at 8:00 A.M.
- The earth **goes** around the sun.

Remember that we say **he/she/it -s**. Don't forget the **s**:

- I **work** . . . *but* He **works** . . .   They **teach** . . . *but* My sister **teaches** . . .

For spelling (**-s** or **-es**), see Appendix 5.

We use **do/does** to make questions and negative sentences:

do	I/we/you/they	**work?**	I/we/you/they	**don't**	**work**
does	he/she/it	**come?**	he/she/it	**doesn't**	**come**
		do?			**do**

- I come from Canada. Where **do** you **come** from?
- "Would you like a cigarette?" "No, thanks. I **don't smoke**."
- What **does** this word **mean**? (*not* What means this word?)
- Rice **doesn't grow** in cold climates.

In the following examples **do** is also the main verb:

- "What **do** you **do**?" (= What's your job?) "I work in a department store."
- He's so lazy. He **doesn't do** anything to help me. (*not* He doesn't anything)

We use the simple present when we say how often we do things:

- I **get** up at 8:00 **every morning**. (*not* I'm getting)
- **How often do** you **go** to the dentist? (*not* How often are you going?)
- Julie **doesn't drink** coffee **very often**.
- In the summer John usually **plays** tennis **once or twice a week**.

Note the position of **always/never/usually**, etc. (before the main verb):

- Sue **always looks** happy. (*not* Sue looks always)
- I **never drink** coffee at night.
- What time do you **usually get** home after work?

For word order, see also Unit 107.

Exercises

2.1 Complete the sentences using one of the following:

cause(s)   close(s)   connect(s)   drink(s)   live(s)   open(s)   ~~speak(s)~~   take(s)

1. Ann _speaks_____ German very well.
2. I never _____ coffee.
3. The swimming pool _____ at 9:00 and _____ at 6:30 every day.
4. Bad driving _____ many accidents.
5. My parents _____ in a very small apartment.
6. The Olympic Games _____ place every four years.
7. The Panama Canal _____ the Atlantic and Pacific oceans.

2.2 Put the verb into the correct form.

1. Jason _doesn't drink_____ (not / drink) coffee very often.
2. What time _____ (the banks / close)?
3. I have a car, but I _____ (not / use) it very often.
4. "What _____ (you / do)?" "I'm an electrical engineer."
5. It _____ (take) me an hour to get to work. How long _____ (it / take) you?
6. I _____ (play) the piano, but I _____ (not / play) very well.
7. I don't understand this sentence. What _____ (this word / mean)?

2.3 Use one of the following verbs to complete these sentences. Sometimes you need the negative.

believe   eat   flow   ~~go~~   ~~grow~~   make   rise   tell   translate

1. The earth _goes_____ around the sun.
2. Rice _doesn't grow__ in Canada.
3. The sun _____ in the east.
4. Bees _____ honey.
5. Vegetarians _____ meat.
6. An atheist _____ in God.
7. An interpreter _____ from one language to another.
8. A liar is someone who _____ the truth.
9. The Amazon River _____ into the Atlantic Ocean.

2.4 Ask Liz questions about herself and her family.

1. You know that Liz plays tennis. You want to know how often. Ask her.
   How often _do you play tennis_____ ?
2. Perhaps Liz's sister plays tennis, too. You want to know. Ask Liz.
   _____ your sister _____ ?
3. You know that Liz reads a newspaper every day. You want to know which one. Ask her.
   _____
4. You know that Liz's brother works. You want to know what he does. Ask Liz.
   _____
5. You know that Liz goes to the movies a lot. You want to know how often. Ask her.
   _____
6. You don't know where Liz's mother lives. Ask Liz.
   _____
7. You know that Liz works every day, but you want to know what time she starts work. Ask her.
   _____

UNIT 3

Present Continuous and Simple Present (1)
(*I am doing* and *I do*)

A

Present continuous (**I am doing**)
We use the *present continuous* for something that is happening at or around the time of speaking. The action is not finished.

I am doing

past	now	future

- The water **is boiling.** Could you turn it off?
- Listen to those people. What language **are** they **speaking?**
- Let's go out. It **isn't raining** now.
- A: Don't disturb me. I'm busy.
  B: Why? What **are** you **doing?**
- **I'm going** to bed now. Good night.
- Maria is in Vancouver now. She's **learning** English.

Use the present continuous for temporary situations:
- **I'm living** with some friends until I find an apartment.
- "You**'re working** hard today." "Yes, I've got a lot to do."

See Unit 1 for more information.

Simple present (**I do**)
We use the *simple present* for things in general or things that happen repeatedly.

I do

past	now	future

- Water **boils** at 100 degrees Celsius.
- Excuse me, **do** you **speak** English?
- It **doesn't rain** very much in the summer.
- What **do** you usually **do** on weekends?
- What **do** you **do?** (= What's your job?)
- I always **go** to bed before midnight.
- Most people **learn** to swim when they are children.

Use the simple present for permanent situations:
- My parents **live** in Boston. They have lived there all their lives.
- John isn't lazy. He **works** very hard most of the time.

See Unit 2 for more information.

B

I always do and **I'm always doing**
Usually we say "I **always do** something" (= I do it every time):
- I **always go** to work by car (*not* I'm always going)

You can also say "I**'m always doing** something," but this has a different meaning.
For example:

I've lost my key again. **I'm always losing** things.

"**I'm always losing** things" does not mean that I lose things every time. It means that I lose things too often or more often than normal.

You**'re always -ing** means that you do something very often, more often than the speaker thinks is normal or reasonable.

- You**'re always watching** TV. You should do something more active.
- John is never satisfied. He**'s always complaining.**

Present Continuous and Simple Present (2) Unit 4   **Present Tenses with a Future Meaning** Unit 18

Exercises

3.1 Are the underlined verbs right or wrong? Correct the verbs that are wrong.

1. Water <u>boils</u> at 100 degrees Celsius.   *RIGHT*
2. The water <u>boils</u>. Could you turn it off?   *is boiling*
3. Look! That man <u>tries</u> to open the door of your car.   _____
4. Can you hear those people? What <u>do</u> they <u>talk</u> about?   _____
5. The moon <u>goes</u> around the earth.   _____
6. I have to go now. It <u>gets</u> late.   _____
7. I usually <u>go</u> to work by car.   _____
8. "Hurry up! It's time to leave." "OK, I <u>come</u>."   _____
9. I hear you've got a new job. How <u>does</u> it <u>go</u>?   _____

3.2 Put the verb in the correct form, present continuous or simple present.

1. Let's go out. It *isn't raining* (not / rain) now.
2. Julia is very good at languages. She *speaks* (speak) four languages very well.
3. Hurry up! Everybody _____ (wait) for you.
4. "_____ (you / listen) to the radio?" "No, you can turn it off."
5. "_____ (you / listen) to the radio every day?" "No, just occasionally."
6. The Nile River _____ (flow) into the Mediterranean.
7. The river _____ (flow) very fast today – much faster than usual.
8. We usually _____ (grow) vegetables in our garden, but this year we _____ (not / grow) any.
9. "How is your English?" "Not bad. It _____ (improve) slowly."
10. Matt is in San Francisco right now. He _____ (stay) at the Pelton Hotel. He _____ (always / stay) there when he's in San Francisco.
11. Can we stop walking soon? I _____ (start) to feel tired.
12. "Do you know how to drive?" "I _____ (learn). My father _____ (teach) me."
13. Usually I _____ (finish) work at 5:00, but this week I _____ (work) until 6:00 to earn some extra money.
14. My parents _____ (live) in Chicago. They were born there and have never lived anywhere else. Where _____ (your parents / live)?
15. Erica _____ (look) for a place to live. She _____ (stay) with her sister until she finds a place.
16. "What _____ (your father / do)?" "He's an architect, but he _____ (not / work) at the moment."
17. The train is never late. It _____ (always / leave) on time.
18. Jim is very messy. He _____ (always / leave) his things all over the place.

3.3 Finish B's sentences. Use *always -ing* (see Section B).

1. *A:* I'm afraid I've lost my key again.
   B: Not again! *You're always losing your key.*
2. *A:* The car has broken down again.
   B: That car is a pain. It _____.
3. *A:* Look! You made the same mistake again.
   B: Oh no, not again! I _____.
4. *A:* Oh, I forgot my books again.
   B: That's typical! You _____.

Present Continuous and Simple Present (2)
(I am doing and I do)

We can use *continuous tenses* only for actions and happenings (they **are eating** / it **is raining**, etc.). Some verbs (for example, **know** and **like**) are not action verbs. You cannot say "I am knowing" or "they are liking"; you can only say **I know, they like.**

The following verbs are not normally used in continuous tenses:

like	love	hate	want	need	prefer	
know	realize	suppose	mean	understand	believe	remember
belong	contain	consist	depend	seem		

- I'm hungry. I **want** something to eat. (*not* I'm wanting)
- **Do** you **understand** what I **mean**?
- Kim **doesn't seem** very happy right now.

When **think** means "believe," do not use the continuous:
- What **do** you **think** (= believe) will happen? (*not* What are you thinking)

but - You look serious. What **are** you **thinking** about? (= What is going on in your mind?)
- I'm **thinking** of quitting my job. (= I am considering)

When **have** means "possess," etc., do not use the continuous (see Unit 16):
- We're enjoying our trip. We **have** a nice room in the hotel. (*not* We're having)

but - We're enjoying our trip. We'**re having** a great time.

See   hear   smell   taste

We normally use the *simple present* (*not* continuous) with these verbs:
- **Do** you **see** that man over there? (*not* Are you seeing)
- This room **smells**. Let's open a window.

We often use **can + see/hear/smell/taste**:
- Listen! **Can** you **hear** something?

Note that you can say **I'm seeing** when the meaning is "having a meeting with" (especially in the future – see Unit 18A):
- I'm **seeing** the manager tomorrow morning.

He is selfish and **He is being selfish**

He'**s being** = He's behaving / He's acting. Compare:
- I can't understand why he'**s being** so selfish. He isn't usually like that.
  (**being** selfish = behaving selfishly at the moment)

but - He never thinks about other people. He **is** very selfish. (*not* He is being)
  (= he is selfish generally, not only at the moment)

We use **am/is/are being** to say how somebody is behaving. It is not usually possible in other sentences:
- It's hot today. (*not* It is being hot)
- Sarah **is** very tired. (*not* is being tired)

Look and **feel**

You can use simple present or continuous to say how somebody looks or feels now:
- You **look** good today.   *or*   You'**re looking** good today.
- How **do** you **feel** now?   *or*   How **are** you **feeling** now?

but - I usually **feel** tired in the morning. (*not* I'm usually feeling)

Present Continuous and Simple Present (1) Unit 3   Present Tenses with a Future Meaning Unit 18

Exercises

4.1 Are the underlined verbs right or wrong? Correct the ones that are wrong.

1. I'm seeing the manager tomorrow morning. *RIGHT*
2. I'm feeling hungry. Is there anything to eat? _____
3. Are you believing in God? _____
4. This sauce is great. It's tasting really good. _____
5. I'm thinking this is your key. Am I right? _____

4.2 Look at the pictures. Use the words in parentheses to make sentences. (You should also study Unit 3 before you do this exercise.)

1. (you / not / seem / very happy today)
   You don't seem very happy today.

2. (what / you / do?)
   _____
   Be quiet! (I / think)

3. (who / this umbrella / belong to?)
   _____
   I have no idea.

4. (dinner / smell / good)
   _____

5. Excuse me. (anybody / sit / here?)
   _____
   No, go ahead.

6. Can I call you back in half an hour? (I / have / dinner)
   _____

4.3 Put the verb into the correct form, present continuous or simple present.

1. Are you hungry? *Do you want* _____ something to eat? (you / want)
2. Don't put the dictionary away. I _____ it. (use)
3. Don't put the dictionary away. I _____ it. (need)
4. Who is that man? What _____ ? (he / want)
5. Who is that man? Why _____ at us? (he / look)
6. George says he's 80 years old, but nobody _____ him. (believe)
7. She told me her name, but I _____ it now. (not / remember)
8. I _____ of selling my car. (think) Would you be interested in buying it?
9. I _____ you should sell your car. (think) You _____ it very often. (not / use)
10. Air _____ mainly of nitrogen and oxygen. (consist)

4.4 Complete the sentences using the most appropriate form of *be*, simple present *(am/is/are)* or present continuous *(am/is/are being)*.

1. I can't understand why *he's being* _____ so selfish. He isn't usually like that.
2. Jack _____ very nice to me tonight. I wonder why.
3. You'll like Jill when you meet her. She _____ very nice.
4. You're usually very patient, so why _____ so unreasonable about waiting five more minutes?
5. Why isn't Sarah at work today? _____ sick?

Simple Past (I did)

A

Study this example:

Wolfgang Amadeus Mozart was an Austrian musician and composer. He **lived** from 1756 to 1791. He **started** composing at the age of five and **wrote** more than 600 pieces of music. He **was** only 35 years old when he **died**.

Lived/started/wrote/was/died are all *simple past*.

B

Very often the simple past ends in **-ed** (*regular* verbs):
- ■ I work in a travel agency now. Before that I **worked** in a department store.
- ■ We **invited** them to our party, but they **decided** not to come.
- ■ The police **stopped** me for speeding.
- ■ She **passed** her exam because she **studied** very hard.

For spelling (**stopped, studied,** etc.), see Appendix 5.

But many verbs are *irregular*. This means that the simple past does not end in **-ed**.
For example:

write	→	**wrote**	■ Mozart **wrote** more than 600 pieces of music.
see	→	**saw**	■ We **saw** Rosa in town a few days ago.
go	→	**went**	■ I **went** to the movies three times last week.
cost	→	**cost**	■ This house **cost** $89,000 in 1996.

For a list of irregular verbs, see Appendix 1.

C

In questions and negatives we use **did/didn't** + *base form* (**enjoy/see/go**, etc.):

I she they	enjoyed saw went		did	you she they	enjoy? see? go?		I she they	didn't	enjoy see go

- ■ *A:* **Did** you **go** out last night?
  B: Yes, I **went** to the movies, but I **didn't enjoy** the film much.
- ■ "When **did** Mr. Thomas **die**?" "About ten years ago."
- ■ They **didn't invite** her to the party, so she **didn't go**.
- ■ "**Did** you **have** time to write the letter?" "No, I **didn't**."

Be careful when **do** is the main verb in the sentence.
- ■ I **didn't do** anything. (*not* I didn't anything)

D

The past of **be** (**am/is/are**) is **was/were**:

I/he/she/it **was/wasn't** we/you/they **were/weren't**	**was** I/he/she/it? **were** we/you/they?

Note that we do not use **did** in negatives and questions with **was/were**:
- ■ I **was** angry because they **were** late.
- ■ **Was** the weather good when you **were** on vacation?
- ■ They **weren't** able to come because they **were** so busy.
- ■ **Did** you **go** out last night, or **were** you too tired?

Exercises

5.1 Read what Debbie says about a typical working day:

DEBBIE

> I usually get up at 7:00 and have a big breakfast. I walk to work, which takes me about half an hour. I start work at 8:45. I never have lunch. I finish work at 5:00. I'm always tired when I get home. I usually make dinner at night. I don't usually go out. I go to bed at about 11:00. I always sleep well.

Yesterday was a typical working day for Debbie. Write what she did or didn't do yesterday.

1. *She got up at 7:00.*
2. She _____ a big breakfast.
3. She _____ .
4. It _____ to get to work.
5. _____ at 8:45.
6. _____ lunch.
7. _____ at 5:00.
8. _____ tired when _____ home.
9. _____ dinner.
10. _____ out last night.
11. _____ at 11:00.
12. _____ well last night.

5.2 Complete the sentences using the following verbs in the correct form:

buy   catch   cost   drink   fall   hurt   sell   spend   teach   throw   win   ~~write~~

1. Mozart *wrote* _____ more than 600 pieces of music.
2. "How did you learn to drive?" "My mother _____ me."
3. We couldn't afford to keep our car, so we _____ it.
4. I was very thirsty. I _____ the water very quickly.
5. Sam and I played tennis yesterday. He's much better than I am, so he _____ easily.
6. Dave _____ down the stairs this morning and _____ his leg.
7. Jim _____ the ball to Sue, who _____ it.
8. Jessica _____ a lot of money yesterday. She _____ a dress that _____ $200.

5.3 A friend has just come back from vacation. Ask him about it. Write your questions.

1. (where / go?) *Where did you go?*
2. (go alone?) _____
3. (food / good?) _____
4. (stay / at a hotel?) _____
5. (rent / a car?) _____
6. (the weather / nice?) _____
7. (what / do in the evenings?) _____

5.4 Complete the sentences. Put the verb into the correct form, positive or negative.

1. It was warm, so I *took* _____ off my coat. (take)
2. The movie wasn't very good. I *didn't enjoy* _____ it very much. (enjoy)
3. I knew Sarah was very busy, so I _____ her. (bother)
4. I was very tired, so I _____ to bed early. (go)
5. The bed was very uncomfortable. I _____ very well. (sleep)
6. We went to Kate's house, but she _____ at home. (be)
7. It was a funny situation, but nobody _____ . (laugh)
8. The window was open, and a bird _____ into the room. (fly)
9. The hotel wasn't very expensive. It _____ very much. (cost)
10. I was in a hurry, so I _____ time to call you. (have)
11. It was hard work carrying the bags. They _____ very heavy. (be)

Past Continuous (*I was doing*)

Study this example situation:

Yesterday Karen and Jim played tennis. They began at 10:00 and finished at 11:30.
So at 10:30 they **were playing** tennis.

They **were playing** = they were in the middle of playing. They had not finished playing.

Was/were -ing is the *past continuous:*

| I/he/she/it **was** | **playing/doing/working**, etc. |
| we/you/they **were** | |

We use the past continuous to say that somebody was in the middle of doing something at a certain time. The action or situation had already started before this time but had not finished:

I started doing   I finished doing

⟵   **I was doing**   ⟶

past   *past*   *now*

- This time last year I **was living** in Brazil.
- What **were** you **doing** at 10:00 last night?
- I waved at her, but she **wasn't looking.**

Compare the *past continuous* (**I was doing**) and *simple past* (**I did**):

Past continuous (in the middle of an action)	*Simple past* (complete action)
■ I **was walking** home when I met Dave. (= in the middle of walking home)	■ I **walked** home after the party last night. (= all the way, completely)
■ Nicole **was watching** TV when the phone rang.	■ Nicole **watched** TV a lot when she was sick last year.

We often use the simple past and the past continuous together to say that something happened in the middle of something else:
- Matt **burned** his hand while he **was cooking** dinner.
- I **saw** you in the park yesterday. You **were sitting** on the grass and **reading** a book.
- While I **was working** in the garden, I **hurt** my back.

But we use the simple past to say that one thing happened after another:
- I **was walking** downtown when I **saw** Dave. So I **stopped** and we **talked** for a while.

Compare:

■ When Beth arrived, we **were having** dinner. (= We had already started dinner.)	■ When Beth arrived, we **had** dinner. (= Beth arrived and then we had dinner.)

Some verbs (for example, **know** and **want**) are not normally used in the continuous (see Unit 4A):
- We were good friends. We **knew** each other well. (*not* We were knowing)
- I was enjoying the party, but Chris **wanted** to go home. (*not* was wanting)

Exercises

6.1 **What were you doing at the following times? Write one sentence as in the examples. The past continuous is not always necessary (see sentence 2).**

1. (at 8:00 last night) *I was having dinner with some friends.*
2. (at 5:00 last Monday) *I was on a bus on my way to class.*
3. (at 10:15 yesterday morning) _____
4. (at 7:45 last night) _____
5. (half an hour ago) _____

6.2 **Use your own ideas to complete these sentences. Use the past continuous.**

1. Matt burned his hand while he *was cooking dinner* .
2. The doorbell rang while I _____ .
3. We saw an accident while we _____ .
4. Lauren fell asleep while she _____ .
5. The television was on, but nobody _____ .

6.3 **Put the verbs into the correct form, past continuous or simple past.**

1

I _saw_ (see) Sue downtown yesterday, but she _____ (not / see) me. She _____ (look) the other way.

2

I _____ (meet) Tom and Ann at the airport a few weeks ago. They _____ (go) to Boston and I _____ (go) to Montreal. We _____ (talk) while we _____ (wait) for our flights.

3

I _____ (ride) my bicycle yesterday when suddenly a man _____ (step) out into the street in front of me. I _____ (go) fairly fast, but luckily I _____ (manage) to stop in time and _____ (not / hit) him.

6.4 **Put the verbs into the correct form, past continuous or simple past.**

1. Jane _was waiting_ (wait) for me when I _arrived_ (arrive).
2. "What _____ (you / do) at this time yesterday?" "I was asleep."
3. "_____ (you / go) out last night?" "No, I was too tired."
4. How fast _____ (you / drive) when the accident _____ (happen)?
5. John _____ (take) a picture of me while I _____ (not / look).
6. We were in a very difficult position. We _____ (not / know) what to do.
7. I haven't seen David for ages. The last time I _____ (see) him, he _____ (try) to find a job in Miami.
8. I _____ (walk) along the street when suddenly I _____ (hear) footsteps behind me. Somebody _____ (follow) me. I was scared, and I _____ (start) to run.
9. When I was young, I _____ (want) to be a pilot.

Present Perfect (1) *(I have done)*

A

Study this example situation:

Tom is looking for his key. He can't find it.
He **has lost** his key. (= He lost it and he still doesn't have it.)
Have/has lost is the *present perfect (simple):*

I/we/they/you **have** (= I've, etc.) he/she/it **has** (= he's, etc.)	**finished** **lost** **done**, etc.

The present perfect is **have/has** + *past participle.* The past participle often ends in **-ed**
(**finished/decided**, etc.), but many important verbs are irregular (**lost/done/been/written**, etc.).
For a list of irregular verbs, see Appendix 1.

B

When we use the present perfect, there is a connection with now. The action in the past has a
result now:
- He told me his name, but **I've forgotten** it. (I can't remember it now.)
- "Is Kimberly here?" "No, she**'s gone** out." (She is out now.)
- I can't find my purse. **Have** you **seen** it? (Do you know where it is now?)

We often use the present perfect to give new information or to announce a recent happening:
- The road is closed. There**'s been** an accident.
- *(from the news)* The police **have arrested** two men in connection with the robbery.

We also use the *simple past* (I **played,** I **did,** etc.) in these situations. So you can say:
- He told me his name, but **I've forgotten** it. *or* . . . but I **forgot** it.
- Kimberly isn't here. She**'s gone** out. *or* . . . She **went** out.

C

We often use the present perfect with **just, already,** and **yet.** You can also use the simple past:

Just = a short time ago:
- "Are you hungry?" "No, **I've just had** lunch." (*or* I **just had** lunch.)

We use **already** to say that something happened sooner than expected (see also Unit 107D):
- "Don't forget to mail the letter." "**I've already mailed** it." (*or* I **already mailed** it.)

Yet = until now. It shows that the speaker is expecting something to happen. Use **yet** only
in questions and negative sentences (see also Unit 107C):
- **Has** it **stopped** raining **yet?** (*or* **Did** it **stop** raining **yet?**)
- I wrote the letter, but I **haven't mailed** it **yet.** (*or* . . . I **didn't mail** it **yet.**)

D

Do not use the present perfect when you talk about a finished time (for example, **last night /
two years ago / yesterday,** etc.). Use the *simple past* (see also Unit 13):
- It **snowed** last night. (*not* has snowed)
- Where **were** you at 3:00? (*not* Where have you been)
- I **started** my new job two weeks ago. (*not* have started)
- Nicole **didn't go** out yesterday. (*not* hasn't gone)

Present Perfect Units 8, 11 **Present Perfect Continuous** Units 9–10
Present Perfect and Simple Past Units 12–13

Exercises

7.1 Read the situations and write sentences with the present perfect. Choose one of the following: break   drop   go up   grow   improve   ~~lose~~   turn on

1. Mike is looking for his key. He can't find it. *He has lost his key.*
2. Jennifer can't walk and her leg is in a cast. She _____ .
3. Maria's English wasn't very good. Now it is much better. _____
4. Jason didn't have a beard last month. Now he has a beard. _____
5. Last week the bus fare was 80 cents. Now it is 90. _____
6. The temperature was 55 degrees. Now it is only 36. The temperature _____ .
7. The light was off. Now it is on. Somebody _____ .

7.2 Complete B's sentences. Use the verb in parentheses + *just/already/yet*.

A   B

1. Would you like something to eat?   No, thanks, I *ve just had* lunch. (just / have)
2. Do you know where Julia is?   Yes, I _____ her. (just / see)
3. What time is David leaving?   He _____ . (already / leave)
4. What's in the newspaper today?   I don't know. I _____ .
                                         (not / read / yet)
5. Is Amy coming to the movies with us? No, she _____ the film.
                                         (already / see)
6. Are your friends here yet?   Yes, they _____ here. (just / get)
7. What does Tim think about your plan? I _____ . (not / tell / yet)

7.3 Read the situations and write sentences with the words in parentheses and *just, already,* or *yet.*

1. After lunch you go to see a friend at her house. She says: "Would you like something to eat?" You say: "No, thank you, *I've just had lunch.* _____" (have lunch)
2. Joe goes out. Five minutes later, the phone rings and the caller says: "Can I speak to Joe?" You say: "I'm sorry, _____ ." (go out)
3. You are eating in a restaurant. The waiter thinks you have finished and starts to take your plate away. You say: "Wait a minute! _____" (not / finish)
4. You are going to a restaurant this evening. You call to reserve a table. Later your friend says: "Should I call to reserve a table?" You say: "No, _____ it." (do)
5. You know that a friend of yours is looking for a job. Perhaps she has been successful. Ask her. You say: "_____ ?" (find)
6. Laura went to the bank, and she returned a few minutes ago. Somebody asks: "Is Laura still at the bank?" You say: "No, _____ ." (come back)

7.4 Are the underlined parts of these sentences right or wrong? Correct the ones that are wrong.

1. It <u>has snowed</u> last night.   *It snowed*
2. <u>Have you seen</u> my purse?   *RIGHT*
3. "Don't forget to pay the gas bill." "<u>I've already done</u> it."   _____
4. The accident <u>has happened</u> three days ago.   _____
5. Sue <u>hasn't been</u> at work yesterday.   _____
6. Jerry gave me his address, but <u>I've lost it</u>.   _____
7. <u>Have you seen</u> Brad on Monday?   _____
8. Where is the newspaper? What <u>have you done</u> with it? _____
9. We <u>have bought</u> our house in 1985.   _____

Present Perfect (2) *(I have done)*

A

Study this example conversation:

Dave: **Have** you **traveled** a lot, Jane?
Jane: Yes, I**'ve been** to lots of places.
Dave: Really? **Have** you ever **been** to China?
Jane: Yes, I**'ve been** to China twice.
Dave: What about India?
Jane: No, I **haven't been** to India.

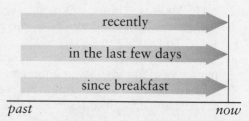

Jane's life
(a period until now)

past   *now*

When we talk about a period of time that continues from the past until now, we use the *present perfect* (**have been / have traveled,** etc.). Here, Dave and Jane are talking about the places Jane has visited in her life (which is a period that continues until now).
Some more examples:

- **Have** you ever **eaten** caviar? *(in your life)*
- We**'ve** never **had** a car.
- "**Have** you **read** *Hamlet?*" "No, I **haven't read** any of Shakespeare's plays."
- Susan really loves that movie. She**'s seen** it eight times!
- What a boring movie! It's the most boring movie I**'ve** ever **seen.**

been (**to**) = visited:

- I've never **been to** China. Have you **been** there?

Here are more examples of speakers talking about a period that continues until now
(**recently / in the last few days / so far / since breakfast,** etc.):

- **Have** you **heard** from Brian **recently?**
- I**'ve met** a lot of people **in the last few days.**
- Everything is going well. We **haven't had** any problems **so far.**
- I'm hungry. I **haven't eaten** anything **since breakfast.** (= from breakfast until now)
- It's nice to see you again. We **haven't seen** each other **for a long time.**

recently

in the last few days

since breakfast

past   *now*

B

We use the present perfect with **today / this morning / this evening,** etc., when these periods are not finished at the time of speaking:

- I**'ve drunk** four cups of coffee today.
- **Have** you **had** a vacation this year?
- I **haven't seen** Tom this morning. **Have** you?

today

past   *now*

C

We say, "It's **the first time** something **has happened**"
(present perfect). For example:

- Don is taking a driving lesson. It's his first one.
  It's the first time he **has driven** a car. (*not* drives)
- *or*   He **has never driven** a car **before.**
- Sarah has lost her passport again. It's the second time this **has happened.** (*not* happens)
- Eric is calling his girlfriend again. This is the third time **he's called** her tonight.

This is the first time I've driven a car.

STUDENT DRIVER

Present Perfect (1) Unit 7   **Present Perfect with *for/since* Unit 12**   **Present Perfect and Simple Past Units 7, 12, 1**

Exercises

8.1 You are asking somebody questions about things he or she has done. Make questions from the words in parentheses.

1. (ever / ride / horse?) *Have you ever ridden a horse?*
2. (ever / be / Mexico?) _____
3. (ever / run / marathon?) _____
4. (ever / speak / famous person?) _____
5. (always / live / in this town?) _____
6. (most beautiful place / ever / visit?) What _____ ?

8.2 Complete B's answers. Some sentences are positive and some negative. Use a verb from this list:

be   be   eat   happen   have   ~~meet~~   play   read   see   see

A   B

1. What's Brian's sister like?   I have no idea. *I've never met* _____ her.
2. How is Amy these days?   I don't know. I _____ her recently.
3. Are you hungry?   Yes, I _____ much today.
4. Can you play chess?   Yes, but _____ for ages.
5. Are you enjoying your vacation?   Yes, it is the best vacation _____ in a long time.
6. What's that book like?   I don't know. _____ it.
7. Is Bangkok an interesting place?   I don't know. _____ there.
8. Mike was late for work again today. Again? He _____ every day this week.
9. The car broke down again yesterday. Not again! That's the second time _____ _____ this week.
10. Who's that woman by the door?   I don't know. _____ before.

8.3 Complete these sentences using *today / this year / this semester,* etc.

1. I saw Tom yesterday, but *I haven't seen him today* .
2. I read a newspaper yesterday, but I _____ today.
3. Last year the company made a profit, but _____ .
4. Tracy worked hard at school last semester, but _____ .
5. It snowed a lot last winter, but _____ .

8.4 Read the situations and write sentences as shown in the examples.

1. James is driving a car, but he's very nervous and not sure what to do.
   You ask: *Have you driven a car before?*
   He says: *No, this is the first time I've driven a car.*
2. Ben is playing tennis. He's not very good, and he doesn't know the rules.
   You ask: Have _____ ?
   He says: No, this is the first _____ .
3. Sue is riding a horse. She doesn't look very confident or comfortable.
   You ask: _____
   She says: _____
4. Maria is in Los Angeles. She has just arrived, and it's very new for her.
   You ask: _____
   She says: _____

Present Perfect Continuous (*I have been doing*)

A

It has been raining. Study this example situation:

Is it raining?
No, but the ground is wet.
It **has been raining**.

Have/has been -ing is the *present perfect continuous*:

I/we/they/you **have**	(= I've, etc.)	**been**	**doing**
he/she/it **has**	(= he's, etc.)		**waiting**
			playing, etc.

We use the present perfect continuous for an activity that has recently stopped or just stopped. There is a connection with now:

- You're out of breath. **Have** you **been running**? (You're out of breath now.)
- Jason is very tired. He's **been working** very hard. (He's tired now.)
- Why are your clothes so dirty? What **have** you **been doing**?
- I've **been talking** to Amanda about the problem, and she agrees with me.

B

It has been raining for two hours. Study this example situation:

It is raining now. It began raining two hours ago.

How long **has** it **been raining**?
It **has been raining** for two hours.

We often use the present perfect continuous in this way, especially with **how long, for,** and **since**. The activity is still happening or has just stopped.

- **How long have** you **been studying** English? (You're still studying English.)
- Tim is still watching TV. He's **been watching** TV **all day**.
- Where have you been? I've **been looking** for you **for the last half hour**.
- Christopher **hasn't been feeling** well **recently**.

You can use the present perfect continuous for actions that are repeated over a period of time:

- Debbie is a very good tennis player. She's **been playing since she was eight**.
- Every morning they meet in the same cafe. They've **been going** there **for years**.

C

Compare **I am doing** (see Unit 1) and **I have been doing**:

I am doing	I have been doing
present continuous	*present perfect continuous*
now	now

- Don't bother me now. **I'm working**.

- We need an umbrella. **It's raining**.
- Hurry up! **We're waiting**.

- I've **been working** hard, so now I'm going to take a break.
- The ground is wet. **It's been raining**.
- We've **been waiting** for an hour.

Present Perfect Simple and Continuous Units 10–11   **Present Perfect with** *for/since* Units 11–12

Exercises

9.1 What have these people been doing or what has been happening?

1. *Now*

They *have been shopping* .

2. *Now*

She _____ .

3. *Now*

They _____ .

4. *Now*

He _____ .

9.2 Write a question for each situation.

1. John looks sunburned. You ask: (you / sit in the sun?) *Have you been sitting in the sun?*
2. You have just arrived to meet a friend who is waiting for you. You ask: (you / wait / long?) _____
3. You meet a friend on the street. His face and hands are very dirty. You ask: (what / you / do?) _____
4. A friend of yours is now living on Main Street. You want to know "How long . . . ?" You ask: (how long / you / live / on Main Street?) _____
5. A friend tells you about her job – she sells computers. You want to know "How long . . . ?" You ask: (how long / you / sell / computers?) _____

9.3 Read the situations and complete the sentences.

1. The rain started two hours ago. It's still raining now.
   It *has been raining* for two hours.
2. We started waiting for the bus 20 minutes ago. We're still waiting now.
   We _____ for 20 minutes.
3. I started Spanish classes in December. I'm still studying Spanish now.
   I _____ since December.
4. Jessica started working in Tokyo on January 18th. She's still working there now.
   _____ since January 18th.
5. Years ago you started writing to a pen pal. You still write to each other regularly.
   We _____ for years.

9.4 Put the verb into the present continuous (*I am -ing*) or present perfect continuous (*I have been -ing*).

1. Maria *has been studying* (study) English for two years.
2. Hello, Tom. I _____ (look) for you all morning. Where have you been?
3. Why _____ (you / look) at me like that? Stop it!
4. We always go to Florida in the winter. We _____ (go) there for years.
5. I _____ (think) about what you said, and I've decided to take your advice.
6. "Is Kim on vacation this week?" "No, she _____ (work)."
7. Sarah is very tired. She _____ (work) very hard recently.

Present Perfect Continuous and Present Perfect Simple (*I have been doing* and *I have done*)

Study these example situations:

Ling's clothes are covered with paint. She **has been painting** the ceiling.

Has been painting is the *present perfect continuous*.

We are interested in the activity. It does not matter whether something has been finished or not. In this example, the activity (painting the ceiling) has not been finished.

The ceiling was white. Now it is blue. She **has painted** the ceiling.

Has painted is the *present perfect simple*.

Here, the important thing is that something has been finished. **Has painted** is a completed action. We are interested in the result of the activity (the painted ceiling), not in the activity itself.

Compare these examples:

- My hands are very dirty. I've **been fixing** the car.
- She's **been eating** too much recently. She should eat less.
- It's nice to see you again. What **have** you **been doing** since the last time we saw you?
- Where have you been? **Have** you **been playing** tennis?

- The car is OK again now. I've **fixed** it.

- Somebody **has eaten** all my candy! The box is empty.
- Where's the book I gave you? What **have** you **done** with it?

- **Have** you ever **played** tennis?

Use the continuous to say how long (for an activity that is still happening):
- How long **have** you **been reading** that book?
- Lisa is still writing letters. She's **been writing** letters all day.
- They've **been playing** tennis since 2:00.

Use the simple to say how much, how many, or how many times (for completed actions):
- How many pages of that book **have** you **read**?
- Lisa **has written** ten letters today.

- They've **played** tennis three times this week.

Some verbs (for example, **know/like/believe**) are not normally used in the continuous:
- I've **known** about it for a long time. (*not* I've been knowing)

For a list of these verbs, see Unit 4A.

Present Perfect (Simple) Units 7–8 **Present Perfect Continuous** Unit 9
Present Perfect with for/since Units 11–12

Exercises

10.1 **Read the situations and write two sentences using the words in parentheses.**

1. Luis started reading a book two hours ago. He is still reading it, and now he is on page 53.
   (read / for two hours) *He has been reading for two hours.*
   (read / 53 pages so far) *He has read 53 pages so far.*
2. Rachel is from Australia. She is traveling around South America at the moment.
   She began her trip three months ago.
   (travel / for three months) She _____ .
   (visit / six countries so far) _____
3. Jimmy is a tennis player. He began playing tennis when he was ten years old. This year
   he is national champion again – for the fourth time.
   (win / the national championship four times) _____
   (play / tennis since he was ten) _____
4. When they graduated from college, Lisa and Amy started making movies together. They
   still make movies.
   (make / ten movies since they graduated from college) They _____ .
   (make / movies since they left college) _____

10.2 **For each situation, ask a question using the words in parentheses.**

1. You have a friend who is studying Arabic. You ask:
   (how long / study / Arabic?) *How long have you been studying Arabic?*
2. You have just arrived to meet a friend. She is waiting for you. You ask:
   (how long / wait?) _____
3. You see somebody fishing by the river. You ask:
   (how many fish / catch?) _____
4. Some friends of yours are having a party next week. You ask:
   (how many people / invite?) _____
5. A friend of yours is a teacher. You ask:
   (how long / teach?) _____
6. You meet somebody who is a writer. You ask:
   (how many books / write?) _____
   (how long / write / books?) _____
7. A friend of yours is saving money to take a trip. You ask:
   (how long / save?) _____
   (how much money / save?) _____

10.3 **Put the verb into the more appropriate form, present perfect simple or continuous.**

1. Where have you been? *Have you been playing* _____ (you / play) tennis?
2. Look! Somebody _____ (break) that window.
3. You look tired. _____ (you / work) hard?
4. "_____ (you / ever / work) in a factory?" "No, never."
5. My brother is an actor. He _____ (appear) in several movies.
6. "Sorry I'm late." "That's all right. I _____ (not / wait) long."
7. "Is it still raining?" "No, it _____ (stop)."
8. I _____ (lose) my address book. _____
   (you / see) it anywhere?
9. I _____ (read) the book you lent me, but I _____
   (not / finish) it yet.
10. I _____ (read) the book you lent me, so you can have it back now.

How long have you (been) . . . ?

Study this example situation:

Bob and Alice are married. They got married exactly 20 years ago, so today is their 20th wedding anniversary.

They **have been** married **for 20 years.**

We say, "They **are** married." *(present)*

but **How long have** they **been** married? *(present perfect)*
(*not* How long are they married?)
They **have been** married **for 20 years.**
(*not* They are married for 20 years.)

We use the present perfect (especially with **how long, for,** and **since**) to talk about something that began in the past and still continues now. Compare the *present* and the *present perfect*:

■ We **know** each other very well.
but We've **known** each other since we were in high school. (*not* We know)

■ **Do** you **have** a pain in your stomach?
but How long **have** you **had** the pain? (*not* How long do you have)

■ **I'm learning** English.
but **I've been learning** English for six months. (*not* I am learning)

■ He's **waiting** for somebody.
but He's **been waiting** all morning.

I have known/had/lived, etc., is the *present perfect simple.*
I have been learning / been waiting / been doing, etc., is the *present perfect continuous.*

In most situations with **how long, since,** and **for,** the continuous is more usual:

■ **I've been studying** English for six months. (more usual than **I've studied**)
■ It's **been raining** since lunchtime.
■ Richard **has been doing** the same job for 20 years.
■ "How long **have** you **been driving?**" "Since I was 17."

But some verbs (for example, **know/like/believe**) are not normally used in the continuous:

■ How long **have** you **known** Jane? (*not* have you been knowing)

For a list of these verbs, see Unit 4A.

You can use either the present perfect continuous or present perfect simple with **live** and **work:**

■ John **has been living / has lived** in Denver for a long time.
■ How long **have** you **been working / have** you **worked** here?

But we use the simple (I've done / I've lived, etc.) with **always:**

■ John **has always lived** in Denver. (*not* has always been living)

We use the present perfect simple in negative sentences like these:

■ I **haven't seen** Tom since Monday. (= Monday was the last time I saw him)
■ Jane **hasn't called** me for two weeks. (= the last time she called was two weeks ago)

Exercises

11.1 Are the underlined verbs right or wrong? Correct them if they are wrong.

1. Bob is a friend of mine. <u>I know him</u> very well.   _RIGHT_
2. Bob is a friend of mine. <u>I know him</u> for a long time.   _I've known him_
3. Sue and Scott <u>are married</u> since July.   _____
4. The weather is awful. <u>It's raining</u> again.   _____
5. The weather is awful. <u>It's raining</u> all day.   _____
6. I like your house. How long <u>are you living</u> there?   _____
7. Mike <u>is working</u> in Las Vegas for the last few months.   _____
8. I'm going to Moscow tomorrow. <u>I'm staying</u> there until next Friday.   _____
9. "Do you still work?" "No, I'm retired. <u>I don't work</u> for years."   _____
10. That's a very old watch. How long <u>do you have</u> it?   _____

11.2 Read the situations and write questions from the words in parentheses.

1. John tells you that his mother is in the hospital. You ask him:
(how long / be / in the hospital?)   _How long has your mother been in the hospital?_
2. You meet a woman who tells you that she teaches English. You ask her:
(how long / teach / English?) _____
3. You know that Jane is a good friend of Carol's. You ask Jane:
(how long / know / Carol?) _____
4. Your friend's brother went to Australia a while ago, and he's still there. You ask your friend: (how long / be / in Australia?) _____
5. Chris always wears the same jacket. It's a very old jacket. You ask him:
(how long / have / that jacket?) _____
6. You are talking to a friend about Scott. Scott now works at the airport. You ask your friend: (how long / work / at the airport?) _____
7. A friend of yours is taking guitar lessons. You ask him:
(how long / take / guitar lessons?) _____
8. You meet somebody on a plane. She tells you that she lives in San Francisco. You ask her: (always / live / in San Francisco?) _____

11.3 Complete B's answers to A's questions.

	A	B
1.	Amy is in the hospital, isn't she?	Yes, she _has been_ in the hospital since Monday.
2.	Do you see Ann very often?	No, I _haven't seen_ her for three months.
3.	Is Margaret married?	Yes, she _____ married for ten years.
4.	Are you waiting for me?	Yes, I _____ for the last half hour.
5.	Do you still play tennis?	No, I _____ tennis for years.
6.	Is Jim watching TV?	Yes, he _____ TV all night.
7.	Do you watch a lot of TV?	No, I _____ TV much recently.
8.	Do you have a headache?	Yes, I _____ a headache all morning.
9.	Are you feeling sick?	Yes, I _____ sick since I got up.
10.	Sue lives in Miami, doesn't she?	Yes, she _____ in Miami for the last few years.
11.	Do you still go to the movies a lot?	No, I _____ to the movies for ages.
12.	Would you like to go to Australia some day?	Yes, I _____ to go to Australia. (*use* always / want)

For and *since*, *When . . . ?*, and *How long . . . ?*

We use **for** and **since** to say how long something has been happening:

We use **for** + a period of time (**two hours, six weeks,** etc.):	We use **since** + the start of a period (**8:00, Monday, 1985,** etc.):
■ I've been waiting **for two hours.**	■ I've been waiting **since 8:00.**

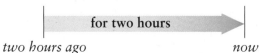

two hours ago   *now*

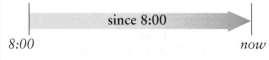

8:00   *now*

for		
two hours	a week	a long time
20 minutes	six months	ages
five days	50 years	years

since		
8:00	April	lunchtime
Monday	1977	I arrived
May 12	Christmas	yesterday

■ Kelly has been working here **for six months.** (*not* since six months)	■ Kelly has been working here **since April.** (= from April until now)
■ I haven't seen Tom **for three days.**	■ I haven't seen Tom **since Monday.**

It is possible to leave out **for** (but not usually in negative sentences):
- ■ They've been married (for) **ten years.** (with or without **for**)
- ■ They haven't had a vacation **for ten years.** (you must use **for**)

We do not use **for** with **all** (**all day / all my life,** etc.):
- ■ I've lived here **all my life.** (*not* for all my life)

Compare **When . . . ?** (+ *simple past*) and **How long . . . ?** (+ *present perfect*):

A: **When did** it **start** raining?
B: It **started** raining   an hour **ago** / **at** one o'clock.

A: **How long has** it been raining?
B: It's **been raining**   **for** an hour / **since** one o'clock.

A: **When did** Joe and Carol **meet** each other?
B: They first **met**   a long time **ago** / **when** they were in high school.

A: **How long have** Joe and Carol **known** each other?
B: They've **known** each other   **for** a long time / **since** they were in high school.

We say "**It's** (= It has) **been a long time / two years** (etc.) **since** something happened":
- ■ **It's been two years since** I last saw Joe. (= I haven't seen Joe for two years.)
- ■ **It's been ages since** we went to the movies. (= We haven't gone to the movies for ages.)

The question is **How long has it been since . . . ?**:
- ■ **How long has it been since** you last saw Joe? (= When did you last see Joe?)
- ■ **How long has it been since** Mrs. Hill died? (= When did Mrs. Hill die?)

How long have you (been) . . . ? **Unit 11**

Exercises

12.1 Put in *for* or *since.*

1. It's been raining _since_____ lunchtime.
2. Joe has lived in Dallas _____ 20 years.
3. Sarah has lived in Chicago _____ 1985.
4. I'm tired of waiting. I've been sitting here _____ an hour.
5. I haven't been to a party _____ a long time.
6. Christine is away. She's been away _____ Friday.
7. Kevin has been looking for a job _____ he finished school.
8. I wonder how Carol is. I haven't seen her _____ ages.

12.2 Write questions with *how long* and *when.*

1. It's raining.
   (how long?) _How long has it been raining?_ _____
   (when?) _When did it start raining?_ _____
2. Karen is studying Japanese.
   (how long?) _____
   (when / start?) _____
3. I know Chris.
   (how long?) _____
   (when / first / meet?) _____
4. Bob and Jessica are married.
   (how long?) _____
   (when?) _____

12.3 Read the situation and complete the sentences.

1. (It's raining now. It's been raining since lunchtime.) It started _raining at lunchtime_____ .
2. (Ann and Sue are friends. They met each other years ago.)
   They've _known each other for years_____ .
3. (Mark is sick. He became sick on Sunday.) He has _____ .
4. (Mark is sick. He became sick a few days ago.) He has _____ .
5. (Sarah is married. She's been married for two years.) She got _____ .
6. (You have a camera. You bought it ten years ago.) I've _____ .
7. (Megan has been in France for the last three weeks.) She went _____ .
8. (You're working in a hotel. You started in June.) I've _____ .

12.4 Write B's sentences using the words in parentheses.

1. *A:* Do you take vacations often?
   B: (no / five years) _No, I haven't taken a vacation for five years._ _____
2. *A:* Do you eat in restaurants often?
   B: (no / ages) No, I _____ .
3. *A:* Do you see Laura often?
   B: (no / about a month) No, _____ .
4. *A:* Do you go to the movies often?
   B: (no / a long time) _____

Now write B's answers again. This time use *It's been . . . since . . .*

5. _No, it's been five years since I took a vacation._ _____
6. No, it's _____ .
7. No, _____ .
8. _____

25

Present Perfect and Past (*I have done* and *I did*)

A

It is often possible to use the *present perfect* (**I have done**) or the *simple past* (**I did**). For example, you can say:

- I've **lost** my key. **Have** you **seen** it? *or* I **lost** my key. **Did** you **see** it?

But do not use the present perfect when you talk about a finished time (for example, **yesterday / ten minutes ago / in 1985**). Use the simple past:

- I **lost** my key yesterday. (*not* I've lost)
- It **was** very hot last summer. (*not* has been)
- They **arrived** ten minutes ago. (*not* have arrived)
- "**Did** you **see** the news on TV last night?" "No, I **went** to bed early."

Use the simple past to ask **When . . . ?** or **What time . . . ?**:

- What time / When **did** you **finish** work yesterday? (*not* have you finished)

B

Do not use the present perfect if there is no connection with the present (for example, things that happened a long time ago):

- The Chinese **invented** printing. (*not* have invented)
- Beethoven **was** a great composer. (*not* has been)

Compare:

- Shakespeare **wrote** many plays.
- My brother is a writer. He **has written** many books. (He still writes books.)

C

Compare *present perfect* and *simple past*:

Present perfect (**have done**)	*Simple past* (**did**)
■ I've **done** a lot of work **today**.	■ I **did** a lot of work **yesterday**.
We use the present perfect for a period of time that continues from the past until now. For example: **today / this week / since 1985**.	We use the simple past for a finished time in the past. For example: **yesterday / last week / from 1985 to 1991**.

┌ *unfinished* ┐	┌ *finished* ┐
today	**yesterday**
past *now*	*past* *now*

■ It **hasn't rained** this week.	■ It **didn't rain** last week.
■ **Have** you **seen** Lisa this morning? (It is still morning.)	■ **Did** you **see** Anna this morning? (It is now afternoon or evening.)
■ **Have** you **seen** Lisa recently?	■ **Did** you **see** Anna on Sunday?
■ We've **been waiting** for an hour. (We are still waiting now.)	■ We **waited** (*or* **were waiting**) for an hour. (We are no longer waiting.)
■ John lives in Los Angeles. He **has lived** there for seven years.	■ John **lived** in New York for ten years. Now he lives in Los Angeles.
■ I **have** never **played** golf. (in my life)	■ I **didn't play** golf last summer.
The present perfect always has a connection with now. See Units 7–12.	The simple past tells us only about the past. See Units 5–6.

Exercises

13.1 Are the underlined parts of these sentences right or wrong? Correct the ones that are wrong.

1. <u>I've lost</u> my key. I can't find it anywhere.   *RIGHT* _____
2. <u>Have you seen</u> the news on television last night?   *Did you see* _____
3. Did you hear about Sue? She<u>'s quit</u> her job. _____
4. Where <u>have you been</u> last night? _____
5. Maria <u>has graduated</u> from high school in 1999. _____
6. I'm looking for Mike. <u>Have you seen</u> him? _____
7. I'm very hungry. <u>I haven't eaten</u> anything today. _____
8. Aristotle <u>has been</u> a Greek philosopher. _____
9. Erica <u>hasn't been</u> at work yesterday. _____
10. When <u>has this book been</u> published? _____

13.2 Make sentences from the words in parentheses. Use the present perfect or simple past.

1. (it / not / rain / this week) *It hasn't rained this week.* _____
2. (the weather / be / cold / recently) The weather _____ .
3. (it / cold / last week) It _____ .
4. (I / not / read / a newspaper yesterday) I _____ .
5. (I / not / read / a newspaper today) _____
6. (Kate / earn / a lot of money / this year) _____
7. (she / not / earn / as much / last year _____
8. (you / take / a vacation recently?) _____

13.3 Put the verb into the correct form, present perfect or simple past.

1. What time *did you finish* _____ (you / finish) work yesterday?
2. When I _____ (get) home last night, I _____
   (be) very tired, so I _____ (go) straight to bed.
3. Robert _____ (not / be) very busy last week.
4. Mr. Lee _____ (work) in a bank for 15 years. Then he quit.
5. Kelly lives in Toronto. She _____ (live) there all her life.
6. "_____ (you / go) to the movies last night?" "Yes, but it
   _____ (be) a mistake. The movie _____ (be) awful."
7. My grandfather _____ (die) 30 years ago. I _____
   (never / meet) him.
8. I don't know Karen's husband. I _____ (never / meet) him.
9. *A:* Where do you live?   *B:* In Rio de Janeiro.
   A: How long _____ (you / live) there?   *B:* Five years.
   A: Where _____ (you / live) before that?   *B:* In Buenos Aires.
   A: And how long _____ (you / live) in Buenos Aires?   *B:* Two years.

13.4 Write sentences about yourself using the ideas in parentheses.

1. (something you haven't done today) *I haven't eaten any fruit today.* _____
2. (something you haven't done today) _____
3. (something you didn't do yesterday) _____
4. (something you did last night) _____
5. (something you haven't done recently) _____
6. (something you've done a lot recently) _____

Past Perfect (*I had done*)

Study this example situation:

At 10:30 Bye!
At 11:00 Hello!

ERIC
SARAH

Sarah went to a party last week. Eric went to the party, too, but they didn't see each other. Eric left the party at 10:30, and Sarah got there at 11:00. So:

When Sarah got to the party, Eric wasn't there. He **had gone** home.

Had gone is the *past perfect (simple)*:

I/we/they/you he/she/it	had	(= I'd, etc.) (= he'd, etc.)	gone seen finished, etc.

The past perfect simple is **had** + *past participle* (**gone/seen/finished,** etc.)

Sometimes we talk about something that happened in the past:
- Sarah **got to** the party.

This is the starting point of the story. Then, if we want to talk about things that happened before this time, we use the past perfect (**had gone**):
- When Sarah **got to** the party, Eric **had** already **gone** home.

Here are some more examples:
- When we got home last night, we found that somebody **had broken** into our apartment.
- Karen didn't want to go to the movies with us because she **had** already **seen** the film.
- At first I thought **I'd done** the right thing, but I soon realized that **I'd made** a mistake.
- The man sitting next to me on the plane was very nervous. He **hadn't flown** before.
  or . . . He **had** never **flown** before.

Compare **have done** *(present perfect)* and **had done** *(past perfect)*:

present perfect	*past perfect*
have done ➤	**had done** ➤
past _____ *now*	*past* _____ *now*
■ Who is that woman? I've never **seen** her before.	■ I didn't know who she was. I'd never **seen** her before. (= before that time)
■ We aren't hungry. We've just **had** lunch.	■ We weren't hungry. We'd just **had** lunch.
■ The house is dirty. They **haven't cleaned** it for weeks.	■ The house was dirty. They **hadn't cleaned** it for weeks.

Compare the *past perfect* (**I had done**) and *simple past* (**I did**):
- "Was Ben at the party when you got there?" "No, he **had** already **gone** home."

but "Was Ben at the party when you got there?" "Yes, but he **went** home soon afterward."
- Amy **had** just **gotten** home when I phoned. She **had been** at her mother's.

but Amy wasn't at home when I phoned. She **was** at her mother's.

Past Perfect Continuous **Unit 15** **Irregular Verbs (*had gone, had seen,* etc.)** **Appendix 1**

Exercises

14.1 Read the situations and write sentences using the words in parentheses.

1. You went to Jill's house, but she wasn't there.
   (she / go / out) *She had gone out.*
2. You went back to your hometown after many years. It wasn't the same as before.
   (it / change / a lot) _____
3. I invited Rachel to the party, but she couldn't come.
   (she / make / plans to do something else) _____
4. It was nice to see Daniel again after such a long time.
   (I / not / see / him for five years) _____
5. You went to the movies last night. You got there late.
   (the movie / already / begin) _____
6. Sam played tennis yesterday. It was his first game, and he wasn't very good at it.
   (he / not / play / before) _____
7. I offered Sue something to eat, but she wasn't hungry.
   (she / just / have / breakfast) _____
8. Last year we went to Mexico. It was our first time there.
   (we / never / be / there before) _____

14.2 Use the sentences on the left to complete the paragraphs on the right. These sentences are in the order in which they happened – so (a) happened before (b), (b) before (c), etc. But your paragraph should begin with the underlined sentence, so sometimes you will need the past perfect.

1. a) Somebody broke into the office during the night.
   b) <u>We arrived at work in the morning.</u>
   c) We called the police.

   We arrived at work in the morning and found that somebody *had broken* into the office during the night. So we _____ .

2. a) Ann went out.
   b) <u>I tried to phone her</u> this morning.
   c) There was no answer.

   I tried to phone Ann this morning, but _____ no answer.
   She _____ out.

3. a) Jim came back from vacation a few days ago.
   b) <u>I met him the same day.</u>
   c) He looked relaxed.

   I met Jim a few days ago. He _____
   just _____ .
   He _____ .

4. a) Kevin wrote to Sally many times.
   b) She never answered his letters.
   c) <u>Yesterday he got a phone call from her.</u>
   d) He was very surprised.

   Yesterday Kevin _____ .
   He _____ very surprised.
   He _____ many times,
   but she _____ .

14.3 Put the verb into the correct form, past perfect (*I had done*) or simple past (*I did*).

1. "Was Ben at the party when you got there?" "No, he *had gone* (go) home."
2. I felt very tired when I got home, so I _____ (go) straight to bed.
3. The house was very quiet when I got home. Everybody _____ (go) to bed.
4. "Sorry I'm late. The car _____ (break) down on my way here."
5. We were driving on the highway when we _____ (see) a car that _____ (break) down, so we _____ (stop) to see if we could help.

Past Perfect Continuous (*I had been doing*)

A

Study this example situation:

Yesterday morning

Yesterday morning I got up and looked out the window. The sun was shining, but the ground was very wet.

It **had been raining.**

It was not raining when I looked out the window; the sun was shining. But it **had been raining** before.

Had been -ing is the *past perfect continuous:*

I/we/you/they he/she/it	had	(= I'd, etc.) (= he'd, etc.)	been	doing working playing, etc.

Here are some more examples:
- When the boys came into the house, their clothes were dirty, their hair was messy, and one of them had a black eye. They**'d been fighting.**
- I was very tired when I got home. I**'d been working** hard all day.

B

You can say that something **had been happening** for a period of time before something else happened:
- We**'d been playing** tennis for about half an hour when it started to rain heavily.
- Jim quit drinking coffee two years ago. He**'d been drinking** coffee for 20 years.

C

Compare **have been -ing** and **had been -ing:**

present perfect continuous	*past perfect continuous*
⟶ **I have been -ing** ⟶	⟶ **I had been -ing** ⟶
past *now*	*past* *now*
■ I hope the bus comes soon. I**'ve been waiting** for 20 minutes. *(before now)*	■ At last the bus came. I**'d been waiting** for 20 minutes. *(before the bus came)*
■ He's out of breath. He **has been running.**	■ He was out of breath. He **had been running.**

D

Compare **had been doing** and **was doing** *(past continuous):*
- It **wasn't raining** when we went out. The sun **was shining.** But it **had been raining,** so the ground was wet.
- Stephanie **was sitting** in an armchair resting. She was tired because she**'d been working** very hard.

E

Some verbs (for example, **know** and **want**) are not normally used in the continuous:
- We were good friends. We **had known** each other for years. (*not* had been knowing)

For a list of these verbs, see Unit 4A.

Present Perfect Continuous Unit 9   Past Perfect Unit 14

Exercises

15.1 Read the situations and make sentences from the words in parentheses.

1. I was very tired when I got home.
   (I / work / hard all day) *I had been working hard all day.*
2. The two boys came into the house. They had a soccer ball, and they were both very tired.
   (they / play / soccer) _____
3. There was nobody in the room, but there was a smell of cigarette smoke.
   (somebody / smoke / in the room) _____
4. Ann woke up in the middle of the night. She was frightened and didn't know where she was.
   (she / dream) _____
5. When I got home, Mike was sitting in front of the TV. He had just turned it off.
   (he / watch / TV) _____

15.2 Read the situations and complete the sentences.

1. We played tennis yesterday. Half an hour after we began playing, it started to rain.
   We *had been playing for half an hour* when *it started to rain* _____ .
2. I had arranged to meet Robert in a restaurant. I arrived and waited for him. After 20
   minutes I suddenly realized that I was in the wrong restaurant.
   I _____ for 20 minutes when I _____
   _____ .
3. Sarah got a job in a factory. Five years later the factory closed down.
   At the time the factory _____ , Sarah _____
   _____ there for five years.
4. I went to a concert last week. The orchestra began playing. After about ten minutes a
   man in the audience suddenly began shouting.
   The orchestra _____ when _____
   _____ .

15.3 Put the verb into the most appropriate form, past continuous (*I was doing*), past perfect
(*I had done*), or past perfect continuous (*I had been doing*).

1. It was very noisy next door. Our neighbors *were having* _____ (have) a party.
2. We were good friends. We *had known* _____ (know) each other for a long
   time.
3. John and I went for a walk. I had trouble keeping up with him because he
   _____ (walk) so fast.
4. Sue was sitting on the ground. She was out of breath. She _____
   (run).
5. When I arrived, everybody was sitting around the table with their mouths full. They
   _____ (eat).
6. When I arrived, everybody was sitting around the table and talking. Their mouths
   were empty, but their stomachs were full. They _____ (eat).
7. Brian was on his hands and knees on the floor. He _____ (look)
   for his contact lens.
8. When I arrived, Kate _____ (wait) for me. She was upset with me
   because I was late and she _____ (wait) for a very long time.
9. I was sad when I sold my car. I _____ (have) it for a very long time.
10. We were extremely tired at the end of our trip. We _____ (travel)
    for more than 24 hours.

Have and *have got*

Have and **have got** (= possess, own, etc.)

We can use **have got** rather than **have** alone. So you can say:

- We **have** a new car.   *or*   We've **got** a new car.
- Nancy **has** two sisters.   *or*   Nancy **has got** two sisters.

We also use **have** or **have got** for illnesses, pains, etc.:

- I **have** a headache.   *or*   I've **got** a headache.

In questions and negative sentences there are two possible forms:

Do you **have** any money?	I **don't have** any money.
Have you **got** any money?	I **haven't got** any money.
Does she **have** a car?	She **doesn't have** a car.
Has she **got** a car?	She **hasn't got** a car.

I have a headache.

I've got a headache, too.

When **have** means "possess," etc., you cannot use continuous forms (**is having / are having,** etc.):

- I **have** / I've **got** a headache. (*not* I'm having)

For the past we use **had** (without got):

- Ann **had** long blond hair when she was a child.

In past questions and past negative sentences we use **did/didn't**:

- **Did** they **have** a car when they were living in Miami?
- I **didn't have** a watch, so I didn't know the time.
- Ann **had** blond hair, **didn't** she?

Have breakfast / have trouble / have a good time, etc.

Have (*but not* have got) is also used for many actions and experiences. For example:

have	breakfast / dinner / a cup of coffee / something to drink a party / a safe trip / a good flight an accident / an experience / a dream a look (at something) a baby (= give birth to a baby) / an operation difficulty / trouble / fun / a nice time

- Good-bye! I hope you **have** a nice time.
- Jennifer **had** a baby recently.

Have got is not possible in these expressions. Compare:

- I usually **have** a sandwich for lunch. (*not* have got; **have** = eat)

but   I've **got** some sandwiches. Would you like one?

In the expressions in the box, **have** is like other verbs. You can use continuous forms (**is having / are having,** etc.) where appropriate:

- I got a postcard from Michael this morning. He's on vacation. He says he's **having** a wonderful time. (*not* he has a wonderful time)

In questions and negative sentences we use **do/does/did**:

- I **don't** usually **have** a big breakfast. (*not* I usually haven't)
- What time **does** Ann **have** lunch? (*not* has Ann lunch)
- **Did** you **have** any trouble finding a place to live?

Exercises

16.1 Write negative sentences with *have*. Some are present *(can't)*, and some are past *(couldn't)*.

1. I can't make a phone call. (any change) *I don't have any change.*
2. I couldn't read the letter. (my glasses) *I didn't have my glasses.*
3. I can't climb up on the roof. (a ladder) I _____ .
4. We couldn't visit the museum. (enough time) We _____ .
5. He couldn't find his way to our house. (a map) _____
6. She can't pay her bills. (any money) _____
7. They can't get into the house. (a key) _____
8. I couldn't take any pictures. (a camera) _____

16.2 Complete these questions with *have*. Some are present and some are past.

1. Excuse me, *do you have* _____ a pen I could borrow?
2. Why are you holding your face like that? _____ a toothache?
3. _____ a bicycle when you were a child?
4. " _____ the time, please?" "Yes, it's ten after seven."
5. When you took the exam, _____ time to answer all the questions?
6. I need a stamp for this letter. _____ one?
7. "It started to rain while I was walking home." "Did it? _____ an umbrella?"

16.3 Write sentences about yourself. Choose four of the following things:

~~a car~~   a bicycle   a moped   a guitar   a computer   a camera   a driver's license
a job   a dog / a cat (or other animal)   a serious illness   long hair

Do you have these things now? Did you have them ten years ago? Write two sentences each time using *I have / I don't have* and *I had / I didn't have*.

	now	*10 years ago (or 5 if you're too young)*
1.	*I have a car.* OR *I've got a car.*	*I didn't have a car.*
2.	_____	_____
3.	_____	_____
4.	_____	_____

16.4 Complete these sentences. Use an expression from the list, and put the verb into the correct form where necessary.

have a cold drink   have a party   have a nice time   have a good flight
have a look   have a baby   have trouble   ~~have lunch~~

1. I don't eat much during the day. I never *have lunch* _____ .
2. We _____ last Saturday. It was great – we invited lots of people.
3. Excuse me, may I _____ at your newspaper, please?
4. I haven't seen you since you came back from your vacation. _____ _____ ?
5. Crystal _____ a few weeks ago. It's her second child.
6. I was very hot after playing tennis, so I _____ .
7. You meet Jason at the airport. He has just arrived. *You say:*
   Hello, Jason. _____ ?
8. What's the matter? _____ opening that jar?

UNIT 17

Used to (do)

A

Study this example situation:

A few years ago

Today

David quit jogging two years ago. He doesn't jog anymore.

But he **used to jog.**
He **used to jog** three miles a day.

He **used to jog** = he jogged regularly for some time in the past, but he doesn't jog now.

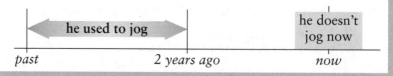

he used to jog		he doesn't jog now
past	*2 years ago*	*now*

B

Something **used to happen** = something happened regularly in the past but no longer happens:
- I **used to play** tennis a lot, but I don't play as much now.
- Diane **used to travel** a lot. These days she doesn't take many trips.
- "Do you go to the movies very often?" "Not anymore, but I **used to.**" (= I used to go)

We also use **used to** for something that was true but is not true anymore:
- This building is now a furniture store. It **used to be** a movie theater.
- I started drinking coffee recently. I never **used to like** it before.
- Nicole **used to have** very long hair when she was a child.

C

Used to do is past. There is no present form. You cannot say "I use to do." To talk about the present, use the present simple (**I do**). Compare:

past	he used to travel	we used to live	there used to be
present	he travels	we live	there is

- We **used to live** in a small town, but now we **live** in Chicago.
- There **used to be** four movie theaters in town. Now there **is** only one.

D

The normal question form is **did (you) use to . . . ?**:
- **Did** you **use to eat** a lot of candy when you were a child?

The negative form is **didn't use to**:
- I **didn't use to** like him.

E

Compare **I used to do** and **I was doing** (see Unit 6):
- I **used to watch** TV a lot. (= I watched TV regularly in the past, but I no longer do this)
- I **was watching** TV when the phone rang. (= I was in the middle of watching TV)

F

Do not confuse **I used to do** and **I am used to doing** (see Unit 58). The structures and meanings are different:
- I **used to live** alone. (= I lived alone in the past, but I no longer live alone)
- I **am used to living** alone. (= I live alone, and I don't find it strange or new because I've been living alone for some time)

***Would** (= used to)* Unit 38D   ***Be/get used to** (doing) something* Unit 58

Exercises

17.1 Complete these sentences with *use(d) to* + an appropriate verb.

1. David quit jogging two years ago. He _used to jog_ four miles a day.
2. Jim _____ a motorcycle, but he sold it last year and bought a car.
3. We moved to Spain a few years ago. We _____ in Paris.
4. I rarely eat ice cream now, but I _____ it when I was a child.
5. Tracy _____ my best friend, but we aren't friends anymore.
6. It only takes me about 40 minutes to get to work since the new highway was opened. It _____ more than an hour.
7. There _____ a hotel near the airport, but it closed a long time ago.
8. When you lived in New York, _____ to the theater very often?

17.2 Matthew changed his lifestyle. He stopped doing some things and started doing other things:

He stopped { studying hard
going to bed early
running three miles every morning

He started { sleeping late
going out every night
spending a lot of money

Write sentences about Matthew with *used to* and *didn't use to*.

1. _He used to study hard._   4. _____
2. _He didn't use to sleep late._   5. _____
3. _____   6. _____

17.3 Compare what Karen said five years ago and what she says today:

Five years ago

I travel a lot.

I play the piano.

I'm very lazy.

I don't like cheese.

I'm a hotel receptionist.

I've got lots of friends.

I never read newspapers.

I don't drink tea.

I have a dog.

Today

I eat lots of cheese now.

I work very hard these days.

I don't see many people these days.

I haven't played the piano for years.

My dog died two years ago.

I read a newspaper every day now.

I work in a bookstore now.

I don't take many trips these days.

Tea's great! I like it now.

Now write sentences about how Karen has changed. Use *used to / didn't use to / never used to* in the first part of your sentence.

1. _She used to travel a lot_ , but _she doesn't take many trips these days_ .
2. She used _____ , but _____ .
3. _____ , but _____ .
4. _____ , but _____ .
5. _____ , but _____ .
6. _____ , but _____ .
7. _____ , but _____ .
8. _____ , but _____ .
9. _____ , but _____ .

Present Tenses (*I am doing / I do*)
with a Future Meaning

A

Present continuous (**I am doing**) with a future meaning

Study this example situation:

This is Ben's appointment book for next week.

He **is playing** tennis on Monday afternoon.
He **is going** to the dentist on Tuesday morning.
He **is having** dinner with Ann on Friday.

In all these examples, Ben has already decided and arranged to do these things.

We use the *present continuous* to say what we have already arranged to do. Do not use the *simple present* (**I do**):

- *A*: What **are** you **doing** on Saturday evening? (*not* What do you do)
  B: **I'm going** to the theater. (*not* I go)
- *B*: What time **is** Cathy **arriving** tomorrow?
  A: At 10:30. **I'm meeting** her at the airport.
- **I'm not working** tomorrow, so we can go somewhere.
- Sam **isn't playing** football on Saturday. He hurt his leg.

"(I'm) **going to** (do)" is also possible in these sentences:
- What **are** you **going to do** Saturday night?

But the present continuous is more natural for arrangements. See also Unit 19B.

Do not use **will** to talk about what you have arranged to do:
- What **are** you **doing** tonight? (*not* What will you do)
- Eric **is getting** married next month. (*not* will get)

B

Simple present (**I do**) with a future meaning

We use the simple present to talk about timetables, schedules, etc. (for example, for public transportation, movies, etc.):
- The plane **leaves** Chicago at 11:30 and **arrives** in Atlanta at 2:45.
- What time **does** the movie **begin**?
- Tomorrow **is** Wednesday.

You can use the simple present for people if their plans are fixed, like a schedule:
- I **start** my new job on Monday.
- What time **do** you **finish** work tomorrow?

But the continuous is more commonly used for personal arrangements:
- What time **are** you **meeting** Ann tomorrow? (*not* do you meet)

Compare:
- What time **are** you **leaving** tomorrow?
but What time **does** the plane **leave** tomorrow?
- **I'm going** to the movies tonight.
but The movie **starts** at 8:15 (tonight).

(I'm) going to Units 19, 22   *Will* Units 20–21   **Simple Present after *when/if*, etc.** Unit 24

Exercises

18.1 A friend of yours is planning to go on vacation soon. Ask her about her plans. Use the words in parentheses to make your questions.

1. (where / go?) _Where are you going?_   Quebec.
2. (how long / stay?) _____ Ten days.
3. (when / go?) _____ Next Friday.
4. (go / alone?) _____ No, with a friend of mine.
5. (travel / by car?) _____ No, by train.
6. (where / stay?) _____ In a hotel.

18.2 Ben wants you to visit him, but you are very busy. Look at your appointment book for the next few days and explain to him why you can't come.

Ben: Can you come on Monday evening?
You: Sorry, but _I'm playing volleyball_ . (1)
Ben: What about Tuesday evening?
You: No, not Tuesday. I _____ . (2)
Ben: And Wednesday evening?
You: _____ (3)
Ben: Well, are you free on Thursday?
You: I'm afraid not. _____ (4)

18.3 Have you arranged to do anything at these times? Write (true) sentences about yourself.

1. (tonight) _I'm going out tonight_ OR _I'm not doing anything tonight._
2. (tomorrow morning) I _____ .
3. (tomorrow night) _____
4. (next Sunday) _____
5. *(choose another day or time)* _____

18.4 Put the verb into the more appropriate form, present continuous or simple present.

1. I _'m going_ (go) to the theater tonight.
2. _Does the movie begin_ (the movie / begin) at 3:30 or 4:30?
3. We _____ (have) a party next Saturday. Would you like to come?
4. The art exhibit _____ (open) on May 3.
5. I _____ (not / go) out this evening. I _____ (stay) at home.
6. "_____ (you / do) anything tomorrow morning?" "No, I'm free."
7. We _____ (go) to a concert tonight. It _____ (begin) at 7:30.
8. *You are on a train to New York and you ask another passenger:* Excuse me. What time _____ (this train / get) to New York?
9. *You are talking to Ann:* Ann, I _____ (go) to the store. _____ (you / come) with me?
10. Sue _____ (come) to New York tomorrow. She _____ (fly) from Vancouver, and her plane _____ (arrive) at 10:15. I _____ (meet) her at the airport.
11. I _____ (not / use) the car tonight, so you can have it.
12. *(watching TV)* I'm bored with this program. When _____ (it / end)?

(I'm) going to (do)

A

I **am going to do** something = I have already decided to do it, I intend to do it:

- A: There's a movie on TV tonight. **Are** you **going to watch** it?
  B: No, **I'm going to write** some letters.
- A: I heard that Lisa won some money. What **is** she **going to do** with it?
  B: **She's going to buy** a new car.
- This cheese looks awful. **I'm not going to eat** it.

B

I am doing and **I am going to do**

We normally use **I am doing** *(present continuous)* when we say what we have arranged to do – for example, arranged to meet somebody, arranged to go somewhere (see Unit 18A):

- What time **are** you **meeting** Amanda this evening?
- **I'm leaving** tomorrow. I have my plane ticket.

I **am going to do** something = I've decided to do it (but perhaps not arranged to do it):

- "The windows are dirty." "Yes, I know. **I'm going to wash** them later." (= I've decided to wash them, but I haven't arranged to wash them)
- I've decided not to stay here any longer. Tomorrow **I'm going to look** for another place to live.

Often the difference is very small, and either form is possible.

C

You can also say that something **is going to happen** in the future. For example:

The man can't see the hole in front of him.

He **is going to fall** into the hole.

When we say that something **is going to happen,** the situation now makes us believe this. The man is walking toward the hole now, so he **is going to fall** into it.

situation now → going to → *future happening*

- Look at those black clouds! It's **going to rain.** (The clouds are there now.)
- I feel terrible. I think **I'm going to be** sick. (I feel terrible now.)

D

I **was going to do** something = I intended to do it but didn't do it:

- We **were going to travel** by train, but then we decided to drive instead.
- Peter **was going to take** the exam, but he changed his mind.
- I **was** just **going to cross** the street when somebody shouted, "Stop!"

You can say something **was going to happen** (but didn't happen):

- I thought it **was going to rain,** but then the sun came out.

Exercises

19.1 **Write a question with *going to* for each situation.**

1. Your friend has won some money. You ask:
   (what / do with it?) *What are you going to do with it?*
2. Your friend is going to a party tonight. You ask:
   (what / wear?) _____
3. Your friend has just bought a new table. You ask:
   (where / put it?) _____
4. Your friend has decided to have a party. You ask:
   (who / invite?) _____

19.2 **Read the situations and complete the dialogs. Use *going to.***

1. You have decided to write some letters this evening.
   Friend: Are you going out this evening?
   You: No, *I'm going to write some letters* .
2. You're taking piano lessons, but you have decided to quit soon.
   Friend: You don't seem to enjoy your piano lessons.
   You: I don't. _____
3. You have been offered a job, but you have decided not to take it.
   Friend: I hear you've been offered a job.
   You: That's right, but _____
4. You are in a restaurant. The food is awful, and you've decided to complain.
   Friend: This food is awful, isn't it?
   You: Yes, it's disgusting. _____
5. You have to call Sarah. It's morning now, and you intend to call her tonight.
   Friend: Have you called Sarah yet?
   You: No, _____ .

19.3 **What is going to happen in these situations? Use the words in parentheses.**

1. There are a lot of black clouds in the sky. (rain) *It's going to rain.* _____
2. It is 8:30. Jack is leaving his house. He has to be at work at 8:45, but the trip takes 30 minutes. (late) He _____ .
3. There is a hole in the bottom of the boat. A lot of water is coming in through the hole. (sink) The boat _____
4. Erica is driving. There is very little gas left in the tank. The nearest gas station is far away. (run out) She _____ .

19.4 **Complete the sentences with *was/were going to* + one of these verbs:**

   call ~~fly~~ have play quit

1. We *were going to fly.* _____ but we decided to drive instead.
2. We _____ tennis yesterday, but it rained all day.
3. I _____ John, but I decided to write him a letter instead.
4. When I last saw Bob, he _____ his job, but in the end he decided not to.
5. We _____ a party last week, but some of our friends couldn't come, so we changed our minds.

Will (1)

We use I'll (= I will) when we decide to do something at the time of speaking:
- Oh, I left the door open. **I'll go** and shut it.
- "What would you like to drink?" "**I'll have** some orange juice, please."
- "Did you call Julie?" "Oh no, I forgot. **I'll call** her now."

You cannot use the *simple present* (**I do** / **I go,** etc.) in these sentences:
- **I'll go** and **shut** the door. (*not* I go and shut)

We often use **I think I'll . . .** and **I don't think I'll . . . :**
- I'm a little hungry. **I think I'll have** something to eat.
- **I don't think I'll go** out tonight. I'm too tired.

In spoken English, the negative of **will** is usually **won't** (= will not):
- I can see you're busy, so I **won't stay** long.

Do not use **will** to talk about what you have already decided or arranged to do (see Units 18–19):
- **I'm leaving** on vacation next Saturday. (*not* I'll leave)
- **Are** you **working** tomorrow? (*not* Will you work)

We often use **will** in these situations:

Offering to do something
- That bag looks heavy. **I'll help** you with it. (*not* I help)

Agreeing to do something
- *A:* You know that book I lent you? Could I have it back if you're finished with it?
- *B:* Of course. **I'll give** it to you this afternoon. (*not* I give)

Promising to do something
- Thanks for lending me the money. **I'll pay** you back on Friday. (*not* I pay)
- I **won't tell** anyone what happened. I promise.

Asking somebody to do something (**Will you . . . ?**)
- **Will you** please **be** quiet? I'm trying to concentrate.
- **Will you shut** the door, please?

You can use **won't** to say that somebody refuses to do something:
- I've tried to give her advice, but she **won't listen.** (= she refuses to listen)
- The car **won't start.** I wonder what's wrong with it. (= the car "refuses" to start)

Shall I . . . ? Shall we . . . ?

Shall is used in the questions **Shall I . . . ?** / **Shall we . . . ?** to ask somebody's opinion (especially in offers or suggestions):
- **Shall I open** the window? (= do you want me to open the window?)
- "Where **shall we have** lunch?" "Let's go to Marino's."

We also use **should** in the same situations:
- **Should I open** the window?
- Where **should we have** lunch?

Will Unit 21   *I will* and *I'm going to* Unit 22

Exercises

20.1 Complete the sentences with *I'll* + an appropriate verb.

1. I'm too tired to walk home. I think _I'll take_ a taxi.
2. "It's a little cold in this room." "You're right. _____ on the heat."
3. "We don't have any milk." "We don't? _____ and get some."
4. "I don't know how to use this computer." "OK, _____ you."
5. "Would you like tea or coffee?" "_____ coffee, please."
6. "Good-bye! Have a nice trip." "Thanks. _____ you a postcard."
7. Thanks for lending me your camera. _____ it back to you on Monday, OK?
8. "Are you coming with us?" "No, I think _____ here."

20.2 Read the situations and write sentences with *I think I'll . . . .* or *I don't think I'll . . . .*

1. It's a little cold. You decide to close the window. You say:
   I think I'll close the window.
2. You're tired, and it's getting late. You decide to go to bed. You say:
   I think _____ .
3. A friend of yours offers you a ride in his car, but you decide to walk. You say:
   Thank you, but I think _____ .
4. You arranged to play tennis today. Now you decide that you don't want to play. You say:
   I don't think _____ .
5. You were going to go swimming. Now you decide that you don't want to go. You say:
   _____

20.3 Which is correct? (If necessary, study Units 18–19 first.)

1. "Did you call Julie?" "Oh no, I forgot. ~~I call~~ / I'll call her now." (*I'll call* is correct.)
2. I can't meet you tomorrow afternoon. I'm playing / ~~I'll play~~ tennis. (*I'm playing* is correct.)
3. "I meet / I'll meet you outside the hotel in half an hour, OK?" "Yes, that's fine."
4. "I need some money." "OK, I'm lending / I'll lend you some. How much do you need?"
5. I'm having / I'll have a party next Saturday. I hope you can come.
6. "Remember to get a newspaper when you go out." "OK. I don't forget / I won't forget."
7. What time does your train leave / will your train leave tomorrow?
8. I asked Sue what happened, but she doesn't tell / won't tell me.
9. "Are you doing / Will you do anything tomorrow evening?" "No, I'm free. Why?"
10. I don't want to go out alone. Do you come / Will you come with me?

20.4 Complete the sentences with *I'll* / *I won't* / *Shall I . . . ?* / *Shall we . . . ?* + an appropriate verb.

1. *A:* Where _shall we have_ lunch?
   B: Let's go to the new restaurant on North Street.
2. *A:* It's Mark's birthday soon, and I have to get him a present. What _____ him?
   B: I don't know. I never know what to give people.
3. *A:* Do you want me to put these things away?
   B: No, it's OK. _____ it later.
4. *A:* Let's go out tonight.
   B: OK, where _____ ?
5. *A:* What I've told you is a secret. I don't want anybody else to know.
   B: Don't worry. _____ anybody else.
6. *A:* I know you're busy, but can you finish this report this afternoon?
   B: Well, _____ , but I can't promise.

Will (2)

We do not use **will** to say what somebody has already arranged or decided to do in the future:

- Ann **is working** next week. (*not* Ann will work)
- Are you **going to watch** TV this evening? (*not* Will you watch)

For **I'm working . . .** and **Are you going to . . . ?** see Units 18–19.

But often, when we talk about the future, we are *not* talking about what somebody has decided to do. For example:

This is a very long line!   Don't worry. We'll get in.

We'll get in does not mean *we have decided to get in.* Joe is saying what he knows or thinks will happen. He is predicting the future. When we predict a future happening or situation, we use **will/won't.**

JOE

Here are some more examples:

- Jill has lived abroad a long time. When she comes back, she**'ll find** a lot of changes.
- "Where **will** you **be** this time next year?" "**I'll be** in Japan."
- That plate is very hot. If you touch it, you**'ll burn** yourself.
- Tom **won't pass** the exam. He hasn't studied hard enough.
- When **will** you **find** out how you did on the exam?

We often use **will** ('ll) with:

probably	■ I'll **probably be** home late tonight.
(I'm) sure	■ Don't worry about the exam. **I'm sure** you'll **pass.**
(I) think	■ Do you **think** Sarah **will like** the present we bought her?
(I) don't think	■ I **don't think** the exam **will be** very difficult.
(I) guess	■ I **guess** your parents **will be** tired after their trip.
(I) suppose	■ When do you **suppose** Jan and Mark **will get** married?
(I) doubt	■ I **doubt** you'll **need** a heavy coat in Las Vegas.
I wonder	■ I **wonder** what **will happen.**

After (I) **hope,** we generally use the present:

- I **hope** Carol **calls** tonight.
- I **hope** it **doesn't rain** tomorrow.

   I will **and** *I'm going to* Unit 22   *Will be doing* **and** *will have done* Unit 23   *Will* Unit 20   *Shall* Unit 20D

Exercises

21.1 Which is correct (or more natural) in these sentences?

1. Ann isn't free on Saturday. ~~She'll work~~ / She's working. (*She's working* is correct.)
2. I'll go / I'm going to a party tomorrow night. Would you like to come, too?
3. I think Amy will get / is getting the job. She has a lot of experience.
4. I can't meet you this evening. A friend of mine will come / is coming to see me.
5. *A:* Have you decided where to go on vacation?
   B: Yes, we will go / we are going to Italy.
6. You don't have to be afraid of the dog. It won't hurt / It isn't hurting you.

21.2 Complete the sentences with *will ('ll)* + one of these verbs:

   be   be   come   get   like   look   meet   ~~pass~~

1. Don't worry about your exam. I'm sure you *'ll pass* .
2. Why don't you try on this jacket? It _____ nice on you.
3. I want you to meet Brandon sometime. I think you _____ him.
4. It's raining. Don't go out. You _____ wet.
5. They've invited me to their house. They _____ offended if I don't go.
6. I've invited Sue to the party, but I don't think she _____ .
7. I wonder where I _____ 20 years from now.
8. Good-bye. I'm sure we _____ again soon.

21.3 Put in *will ('ll)* or *won't*.

1. Can you wait for me? I *won't* be very long.
2. You don't need to take an umbrella with you. It _____ rain.
3. If you don't eat anything now, you _____ be hungry later.
4. I'm sorry about what happened yesterday. It _____ happen again.
5. I've got some incredible news! You _____ never believe what happened.
6. Don't ask Amanda for advice. She _____ know what to do.
7. There's no more bread. I guess we _____ have to go to the store before we eat.
8. Jack doesn't like crowds. I don't think he _____ come to our party.

21.4 Where do you think you will be at these times? Write true sentences using one of these:

   I'll be . . .   I'll probably be . . .   I don't know where I'll be . . .   I guess I'll be . . .

1. (next Monday night at 7:45) *I'll probably be at home.* OR *I don't know where I'll be.*
2. (at 5:00 tomorrow morning) _____
3. (at 10:30 tomorrow morning) _____
4. (next Saturday afternoon at 4:15) _____
5. (this time next year) _____

21.5 Write questions using *Do you think . . . will . . . ?* with one of these verbs:

   be back   cost   get married   happen   ~~like~~   rain

1. I bought Rosa a present. *Do you think she'll like it?*
2. The weather doesn't look very good. Do you _____ ?
3. My car needs to be fixed. How much _____ ?
4. Sarah and David are in love. Do _____ ?
5. "I'm going out now." "OK. What time _____ ?"
6. The future is uncertain. What _____ ?

I will and *I'm going to*

Future actions

Study the difference between **will** and **going to**:

Sue is talking to Erica:

Let's have a party.

That's a great idea. We'll **invite** some people from work.

SUE   ERICA

will ('**ll**): We use **will** when we decide to do something at the time of speaking. The speaker has not decided before. The party is a new idea.

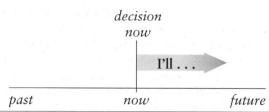

decision now

I'll . . .

past   now   future

Later that day, Erica meets Dave:

Sue and I have decided to have a party. We're **going to invite** some people from work.

ERICA   DAVE

going to: We use (**be**) **going to** when we have already decided to do something. Erica had already decided to invite some people from work before she spoke to Dave.

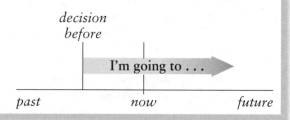

decision before

I'm going to . . .

past   now   future

Compare:
- "Daniel called while you were out." "OK. I'll **call** him back."

but   "Daniel called while you were out." "Yes, I know. I'm **going to call** him back."
- "Anna is in the hospital." "Oh, really? I didn't know. I'll **go** and **visit** her tonight."

but   "Anna is in the hospital." "Yes, I know. I'm **going to visit** her tonight."

Future happenings and situations (predicting the future)

Sometimes there is not much difference between **will** and **going to**. For example, you can say:
- I think the weather **will be** nice later.
- I think the weather **is going to be** nice later.

When we say something **is going to happen,** we think this because of the situation now:
- Look at those black clouds. It's **going to rain.** (*not* It will rain – We can see the clouds now.)
- I feel terrible. I think I'm **going to be** sick. (*not* I think I'll be sick – I feel terrible now.)

Do not use **will** in situations like these. (See also Unit 19C.)

In other situations, **will** is more usual:
- Tom **will** probably **arrive** at about 8:00.
- I think Jessica **will like** the present we bought for her.

Exercises

22.1 Complete the sentences using *will ('ll)* or *going to.*

1. *A:* Why are you turning on the television?
   B: _I'm going to watch_ the news. (I / watch)
2. *A:* Oh, I just realized that I don't have any money.
   B: You don't? Well, don't worry. _____ you some. (I / lend)
3. *A:* I have a headache.
   B: You do? Wait a second and _____ an aspirin for you. (I / get)
4. *A:* Why are you filling that bucket with water?
   B: _____ the car. (I / wash)
5. *A:* I've decided to paint this room.
   B: Oh, really? What color _____ it? (you / paint)
6. *A:* Where are you going? Are you going shopping?
   B: Yes, _____ something for dinner. (I / buy)
7. *A:* I don't know how to use this camera.
   B: It's easy. _____ you. (I / show)
8. *A:* Did you mail that letter for me?
   B: Oh, I'm sorry. I completely forgot. _____ it now. (I / do)
9. *A:* Has Dan decided what to do when he finishes high school?
   B: Oh, yes. Everything is planned. _____ a few months off (he / take)
   and then _____ classes at the community college. (he / start)

22.2 Read the situations and complete the sentences using *will ('ll)* or *going to.*

1. The phone rings and you answer. Somebody wants to speak to Jim.
   Caller: Hello. May I speak to Jim, please?
   You: Just a moment. _I'll get_ him. (I / get)
2. It's a nice day. You've decided to take a walk. Before going outside, you tell your friend.
   You: The weather's too nice to stay indoors. _____ a
   walk. (I / take)
   Friend: That's a good idea. I think _____ you. (I / join)
3. Your friend is worried because she has lost an important letter.
   You: Don't worry about the letter. I'm sure _____ it.
   (you / find)
   Friend: I hope so.
4. There was a job advertised in the newspaper recently. At first you were interested, but
   then you decided not to apply.
   Friend: Have you decided what to do about that job that was advertised?
   You: Yes, _____ for it. (I / not / apply)
5. You and a friend come home very late. Other people in the house are asleep. Your
   friend is noisy.
   You: Shh! Don't make so much noise. _____ everybody
   up. (you / wake)
6. John has to go to the airport to catch a plane tomorrow morning.
   John: Ann, I need a ride to the airport tomorrow morning.
   Ann: That's no problem. _____ you. (I / take) What
   time is your flight?
   John: 10:50.
   Ann: OK, then _____ at about 8:00. (we / leave)
   Later that day, Joe offers to take John to the airport.
   Joe: John, do you want me to take you to the airport?
   John: No thanks, Joe. _____ me. (Ann / take)

Will be doing and will have done

Study this example situation:

Kevin loves football and tonight there is a big football game
on TV. The game begins at 7:30 and ends at 9:15. Paul wants to
see Kevin tonight and wants to know what time to come over.

  Paul: Is it all right if I come at about 8:30?
Kevin: No, I'**ll be watching** the game then.
  Paul: Well, what about 9:30?
Kevin: Fine. The game **will have ended** by then.

I will be doing something *(future continuous)* = I will be in the middle of doing something.
The football game begins at 7:30 and ends at 9:15. So during this time, for example at 8:30,
Kevin **will be watching** the game. Another example:
- I'm leaving on vacation this Saturday. This time next week I'**ll be lying** on a beach or
  swimming in the ocean.

Compare **will be doing** and **will do**:
- Don't call me between 7 and 8. We'**ll be having** dinner then.
- Let's wait for Maria to arrive, and then we'll **have** dinner.

Compare **will be doing** with other continuous forms:
- At 10:00 yesterday, Kelly **was** in her office. She **was working.** *(past)*
  It's 10:00 now. She **is** in her office. She **is working.** *(present)*
  At 10:00 tomorrow, she **will be** in her office. She **will be working.** *(future)*

We also use **will be doing** in a different way: to talk about complete actions in the future:
- I'**ll be seeing** Kelly at the meeting this evening.
- What time **will** your friends **be arriving** tomorrow?

In these examples, **will be doing** is similar to the present continuous with a future meaning.
(See Unit 18A.)

You can use **Will you be -ing . . . ?** to ask about somebody's plans, especially if you want
something or want them to do something. For example:
- *A:* **Will you be using** your car tonight?
- *B:* Why? Do you want to borrow it?

We use **will have done** *(future perfect)* to say that something will already be complete before
a time in the future. Kevin's football game ends at 9:15. So after this time, for example at
9:30, the game **will have ended.** Some more examples:
- Kelly always leaves for work at 8:30 in the morning, so she won't be home at 9:00.
  She'**ll have gone** to work.
- We're late. The movie **will** already **have started** by the time we get to the theater.

Compare **will have done** with other perfect forms:
- Ted and Amy **have been married** for 24 years. *(present perfect)*
  Next year they **will have been married** for 25 years. *(future perfect)*
  When their first child was born, they **had been married** for three years. *(past perfect)*

By the time / by then Unit 116C

Exercises

23.1 Read about Josh. Then put a check (✓) by the sentences that are true. In each group of sentences, at least one is true.

Josh goes to work every day. After breakfast, he leaves home at 8:00 and arrives at work at about 8:45. He starts work immediately and continues until 12:30, when he has lunch (which takes about half an hour). He starts work again at 1:15 and goes home at exactly 4:30. Every day he follows the same routine, and tomorrow will be no exception.

1. **At 7:45**
   a) he'll be leaving the house.
   b) he'll have left the house.
   c) he'll be at home. ✓
   d) he'll be having breakfast. ✓

4. **At 12:45**
   a) he'll have lunch.
   b) he'll be having lunch.
   c) he'll have finished his lunch.
   d) he'll have started his lunch.

2. **At 8:15**
   a) he'll be leaving the house.
   b) he'll have left the house.
   c) he'll have arrived at work.
   d) he'll be arriving at work.

5. **At 4:00**
   a) he'll have finished work.
   b) he'll finish work.
   c) he'll be working.
   d) he won't have finished work.

3. **At 9:15**
   a) he'll be working.
   b) he'll start work.
   c) he'll have started work.
   d) he'll be arriving at work.

6. **At 4:45**
   a) he'll leave work.
   b) he'll be leaving work.
   c) he'll have left work.
   d) he'll have arrived home.

23.2 Put the verb into the correct form, *will be (do)ing* or *will have (done)*.

1. Don't phone me between 7 and 8. _We'll be having_ (we / have) dinner then.
2. Call me after 8:00. _____ (we / finish) dinner by then.
3. Tomorrow afternoon we're going to play tennis from 3:00 until 4:30. So at 4 :00, _____ (we / play) tennis.
4. *A:* Can we meet tomorrow afternoon?
   B: I'm afraid not. _____ (I / work).
5. (B has to go to a meeting that begins at 10:00. It will last about an hour.)
   A: Will you be free at 11:30?
   B: Yes, _____ (the meeting / end) by then.
6. Ben is on vacation, and he is spending his money very quickly. If he continues like this, _____ (he / spend) all his money before the end of his vacation.
7. Do you think _____ (you / still / do) the same job in ten years' time?
8. Lisa is from New Zealand. She is traveling around Canada at the moment. So far she has traveled about 1,000 miles. By the end of the trip, _____ (she / travel) more than 3,000 miles.
9. If you need to contact me, _____ (I / stay) at the Bellmore Hotel until Friday.
10. *A:* _____ (you / see) Tracy tomorrow?
    B: Yes, probably. Why?
    A: I borrowed this book from her. Could you give it back to her?

When I do / When I've done
When and if

A

Study these examples:

What time will you phone me tomorrow?

I'll call you **when I get** home from work.

"I'll call you when I get home from work" is a sentence with two parts:

the main part: I'll call you
the **when** part: when I get home from work (tomorrow)

The time in the sentence is *future* (tomorrow), but we use a *present tense* (**get**) in the **when** part of the sentence.

We do not use **will** in the **when** part of the sentence:
- We'll go out **when** it **stops** raining. (*not* when it will stop)
- **When** you **are** in Los Angeles again, give us a call. (*not* When you will be)
- (*said to a child*) What do you want to be **when** you **grow** up? (*not* will grow)

The same thing happens after **while / before / after / as soon as / until** or **till**:
- I'm going to read a lot of books **while I'm** on vacation. (*not* while I will be)
- I'm going back home on Sunday. **Before I go,** I'd like to visit the museum.
- Wait here **until** (*or* **till**) I **come** back.

B

You can also use the *present perfect* (**have done**) after **when / after / until / as soon as**:
- Can I borrow that book **when** you've **finished** it?
- Don't say anything while Ben is here. Wait **until** he **has gone**.

It is often possible to use the *simple present* or the *present perfect*:
- I'll come **as soon as I finish**.   *or*   I'll come **as soon as I've finished**.
- You'll feel better **after** you **have**   *or*   You'll feel better **after** you've **had**
  something to eat.   something to eat.

But do not use the present perfect if two things happen together. The present perfect shows that one thing will be complete before the other (so the two things do not happen together). Compare:
- **When I've called** Kate, we can have dinner.
  (= First I'll call Kate, and after that we can have dinner.)
but   **When I call** Kate this evening, I'll invite her to the party. (*not* When I've called)
  (In this example, the two things happen together.)

C

After **if,** we normally use the simple present (**do/see,** etc.) for the future:
- It's raining hard. We'll get wet **if** we **go** out. (*not* if we will go)
- Hurry up! **If** we **don't hurry,** we'll be late.

Compare **when** and **if:**
We use **when** for things that are sure to happen:
- I'm going shopping this afternoon. (for sure)   **When** I go shopping, I'll buy some food.

We use **if** (*not* when) for things that will possibly happen:
- I might go shopping this afternoon. (it's possible)   **If** I go shopping, I'll buy some food.
- Don't worry **if** I'm late tonight. (*not* when I'm late)
- **If** they don't come soon, I'm not going to wait. (*not* When they don't come)

Exercises

24.1 Complete these sentences using the verbs in parentheses. All the sentences are about the future. Use *will/won't* or the simple present (*I see / he plays / it is,* etc.).

1. I _'ll call_____ (call) you when I _get_____ (get) home from work.
2. I want to see Jennifer before she _____ (go) out.
3. We're going on a trip tomorrow. I _____ (tell) you all about it when we _____ (come) back.
4. Brian looks very different now. When you _____ (see) him again, you _____ (not / recognize) him.
5. We should do something soon before it _____ (be) too late.
6. I don't want to go without you. I _____ (wait) until you _____ (be) ready.
7. Sue has applied for the job, but she isn't very well qualified for it. I _____ (be) surprised if she _____ (get) it.
8. I'd like to play tennis tomorrow if the weather _____ (be) nice.
9. I'm going out now. If anybody _____ (call) while I _____ (be) out, can you take a message?

24.2 Make one sentence from two.

1. You will be in Los Angeles again. Give us a call.
   _Give us a call_____ when _you are in Los Angeles again_____ .
2. I'll find a place to live. Then I'll give you my address.
   I _____ when _____ .
3. I'll do the shopping. Then I'll come straight home.
   _____ after _____ .
4. It's going to start raining. Let's go home before that.
   _____ before _____ .
5. She has to apologize to me first. I won't speak to her until then.
   _____ until _____ .

24.3 Read the situations and complete the sentences.

1. A friend of yours is going to visit Hong Kong. You want to know where she is going to stay. You ask:
   Where are you going to stay when _you are in Hong Kong_____ ?
2. A friend of yours is visiting you. She has to leave soon, but you'd like to show her some pictures. You ask:
   Do you have time to look at some pictures before _____ ?
3. Your friend is reading the newspaper. You'd like to read it next. You ask:
   Could I have the newspaper when _____ ?
4. You want to sell your car. Jim is interested in buying it, but he hasn't decided yet. You ask:
   Can you let me know as soon as _____ ?

24.4 Put in *when* or *if*.

1. Don't worry _if___ I'm late tonight.
2. Chris might call while I'm out this evening. _____ he does, can you take a message?
3. I'm going to Tokyo next week. _____ I'm there, I hope to visit a friend of mine.
4. I think Beth will get the job. I'll be very surprised _____ she doesn't get it.
5. I'm going shopping. _____ you want anything, I can get it for you.
6. I'm going away for a few days. I'll call you _____ I get back.
7. I want you to come to the party, but _____ you don't want to come, that's all right.
8. We can eat at home or, _____ you prefer, we can go to a restaurant.

Can, could, and (be) able to

We use **can** to say that something is possible or that somebody has the ability to do something:

- We **can see** the ocean from our hotel window.
- **Can** you **speak** any foreign languages?
- I **can come** and help you tomorrow if you want.
- The word "dream" **can be** a noun or a verb.

The negative is **can't** (= cannot):

- I'm afraid I **can't come** to your party on Friday.

(Be) able to is possible instead of **can,** but **can** is more usual:

- Are you **able to speak** any foreign languages?

But **can** has only two forms: **can** *(present)* and **could** *(past)*. So sometimes it is necessary to use **(be) able to.** Compare:

- I **can't** sleep.
but I **haven't been able to** sleep recently.
- Tom **can** come tomorrow.
but Tom **might be able to** come tomorrow.

Could and **was able to**

Sometimes **could** is the past of **can.** We use **could** especially with:
see   hear   smell   taste   feel   remember   understand

- When we went into the house, we **could smell** something burning.
- She spoke in a very soft voice, but I **could understand** what she said.

We also use **could** to say that somebody had the general ability or permission to do something:

- My grandfather **could speak** five languages.
- We were totally free. We **could do** whatever we wanted. (= We were allowed to do)

We use **could** for general ability. But if we are talking about what happened in a particular situation, we use **was/were able to** or **managed to** (*not* could):

- The fire spread through the building quickly, but everybody **was able to escape.**
or . . . everybody **managed to escape.** (*not* could escape)
- They didn't want to come with us at first, but we **managed to persuade** them.
or . . . we **were able to persuade** them. (*not* could persuade)

Compare:

- Jack was an excellent tennis player. He **could beat** anybody.
(= he had the general ability to beat anybody)
but Jack and Ted played tennis yesterday. Ted played very well, but in the end Jack **managed to beat** him.
or . . . **was able to beat** him. (= he managed to beat him this time)

The negative **couldn't** (= could not) is possible in all situations:

- My grandfather **couldn't swim.**
- We tried hard, but we **couldn't persuade** them to come with us.
- Ted played well, but he **couldn't beat** Jack.

Could (do) and *could have (done)* Unit 26   *Must and can't* Unit 27   *Can/Could you . . . ?* Unit 34

Exercises

25.1 Complete the sentences using *can* or *(be) able to*. Use *can* if possible; otherwise, use *(be) able to.*

1. Eric has traveled a lot. He _can_____ speak four languages.
2. I haven't _been able to_____ sleep very well recently.
3. Nicole _____ drive, but she doesn't have a car.
4. I can't understand Michael. I've never _____ understand him.
5. I used to _____ stand on my head, but I can't do it now.
6. I can't see you on Friday, but I _____ meet you on Saturday morning.
7. Ask Catherine about your problem. She might _____ help you.

25.2 Write sentences about yourself using the ideas in parentheses.

1. (something you used to be able to do) _I used to be able to sing well._
2. (something you used to be able to do) I used _____.
3. (something you would like to be able to do) I'd _____.
4. (something you have never been able to do) I've _____.

25.3 Complete the sentences with *can/can't/could/couldn't* + one of these verbs:

~~come~~ eat hear run sleep wait

1. I'm afraid I _can't come_____ to your party next week.
2. When Bob was 16, he was a fast runner. He _____ 100 meters in 11 seconds.
3. "Are you in a hurry?" "No, I've got plenty of time. I _____."
4. I felt sick yesterday. I _____ anything.
5. Can you speak a little louder? I _____ you very well.
6. "You look tired." "Yes, I _____ last night."

25.4 Complete the answers to the questions using *was/were able to.*

1. *A:* Did everybody escape from the fire?
   B: Yes. Although the fire spread quickly, everybody _was able to escape_____.
2. *A:* Did you have any trouble finding Amy's house?
   B: Not really. She had given us good directions, so we _____.
3. *A:* Did you finish your work this afternoon?
   B: Yes. Nobody was around to bother me, so _____.
4. *A:* Did the thief get away?
   B: Yes. No one realized what was happening, and the thief _____.

25.5 Complete the sentences using *could, couldn't,* or *was/were able to.*

1. My grandfather was a very clever man. He _could_____ speak five languages.
2. I looked everywhere for the book, but I _couldn't_____ find it.
3. They didn't want to come with us at first, but we _were able to_____ persuade them.
4. Laura had hurt her leg and _____ walk very well.
5. Sue wasn't at home when I called, but I _____ contact her at her office.
6. I looked very carefully, and I _____ see a figure in the distance.
7. I wanted to buy some tomatoes. The first store I went to didn't have any good ones, but I _____ get some at the next place.
8. My grandmother loved music. She _____ play the piano very well.
9. A girl fell into the river, but fortunately we _____ rescue her.
10. I had forgotten to bring my camera, so I _____ take any photographs.

Could (do) and could have (done)

We use **could** in a number of ways. Sometimes **could** is the past of **can** (see Unit 25C):
- Listen. I **can hear** something. *(now)*
- I listened. I **could hear** something. *(past)*

But **could** is not used only in this way. We also use **could** to talk about possible actions now or in the future (especially to make a suggestion). For example:

What would you like to do tonight?

We could go to the movies.

- A: What would you like to do tonight?
  B: We **could go** to the movies.
- It's a nice day. We **could go** for a walk.
- When you go to New York next month, you **could stay** with Candice.
- A: If you need a car, you **could borrow** Lauren's.
  B: Yes, I guess I **could.**

Can is also possible in these sentences (We **can go** for a walk, etc.). **Could** is less sure than **can.** Use **could** (*not* can) when you don't really mean what you say. For example:
- I'm so angry with him. I **could kill** him! (*not* I can kill him!)

We also use **could** to say that something is possible now or in the future:
- The phone is ringing. It **could be** Alex. (*not* It can be Alex)
- I don't know when they'll be here. They **could get** here at any time.

Can is not possible in these examples. In these sentences **could** is similar to **might** (see Units 28–29):
- The phone is ringing. It **might be** Alex.

Compare **could** (**do**) and **could have** (**done**):
- I'm so tired. I **could sleep** for a week. *(now)*
- I was so tired. I **could have slept** for a week. *(past)*

We normally use **could have** (**done**) for things that were possible but did not happen:
- Why did you stay at a hotel when you went to New York? You **could have stayed** with Candice. (= you had the opportunity to stay with her, but you didn't)
- Dave fell off a ladder yesterday, but he's all right. He's lucky – he **could have hurt** himself badly. (but he didn't hurt himself)
- The situation was bad, but it **could have been** worse.

Sometimes **could** means "would be able to":
- We **could take** a trip if we had enough money. (= we would be able to go away)
- I don't know how you work so hard. I **couldn't do** it.

Could have (**done**) = would have been able to (do):
- Why didn't Liz apply for the job? She **could have gotten** it.
- We **could have taken** a trip if we'd had enough money.
- The trip was canceled last week. I **couldn't have gone** anyway because I was sick. (= I wouldn't have been able to go)

Could, may, and *might* Unit 28C   *Could you . . . ?* Unit 34   *Could* with *if* Units 35C, 36E, 37D

Exercises

26.1 Answer the questions with a suggestion. Use *could* and the words in parentheses.

1. Where should we go for the long weekend?   (to San Antonio) _We could go to San Antonio._
2. What should we have for dinner tonight?   (fish) We _____ .
3. What should I give Amy for her birthday?   (a book) You _____ .
4. When should I call Angela?   (now) _____
5. When should we go and see Tom?   (on Friday) _____

26.2 Put in *can* or *could*. Sometimes either word is possible.

1. "The phone is ringing. Who do you think it is?" "It _could_ be Alex."
2. I'm really hungry. I _____ eat a horse!
3. If you're very hungry, we _____ have dinner now.
4. It's so nice here. I _____ stay here all day, but unfortunately I have to go.
5. "I can't find my bag. Have you seen it?" "No, but it _____ be in the car."
6. David is a good musician. He plays the flute, and he _____ also play the piano.
7. "What do you want to do?" "There's a movie on television. We _____ watch that."
8. The weather is nice now, but it _____ change later.

26.3 Complete the sentences. Use *could* or *could have* + an appropriate verb.

1. *A:* What should we do this evening? *B:* I don't know. We _could go_ to the movies.
2. *A:* I was so bored at home last night.
   B: Why did you stay at home? You _____ to the movies.
3. *A:* There's an interesting job advertised in the paper. You _____ for it.
   B: What kind of job is it? Show me the ad.
4. *A:* Did you go to the concert last night?
   B: No. We _____ , but we decided not to.
5. *A:* Where should we meet tomorrow?
   B: Well, I _____ to your house if you want.

26.4 Read this information about Ken:

Ken didn't do anything on Saturday night.   Ken ran out of money last week.
Ken doesn't know anything about machines.   ~~Ken's car was stolen on Monday.~~
Ken had Monday afternoon off.   Ken had to work Friday night.

Some people wanted Ken to do different things last week, but they couldn't contact him. You have to say whether he could have done or couldn't have done them.

1. Ken's aunt wanted him to drive her to the airport on Tuesday.
   He couldn't have driven her to the airport (because his car had been stolen).
2. A friend of his wanted him to go out for dinner on Friday night.
   Ken _____ .
3. Another friend wanted him to play tennis on Monday afternoon.
   Ken _____ .
4. Jack wanted Ken to lend him $50 last week.
   _____
5. Lisa wanted Ken to come to her party on Saturday night.
   He _____ .
6. Ken's mother wanted him to fix her washing machine.
   _____

Must (You must be tired, etc.)

Must (not)

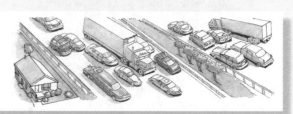

We use **must** to say that we feel sure something is true:

■ You've been traveling all day. You **must be** tired. (Traveling is tiring and you've been traveling all day, so you are probably tired.)

■ "Jim is a hard worker." "Jim? A hard worker? You **must be joking.** He's very lazy."

■ Debbie **must get** very bored with her job. She does the same thing every day.

We use **must not** to say that we feel sure something is not true:

■ Their car isn't outside their house. They **must not be** home. (= They must be out.)

■ Brian said he would definitely be here before 9:30. It's 10:00 now, and he's never late. He **must not be coming.**

■ They haven't lived here very long. They **must not know** many people.

Study the structure:

I/you/he (etc.) **must (not)**	**be** (tired/hungry/home, etc.) **be** (doing/coming/joking, etc.) **do/get/know/have,** etc.

Must (not) have done

For the past, we use **must (not) have done:**

■ "We used to live close to the freeway." "Did you? It **must have been** noisy."

■ There's nobody at home. They **must have gone** out.

■ I've lost one of my gloves. I **must have dropped** it somewhere.

■ She walked past me without speaking. She **must not have seen** me.

■ Tom walked straight into a wall. He **must not have been looking** where he was going.

Study the structure:

I/you/he (etc.) **must (not) have**	**been** (tired/hungry/noisy, etc.) **been** (doing/coming/looking, etc.) **done/gone/known/had,** etc.

Can't and must not

It **can't be** true = I believe it is impossible:

■ How can you say such a thing? You **can't be** serious!

Compare **can't** and **must not:**

■ A: Joe wants something to eat.
B: But he just had lunch. He **can't be** hungry already. (= it's impossible that he is hungry because he just had lunch)

■ A: I offered Bill something to eat, but he didn't want anything.
B: He **must not be** hungry. (= I'm sure he is not hungry – otherwise he would eat something)

Can't (I can't swim, etc.) **Unit 25A, B**   *Must (I must go, etc.)* **Unit 30D, E**

Exercises

27.1 Put in *must* or *must not.*

1. You've been traveling all day. You _must_ be very tired.
2. That restaurant _____ be very good. It's always full of people.
3. That restaurant _____ be very good. It's always empty.
4. You _____ be looking forward to going on vacation next week.
5. It rained every day during their vacation, so they _____ have had a very good time.
6. You got here very quickly. You _____ have walked very fast.

27.2 Complete the sentences with a verb in the correct form.

1. I've lost one of my gloves. I must _have dropped_ it somewhere.
2. They haven't lived here very long. They must not _know_ many people.
3. Ted isn't at work today. He must _____ sick.
4. Ted wasn't at work last week. He must _____ sick.
5. Sarah knows a lot about movies. She must _____ to the movies a lot.
6. Look – James is putting on his coat. He must _____ out.
7. I left my bike outside last night, and this morning it isn't there anymore. Somebody must _____ it.
8. Megan was in a very difficult situation. It must not _____ easy for her.
9. There is a man walking behind us. He has been walking behind us for the last 20 minutes. He must _____ us.

27.3 Read the situations and use the words in parentheses to write sentences with *must have* and *must not have.*

1. The phone rang but I didn't hear it. (I / asleep) _I must have been asleep._
2. Julie walked past me without speaking. (she / see / me) _She must not have seen me._
3. The jacket you bought is very good quality. (it / very expensive)
   _____
4. I can't find my umbrella. (I / leave / it in the restaurant last night)
   _____
5. Dave passed the exam without studying for it. (the exam / very difficult)
   _____
6. She knew everything about our plans. (she / listen / to our conversation)
   _____
7. Rachel did the opposite of what I asked her to do. (she / understand / what I said)
   _____
8. When I woke up this morning, the light was on. (I / forget / to turn it off)
   _____
9. The light was red, but the car didn't stop. (the driver / see / the red light)
   _____

27.4 Complete the sentences with *must not* or *can't.*

1. How can you say such a thing? You _can't_ be serious.
2. Their car isn't outside their house. They _must not_ be home.
3. I just bought a box of cereal yesterday. It _____ be empty already.
4. The Smiths always go on vacation this time of year, but they are still home.
   They _____ be taking a vacation this year.
5. You just started filling out your tax forms 10 minutes ago.
   You _____ be finished with them already!
6. Eric is a good friend of Ann's, but he hasn't visited her in the hospital.
   He _____ know she's in the hospital.

May and *might* (1)

A

Study this example situation:

You are looking for Bob. Nobody is sure where he is, but you get some suggestions.

Where's Bob?

YOU

He **may be** in his office. — (= perhaps he is in his office)

He **might be having** lunch. — (= perhaps he is having lunch)

Ask Ann. She **might know.** — (= perhaps she knows)

We use **may** or **might** to say that something is a possibility:
- It **may be** true.   *or*   It **might be** true. (= perhaps it is true)
- She **might know.**   *or*   She **may know.**

The negative forms are **may not** and **might not**:
- It **might not be** true. (= perhaps it isn't true)
- I'm not sure whether I can lend you any money. I **may not have** enough. (= perhaps I don't have enough)

Study the structure:

I/you/he (etc.)	may might	(not)	be (wrong / in his office, etc.) be (doing/working/having, etc.) do/know/have/want, etc.

B

For the past we use **may have done** or **might have done**:
- *A:* I wonder why Amy didn't answer the phone.
  B: She **may have been** asleep. (= perhaps she was asleep)
- *A:* I can't find my bag anywhere.
  B: You **might have left** it in the store. (= perhaps you left it in the store)
- *A:* I was surprised that Sarah wasn't at the meeting.
  B: She **might not have known** about it. (= perhaps she didn't know)
- *A:* I wonder why David was in such a bad mood yesterday.
  B: He **may not have been** feeling well. (= perhaps he wasn't feeling well)

Study the structure:

I/you/he (etc.)	may might	(not) have	been (asleep / at home, etc.) been (doing/waiting, etc.) done/known/had/seen, etc.

C

Sometimes **could** has a similar meaning to **may** and **might**:
- The phone's ringing. It **could be** Matt. (= it may/might be Matt)
- You **could have left** your bag in the store. (= you may/might have left it there)

But **couldn't** (*negative*) is different from **may not** and **might not**. Compare:
- He was too far away, so he **couldn't have seen** you. (= it is not possible that he saw you)
- *A:* I wonder why she didn't say hello.
  B: She **might not have seen** you. (= perhaps she didn't see you; perhaps she did)

Could Unit 26   ***May and might* (2)** Unit 29   ***May I . . . ?*** Unit 34

Exercises

28.1 Write these sentences in a different way using *may* or *might*.

1. Perhaps Elizabeth is in her office. *She might be in her office.* OR *She may be . . .*
2. Perhaps Elizabeth is busy. _____
3. Perhaps she is working. _____
4. Perhaps she wants to be alone. _____
5. Perhaps she was sick yesterday. _____
6. Perhaps she went home early. _____
7. Perhaps she had to go home early. _____
8. Perhaps she was working yesterday. _____

In sentences 9–11, use *may not* or *might not*.

9. Perhaps she doesn't want to see me. _____
10. Perhaps she isn't working today. _____
11. Perhaps she wasn't feeling well yesterday. _____

28.2 Complete the sentences with a verb in the correct form.

1. *A:* Where's Bob?   *B:* I'm not sure. He might *be having* _____ lunch.
2. *A:* Who is that man with Anna?
   B: I'm not sure. It might _____ her brother.
3. *A:* Who was the man we saw with Anna yesterday?
   B: I'm not sure. It might _____ her brother.
4. *A:* What are those people doing on the sidewalk?
   B: They might _____ for a bus.
5. *A:* Should I buy this book for Sam?
   B: You'd better not. He might already _____ it.

28.3 Read the situations and make sentences from the words in parentheses. Use *may* or *might*.

1. I can't find Jeff anywhere. I wonder where he is.
   a) (he / go / shopping) *He may have gone shopping.* _____
   b) (he / play / tennis) *He might be playing tennis.* _____
2. I'm looking for Tiffany. Do you know where she is?
   a) (she / watch / TV / in her room) _____
   b) (she / go / out) _____
3. I can't find my umbrella. Have you seen it?
   a) (it / be / in the car) _____
   b) (you / leave / in the restaurant last night) _____
4. Why didn't Dave answer the doorbell? I'm sure he was home at the time.
   a) (he / be / in the shower) _____
   b) (he / not / hear / the bell) _____

28.4 Complete the sentences using *might not* or *couldn't*.

1. *A:* Do you think she saw you?
   B: No, she was too far away. *She couldn't have seen me.* _____
2. *A:* I wonder why Ann didn't come to the party. Perhaps she wasn't invited.
   B: Yes, it's possible. She _____ .
3. *A:* Tom loves parties. I'm sure he would have come to the party if he'd been invited.
   B: I agree. He _____ .
4. *A:* I wonder how the fire started. Maybe it was an accident.
   B: No, the police say it _____ .
5. *A:* How did the fire start? Do you think it was an accident?
   B: Well, the police aren't sure. They say it _____ .

May and *might* (2)

A

We use **may** and **might** to talk about possible actions or happenings in the future:

- I haven't decided what I'm doing for spring break. I **may go** to Mexico. (= perhaps I will go to Mexico)
- Take an umbrella with you when you go out. It **might rain** later. (= perhaps it will rain)
- The bus doesn't always come on time. We **might have to wait** a few minutes.

The negative forms are **may not** and **might not**:

- Ann **may not go** out tonight. She isn't feeling well. (= perhaps she will not go out)
- There **might not be** a meeting on Friday because the director is sick.

B

Usually it doesn't matter whether you use **may** or **might**. So you can say:

- I **may go** to Mexico. *or* I **might go** to Mexico.
- Lisa **might be** able to help you. *or* Lisa **may be** able to help you.

But we use only **might** (*not* may) when the situation is not real:

- If I knew them better, I **might invite** them to dinner.
  (The situation here is not real because I don't know them very well, so I'm not going to invite them. **May** is not possible in this example.)

C

There is also a continuous form: **may/might be -ing**. Compare this with **will be -ing**:

- Don't phone me at 8:30. I'**ll be watching** the baseball game on TV.
- Don't phone me at 8:30. I **might be watching** (*or* I **may be watching**) the baseball game on TV. (= perhaps I'll be watching it)

For **will be -ing**, see Unit 23.

We also use **may/might be -ing** for possible plans. Compare:

- I'm going to Mexico in July. (for sure)
- I **may be going** (*or* I **might be going**) to Mexico in July. (possible)

But you can also say "I **may go** (*or* I **might go**) to Mexico" with little difference in meaning.

D

Might as well / may as well

Rosa and Maria have just missed the bus. The buses run every hour.

What should we do? Should we walk?

We **might as well**. It's a nice day, and I don't want to wait here for an hour.

We **might as well do** something = We should do something because there is nothing better to do and there is no reason not to do it.

You can also say **may as well**.

- *A:* What time are you going?
  B: Well, I'm ready, so I **might as well go** now.
- Rents are so high these days, you **may as well buy** a house.

May and might (1) Unit 28   *May I . . . ?* Unit 34   *Might* with *if* Units 35C, 37D

Exercises

29.1 Write sentences with *may* or *might*.

1. Where are you going for spring break? (to Mexico???)
   I haven't decided yet. *I may go to Mexico.*
2. What kind of car are you going to buy? (a Toyota???)
   I'm not sure yet. I _____ .
3. Where are you going to hang that picture? (in the dining room???)
   I haven't made up my mind yet. _____
4. When is Jim coming to see us? (on Saturday???)
   I don't know yet. _____
5. What is Julia going to do when she graduates from high school? (go to college???)
   She hasn't decided yet. _____

29.2 Complete the sentences using *might* + one of these verbs:

  bite   break   need   ~~rain~~   slip   wake

1. Take an umbrella with you when you go out. It *might rain* _____ later.
2. Don't make too much noise. You _____ the baby.
3. Watch out for that dog. It _____ you.
4. I don't think we should throw that letter away. We _____ it later.
5. Be careful. The sidewalk is very icy. You _____ .
6. I don't want the children to play in this room. They _____ something.

29.3 Complete the sentences using *might be able to* or *might have to* + an appropriate verb.

1. I can't help you, but why don't you ask Liz? She *might be able to help* _____ you.
2. I can't meet you tonight, but I _____ you tomorrow night.
3. I'm not working on Saturday, but I _____ on Sunday.
4. Michael is very sick. He _____ to the hospital.

29.4 Read the situations and write sentences with *may not* or *might not*.

1. You don't know if Ann will come to the party.
   Ann may not come to the party.
2. You don't know if you'll go out this evening.
   I _____ .
3. You don't know if Sam will like the present you bought for him.
   Sam _____ .
4. You don't know if Sue will be able to meet you tonight.
   _____

29.5 Read the situations and make sentences with *may/might as well*.

1. You and a friend have just missed the bus. The buses run every hour. You say:
   We'll have to wait an hour for the next bus. *We might as well walk.*
2. You have a free ticket for a concert. You're not very excited about the concert but you
   decide to go. You say: I _____ to the concert. It's a
   shame to waste a free ticket.
3. You and a friend were thinking of eating in a restaurant, but you have a lot of food in
   the refrigerator. You say: We _____ at home. There's a
   lot of food in the fridge.
4. You and a friend are at home. You are bored. There's a movie on TV starting in a few
   minutes. You say: _____ . There's nothing else to do.

Have to and *must*

A

We use **have to do** to say that it is necessary to do something:

- I **have to get up** early tomorrow. My flight leaves at 7:30.
- This street ends at the next block, so you **have to turn.**
- Jason can't meet us this evening. He **has to work** late.
- Last week Nicole broke her arm and **had to go** to the hospital.
- Have you ever **had to go** to the hospital?
- I might **have to leave** the meeting early.

B

In *simple present* and *simple past* questions, we use **do/does/did:**

- What **do I have to do** to get a driver's license? (*not* What have I to do?)
- **Does** Kimberly **have to work** tomorrow?
- Why **did** you **have to go** to the hospital?

In negative sentences, we use **don't/doesn't/didn't:**

- I **don't have to get up** early tomorrow. (*not* I haven't to get up)
- Kimberly **doesn't have to work** on Saturdays.
- We **didn't have to pay** to park the car.

C

You can use **have got to** instead of **have to** for the present. So you can say:

- I've **got to** work now. *or* I **have to** work now.
- He's **got to** visit his aunt *or* He **has to** visit his aunt
  in the hospital tonight. in the hospital tonight.

D

We can also use **must** to say that it is necessary to do something:

- I **must** get to the store before it closes.
- When you go to San Francisco next week, you really **must** visit Golden Gate Park.

Must is often used in written rules and instructions:

- You **must** apply by April 15. (= your application won't be accepted after that date)
- This medicine **must** be taken with food. (or your stomach will be upset)

You can also use **have to** in these situations.

We use **must** to talk about the present or future but not the past:

- I **had to** get up early **yesterday.** (*not* I must)

E

Mustn't (= must not) and **don't / doesn't have to** are completely different in meaning:

You **mustn't** do something = it is necessary that you not do it, so don't do it: ■ You must keep it a secret. You **mustn't** tell anyone. (= don't tell anyone) ■ I promised I would be on time. I **mustn't** be late. (= I must be on time)	You **don't have to** do something = you don't need to do it (but you can if you want): ■ You **don't have to** tell him, but you can if you want to. ■ Sue isn't working tomorrow, so she **doesn't have to** get up early.

Must (You must be tired, etc.) Unit 27

Exercises

30.1 Complete the sentences with *have to / has to / had to.*

1. Jason can't meet us this evening. He _has to_ work late.
2. Beth left before the end of the meeting. She _____ go home early.
3. I don't have much time. I _____ go soon.
4. Kathy may _____ go away next week.
5. Eric is usually free on weekends, but sometimes he _____ work.
6. There was nobody to help me. I _____ do everything by myself.
7. Julie has _____ wear glasses since she was a small child.
8. Jeff has money problems. He's going to _____ sell his car.

30.2 Complete the questions using the words in parentheses.

1. "I broke my arm last week." "_Did you have to go_ (you / have / go) to the hospital?"
2. "I'm afraid I can't stay very long." "What time _____ (you / have / go)?"
3. _____ (you / have / wait) long for the bus last night?
4. How old _____ (you / have / be) to drive in your country?
5. How does Chris like his new job? _____ (he / have / travel) a lot?

30.3 Complete these sentences using *have to* + one of the verbs in the list. Some sentences are positive (*I have to . . .*) and some are negative (*I don't have to . . .*).

> ask   do   ~~get up~~   go   make   make   shave   ~~show~~

1. I'm not working tomorrow, so I _don't have to get up_ early.
2. Steve didn't know how to use the computer, so I _had to show_ him.
3. Excuse me for a minute – I _____ a phone call. I won't be long.
4. I couldn't find the street I was looking for. I _____ somebody for directions.
5. Jack has a beard, so he _____ .
6. A man was injured in the accident, but he _____ to the hospital because it wasn't serious.
7. Sue is a vice-president in the company. She _____ important decisions.
8. I'm not very busy. I've got a few things to do, but I _____ them now.

30.4 Match the two halves of the sentences.

1. You really must
2. This letter must
3. Eric says he has
4. My wife and I both have
5. I can't talk to you now. I have
6. All the students must

a) be mailed by tomorrow.
b) to get our eyes tested.
c) finish their exams in one hour.
d) visit the museum while you're here.
e) to take his aunt to the hospital.
f) to make an important phone call right away.

30.5 Complete these sentences with *mustn't* or *don't/doesn't have to.*

1. I don't want anyone to know. You _mustn't_ tell anyone.
2. He _doesn't have to_ wear a suit to work, but he usually does.
3. I can sleep late tomorrow morning because I _____ go to work.
4. Whatever you do, you _____ touch that switch. It's very dangerous.
5. There's an elevator in the building, so we _____ climb the stairs.
6. You _____ forget what I told you. It's very important.
7. Lauren _____ get up early. She gets up early because she wants to.
8. Don't make so much noise. We _____ wake the baby.
9. You _____ be a good player to enjoy a game of tennis.

Should

A

You **should do** something = it is a good thing to do or the right thing to do. You can use **should** to give advice or to give an opinion:

- You look tired. You **should go** to bed.
- The government **should do** more to help homeless people.
- "**Should** we **invite** Susan to the party?" "Yes, I think we **should.**"

We often use **should** with **I think / I don't think / Do you think . . . ?**:

- **I think** the government **should do** more to help homeless people.
- **I don't think** you **should work** so hard.
- "**Do you think** I **should apply** for this job?" "Yes, **I think** you **should.**"

You **shouldn't do** something = it isn't a good thing to do:

- You **shouldn't believe** everything you read in the newspapers.

Should is not as strong as **must**:

- You **should apologize.** (= it would be a good thing to do)
- You **must apologize.** (= you have no alternative)

B

We also use **should** when something is not right or not what we expect:

- I wonder where Liz is. She **should be** here by now. (= she isn't here yet, and this is not normal)
- The price on this package is wrong. It **should be** $1.29, not $1.59.
- Those boys **shouldn't be playing** football right now. They **should be** in school.

We use **should** to say that we expect something to happen:

- She's been studying hard for the exam, so she **should pass.** (= I expect her to pass)
- There are plenty of hotels in this city. It **shouldn't be** difficult to find a place to stay. (= I don't expect that it will be difficult)

C

You **should have done** something = you didn't do it but it would have been the right thing to do:

- It was a great party last night. You **should have come.** Why didn't you? (= you didn't come, but it would have been good to come)
- I feel sick. **I shouldn't have eaten** so much chocolate. (= I ate too much chocolate)
- I wonder why they're so late. They **should have been** here an hour ago.
- She **shouldn't have been listening** to our conversation. It was private.

Compare **should (do)** and **should have (done)**:

- You look tired. You **should go** to bed now.
- You went to bed very late last night. You **should have gone** to bed earlier.

D

Ought to

You can use **ought** (with **to**) instead of **should**:

- Do you think **I ought to apply** for this job? (= Do you think I should apply?)
- She's been studying hard for the exam, so she **ought to pass.**

Should and *had better*   Unit 33B

Exercises

31.1 For each situation, write a sentence with *should* or *shouldn't* + one of the following:

> go away for a few days   go to bed so late   look for another job
> take a photograph   use her car so much

1. Liz needs a change. She *should go away for a few days* .
2. Your salary is too low. You _____ .
3. Eric always has trouble getting up. He _____ .
4. What a beautiful view! You _____ .
5. Sue drives everywhere. She never walks. She _____ .

31.2 Read the situations and write sentences with *I think / I don't think . . . should . . .*

1. Chris and Amy are planning to get married. You think it's a bad idea.
   (get married) *I don't think they should get married.*
2. I have a very bad cold, but I plan to go out this evening. You don't think this is a good
   idea. You say to me: (go out) _____
3. You don't like smoking, especially in restaurants.
   (be banned) I think _____ .
4. The government wants to raise taxes, but you don't think this is a good idea.
   (raise) _____

31.3 Complete the sentences with *should* or *should have* + the verb in parentheses.

1. Tracy *should pass* the exam. She's been studying very hard. (pass)
2. You missed a great party last night. You *should have come* . (come)
3. We don't see you enough. You _____ and see us more often. (come)
4. I'm in a difficult position. What do you think I _____ ? (do)
5. I'm sorry that I didn't follow your advice. I _____ what you said. (do)
6. We lost the game, but we _____ . Our team was better than theirs.
   (win)
7. "Is John here yet?" "Not yet, but he _____ here soon." (be)
8. I mailed the letter three days ago, so it _____ by now. (arrive)

31.4 Read the situations and write sentences with *should/shouldn't*. Some of the sentences
are past, and some are present.

1. I'm feeling sick. I ate too much. *I shouldn't have eaten so much.*
2. That man on the motorcycle isn't wearing a helmet. That's dangerous.
   He *should be wearing a helmet* .
3. When we got to the restaurant, there were no free tables. We hadn't reserved one.
   We _____ .
4. The sign says that the store opens every day at 8:30. It's 9:00 now, but the store isn't
   open yet. _____
5. The speed limit is 30 miles an hour, but Catherine is driving 50 miles an hour.
   She _____ .
6. I went to Dallas. A friend of mine lives in Dallas, but I didn't go to see him while I was
   there. When I saw him later, he said:
   You _____ .
7. I was driving right behind another car. Suddenly the driver in front of me stopped and I
   drove into the back of his car. It was my fault.

   _____
8. I walked into a wall. I wasn't looking where I was going.

   _____

Subjunctive *(I suggest you do)*

A

Study this example:

Why don't you buy some new clothes?

Lisa said to Mary, "Why don't you buy some new clothes?"

Lisa suggested (that) Mary **buy** some new clothes.

The *subjunctive* is always the same as the *base form* (**I buy, he buy, she buy,** etc.).

I/he/she/it we/you/they	do/buy/be, etc.

B

We use the subjunctive after these verbs:
suggest   propose   recommend   insist   demand

■ I **suggest** (that) **you take** a vacation.
■ The doctor **recommended** (that) **I rest** for a few days.
■ They **insisted** (that) **we have** dinner with them.
■ I **insisted** (that) **he have** dinner with us.
■ He **demanded** (that) **she apologize** to him.

The negative is **not** + the base form (**I not be, you not leave, she not go,** etc.):
■ The doctor recommended that **I not go** to work for two days.
■ They insisted that **he not bring** them a present.

You can use the subjunctive for the present, past, or future:
■ I **insist** (that) **you come** with us.
■ They **insisted** (that) **I go** with them.

Note the subjunctive **be** (often *passive*):
■ I insisted (that) something **be done** about the problem.
■ The chairperson proposed (that) the plans **be changed.**
■ The airline recommends that passengers **be** two hours early.

C

Other structures are possible after **insist** and **suggest**:
■ They **insisted on my having** dinner with them. (See Unit 59A.)
■ It was a beautiful evening, so I **suggested going** for a walk. (See Unit 50.)

You cannot use the *infinitive* after **suggest**:
■ She **suggested that he buy** some new clothes. (*not* suggested him to buy)
■ What do you **suggest I do**? (*not* suggest me to do)

Exercises

32.1 Write a sentence that means the same as the first sentence. Begin in the way shown. Some sentences are negative.

1. "Why don't you buy some new clothes?" said Lisa to Mary.
   Lisa suggested that _Mary buy some new clothes_____ .
2. "You really must stay a little longer," she said to me.
   She insisted that _____ .
3. "Why don't you visit the museum after lunch?" I said to her.
   I suggested that _____ .
4. "I think it would be a good idea to see a specialist," the doctor said to me.
   The doctor recommended that _____ .
5. "It would be a good idea for you not to lift anything heavy," the specialist said to me.
   The specialist recommended that _____ .
6. "You have to pay the rent by Friday at the latest," the landlord said to the tenant.
   The landlord demanded that _____ .
7. "Why don't you go away for a few days?" Josh said to me.
   Josh suggested that _____ .
8. "You shouldn't give your children snacks right before mealtime," the doctor told me.
   The doctor suggested that _____ .
9. "Let's have dinner early," Sarah said to us.
   Sarah proposed that _____ .

32.2 Complete these sentences with an appropriate verb.

1. I suggest that you _take_____ a vacation.
2. I insisted that something _be_____ done about the problem.
3. Our friends recommended that we _____ our vacation in the mountains.
4. Since Dave hurt Tracy's feelings, I strongly recommended that he _____ to her.
5. The workers at the factory are demanding that their wages _____ raised.
6. She doesn't use her car very often, so I suggested that she _____ it and use the money for something else.
7. Lisa wanted to walk home alone, but we insisted that she _____ for us.
8. The city council has proposed that a new shopping center _____ built.
9. What do you suggest I _____ to the party? A dress?
10. I didn't want her to come to the party, but Sam insisted that she _____ invited.

32.3 Tom is out of shape, and his friends made some suggestions:

Why don't you try jogging?	How about walking to work in the morning?	Eat more fruit and vegetables.	Why don't you take vitamins?
LINDA	SANDRA	BILL	ANNA

Write sentences telling what Tom's friends suggested.

1. Linda suggested that he _try jogging_____ .
2. Sandra suggested that he _____ .
3. Bill suggested _____ .
4. Anna _____ .

Had better
It's time . . .

A

Had better (I'd better / you'd better, etc.)

I'd better do something = it is advisable to do it. If I don't, there will be a problem or a danger:

- I have to meet Amy in ten minutes. **I'd better go** now or I'll be late.
- "Do you think I should take an umbrella?" "Yes, **you'd better**. It might rain."
- **We'd better stop** for gas soon. The tank is almost empty.

The negative is **I'd better not** (= I had better not):

- "Are you going out tonight?" "**I'd better not.** I've got a lot of work to do."
- You don't look very well. **You'd better not go** to work today.

You can use **had better** when you warn somebody that they must do something:

- **You'd better** be on time. / **You'd better not** be late. (or I'll be very angry)

> Note that the form is "**had** better" (usually I'd better / you'd better, etc., in spoken English):
> - **I'd better** go now = I **had** better go now.
>
> **Had** is a past form, but in this expression the meaning is present or future, not past:
> - **I'd better go** to the bank now/tomorrow.
>
> We say **I'd better do** . . . (not to do):
> - It might rain. **We'd better take** an umbrella. (not We'd better to take)

B

Had better and **should**

Had better is similar to **should** (see Unit 31A) but not exactly the same. We use **had better** only for specific occasions (not for things in general). You can use **should** in all types of situations to give an opinion or to give advice:

- It's cold today. **You'd better** wear a coat when you go out. (a specific occasion)
- I think all drivers **should** wear seat belts. (in general – not "had better wear")

Also, with **had better**, there is always a danger or a problem if you don't follow the advice. **Should** means "it is a good thing to do." Compare:

- It's a great movie. You **should** go and see it. (but no problem if you don't)
- The movie starts at 8:30. **You'd better** go now, or you'll be late.

C

It's time . . .

You can say, "**It's time** (for somebody) **to do** something":

- It's time to go home. / It's time for us to go home.

You can also say:

- It's late. It's time we **went** home.

Here we use the past (**went**), but the meaning is present, not past:

- It's 10:00 and he's still in bed. It's time he **got** up. (not It's time he gets up)

It's time you did something = you should have done it already or started it. We often use the structure **it's time** to criticize or to complain:

- **It's time** the children **were** in bed. It's long past their bedtime.
- The windows are very dirty. I think **it's time** somebody **washed** them.

You can also say **It's about time** . . . . This makes the criticism stronger:

- Jack is a great talker. But **it's about time** he **did** something instead of just talking.

Exercises

33.1 Read the situations and write sentences with *had better*. Use the words in parentheses.

1. You're going out for a walk with Tom. It might rain. You say to Tom:
   (an umbrella) *We'd better take an umbrella.*
2. Alex has just cut himself. It's a bad cut. You say to him:
   (a bandage) _____
3. You and Kate plan to go to a restaurant this evening. It's a very popular restaurant. You
   say to Kate: (make a reservation) We _____ .
4. Jill doesn't look very well – not well enough to go to work. You say to her:
   (work) _____
5. You received your phone bill four weeks ago, but you haven't paid it yet. If you don't
   pay very soon, you could be in trouble. You say to yourself:
   (pay) _____
6. You want to go out, but you're expecting an important phone call. You say to your friend:
   (go out) I _____ .
7. You and Jeff are going to the theater. You've missed the bus, and you don't want to be late.
   You say to Jeff: (a taxi) _____

33.2 Put in *had better* or *should*. Sometimes either is possible.

1. I have an appointment in ten minutes. I *'d better* _____ go now or I'll be late.
2. It's a great movie. You *should* _____ go and see it. You'll really like it.
3. I _____ get up early tomorrow. I've got a lot to do.
4. When people are driving, they _____ keep their eyes on the road.
5. Thank you for coming to see us. You _____ come more often.
6. She'll be upset if we don't invite her to the wedding, so we _____ invite her.
7. These cookies are delicious. You _____ try one.
8. I think everybody _____ learn a foreign language.

33.3 Complete the sentences. Sometimes you need only one word, sometimes two.

1. a) I need some money. I'd better *go* _____ to the bank.
   b) John is expecting you to call him. You _____ better do it now.
   c) "Should I leave the window open?" "No, you'd better _____ it."
2. a) It's time the government _____ something about the problem.
   b) It's time something _____ about the problem.
   c) I think it's about time you _____ about me instead of thinking only about
      yourself.

33.4 Read the situations and write sentences with *It's time . . . .*

1. You think the children should be in bed. It's already 11:00.
   It's time the children were in bed.
2. You haven't taken a vacation for a very long time. You need one now.
   It's time I _____ .
3. You're sitting on a train waiting for it to leave the station. It's already five minutes late.

   _____

4. You enjoy having parties. You haven't had one for a long time.

   _____

5. The company you work for is badly managed. You think there should be some changes.

   _____

Can/Could/Would you . . . ?, etc.
(Requests, Offers, Permission, and Invitations)

A

Asking people to do things (requests)

We often use **can** or **could** to ask people to do things:

- **Can you** wait a minute, please? *or*
  Could you wait a minute, please?
- Liz, **can you** do me a favor?
- Excuse me, **could you** tell me how to get to the airport?
- I wonder if **you could** help me.

> Could you open the door, please?

Note that we say "Do you think you **could** . . . ?"
(*not usually* can):

- Do you think you could lend me some money until next week?

We also use **will** and **would** to ask people to do things (but **can/could** are more usual):

- Liz, **will you** do me a favor?
- **Would you** please be quiet? I'm trying to concentrate.

B

Asking for things

To ask for something we use **Can I have . . . ?** or **Could I have . . . ?**:

- *(in a gift shop)* **Can I have** these postcards, please?
- *(during a meal)* **Could I have** the salt, please?

May I have . . . ? is also possible (but less usual):

- **May I have** the salt, please?

C

Asking for and giving permission

To ask for permission to do something, we use **can**, **could**, or **may**:

- *(on the phone)* Hello, **can I** speak to Tom, please?
- "**Could I** use your phone?" "Yes, of course."
- Do you think **I could** borrow your bike?
- "**May I** come in?" "Yes, please do."

May is formal and less usual than **can** or **could**.

D

Offering to do things

We use **Can I . . . ?** or **May I . . . ?** when we offer to do things. (**May** is more formal.):

- "**Can I** get you a cup of coffee?" "Yes, that would be very nice."
- *(in a store)* "**May I** help you?" "No, thanks. I'm being helped."

E

Offering and inviting

To offer or to invite we use **Would you like . . . ?** (*not* Do you like):

- "**Would you like** a cup of coffee?" "Yes, please."
- "**Would you like** to go to the movies with us Saturday night?" "Yes, I'd love to."

I'd like . . . is a polite way of saying what you want:

- *(at a tourist information office)* **I'd like** some information about hotels, please.
- *(in a store)* **I'd like** to try on this jacket, please.

Exercises

34.1 Read the situations and write questions beginning with *Can* or *Could.*

1. You're carrying a lot of things. You can't open the door yourself. There's a man standing near the door. You say to him:
   Can you open the door, please? OR *Could you open the door, please?*

2. You phone Ann, but somebody else answers. Ann isn't there. You want to leave a message for her. You say: _____

3. You are a tourist. You want to go to the post office, but you don't know where it is. You ask at your hotel. You say: _____

4. You are in a department store. You see some pants you like, and you want to try them on. You say to the salesperson: _____

5. You need a ride home from a party. John drove to the party and lives near you. You say to John: _____

34.2 Read the situations and write questions beginning with *Do you think.*

1. You want to borrow your friend's camera. What do you say to him?
   Do you think *I could borrow your camera* _____ ?

2. You are at a friend's house and you want to use her phone. What do you say?

   _____

3. You've written a letter in English. Before you send it, you want a friend to check it. What do you ask him? _____

4. You want to leave work early because you have something important to do. What do you ask your boss? _____

5. The woman in the next room is playing music. It's very loud. You want her to turn it down. What do you say to her?

   _____

6. You are phoning the owner of an apartment that was advertised in the newspaper. You are interested in the apartment and want to see it today. What do you say to the owner?

   _____

34.3 What would you say in these situations?

1. John has come to see you. You offer him something to eat.
   You: *Would you like something to eat?* _____
   John: No, thank you. I've just eaten.

2. You need help to change the film in your camera. You ask Ann.
   You: Ann, I don't know how to change the film. _____
   Ann: Sure. It's easy. All you have to do is this.

3. You're on a plane. The woman next to you has finished reading her newspaper. You want to have a look at it. You ask her.
   You: Excuse me, _____ ?
   Woman: Yes, of course. I'm finished with it.

4. You're on a bus. You have a seat, but an elderly man is standing. You offer him your seat.
   You: _____
   Man: Oh, that's very nice of you. Thank you very much.

5. You're the passenger in a car. Your friend is driving very fast. You ask her to slow down.
   You: You're making me very nervous. _____
   Driver: Oh, I'm sorry. I didn't realize I was going so fast.

6. A friend of yours is interested in one of your books. You invite him to borrow it.
   Friend: This book looks very interesting.
   You: Yes, it's very good. _____

If I do . . . and If I did . . .

A

Compare these two examples:

Sue has lost her watch. She thinks it may be at Ann's house.

Sue: I think I left my watch at your house. Have you seen it?
Ann: No, but I'll look when I get home. **If I find** it, I'll tell you.

In this example, Ann feels there is a possibility that she will find the watch. So she says: **If I find . . . , I'll . . .**

Carol says: **If I found** a wallet in the street, I'd take it to the police.

In this example, Carol is not thinking about a real possibility. She is imagining the situation and doesn't expect to find a wallet in the street. So she says: **If I found . . . , I'd** (= I would) **. . .** (*not* If I find . . . , I'll . . .).

When you imagine something like this, you use **if + past** (**if** I **found** / **if** you **were** / **if** we **didn't**, etc.). But the meaning is not past:

If I won a million dollars . . .

- What would you do **if** you **won** a million dollars? (We don't really expect this to happen.)
- I don't really want to go to their party, but I probably will go. They'd be hurt **if I didn't go.**
- Sarah has decided not to apply for the job. She isn't really qualified for it, so she probably wouldn't get it **if she applied.**

B

We do not normally use **would** in the **if** part of the sentence:

- I'd be very frightened **if** somebody **pointed** a gun at me. (*not* if somebody would point)
- **If I didn't go** to their party, they'd be hurt. (*not* If I wouldn't go)

C

In the other part of the sentence (not the **if** part), we use **would** ('**d**) / **wouldn't**:

- If you got more exercise, you'**d** (= you would) probably **feel** better.
- **Would** you **mind** if I used your phone?
- I'm not tired enough to go to bed yet. I **wouldn't sleep** (if I went to bed now).

Could and **might** are also possible:

- If you got more exercise, you **might feel** better. (= it is possible that you would feel better)
- If it stopped raining, we **could go** out. (= we would be able to go out)

D

Do not use **when** in sentences like those on this page:

- They would be hurt **if** we didn't accept their invitation. (*not* when we didn't)
- What would you do **if** you were bitten by a snake? (*not* when you were bitten)

For **if** and **when**, see also Unit 24C.

Exercises

35.1 Put the verb into the correct form.

1. They would be hurt if I _didn't go_ to see them. (not / go)
2. If you got more exercise, you _would feel_ better. (feel)
3. If they offered me the job, I think I _____ it. (take)
4. I'm sure Amy will lend you the money. I'd be very surprised if she _____ . (refuse)
5. If I sold my car, I _____ much money for it. (not / get)
6. A lot of people would be out of work if the factory _____ . (close down)
7. *(in an elevator)* What would happen if I _____ that red button? (press)
8. Liz gave me this ring. She _____ very upset if I lost it. (be)
9. Dave and Kate are expecting us. They would be disappointed if we _____ . (not / come)
10. Would Bob mind if I _____ his book without asking him? (borrow)
11. If somebody _____ in here with a gun, I'd be very scared. (walk)
12. I'm sure Sue _____ if you explained the situation to her. (understand)

35.2 You ask a friend questions. Use *What would you do if . . . ?*

1. (Maybe one day your friend will win a lot of money.)
   What would you do if you won a lot of money?
2. (Maybe one day someone will offer your friend a job in Rio de Janeiro.)
   What _____ ?
3. (Perhaps one day your friend will lose his / her passport.)
   _____
4. (There has never been a fire in the building. Ask your friend "What . . . if . . . ?")
   _____

35.3 Answer the questions in the way shown.

1. *A:* Should we take the 10:30 train?
   B: No. (arrive / too early) _If we took the 10:30 train, we'd arrive too early._
2. *A:* Is Ken going to take the driver's test?
   B: No. (fail) If he _____ .
3. *A:* Why don't we stay in a hotel?
   B: No. (cost too much money) _____
4. *A:* Is Sally going to apply for the job?
   B: No. (not / get it) _____
5. *A:* Let's tell them the truth.
   B: No. (not / believe us) _____
6. *A:* Why don't we invite Bill to the party?
   B: No. (have to invite his friends, too) _____

35.4 Use your own ideas to complete these sentences.

1. If you got more exercise, _you'd feel better_ .
2. I'd feel very angry if _____ .
3. If I didn't go to work tomorrow, _____ .
4. Would you go to the party if _____ ?
5. If you bought a car, _____ .
6. Would you mind if _____ ?

If I knew . . .
I wish I knew . . .

Study this example situation:

> Sue wants to call Paul, but she can't because she doesn't know his phone number. She says:
>
> **If** I **knew** his number, I **would call** him.
>
> Sue says: **If** I **knew** his number . . . This tells us that she doesn't know his number. She is imagining the situation.

If I knew his number . . .

When you imagine a situation like this, you use **if** + *past* (**if** I **knew** / **if** you **were** / **if** we **didn't**, etc.). But the meaning is present, not past:

- Tom would read more **if** he **had** more time. (but he doesn't have much time)
- **If** I **didn't want** to go to the party, I wouldn't go. (but I want to go)
- We wouldn't have any money **if** we **didn't work.** (but we work)
- **If** you **were** in my position, what would you do?
- It's a shame you can't drive. It would be helpful **if** you **could.**

We use the past in the same way after **wish** (I **wish** I **knew** / I **wish** you **were,** etc.). We use **wish** to say that we regret something, that something is not as we would like it to be:

- I **wish** I **knew** Paul's phone number. (= I don't know it and I regret this.)
- Do you ever **wish** you **could fly?** (You can't fly.)
- It rains a lot here. I **wish** it **didn't rain** so often.
- It's very crowded here. I **wish** there **weren't** so many people.
- I **wish** I **didn't have** to work. (but I have to work)

I wish I had an umbrella.

After **if** and **wish**, we normally use **were** with I/he/she/it. **Was** is also possible. So we say:

- If I **were** you, I wouldn't buy that coat.   *or*   If I **was** you, . . .
- I'd go out **if** it **weren't** raining.   *or*   . . . if it **wasn't** raining.
- I **wish** Carol **were** here.   *or*   I **wish** Carol **was** here.

We do not normally use **would** in the **if** part of the sentence or after **wish**:

- If I **were** rich, I would have a yacht. (*not* If I would be rich)
- I **wish** I **had** something to read. (*not* I wish I would have)

Sometimes **wish . . . would** is possible: I **wish** you **would listen.** See Unit 38C.

Note that **could** sometimes means "would be able to" and sometimes "was/were able to":

- You **could get** a job more easily   (= you would be able to get)
  if you **could use** a computer.   (= you were able to use)

If I do and *If I did . . .*   Unit 35   *If I had known* and *I wish I had known . . .*   Unit 37   *I wish . . . would* Unit 38C

Exercises

36.1 **Put the verb into the correct form.**

1. If I _knew_____ his phone number, I would call him. (know)
2. I _wouldn't buy_____ that coat if I were you. (not / buy)
3. I _____ you if I could, but I'm afraid I can't. (help)
4. We would need less money if we _____ in the country. (live)
5. If we had the choice, we _____ in the country. (live)
6. This soup isn't very good. It _____ better if it weren't so salty. (taste)
7. I wouldn't mind living in Maine if the weather _____ better. (be)
8. If I were you, I _____ . (not / wait) I _____ now. (go)
9. You're always tired. If you _____ to bed so late every night, you wouldn't be tired all the time. (not / go)
10. I think there are too many cars. If there _____ so many cars (not / be), there _____ so much pollution. (not / be)

36.2 **Write a sentence with *If . . .* for each situation.**

1. We don't visit you very often because you live so far away.
   If you didn't live so far away, we'd visit you more often.
2. That book is too expensive, so I'm not going to buy it.
   If the book _____ , I _____ .
3. We don't go out very often because we can't afford it.
   _____
4. It's raining, so we can't have lunch on the patio.
   _____
5. I have to work late tomorrow, so I can't meet you for dinner.
   _____

36.3 **Write sentences beginning *I wish.***

1. I don't know many people (and I'm lonely). _I wish I knew more people._
2. I don't have a key (and I need one). I wish _____ .
3. Amanda isn't here (and I need to see her). _____
4. It's cold (and I hate cold weather). _____
5. I live in a big city (and I don't like it). _____
6. I can't go to the party (and I'd like to). _____
7. I have to work tomorrow (but I'd like to stay in bed).
   _____
8. I don't know anything about cars (and my car has just broken down).
   _____
9. I'm not lying on a beautiful sunny beach (and that's a shame).
   _____

36.4 **Write your own sentences beginning *I wish.***

1. (somewhere you'd like to be now – on the beach, in New York, in bed, etc.)
   I wish I _____ .
2. (something you'd like to have – a computer, a job, lots of money, etc.)
   _____
3. (something you'd like to be able to do – sing, speak a language, fly, etc.)
   _____
4. (something you'd like to be – beautiful, strong, rich, etc.)
   _____

If I had known . . .
I wish I had known . . .

A

Study this example situation:

> Last month Brian was in the hospital for an operation. Liz didn't know this, so she didn't go to see him. They met a few days ago. Liz said:
>
> If I **had known** you were in the hospital, I **would have gone** to see you.
>
> Liz said, "If I **had known** you were in the hospital . . . " So she *didn't* know.

When you are talking about the past, you use **if + had** (**'d**) . . . (**if I had known/been/done**, etc.):
- I didn't see you when you passed me on the street. **If I'd seen** you, of course I would have said hello. (but I didn't see you)
- I didn't go out last night. I would have gone out **if I hadn't been** so tired. (but I was tired)
- **If he had been looking** where he was going, he wouldn't have walked into the wall. (but he wasn't looking)
- The view was wonderful. **If I'd had** a camera, I would have taken some pictures. (but I didn't have a camera)

Compare:
- I'm not hungry. **If I were** hungry, I would eat something. *(now)*
- I wasn't hungry. **If I had been** hungry, I would have eaten something. *(past)*

B

Do not use **would** in the **if** part of the sentence. We use **would** in the other part of the sentence:
- If I had seen you, I **would** have said hello. (*not* If I would have seen you)

Note that **'d** can be **would** or **had**:
- If I'd seen you,   (= I had seen)
  I'd have said hello.   (= I would have said)

C

We use **had done** in the same way after **wish**. I **wish** something **had happened** = I am sorry that it didn't happen:
- I **wish I'd known** that Brian was sick. I would have gone to see him. (but I didn't know)
- I feel sick. I **wish I hadn't eaten** so much cake. (I ate too much cake.)
- Do you **wish** you **had studied** science instead of languages? (You didn't study science.)
- The weather was cold on our vacation. I **wish** it **had been** warmer.

Do not use **would have** . . . after **wish** in these sentences:
- I wish it **had been** warmer. (*not* I wish it would have been)

D

Compare **would do** and **would have done**:
- If I had gone to the party last night, I **would be** tired now. (I am not tired now – *present*)
- If I had gone to the party last night, I **would have met** lots of people. (I didn't meet lots of people – *past*)

Compare **would have**, **could have**, and **might have**:
- If the weather hadn't been so bad,
  - we **would have gone** out.
  - we **could have gone** out. (= we would have been able to go out)
  - we **might have gone** out. (= perhaps we would have gone out)

Exercises

37.1 Put the verb into the correct form.

1. I didn't know you were in the hospital. If *I'd known* _____ (I / know),
   I would have gone _____ (I / go) to see you.
2. John got to the station in time to catch his train. If _____
   (he / miss) it, _____ (he / be) late for his interview.
3. I'm glad that you reminded me about Rachel's birthday. _____
   (I / forget) if _____ (you / not / remind) me.
4. Unfortunately, I didn't have my address book with me when I was on vacation. If
   _____ (I / have) your address, _____
   (I / send) you a postcard.
5. *A:* How was your trip? Did you have a nice time?
   B: It was OK, but _____ (it / be) better if
   _____ (the weather / be) nicer.
6. I'm not tired. If _____ (I / be) tired, I'd go home now.
7. I wasn't tired last night. If _____ (I / be) tired, I would
   have gone home earlier.

37.2 Write a sentence with *if* for each situation.

1. I wasn't hungry, so I didn't eat anything.
   If I'd been hungry, I would have eaten something.
2. The accident happened because the driver in front stopped so suddenly.
   If the driver in front _____.
3. I didn't know that Matt had to get up early, so I didn't wake him up.
   If I _____.
4. I was able to buy the car only because Jim lent me the money.
   _____
5. Michelle wasn't injured in the accident because she was wearing a seat belt.
   _____
6. You didn't have any breakfast – that's why you're hungry now.
   _____

37.3 Imagine that you are in these situations. For each situation, write a sentence with *I wish*.

1. You've eaten too much and now you feel sick. You say:
   I wish I hadn't eaten so much.
2. There was a job advertised in the newspaper. You decided not to apply for it. Now you
   think that your decision was wrong. You say:
   I wish I _____.
3. When you were younger, you didn't learn to play a musical instrument. Now you regret
   this. You say:
   _____
4. You've painted the door red. Now you think that it doesn't look very good. You say:
   _____
5. You are walking in the country. You would like to take some pictures, but you didn't
   bring your camera. You say:
   _____
6. You have some unexpected guests. They didn't tell you they were coming. You are very
   busy and you are not prepared for them. You say (to yourself):
   _____

UNIT 38

Would   I wish . . . would

A

We use **would** ('d) when we imagine a situation or action:
- It **would be** nice to buy a new car, but we can't afford it.
- I'm not going to invite them to the party. They **wouldn't come** anyway.

We use **would have done** when we imagine situations or actions in the past:
- They helped me a lot. I don't know what I **would have done** without their help.
- I didn't invite them to the party. They **wouldn't have come** anyway.

For **would** in sentences with **if,** see Units 35–37.

B

Compare **will** ('ll) and **would** ('d):
- I'll **stay** a little longer. I've got plenty of time.
- I'd **stay** a little longer, but I really have to go now. (so I can't stay longer)

Sometimes **would/wouldn't** is the past of **will/won't.** Compare:

present		*past*
■ *Tom:* I'll **call** you on Sunday.	→	■ Tom said he'd **call** me on Sunday.
■ *Ann:* I promise I **won't be** late.	→	■ Ann promised that she **wouldn't be** late.
■ *Liz:* Darn! The car **won't start.**	→	■ Liz was upset because the car **wouldn't start.**

C

I wish . . . would . . .

I wish it would stop raining.

It is raining. Jill wants to go out, but not in the rain. She says:

I wish it **would stop** raining.

This means that Jill is complaining about the rain and wants it to stop.

We use **I wish . . . would . . .** when we want something to happen or when we want somebody to do something. The speaker is not happy with the present situation.

- The phone has been ringing for five minutes. **I wish** somebody **would answer** it.
- **I wish** you **would do** something instead of just sitting and doing nothing.

You can use **I wish . . . wouldn't . . .** to complain about things people do repeatedly:
- **I wish** you **wouldn't keep** interrupting me.

We use **I wish . . . would . . .** for actions and changes, *not* situations. Compare:
- I wish Sarah **would come.** (= I want her to come)

but I wish Sarah **were** here now. (*not* I wish Sarah would be)
- I wish somebody **would buy** me a car.

but I wish I **had** a car. (*not* I wish I would have)

For **I wish . . . were / had** (etc.), see Units 36B and 37C.

D

You can also use **would** when you talk about things that happened regularly in the past:
- When we were children, we lived by the ocean. In the summer, if the weather was nice, we **would** all **get up** early and go for a swim. (= we did this regularly)
- Whenever Arthur got angry, he **would walk** out of the room.

With this meaning, **would** is similar to **used to** (see Unit 17):
- Whenever Arthur was angry, he **used to walk** out of the room.

Exercises

38.1 Complete the sentences using *would* + one of the following verbs in the correct form:

be   call   ~~do~~   enjoy   enjoy   stop

1. They helped me a lot. I don't know what I _would have done_ without their help.
2. You should go and see the movie. You _____ it.
3. It's too bad you couldn't come to the party last night. You _____ it.
4. I _____ you last night, but I didn't have your phone number.
5. Why don't you go and visit Maria? She _____ very happy to see you.
6. I was in a hurry when I saw you. Otherwise I _____ to talk.

38.2 What do you say in these situations? Write sentences with *I wish . . . would . . . .*

1. It's raining. You want to go out, but not in the rain. You say:
   I wish it would stop raining.
2. You're waiting for John to come. He's late and you're getting impatient. You say (to yourself): I wish _____ .
3. You can hear a baby crying, and you're trying to study. You say:
   _____
4. You're looking for a job – so far without success. Nobody will give you a job. You say:
   I wish somebody _____ .
5. Brian has been wearing the same clothes for years. You think he needs some new clothes. You say (to Brian): _____

For the following situations, write sentences with *I wish . . . wouldn't . . . .*

6. Your friend drives very fast. You don't like it. You say (to your friend):
   I wish you _____ .
7. Jack always leaves the door open. This bothers you. You say (to Jack):
   _____
8. A lot of people drop their litter in the street. You don't like it. You say:
   I wish people _____ .

38.3 Are these sentences right or wrong? Correct the ones that are wrong.

1. I wish Sarah would be here now.   _I wish Sarah were here now._
2. I wish you would listen to me.   _____
3. I wish I would have more money.   _____
4. I wish it wouldn't be so cold today.   _____
5. I wish the weather would change.   _____
6. I wish you wouldn't complain all the time. _____
7. I wish everything wouldn't be so expensive. _____

38.4 These sentences are about things that often happened in the past. Complete the sentences using *would* + one of these verbs:

forget   shake   share   ~~walk~~

1. Whenever Arthur got angry, he _would walk_ out of the room.
2. I used to live next to the railroad tracks. Whenever a train went by, the house
   _____ .
3. You could never rely on Joe. It didn't matter how many times you reminded him to do something, he _____ always _____ .
4. Brandi was always very generous. She didn't have much, but she _____ what she had with everyone else.

Passive (1) *(is done / was done)*

Study this example:

This house **was built** in 1930.

Was built is *passive*. Compare *active* and *passive*:

Somebody **built** this house in 1930. *(active)*
     subject   *object*

This house **was built** in 1930. *(passive)*
  subject

We use an active verb to say what the subject does:

- My grandfather was a builder. He **built** this house in 1930.
- It's a big company. It **employs** two hundred people.

We use a passive verb to say what happens to the subject:

- This house is quite old. It **was built** in 1930.
- Two hundred people **are employed** by the company.

When we use the passive, who or what causes the action is often unknown or unimportant:

- A lot of money **was stolen** in the robbery. (Somebody stole it, but we don't know *who*.)

If we want to say who does or what causes the action, we use **by**:

- This house was built **by my grandfather.**
- Two hundred people are employed **by the company.**

The passive is **be** (**is/was/have been**, etc.) + the *past participle* (**done/cleaned/seen**, etc.):
(**be**) **done**   (**be**) **cleaned**   (**be**) **seen**   (**be**) **damaged**   (**be**) **built**, etc.
For irregular past participles (**done/known/seen**, etc.), see Appendix 1.

Study the active and passive forms of the *simple present* and *simple past*:

Simple present
  active: **clean(s)/see(s)**, etc.   Somebody **cleans** this room every day.

  passive: **am/is/are** + **cleaned/seen**, etc.   This room **is cleaned** every day.

- Many accidents **are caused** by careless driving.
- I'm not often **invited** to parties.
- How **is** this word **pronounced?**

Simple past
  active: **cleaned/saw**, etc.   Somebody **cleaned** this room yesterday.

  passive: **was/were** + **cleaned/seen**, etc.   This room **was cleaned** yesterday.

- We **were woken up** by a loud noise during the night.
- "Did you go to the party?" "No, I **wasn't invited.**"
- How much money **was stolen?**

Exercises

39.1 Complete the sentences using one of these verbs in the correct form, present or past:

~~cause~~   damage   find   hold   include   invite   make   show   translate   write

1. Many accidents _are caused_____ by dangerous driving.
2. Cheese _____ from milk.
3. The roof of the building _____ in a storm a few days ago.
4. You don't have to leave a tip. Service _____ in the bill.
5. You _____ to the wedding. Why didn't you go?
6. A movie theater is a place where movies _____ .
7. In the United States, elections for President _____ every four years.
8. Originally the book _____ in Spanish, and a few years ago it _____ into English.
9. My keys _____ in the parking lot at the mall.

39.2 Write questions using the passive. Some are present, and some are past.

1. Ask about the telephone. (when / invent?) _When was the telephone invented?_____
2. Ask about glass. (how / make?) How _____ ?
3. Ask about the planet Pluto. (when / discover?) _____
4. Ask about silver. (what / use for?) _____
5. Ask about television. (when / invent?) _____

39.3 Put the verb into the correct form, simple present or simple past, active or passive.

1. It's a big factory. Five hundred people _are employed_____ (employ) there.
2. Water _____ (cover) most of the Earth's surface.
3. Most of the Earth's surface _____ (cover) by water.
4. The park gates _____ (lock) at 6:30 every evening.
5. The letter _____ (mail) a week ago, and it _____ (arrive) yesterday.
6. Ron's parents _____ (die) when he was very young. He and his sister _____ (bring up) by their grandparents.
7. I was born in Chicago, but I _____ (grow up) in Houston.
8. While I was on vacation, my camera _____ (steal) from my hotel room.
9. While I was on vacation, my camera _____ (disappear) from my hotel room.
10. Why _____ (Sue / resign) from her job? Didn't she like it?
11. Why _____ (Bill / fire) from his job? What did he do wrong?
12. The business is not independent. It _____ (own) by a much larger company.
13. I saw an accident last night. Somebody _____ (call) an ambulance, but nobody _____ (injure), so the ambulance _____ (not / need).
14. Where _____ (these pictures / take)? In Hong Kong? _____ (you / take) them?

39.4 Rewrite these sentences. Instead of using *somebody/they/people*, etc., write a passive sentence.

1. Somebody cleans the room every day. _The room is cleaned every day._____
2. They canceled all flights because of fog. All _____ .
3. People don't use this road very often. _____
4. Somebody accused me of stealing money. I _____ .
5. How do people learn languages? How _____ ?
6. People warned us not to go out alone. _____

Passive (2) *(be/been/being done)*

Study the following *active* and *passive* forms:

A

After **will / can / must / going to / want to**, etc.

active: **do/clean/see**, etc.   Somebody **will clean** the room later.
passive: **be done/cleaned/seen**, etc.   The room **will be cleaned** later.

- The situation is serious. Something must **be done** before it's too late.
- A mystery is something that can't **be explained**.
- The music was very loud and could **be heard** from a long way away.
- A new supermarket is going to **be built** next year.
- Please go away. I want to **be left** alone.

B

After **should have / might have / would have / seem to have**, etc.

active: **done/cleaned/seen**, etc.   Somebody **should have cleaned** the room.
passive: **been done/cleaned/seen**, etc.   The room **should have been cleaned**.

- I haven't received the letter yet. It might have **been sent** to the wrong address.
- If you hadn't left the car unlocked, it wouldn't have **been stolen**.
- There were some problems at first, but they seem to have **been solved**.

C

Present perfect

active: **has/have done**   The room looks nice. Somebody **has cleaned** it.
passive: **has/have been done**   The room looks nice. It **has been cleaned**.

- **Have** you ever **been bitten** by a dog?
- "Are you going to the party?" "No, I **haven't been invited**."

Past perfect

active: **had done**   The room looked nice. Somebody **had cleaned** it.
passive: **had been done**   The room looked nice. It **had been cleaned**.

- The vegetables didn't taste very good. They **had been cooked** too long.
- The car was three years old but **hadn't been used** very much.

D

Present continuous

active: **am/is/are doing**   Somebody **is cleaning** the room right now.
passive: **am/is/are being done**   The room **is being cleaned** right now.

- There's somebody walking behind us. I think we **are being followed**.
- *(in a store)* "Can I help you, ma'am?" "No, thank you. **I'm being helped**."

Past continuous

active: **was/were doing**   Somebody **was cleaning** the room when I arrived.
passive: **was/were being done**   The room **was being cleaned** when I arrived.

- There was somebody walking behind us. We **were being followed**.

Exercises

40.1 What do these words mean? Use *it can* or *it can't*. Use a dictionary if necessary.

If something is:
1. **washable,** *it can be washed* .
2. **unbreakable,** it _____ .
3. **edible,** it _____ .
4. **unusable,** _____ .
5. **invisible,** _____ .
6. **portable,** _____ .

40.2 Complete these sentences with one of the following verbs (in the correct form):

carry   cause   ~~do~~   make   repair   ~~send~~   spend   wake up

Sometimes you need *have* (*might have, could have*, etc.).

1. The situation is serious. Something must *be done* before it's too late.
2. I haven't received the letter. It might *have been sent* to the wrong address.
3. A decision will not _____ until the next meeting.
4. I told the hotel desk clerk that I wanted to _____ at 6:30 the next morning.
5. Do you think that less money should _____ on the military?
6. This road is in very bad condition. It should _____ a long time ago.
7. The injured man couldn't walk and had to _____ .
8. It's not certain how the fire started, but it might _____ by an electrical short circuit.

40.3 Rewrite these sentences. Instead of using *somebody* or *they*, write a passive sentence.

1. Somebody has cleaned the room. *The room has been cleaned.*
2. Somebody is using the computer at the moment.
   The computer _____ .
3. I didn't realize that somebody was recording our conversation.
   I didn't realize that _____ .
4. When we got to the stadium, we found that they had canceled the game.
   When we got to the stadium, we found that _____ .
5. They are building a new highway around the city.
   _____
6. They have built a new hospital near the airport.
   _____

40.4 Make sentences from the words in parentheses. Sometimes the verb is active, sometimes passive. (This exercise also includes the simple past – see Unit 39C.)

1. There's somebody behind us. (I think / we / follow) *I think we're being followed.*
2. This room looks different. (you / paint?) *Have you painted it?*
3. Tom gets a higher salary now. (he / promote) _____
4. My umbrella has disappeared. (somebody / take) _____
5. Ann can't use her office right now. (it / redecorate) _____
6. Our car wasn't where we had left it. (it / steal) _____
7. The photocopier broke down yesterday, but now it's OK. (it / work / again; it / repair)
   _____
8. The police have found the people they were looking for. (two people / arrest / last night)
   _____
9. The man next door disappeared six months ago. (nobody / see / since then)
   _____
10. I was mugged on my way home a few nights ago. (you / ever / mug?)
    _____

Passive (3)

A

I was born . . .

We say **I was born** (*not* I am born):

- ■ I **was born** in Chicago.
- ■ Where **were** you **born**? (*not* Where are you born?) } *simple past*

but ■ How many babies **are born** every day? *simple present*

B

Some verbs can have two objects – for example, **give**:

- ■ We gave the police the information. (= We gave the information to the police.)

  object 1   object 2

So it is possible to make two passive sentences:

- ■ **The police** were given the information. *or* **The information** was given to the police.

Other verbs that can have two objects are: **ask   offer   pay   show   teach   tell**

When we use these verbs in the passive, most often we begin with the person:

- ■ **I was offered** the job, but I refused it. (= they offered me the job)
- ■ **You will be given** plenty of time to decide. (= we will give you plenty of time)
- ■ **Have you been shown** the new machine? (= Has anybody shown you . . . ?)
- ■ **The men were paid** $200 to do the work. (= somebody paid the men $200)

C

I don't like being . . .

The passive of **doing/seeing**, etc., is **being done / being seen**, etc. Compare:

active: I don't like people **telling** me what to do.
passive: I don't like **being told** what to do.

- ■ I remember **being given** a toy drum on my fifth birthday. (= I remember somebody giving me a toy drum)
- ■ Mr. Miller hates **being kept** waiting. (= he hates people keeping him waiting)
- ■ We managed to climb over the wall without **being seen**. (= without anybody seeing us)

D

Get

Sometimes you can use **get** instead of **be** in the passive:

- ■ There was a fight at the party, but nobody **got hurt**. (= nobody was hurt)
- ■ I don't often **get invited** to parties. (= I'm not often invited)
- ■ I'm surprised Ann **didn't get offered** the job. (= Ann wasn't offered the job)

You can use **get** to say that something happens to somebody or something, especially if this is unplanned or unexpected:

- ■ Our dog **got run over** by a car.

You can use **get** only when things happen or change. For example, you cannot use **get** in these sentences:

- ■ Jill **is liked** by everybody. (*not* gets liked – this is not a "happening")
- ■ He was a mysterious man. Nothing **was known** about him. (*not* got known)

We use **get** mainly in informal spoken English. You can use **be** in all situations.

Exercises

41.1 When were they born? Choose five of these people and write a sentence for each.

Beethoven	Galileo	Elvis Presley	1452	1869	1935
Diana, Princess of Wales	Mahatma Gandhi	Leonardo da Vinci	1564	~~1901~~	1961
~~Walt Disney~~	Martin Luther King, Jr.		1770	1929	

1. _Walt Disney was born in 1901._ _____
2. _____
3. _____
4. _____
5. _____
6. And you? I _____ .

41.2 Write these sentences using the passive, beginning in the way shown.

1. They didn't give me the money. I _wasn't given the money_ _____ .
2. They asked me some difficult questions at the interview.
   I _____ .
3. Jessica's colleagues gave her a present when she retired.
   Jessica _____ .
4. Nobody told me that Michael was sick.
   I wasn't _____ .
5. How much will they pay you?
   How much will you _____ ?
6. I think they should have offered John the job.
   I think John _____ .
7. Has anybody shown you what to do?
   Have you _____ ?

41.3 Complete the sentences using *being* + one of these verbs:

ask   attack   give   invite   ~~keep~~   pay

1. Mr. Miller doesn't like _being kept_ _____ waiting.
2. They went to the party without _____ .
3. Most people like _____ presents.
4. It's a dangerous city. People won't go out after dark because they are afraid of
   _____ .
5. I don't like _____ stupid questions.
6. Few people are prepared to work without _____ .

41.4 Complete the sentences using *get/got* + one of these verbs (in the correct form):

ask   break   damage   ~~hurt~~   pay   steal   sting   stop   use

1. There was a fight at the party, but nobody _got hurt_ _____ .
2. Ted _____ by a bee while he was sitting in the yard.
3. How did that window _____ ?
4. These tennis courts don't _____ very often. Not many people want to play.
5. I used to have a bicycle, but it _____ .
6. Last night I _____ by the police while I was driving home.
7. How much did you _____ last month?
8. Please pack these things very carefully. I don't want them to _____ .
9. People always want to know what my job is. I often _____ that question.

It is said that . . . He is said to . . . (be) supposed to . . .

Study this example situation:

Henry is very old. Nobody knows exactly how old he is, but:

It is said that he is 108 years old.

or He **is said to** be 108 years old.

Both these sentences mean: People say that he is 108 years old.

HENRY

You can use these structures with a number of other verbs, especially:
thought   believed   considered   reported   known   expected   alleged   understood

Compare the two structures:

- Cathy works very hard.
    It is said that she works 16 hours a day.   *or* **She is said to** work 16 hours a day.
- The police are looking for a missing boy.
    It is believed that the boy is wearing a   *or* **The boy is believed to** be wearing a
    white sweater and blue jeans.   white sweater and blue jeans.
- The strike started three weeks ago.
    It is expected that it will end soon.   *or* **The strike is expected to** end soon.
- A friend of mine has been arrested.
    It is alleged that he kicked a police   *or* **He is alleged to** have kicked a police
    officer.   officer.
- Those two houses belong to the same family.
    It is said that there is a secret tunnel   *or* **There is said to** be a secret tunnel
    between them.   between them.

These structures are often used in news reports.

- **It is reported that** two people were   *or* Two people **are reported to** have been
    injured in the explosion.   injured in the explosion.

(Be) supposed to

Sometimes **it is supposed to . . .** = it is said to . . . :

- Let's go and see that movie. It's **supposed to** be very good. (= it is said to be very good)
- Mark **is supposed to** have kicked a police officer. (= he is said to have kicked)

But sometimes **supposed to** has a different meaning. Something **is supposed to** happen = it is planned, arranged, or expected. Often this is different from what really happens:

- I'd better hurry. It's almost 8:00 and **I'm supposed to** meet Ann at 8:15. (= I have arranged to meet Ann; I said I would meet her)
- The train **was supposed to** arrive at 11:30, but it was an hour late. (= the train was expected to arrive at 11:30 according to the schedule)

You're **not supposed to** do something = it is not allowed or advisable for you to do it:

- You're **not supposed to** park your car here. (= You're not allowed to park here.)
- Mr. Bruno is much better after his operation, but he's still **not supposed to** do any heavy work. (= his doctors have advised him not to)

Exercises

42.1 Write these sentences in another way, beginning as shown. Use the underlined word in your sentence.

1. It is <u>expected</u> that the strike will end soon.
   The strike *is expected to end soon* .

2. It is <u>thought</u> that the prisoner escaped by climbing over a wall.
   The prisoner *is thought to have escaped by climbing over a wall* .

3. It is <u>reported</u> that many people are homeless after the floods.
   Many people _____ .

4. It is <u>alleged</u> that the man robbed the store of $3,000 in cash.
   The man is _____ .

5. It is <u>reported</u> that the building was badly damaged by the fire.
   The building _____ .

6. a) It is <u>said</u> that the company is losing a lot of money.
      The company _____ .
   b) It is <u>believed</u> that the company lost a lot of money last year.
      The company _____ .
   c) It is <u>expected</u> that the company will lose money this year.
      The company _____ .

42.2 People say a lot of things about Michael. For example:

1. Michael eats spiders.

2. He is very rich.

3. He has 12 children.

4. He knows a lot of famous people.

5. He robbed a bank a long time ago.

MICHAEL

Nobody knows for sure whether these things are true or not. Write sentences about Michael using *supposed to.*

1. *Michael is supposed to eat spiders.*
2. He _____ .
3. _____
4. _____
5. _____

42.3 Now use *supposed to* with its other meaning. In each example what happens is different from what is supposed to happen. Use *(be) supposed to* + one of these verbs:

~~arrive~~   be   block   call   come   ~~park~~   start

Some of the sentences are negative (like the first example).

1. You *'re not supposed to park* here. It's for private parking only.
2. The train *was supposed to arrive* at 11:30, but it was an hour late.
3. What are the children doing at home? They _____ at school now.
4. We _____ work at 8:15, but we rarely do anything before 8:30.
5. This door is a fire exit. You _____ it.
6. Oh no! I _____ Ann, but I completely forgot.
7. They came very early – at 2:00. They _____ until 3:30.

Have something done

A

Study this example situation:

LISA

The roof of Lisa's house was damaged in a storm, so she arranged for somebody to repair it. Yesterday a worker came and did the job.

Lisa **had the roof repaired** yesterday.

This means: Lisa arranged for somebody else to repair the roof. She didn't repair it herself.

We use **have something done** to say that we arrange for somebody else to do something for us. Compare:
- Lisa **repaired** the roof. (= she repaired it herself)
- Lisa **had** the roof **repaired**. (= she arranged for somebody else to repair it)

Study these sentences:
- Did Ann make the cake herself, or **did** she **have** it **made?**
- "Are you going to repair the car yourself?" "No, I'm going to **have** it **repaired.**"

Be careful with word order. The *past participle* (**repaired/cut**, etc.) comes after the *object*:

	have	+	object	+	past participle	
Lisa	had		the roof		repaired	yesterday.
Where	did you have		your hair		cut?	
Our neighbors	have just had		air conditioning		installed	in their house.
We	are having		the house		painted	at the moment.
How often	do you have		your car		serviced?	
Why	don't you have		that coat		cleaned?	
I don't like	having		my picture		taken.	

B

You can also say "**get** something done" instead of "**have** something done" (mainly in informal spoken English):
- When are you going to **get the roof repaired?** (= have the roof repaired)
- I think you should **get your hair cut.**

C

Sometimes **have something done** has a different meaning. For example:
- Lisa and Eric **had all their money stolen** while they were on vacation.

Of course this does not mean that they arranged for somebody to steal their money. "They **had all their money stolen**" means: All their money was stolen from them.

With this meaning, we use **have something done** to say that something happens to somebody or their belongings. Usually what happens is not nice:
- James **had his nose broken** in a fight.
- Have you ever **had your passport stolen?**

Exercises

43.1 Check (✓) the correct sentence, (a) or (b), for each picture.

1. 	2. 	3. 	4. 
SARAH	BILL	JOHN	SUE
a) Sarah is cutting her hair.	a) Bill is cutting his hair.	a) John is shining his shoes.	a) Sue is taking a picture.
b) Sarah is having her hair cut.	b) Bill is having his hair cut.	b) John is having his shoes shined.	b) Sue is having her picture taken.

43.2 Answer the questions using the structure *have something done.* Use one of these verbs:

clean   cut   repair   ~~service~~

1. Why did you take your car to the garage?   *To have it serviced.*
2. Why did you take your jacket to the cleaner's?   To _____
3. Why did you take your watch to the jeweler's?   _____
4. Why did you go to the hair salon?   _____

43.3 Write sentences in the way shown.

1. Lisa didn't repair the roof herself. She *had it repaired* _____ .
2. I didn't cut my hair myself. I _____ .
3. They didn't paint the house themselves. They _____ .
4. Sue didn't make the curtains herself. _____

43.4 Use the words in parentheses to complete the sentences. Use the structure *have something done.*

1. We *are having the house painted* _____ (the house / paint) at the moment.
2. I lost my key. I'll have to _____ (another key / make).
3. When was the last time you _____ (your hair / cut)?
4. _____ (you / a newspaper / deliver) to your home, or do you buy one on your way to work?
5. *A:* What are those workers doing at your house?
   B: Oh, we _____ (air conditioning / install).
6. *A:* Can I see the pictures you took when you were on vacation?
   B: I'm afraid I _____ (not / the film / develop) yet.
7. This coat is dirty. I should _____ (it / clean).

43.5 Now use *have something done* with its second meaning (see Section C).

1. Bill's nose was broken in a fight.
   What happened to Bill?   *He had his nose broken in a fight.*
2. Sarah's bag was stolen on a train.
   What happened to Sarah?   She _____ .
3. John's electricity was turned off because he didn't pay the bill.
   What happened to John?   _____
4. Diane's passport was taken away by the police.
   What happened to Diane?   _____

UNIT 44

Reported Speech (1) *(He said that . . .)*

A

Study this example situation:

I'm feeling sick.

TOM

You want to tell somebody else what Tom said. There are two ways of doing this:

You can repeat Tom's words *(direct speech):*
Tom said, "I'm feeling sick."

Or you can use *reported speech:*
Tom said that he was feeling sick.

Compare:

> *direct:* Tom said, " **I** **am** feeling sick."
>
> *reported:* Tom said that **he** **was** feeling sick.

In writing we use quotation marks to show direct speech.

B

When we use reported speech, the main verb of the sentence is usually past (Tom **said** that . . . / I **told** her that . . . , etc.). The rest of the sentence is usually past, too:

- Tom **said** that he **was feeling** sick.
- I **told** her that I **didn't have** any money.

You can leave out **that:**

- Tom **said** (that) he was feeling sick.

In general, the *present* form in direct speech changes to the *past* form in reported speech:

am/is → **was**	have/has → **had**	will → **would**	can → **could**
are → **were**	do/does → **did**	want/know/go, etc. → **wanted/knew/went,** etc.	

Compare direct speech and reported speech:

You met Jenny. Here are some of the things she said to you in direct speech.

"My parents **are** fine."

"I'm going to learn to drive."

"John **has** quit his job."

"I **can't** come to the party on Friday."

"I **want** to go away for the weekend, but I **don't** know where to go."

"I'm going away for a few days. I'll call you when I **get** back."

JENNY

Later you tell somebody what Jenny said. You use reported speech:

- Jenny said that her parents **were** fine.
- She said that she **was** going to learn to drive.
- She said that John **had** quit his job.
- She said that she **couldn't** come to the party on Friday.
- She said that she **wanted** to go away for the weekend, but (she) **didn't** know where to go.
- She said that she **was** going away for a few days and **would** call me when she **got** back.

C

The *simple past* (**did/saw/knew,** etc.) can usually stay the same in reported speech, or you can change it to the *past perfect* (**had done / had seen / had known,** etc.):

- *direct:* Tom said, "I **woke** up feeling sick, so I **stayed** in bed."
  reported: Tom said (that) he **woke** up feeling sick, so he **stayed** in bed. *or*
  Tom said (that) he **had woken** up feeling sick, so he **stayed** in bed.

Reported Speech (2) Unit 45   **Reported Questions** Unit 47B

Exercises

44.1 Yesterday you met a friend of yours, Robert. Here are some of the things Robert said to you:

ROBERT

1. I'm living in my own apartment now.
2. My father isn't very well.
3. Amanda and Paul are getting married next month.
4. Michelle has had a baby.
5. I don't know what Eric is doing.
6. I saw Nicole at a party in June, and she seemed fine.
7. I haven't seen Diane recently.
8. I'm not enjoying my job very much.
9. You can come and stay at my place if you are ever in Chicago.
10. My car was stolen a few weeks ago.
11. I want to take a vacation, but I can't afford it.
12. I'll tell Amy I saw you.

Later that day you tell another friend what Robert said. Use reported speech.

1. *Robert said that he was living in his own apartment now.*
2. He said that _____ .
3. He _____ .
4. _____
5. _____
6. _____
7. _____
8. _____
9. _____
10. _____
11. _____
12. _____

44.2 Somebody says something to you that is the opposite of what they said before. Write an appropriate answer beginning with *I thought you said . . . .*

1. *A:* That restaurant is expensive.
    B: It is? *I thought you said it was cheap.*
2. *A:* Ann is coming to the party tonight.
    B: She is? I thought you said she _____ .
3. *A:* Ann likes Paul.
    B: She does? I thought you said _____ .
4. *A:* I know lots of people.
    B: You do? I thought you said you _____ .
5. *A:* Pat will be here next week.
    B: She will? _____
6. *A:* I'm going out this evening.
    B: You are? _____
7. *A:* I can speak a little French.
    B: You can? _____
8. *A:* I haven't been to the movies in a long time.
    B: You haven't? _____

Reported Speech (2)

It is not always necessary to change the verb when you use reported speech. If you report something and it is still true, you do not need to change the verb:

-     *direct:* Tom said, "New York **is** more exciting than London."
     reported: Tom said that New York **is** more exciting than London.
             (New York is still more exciting. The situation hasn't changed.)
-     *direct:* Ann said, "I **want** to go to New York next year."
     reported: Ann said that she **wants** to go to New York next year.
             (Ann still wants to go to New York next year.)

Note that it is also correct to change the verb into the past:

- Tom said that New York **was** more exciting than London.
- Ann said that she **wanted** to go to New York next year.

But you must use a past form when there is a difference between what was said and what is really true. Study this example situation:

You met Kelly a few days ago.
She said, **"Jim is sick."** *(direct speech)*

Later that day you see Jim. He is looking fine and carrying a tennis racquet. You say: "I didn't expect to see you, Jim. Kelly said you **were** sick." (*not* "Kelly said you are sick," because obviously he is not sick)

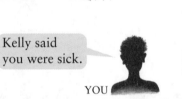

Say and **tell**

Use **tell** when you say who you are talking to:

- Kelly **told me** that you were sick. (*not* Kelly said me)   **TELL** <u>SOMEBODY</u>
- What did you **tell the police**? (*not* say the police)

Otherwise use **say**:

- Kelly **said** that you were sick. (*not* Kelly told that . . .)   **SAY** ~~SOMEBODY~~
- What did you **say**?

But you can **say** something **to** somebody:

- Ann **said** good-bye **to** me and left. (*not* Ann said me good-bye)
- What did you **say to** the police?

Tell/ask somebody **to do** something

We also use the *infinitive* (**to do** / **to stay**, etc.) in reported speech, especially with **tell** and **ask** (for orders and requests):

-     *direct:* "Stay in bed for a few days," the doctor said to me.
     reported: The doctor **told** me **to stay** in bed for a few days.
-     *direct:* "Don't shout," I said to Jim.
     reported: I **told** Jim **not to shout.**
-     *direct:* "Please don't tell anybody what happened," Ann said to me.
     reported: Ann **asked** me **not to tell** anybody what (had) happened.

Exercises

45.1 Here are some things that Ann said to you:

> I've never been to South America.
> I don't have any brothers or sisters.
> I can't drive.
> Rosa is a friend of mine.
> I don't like fish.
> ~~Dave is lazy.~~
> I'm working tomorrow night.
> Rosa has a very well-paid job.

ANN

YOU

But later Ann says something different to you. What do you say?

1. Dave works very hard. — *But you said he was lazy.*
2. Let's have fish for dinner. _____
3. I'm going to buy a car. _____
4. Rosa is always short of money. _____
5. My sister lives in Tokyo. _____
6. I think Buenos Aires is a great place. _____
7. Let's go out for dinner tomorrow night. _____
8. I've never spoken to Rosa. _____

45.2 Complete the sentences with *say* or *tell* in the correct form. Use only one word each time.

1. Ann *said* _____ good-bye to me and left.
2. _____ us about your vacation. Did you have a good time?
3. Don't just stand there! _____ something!
4. I wonder where Sue is. She _____ she would be here at 8:00.
5. Jack _____ me that he was fed up with his job.
6. The doctor _____ that I should rest for at least a week.
7. Don't _____ anybody what I _____ . It's a secret just between us.
8. "Did she _____ you what happened?" "No, she didn't _____ anything to me."
9. Jason couldn't help me. He _____ me to ask Kate.

45.3 The following sentences are direct speech:

> Don't wait for me if I'm late.
> Will you marry me?
> ~~Hurry up!~~
> Can you open your bag, please?
> Mind your own business.
> Please slow down!
> Don't worry, Sue.
> Could you give me a hand, Tom?

Now choose one of these to complete each sentence below. Use reported speech (see Section C).

1. Bill was taking a long time to get ready, so I *told him to hurry up* _____ .
2. Sarah was driving too fast, so I asked _____ .
3. Sue was very nervous about the situation. I told _____ .
4. I couldn't move the piano alone, so I _____ .
5. The customs officer looked at me suspiciously and _____ .
6. I didn't want to delay Ann, so I _____ .
7. John was in love with Maria, so he _____ .
8. He started asking me personal questions, so _____ .

Questions (1)

A

In questions, we usually put the first *auxiliary verb (AV)* before the *subject (S)*:

$$S + AV \qquad AV + S$$

Tom	will	→	will	Tom?
you	have	→	have	you?
I	can	→	can	I?
the house	was	→	was	the house?

- **Will Tom** be here tomorrow?
- **Have you** been working hard?
- What **can I** do?
- When **was the house** built?

B

In *simple present* questions, we use **do/does**:

you	live	→	**do**	you live?
the movie	begins	→	**does**	the movie begin?

- **Do you live** near here?
- What time **does** the movie **begin**? (*not* What time begins)

In *simple past* questions, we use **did**:

you	sold	→	**did**	you sell?
the accident	happened	→	**did**	the accident **happen?**

- **Did you sell** your car?
- How **did** the accident **happen?**

But do not use **do/does/did** if **who/what/which** is the subject of the sentence. Compare:

who *object*	**who** *subject*
Emma phoned somebody .	Somebody phoned Emma.
— object —	— subject —
Who **did** Emma **phone?**	Who **phoned** Emma?

In these examples, **who/what/which** is the subject:
- **Who wants** something to eat? (*not* Who does want)
- **What happened** to you last night? (*not* What did happen)
- **Which bus** goes downtown? (*not* Which bus does go)

C

Note the position of prepositions in questions beginning **Who/What/Which/Where . . . ?**:
- **Who** do you want to speak **to?**
- **Which** job has Jane applied **for?**
- **What** was the weather **like** yesterday?
- **Where** are you **from?**

D

Negative questions (**isn't it . . . ?** / **didn't you . . . ?**)

We use negative questions especially to show surprise:
- **Didn't you hear** the doorbell? I rang it four times.

We also use them when we expect the listener to agree with us:
- "**Haven't we met** somewhere before?" "Yes, I think we have."
- **Isn't it** a beautiful day! (= It's a beautiful day, isn't it?)

Note the meaning of **yes** and **no** in answers to negative questions:
- Don't you want to go to the party? { **Yes.** (= Yes, I want to go.)
  { **No.** (= No, I don't want to go.)

Note the word order in negative questions beginning **Why . . . ?**:
- **Why don't we go** out for dinner tonight? (*not* Why we don't)
- **Why wasn't Mary** at work yesterday? (*not* Why Mary wasn't)

Questions (2) Unit 47

Exercises

46.1 Ask Joe questions. (Look at his answers before you write the questions.)

JOE

1. (where / from?) *Where are you from?*   From Toronto originally.
2. (where / live / now?) Where _____?   In Vancouver.
3. (married?) _____   Yes.
4. (how long / married?) _____   Twelve years.
5. (children?) _____   Yes, three boys.
6. (how old / they?) _____   They're 4, 7, and 9.
7. (what / wife / do?) _____   She's a police officer.
8. (she / like her job?) _____   Yes, very much.

46.2 Make questions with *who* or *what*.

1. Somebody hit me.   *Who hit you?*
2. I hit somebody.   *Who did you hit?*
3. Somebody gave me the key.   Who _____?
4. Something happened.   What _____?
5. Diane told me something.   _____
6. This book belongs to somebody.   _____
7. Somebody lives in that house.   _____
8. I fell over something.   _____
9. Something fell on the floor.   _____
10. This word means something.   _____
11. I borrowed the money from somebody.   _____
12. I'm worried about something.   _____

46.3 Put the words in parentheses in the correct order. All the sentences are questions.

1. (when / was / built / this house) *When was this house built?*
2. (how / cheese / is / made) _____
3. (when / invented / the computer / was) _____
4. (why / Sue / working / isn't / today) _____
5. (what time / coming / your friends / are) _____
6. (why / was / canceled / the concert) _____
7. (where / your mother / was / born) _____
8. (why / you / to the party / didn't / come) _____
9. (how / the accident / did / happen) _____
10. (why / this machine / doesn't / work) _____

46.4 Write negative questions from the words in parentheses. In each situation you are surprised.

1. *A:* We're not going to see Ann tonight.
   B: Why not? (she / not / come to the party?) *Isn't she coming to the party?*
2. *A:* I hope we don't see Brian tonight.
   B: Why not? (you / not / like / him?) _____
3. *A:* Don't go and see that movie.
   B: Why not? (it / not / good) _____
4. *A:* I'll have to borrow some money.
   B: Why? (you / not / have / any?) _____

Questions (2) (Do you know where . . . ? / She asked me where . . .)

A

We say:

■ Where **has Tom** gone?

but   Do you know where **Tom has** gone? (*not* Do you know where has Tom gone?)

When a question (**Where has Tom gone?**) is part of a longer sentence (**Do you know . . . ? / I don't know . . . / Can you tell me . . . ?**, etc.), the word order changes. Compare:

■ What time **is it**?	*but*	Do you know what time **it is**?
■ Who **is that woman**?		I don't know who **that woman is**.
■ Where **can I find** Linda?		Can you tell me where **I can find** Linda?
■ How much **will it cost**?		Do you have any idea how much **it will cost**?

Be careful with **do/does/did** questions (*simple present* and *past*). We say:

■ What time **does the movie begin**?	*but*	Do you know what time **the movie begins**? (*not* Do you know what time does)
■ What **do you mean**?		Please explain what **you mean**.
■ Why **did Ann leave** early?		I wonder why **Ann left** early.

Use **if** or **whether** where there is no other question word (**what, why,** etc.):

■ Did anybody see you?   *but*   Do you know **if** (*or* **whether**) anybody saw you?

B

The same changes in word order happen in *reported* questions:

■   *direct:* The police officer said to us, "Where are you going ?"

reported: The police officer asked us where we were going .

■   *direct:* Claire asked, "What time do the banks close ?"

reported: Claire wanted to know what time the banks closed .

In reported questions, the verb usually changes to the past (**were/closed**, etc.). See Unit 44.

Study these examples. You had an interview for a job, and these were some of the questions the interviewer asked you:

Are you willing to travel?

What **do you do** in your spare time?

Do you have a driver's license?

Can you use a computer?

INTERVIEWER

How long **have you** been working at your present job?

Where **did you** go to school?

YOU

Later you tell a friend what the interviewer asked you. You use reported speech:

■ She asked (me) if **I was** willing to travel.
■ She wanted to know what **I did** in my spare time.
■ She asked (me) how long **I had** been working at my present job.
■ She asked (me) where **I had** gone to school. (*or* . . . where I went)
■ She wanted to know whether (*or* if) **I could** use a computer.
■ She asked whether (*or* if) **I had** a driver's license.

Exercises

47.1 Make a new sentence from the question in parentheses.

1. (Where has Tom gone?) _Do you know where Tom has gone?_
2. (Where is the post office?) Could you tell me where _____ ?
3. (What does this word mean?) I'd like to know _____ .
4. (Is Sue going out tonight?) I don't know _____ .
5. (Where does Carol live?) Do you have any idea _____ ?
6. (Where did I park the car?) I can't remember _____ .
7. (Is there a bank near here?) Can you tell me _____ ?
8. (What do you want?) Tell me _____ .
9. (Why didn't Liz come to the party?) I wonder _____ .
10. (Who is that woman?) I have no idea _____ .
11. (Did Ann get my letter?) Do you know _____ ?
12. (How far is it to the airport?) Can you tell me _____ ?

47.2 You are making a phone call. You want to speak to Amy, but she isn't there. Somebody else answers the phone. You want to know three things:
(1) _Where is Amy?_ (2) _When will she be back?_ and (3) _Did she go out alone?_
Complete the conversation:

A: Do you know where _____ ? (1)
B: Sorry, I have no idea.
A: That's all right. I don't suppose you know _____ . (2)
B: No, I'm afraid I don't.
A: One more thing. Do you happen to know _____ ? (3)
B: I'm afraid I didn't see her go out.
A: OK. Well, thank you anyway. Good-bye.

47.3 You have been away for a while and have just come back to your hometown. You meet Tony, a friend of yours. He asks you a lot of questions:

1. How are you?
2. Where have you been?
3. How long have you been back?
4. What are you doing now?
5. Where are you living?
6. Why did you come back?
7. Are you glad to be back?
8. Do you plan to stay for a while?
9. Can you lend me some money?

TONY

Now tell another friend what Tony asked you. Use reported speech.

1. _He asked me how I was._
2. He asked me _____ .
3. He _____ .
4. _____
5. _____
6. _____
7. _____
8. _____
9. _____

Auxiliary Verbs (*have/do/can*, etc.)
I think so / I hope so, etc.

A

There are two verbs in each of these sentences:

I	**have**	lost	my keys.
She	**can't**	come	to the party.
The hotel	**was**	built	ten years ago.
Where	**do** you	live?	

In these examples **have/can't/was/do** are *auxiliary* (= helping) *verbs*.

You can use an auxiliary verb when you don't want to repeat something:

- "Have you locked the door?" "Yes, I **have**." (= I have locked the door)
- Matt wasn't working, but Jenny **was**. (= Jenny was working)
- She could lend me the money, but she **won't**. (= she won't lend me the money)
- "Are you angry with me?" "Of course I'm **not**." (= I'm not angry)

Use **do/does/did** for the *simple present* and *past*:

- "Do you like onions?" "Yes, I **do**." (= I like onions)
- "Does Mark play soccer?" "He **did**, but he **doesn't** anymore."

B

We use **You have?** / **She isn't?** / **They do?** etc., to show polite interest in what somebody has said:

- "I've just seen David." "**You have?** How is he?"
- "Liz isn't feeling very well today." "**She isn't?** What's wrong with her?"
- "It rained every day during our vacation." "**It did?** What a shame!"

Sometimes we use inverted word order (**Have you?** / **Isn't she?**) to show surprise:

- "Toshi and Keiko are getting married." "**Are they?** That's great!"

C

We use auxiliary verbs with **so** and **neither**:

- "I'm tired." "**So am I.**" (= I'm tired, too)
- "I never read newspapers." "**Neither do I.**" (= I never read newspapers either)
- Sue doesn't have a car, and **neither does Mark**.

Note the word order after **so** and **neither** (verb before subject):

- I passed the exam, and **so did Tom**. (*not* so Tom did)

You can use **not either** instead of **neither**:

- "I don't have any money." "**Neither do I.**" *or* "**I don't either.**"

D

I think so / I guess so, etc.

After some verbs you can use **so** when you don't want to repeat something:

- "Are those people Australian?" "**I think so.**" (= I think they are Australian)
- "Will you be home tomorrow morning?" "**I guess so.**" (= I guess I'll be home)
- "Do you think Kate has been invited to the party?" "**I suppose so.**"

You can also say **I hope so, I expect so,** and **I'm afraid so**.

The usual negative forms are:

I think so / I expect so	→	I don't think so / I don't expect so
I hope so / I'm afraid so / I guess so /	→	I hope not / I'm afraid not / I guess not /
I suppose so		I suppose not

- "Is that woman American?" "**I think so. / I don't think so.**"
- "Do you think it's going to rain?" "**I hope so. / I hope not.**" (*not* I don't hope so)

Exercises

48.1 Complete the sentences with an auxiliary verb (*do/was/could/should*, etc.). Sometimes the verb must be negative (*don't/wasn't,* etc.).

1. I wasn't tired, but my friends _were_ .
2. I like hot weather, but Ann _____ .
3. "Is Eric here?" "He _____ five minutes ago, but I think he's gone home."
4. She might call later on tonight, but I don't think she _____ .
5. "Are you and Chris coming to the party?" "I _____ , but Chris _____ ."
6. I don't know whether to apply for the job or not. Do you think I _____ ?
7. "Please don't tell anybody what I said." "Don't worry. I _____ ."
8. "You never listen to me." "Yes, I _____ !"
9. "Can you play a musical instrument?" "No, but I wish I _____ ."
10. "Please help me." "I'm sorry. I _____ if I _____ , but I _____ ."

48.2 You never agree with Alex. Answer in the way shown.

1. I'm hungry.   → You are? I'm not.
2. I'm not tired.   → You aren't? I am.
3. I like baseball.
4. I didn't like the movie.
5. I've never been to South America.
6. I thought the exam was easy.

ALEX / YOU

48.3 You are talking to Lisa. Write true sentences about yourself. Reply with *So . . .* or *Neither . . .* if appropriate. Study the two examples carefully.

1. I feel really tired.   → So do I.
2. I'm working hard.   → You are? I'm not.
3. I watched TV last week.
4. I won't be in class next week.
5. I live in a small town.
6. I'd like to go to the moon.
7. I can't play the trumpet.

LISA / YOU

48.4 In these conversations, you are B. Read the information in parentheses and then answer with *I think so, I hope not,* etc.

1. (You don't like rain.) *A:* Is it going to rain? *B:* (hope) _I hope not._
2. (Sarah has applied for a job. You want her to get it.)
   A: I wonder if Sarah will get the job. *B:* (hope) _____
3. (You're not sure whether Amy is married – probably not.)
   A: Is Amy married? *B:* (think) _____
4. (You are the desk clerk at a hotel. The hotel is full.)
   A: Do you have a room for tonight? *B:* (afraid) _____
5. (You're at a party. You have to leave early.)
   A: Do you have to leave already? *B:* (afraid) _____
6. (Ann usually works every day, Monday to Friday. Tomorrow is Wednesday.)
   A: Is Ann working tomorrow? *B:* (guess) _____
7. (You are going to a party. You can't stand John.)
   A: Do you think John will be at the party? *B:* (hope) _____
8. (You're not sure what time the concert is – probably 7:30.)
   A: Is the concert at 7:30? *B:* (think) _____

Tag Questions (*do you? / isn't it?*, etc.)

A

Study these examples:

You haven't seen Maria today, **have you?**

No, I haven't.

It was a good movie, **wasn't it?**   Yes, I loved it.

Have you? and **wasn't it?** are *tag questions* (= mini-questions that we often put at the end of a sentence in spoken English). In tag questions, we use an *auxiliary verb* (**have/was/will**, etc.). We use **do/does/did** for the *simple present* and *past* (see also Unit 48):

- "Lauren plays the piano, **doesn't she?**" "Well, yes, but not very well."
- "You didn't lock the door, **did you?**" "No, I forgot."

B

Normally we use a *negative* tag question after a *positive* sentence:

positive sentence + negative tag

Maria **will** be here soon, **won't she?**
There **was** a lot of traffic, **wasn't there?**
Jim **should** take his medicine, **shouldn't he?**

. . . and a *positive* tag question after a *negative* sentence:

negative sentence + positive tag

Maria **won't** be late, **will she?**
They **don't** like us, **do they?**
You **haven't** paid the gas bill, **have you?**

Notice the meaning of **yes** and **no** in answer to a negative sentence:

- You're not going out today, are you?
  - **Yes.** (= Yes, I am going out.)
  - **No.** (= No, I am not going out.)

C

The meaning of a tag question depends on how you say it. If your voice goes down, you aren't really asking a question; you are only inviting the listener to agree with you:

- "It's a nice day, isn't it?" "Yes, beautiful."
- "Eric doesn't look too good today, does he?" "No, he looks very tired."
- She's very funny. She has a wonderful sense of humor, doesn't she?

But if the voice goes up, it is a real question:

- "You haven't seen Lisa today, have you?" "No, I haven't."
  (= Have you seen Lisa today by any chance?)

We often use a negative sentence + positive tag to ask for things or information or to ask somebody to do something. The voice goes up at the end of the tag in sentences like these:

- "You wouldn't have a pen, would you?" "Yes, here you are."
- "You couldn't lend me some money, could you?" "It depends how much."
- "You don't know where Lauren is, do you?" "Sorry, I have no idea."

D

After **Let's . . .** the question tag is **shall we?**:

- **Let's** go for a walk, **shall we?**

After the imperative (**Do . . . / Listen . . . / Give . . .** , etc.), the tag is usually **will you?**:

- **Open** the door, **will you?**

Note that we say **aren't I?** (= am I not?):

- I'm late, **aren't I?**

Exercises

49.1 Put a tag question at the end of these sentences.

1.	Tom won't be late, _will he_ ?	No, he's never late.
2.	You're tired, _aren't you_ ?	Yes, a little.
3.	Tracy has lived here a long time, _____ ?	Yes, 20 years.
4.	You weren't listening, _____ ?	Yes, I was!
5.	Sue doesn't know Ann, _____ ?	No, they've never met.
6.	Jack's on vacation, _____ ?	Yes, he's in Puerto Rico.
7.	Mike hasn't phoned today, _____ ?	No, I don't think so.
8.	You can speak Spanish, _____ ?	Yes, but not fluently.
9.	He won't mind if I use his phone, _____ ?	No, of course he won't.
10.	There are a lot of people here, _____ ?	Yes, more than I expected.
11.	Let's go out tonight, _____ ?	Yes, that would be great.
12.	This isn't very interesting, _____ ?	No, not very.
13.	I'm too impatient, _____ ?	Yes, you are sometimes.
14.	You wouldn't tell anyone, _____ ?	No, of course not.
15.	Listen, _____ ?	OK, I'm listening.
16.	I shouldn't have lost my temper, _____ ?	No, but that's all right.
17.	He'd never met her before, _____ ?	No, that was the first time.

49.2 Read the situation and write a sentence with a tag question. In each situation you are asking your friend to agree with you.

1. You look out of the window. The sky is blue and the sun is shining. What do you say to your friend? (beautiful day) _It's a beautiful day, isn't it?_

2. You're with a friend outside a restaurant. You're looking at the prices, which are very high. What do you say? (expensive) It _____ ?

3. You've just come out of a movie theater with a friend. You really enjoyed the movie. What do you say to your friend? (great) The movie _____ ?

4. You and a friend are listening to a woman singing. You like her voice very much. What do you say to your friend? (a beautiful voice)
   She _____ ?

5. You are trying on a jacket. You look in the mirror and you don't like what you see. What do you say to your friend? (not / look / very good)
   It _____ ?

6. Your friend's hair is much shorter than when you last met. What do you say? (have / your hair / cut) You _____ ?

7. You and a friend are walking over a wooden bridge. It is very old, and some parts are broken. What do you say? (not / very safe)
   This bridge _____ ?

49.3 In these situations you are asking for information and asking people to do things.

1. You need a pen. Perhaps Kelly has one. Ask her. _Kelly, you don't have a pen, do you?_

2. The cashier is putting your groceries in a plastic bag, but perhaps he could give you a paper bag. Ask him. _____

3. You're looking for Ann. Perhaps Kate knows where she is. Ask her.
   Kate, you _____ ?

4. You need a bicycle pump. Perhaps Nicole has one. Ask her.
   Nicole, _____ ?

5. You're looking for your keys. Perhaps Robert has seen them. Ask him.
   _____

Verb + *-ing* (*enjoy doing / stop doing*, etc.)

A

Look at these examples:
- I **enjoy dancing**. (*not* I enjoy to dance)
- Would you **mind closing** the door? (*not* mind to close)
- Sam **suggested going** to the movies. (*not* suggested to go)

After **enjoy, mind,** and **suggest**, we use **-ing** (*not* to . . .).

Here are some more verbs that are followed by **-ing**:

stop	finish	avoid	consider	admit	miss	involve
quit	postpone	delay	imagine	deny	risk	practice

- Suddenly everybody **stopped talking**. There was silence.
- I'll do the shopping when I've **finished cleaning** the apartment.
- He tried to **avoid answering** my question.
- Have you ever **considered going** to live in another country?

Note the negative form **not -ing**:
- When I'm on vacation, I **enjoy not having** to get up early.

B

We also use **-ing** after:

> **give up** (= quit)
> **put off** (= postpone)
> **go on** (= continue)
> **keep** *or* **keep on** (= do something continuously or repeatedly)

- Paula has **given up trying** to lose weight.
- We have to do something. We can't **go on living** like this!
- Don't **keep interrupting** me while I'm talking. (*or* Don't **keep on interrupting** . . .)

C

With some verbs you can use the structure *verb* + somebody + **-ing**:
- I can't **imagine George riding** a motorbike.
- "Sorry to **keep you waiting** so long." "That's all right."

Note the passive form (**being done/seen/kept**, etc.):
- I don't mind **being kept** waiting. (= I don't mind people keeping me waiting)

D

When you are talking about finished actions, you can say **having done/stolen/said**, etc.:
- She admitted **having stolen** the money.

But it is not necessary to use **having done**. You can also use the simple **-ing** form for finished actions:
- She admitted **stealing** the money.
- I now regret **saying** (*or* **having said**) it.

For **regret**, see Unit 53B.

E

After some of the verbs on this page (especially **admit/deny/suggest**), you can use **that**:
- She **denied that** she had stolen the money. (*or* She **denied stealing** . . .)
- Sam **suggested that** we go to the movies. (*or* Sam **suggested going** . . .)

For **suggest**, see also Unit 32.

Verb + to . . . Unit 51   *Verb + to . . . and -ing* Units 52C, 53–55   *Regret / go on + ing* Unit 53B

Exercises

50.1 Complete each sentence with one of these verbs:

~~answer~~ apply be get listen make splash try use wash work write

1. He tried to avoid _answering_ my question.
2. Could you please stop _____ so much noise?
3. I enjoy _____ to music.
4. I considered _____ for the job, but in the end I decided against it.
5. Have you finished _____ your hair yet?
6. If you walk out into the street without looking, you risk _____ run over.
7. Jim is 65, but he isn't going to retire yet. He wants to go on _____ .
8. I don't mind you _____ the phone as long as you pay for all your calls.
9. If you use the shower, try and avoid _____ water on the floor.
10. I've put off _____ the letter several times. I really have to do it today.
11. What a mean thing to do! Can you imagine anybody _____ so mean?
12. Sarah gave up _____ to find a job in this country and decided to go abroad.

50.2 Complete the sentences for each situation using -ing.

1. What should we do?   We could go to the movies.   She suggested _going to the movies_ .

2. You were driving too fast.   Yes, I was. Sorry!   She admitted _____ .

3. Let's go swimming.   Good idea!   She suggested _____ .

4. You broke my CD player.   No, I didn't!   He denied _____ .

5. Can you wait a few minutes?   Sure, no problem.   They didn't mind _____ .

50.3 Complete the sentences so that they mean the same as the first sentence. Use -ing.

1. We can't live like this anymore. We can't go on _living like this_ .
2. It's not a good idea to travel during rush hour.
   It's best to avoid _____ .
3. Should we leave tomorrow instead of today?
   Should we postpone _____ until _____ ?
4. The driver of the car said it was true that he didn't have a license.
   The driver of the car admitted _____ .
5. Could you turn the radio down, please?
   Would you mind _____ ?
6. Please don't interrupt me all the time.
   Would you mind _____ ?

50.4 Use your own ideas to complete these sentences. Use -ing.

1. She's a very interesting person. I always enjoy _talking to her_ .
2. I'm afraid there aren't any chairs. I hope you don't mind _____ .
3. It was a beautiful day, so I suggested _____ .
4. It was very funny. I couldn't stop _____ .
5. My car isn't very reliable. It keeps _____ .

Verb + *to . . . (decide to do / forget to do,* etc.)

A

offer	decide	hope	deserve	attempt	mean	promise
agree	plan	aim	afford	manage	intend	threaten
refuse	arrange	learn	need	fail		forget

If these verbs are followed by another verb, the structure is usually *verb* + **to** . . . *(infinitive):*
- It was late, so we **decided to take** a taxi home.
- David was in a difficult situation, so I **agreed to lend** him some money.
- How old were you when you **learned to drive?** (*or* learned **how** to drive)
- Karen **failed to make** a good impression at the job interview.

Note these examples with the negative **not to:**
- We **decided not to go** out because of the weather.
- I **promised not to be** late.

With many verbs you cannot normally use **to** – for example, **enjoy/think/suggest:**
- I **enjoy dancing.** (*not* enjoy to dance)
- Sam **suggested going** to the movies. (*not* suggested to go)
- Are you **thinking of buying** a car? (*not* thinking to buy)

For *verb* + **-ing,** see Unit 50. For *verb* + *preposition* + **-ing,** see Unit 59.

B

We also use **to** . . . after: **seem   appear   tend   pretend   claim.**   For example:
- They **seem to have** plenty of money.
- I like Dan, but he **tends to talk** too much.
- Ann **pretended not to see** me when she passed me on the street.

There is also a *continuous infinitive* (**to be doing**) and a *perfect infinitive* (**to have done**):
- I **pretended to be reading** the newspaper. (= I pretended that I was reading)
- You seem **to have lost** weight. (= it seems that you have lost weight)

C

We say **decide to do** (something), **promise to do** (something), etc. In the same way, we say a **decision to do** (something), a **promise to do** (something), etc. (*noun* + **to**):
- I think his **decision to quit** his job was foolish.
- John has a **tendency to talk** too much.

D

After **dare** you can use the verb with or without **to:**
- I wouldn't **dare to tell** him. *or* I wouldn't **dare tell** him.

E

After the following verbs you can use a question word (**what/whether/how,** etc.) + **to** . . . :
ask   decide   know   remember   forget   explain   learn   understand   wonder

We **asked**	how	to get	to the station.
Have you **decided**	where	to go	for your vacation?
I don't **know**	whether	to apply	for the job or not.
Do you **understand**	what	to do?	

Also: **show/tell/ask/advise/teach** somebody **what/how/where** to do something:
- Can somebody **show me how to change** the film in this camera?
- Ask Jeff. He'll **tell you what to do.**

Exercises

51.1 Complete the sentence for each situation.

1. Shall we get married? — Yes.
They decided *to get married* .

2. Please help me. — OK.
She agreed _____
_____ .

3. Can I carry your bags for you? — No, thanks. I can manage.
He offered _____
_____ .

4. Let's meet at 8:00. — OK, fine.
They arranged _____
_____ .

5. What's your name? — I'm not going to tell you.
She refused _____
_____ .

6. Please don't tell anyone. — I won't. I promise.
She promised _____
_____ .

51.2 Put the verb into the correct form, *to . . .* or *-ing.* (See Unit 50 for verb + *-ing.*)
1. When I'm tired, I enjoy *watching* TV. It's relaxing. (watch)
2. It was a nice day, so we decided _____ for a walk. (go)
3. There was a lot of traffic, but we managed _____ to the airport in time. (get)
4. I'm not in a hurry. I don't mind _____ . (wait)
5. They don't have much money. They can't afford _____ out very often. (go)
6. We've got a new computer in our office. I haven't learned how _____ it yet. (use)
7. I wish that dog would stop _____ . It's driving me crazy. (bark)
8. Our neighbor threatened _____ the police if we didn't stop the noise. (call)
9. We were hungry, so I suggested _____ dinner early. (have)
10. We were all afraid to speak. Nobody dared _____ anything. (say)
11. Hurry up! I don't want to risk _____ the train. (miss)
12. I'm still looking for a job, but I hope _____ something soon. (find)

51.3 Make a new sentence using the verb in parentheses.
1. He has lost weight. (seem) *He seems to have lost weight.*
2. Tom is worried about something. (appear) Tom appears _____ .
3. You know a lot of people. (seem) You _____ .
4. My English is getting better. (seem) _____
5. That car has broken down. (appear) _____
6. David forgets things. (tend) _____
7. They have solved the problem. (claim) _____

51.4 Complete each sentence using *what/how/whether* + one of these verbs:

do ~~get~~ go ride say use

1. Do you know *how to get* to John's house?
2. Can you show me _____ this washing machine?
3. Would you know _____ if there was a fire in the building?
4. You'll never forget _____ a bicycle once you have learned.
5. I was really astonished. I didn't know _____ .
6. I've been invited to the party, but I don't know _____ or not.

Verb + (Object) + *to* . . . (*I want to do / I want you to do,* etc.)

A

| want | ask | help | expect | beg | would like | would prefer |

These verbs are followed by **to** . . . (*infinitive*). The structure can be:

verb + **to** . . .   or   *verb* + *object* + **to** . . .
- We **expected to be** late.   - We **expected Tom to be** late.
- **Would** you **like to go** now?   - Would you like **me to go** now?
- He doesn't **want to know.**   - He doesn't want **anybody to know.**

Be careful with **want.** Do not say "want that":
- Do you **want me to come** with you? (*not* Do you want that I come)

After **help** you can use the verb with or without **to**. So you can say:
- Can you help me **to move** this table? *or* Can you help me **move** this table?

B

| tell | remind | force | enable | teach |
| order | warn | invite | persuade | get (= persuade, arrange for) |

These verbs have the structure *verb* + *object* + **to** . . . :
- Can you **remind me to call** Ann tomorrow?
- Who **taught you to drive?**
- I didn't move the piano by myself. I **got somebody to help** me.
- Jim said the electrical outlet was dangerous and **warned me not to touch** it.

In the next example, the verb is *passive* (**was warned**):
- I **was warned not to touch** the electrical outlet.

Note that you cannot use **suggest** with the structure *verb* + *object* + **to** . . . :
- Jane **suggested that I buy** a car. (*not* Jane suggested me to buy)

For **suggest,** see Units 32 and 50.

C

| advise | encourage | allow | permit | forbid |

There are two possible structures after these verbs. Compare:
verb + **-ing** (without an object)   *verb* + *object* + **to** . . .
- I wouldn't **advise staying** in that hotel. - I wouldn't **advise anybody to stay** in that hotel.

- She doesn't **allow smoking** in the house.   - She doesn't **allow anyone to smoke** in the house.

Compare these examples with **(be) allowed** (*passive*):
- Smoking **isn't allowed** in the house.   - We **aren't allowed to smoke** in the house.

D

Make and **let**

These verbs have the structure *verb* + *object* + *base form* (**do/open/feel,** etc.):
- The customs officer **made Sally open** her case. (*not* to open)
- Hot weather **makes me feel** tired. (= causes me to feel tired)
- Her parents wouldn't **let her go** out alone. (= wouldn't allow her to go out)
- **Let me carry** your bag for you.

We say **make somebody do** . . . (*not* to do), but the passive is **(be) made to do** . . . (with **to**):
- I only did it because I **was made to do** it.

Exercises

52.1 Complete the questions. Use *do you want me to . . . ?* or *would you like me to . . . ?*
with one of these verbs (and any other necessary words):

~~come~~ lend repeat show shut

1. Do you want to go alone, or *do you want me to come with you* ?
2. Do you have enough money, or do you want _____ ?
3. Should I leave the window open, or would you _____ ?
4. Do you know how to use the machine, or would _____ ?
5. Did you hear what I said, or do _____ ?

52.2 Complete the sentence for each situation.

1.
Lock the door. → OK.

She told *him to lock the door* .

2.
Why don't you stay with us for a few days? → Yes, I'd like to.

They invited him _____ _____ .

3.
Can I use your phone? → No!

She wouldn't let _____ _____ .

4.
Be careful. → Don't worry. I will.

She warned _____ _____ .

5.
Can you give me a hand? → Sure.

He asked _____ _____ .

52.3 Complete these sentences so that the meaning is similar to the first sentence.

1. My father said I could use his car. My father allowed *me to use his car* .
2. I was surprised that it rained. I didn't expect it _____ .
3. Don't stop him from doing what he wants. Let _____ .
4. He looks older when he wears glasses. Glasses make _____ .
5. I think you should know the truth. I want you _____ .
6. Don't let me forget to call my sister. Remind _____ .
7. At first I didn't want to apply for the job, but Sarah persuaded me.
   Sarah persuaded _____ .
8. My lawyer said I shouldn't say anything to the police.
   My lawyer advised _____ .
9. I was told that I shouldn't believe everything he says.
   I was warned _____ .
10. If you have a car, you are able to go places more easily.
    Having a car enables _____ .

52.4 Put the verb in the right form: *-ing*, infinitive (*to do / to read*, etc.), or base form
(*do/read*, etc.).

1. She doesn't allow *smoking* in the house. (smoke)
2. I've never been to Hong Kong, but I'd like _____ there. (go)
3. I'm in a difficult position. What do you advise me _____ ? (do)
4. She said the letter was personal and wouldn't let me _____ it. (read)
5. We were kept at the police station for an hour, and then we were allowed
   _____ . (go)
6. I wouldn't advise _____ in that restaurant. The food is awful. (eat)
7. The movie was very sad. It made me _____ . (cry)
8. Lauren's parents always encouraged her _____ hard at school. (study)

Verb + -ing or to . . . (1) (remember/regret, etc.)

A

Compare *verb* + -ing and *verb* + to . . . :

verb + -ing	*verb* + to . . .
■ They **denied stealing** the money.	■ They **decided to steal** the money.
■ I **enjoy going** out.	■ I **want to go** out.
Often we use -ing for an action that happens before the first verb or at the same time. So you **deny doing** something *after* you do it, you **enjoy doing** something *while* you do it.	Often we use to . . . for an action that follows the first verb. So you **decide to do** something *before* you do it, you **want to do** something *before* you do it.

This difference is often helpful (see Section B) but does not explain all uses of -ing and to . . .

B

Some verbs can be followed by -ing or to . . . with a difference of meaning:

remember

I remember doing something = I did it and now I remember this. You **remember doing** something *after* you have done it:	**I remembered to do** something = I remembered that I had to do it, and so I did it. You **remember to do** something *before* you do it:
■ I'm absolutely sure I locked the door. I distinctly **remember locking** it. (= I locked it, and now I remember this.)	■ I **remembered to lock** the door when I left, but I forgot to shut the windows. (= I remembered that I had to lock the door, and so I locked it.)
■ He could **remember driving** along the road just before the accident happened, but he couldn't remember the accident itself.	■ Please **remember to mail** the letter. (= Don't forget to mail it.)

regret

I regret doing something = I did it, and now I'm sorry about it:	**I regret to say / to tell you / to inform you** = I'm sorry that I have to say (etc.):
■ I now **regret saying** what I said. I shouldn't have said it.	■ *(from a letter)* We **regret to inform** you that we are unable to offer you the job.

go on

Go on doing something = continue doing it:	**Go on to do** something = do something new:
■ The president **went on talking** for hours.	■ After discussing the economy, the president then **went on to talk** about foreign policy.
■ We must change our ways. We can't **go on living** like this.	

C

begin   start   continue   bother

These verbs can be followed by -ing or to . . . with little or no difference in meaning. So you can say:

■ It has **started raining**.   *or*   It has **started to rain**.
■ Don't **bother locking** the door.   *or*   Don't **bother to lock** . . .

But we do not use -ing after -ing:

■ It's **starting to rain**. (*not* It's starting raining)

Exercises

53.1 Put the verb into the correct form, *-ing* or *to* . . . Sometimes either form is possible.

1. They denied *stealing* _____ the money. (steal)
2. I don't enjoy _____ very much. (drive)
3. I don't want _____ out tonight. I'm too tired. (go)
4. I can't afford _____ out tonight. I don't have enough money. (go)
5. Has it stopped _____ yet? (rain)
6. Can you remind me _____ some coffee when we go out? (buy)
7. Why do you keep _____ me questions? Can't you leave me alone? (ask)
8. Please stop _____ me questions! (ask)
9. I refuse _____ any more questions. (answer)
10. One of the boys admitted _____ the window. (break)
11. The boy's father promised _____ for the window to be repaired. (pay)
12. "How did the thief get into the house?" "I forgot _____ the window." (lock)
13. I enjoyed _____ you. (meet) I hope _____ you again soon. (see)
14. The baby began _____ in the middle of the night. (cry)
15. Julie has been sick, but now she's beginning _____ better. (get)

53.2 Here is some information about Tom when he was a child.

1. He was in the hospital when he was four.
2. He went to Miami when he was eight.
3. Once he fell into a river.
4. He cried on his first day at school.
5. He said he wanted to be a doctor.
6. Once he was bitten by a dog.

He can still remember 1, 2, and 4. But he can't remember 3, 5, and 6. Write sentences beginning *He can remember* . . . or *He can't remember* . . .

1. *He can remember being in the hospital when he was four.*
2. _____
3. _____
4. _____
5. _____
6. _____

53.3 Complete these sentences with an appropriate verb in the correct form, *-ing* or *to* . . .

1. a) Please remember *to lock* _____ the door when you go out.
   b) *A:* You lent me some money a few months ago.
      B: I did? Are you sure? I don't remember _____ you any money.
   c) *A:* Did you remember _____ your sister?
      B: Oh no, I completely forgot. I'll phone her tomorrow.
   d) When you see Amanda, remember _____ hello for me, OK?
   e) Someone must have taken my bag. I distinctly remember _____ it by the window, and now it's gone.
2. a) I believe that what I said was fair. I don't regret _____ it.
   b) (after a driving test) I regret _____ that you have failed the test.
3. a) Ben joined the company nine years ago. He became assistant manager after two years. A few years later he went on _____ manager of the company.
   b) I can't go on _____ here anymore. I want a different job.
   c) When I came into the room, Liz was reading a newspaper. She looked up and said hello to me and then went on _____ her newspaper.

Verb + *-ing* or *to* . . . (2) *(try/need/help)*

A

Try to do and try doing

Try to do = attempt to do, make an effort to do:
- I was very tired. I **tried to keep** my eyes open, but I couldn't.
- Please **try to be** quiet when you come home. Everyone will be asleep.

Try also means "do something as an experiment or a test." For example:
- These cookies are delicious. You should **try** one. (= you should have one to see if you like it)
- We couldn't find anywhere to stay. We **tried** every hotel in town, but they were all full. (= we went to every hotel to see if they had a room)

If **try** (with this meaning) is followed by a verb, we use **try -ing**:
- *A:* The photocopier doesn't seem to be working.
- *B:* **Try pressing** the green button. (= press the green button – maybe this will help to solve the problem)

Compare:
- I **tried to move** the table, but it was too heavy. (so I couldn't move it)
- I didn't like the way the furniture was arranged, so I **tried moving** the table to the other side of the room. But it still didn't look right, so I moved it back again.

B

Need to do, need to be done, need doing

I **need to do** something = it is necessary for me to do it:
- I **need to get** more exercise.
- He **needs to work** harder if he wants to make progress.

Something **needs to be done** = someone needs to do something:
- The batteries in the radio **need to be changed**.
- Do you think my jacket **needs to be washed?**

Sometimes we use **need doing** instead of **need to be done**.
- The batteries in the radio **need changing**.
- The tire **needs changing**. (*or* The tire **needs to be changed**.)

C

Help and can't help

You can say **help to do** or **help do** (with or without **to**):
- Everybody **helped to clean up** after the party. *or* Everybody **helped clean up** . . .
- Can you **help** me **to move** this table? *or* Can you **help** me **move** . . .

There is also an expression: **can't/couldn't help doing** something. I **can't help doing** it = I can't stop myself from doing it:
- I don't like him, but he has a lot of problems. I **can't help feeling** sorry for him.
- She tried to be serious, but she **couldn't help laughing**. (= she couldn't stop herself from laughing)
- I'm sorry I'm so nervous. I **can't help it**. (= I can't help being nervous)

Verb + *-ing* Unit 50   **Verb +** *to* . . . Units 51–52   **Verb +** *-ing* **or** *to* . . . Units 53–55

Exercises

54.1 Make suggestions. Write sentences using *try* + one of the following suggestions:

call him at work   ~~change the batteries~~   take an aspirin   turn it the other way

1. The radio isn't working. I wonder what's wrong with it.
2. I can't open the door. The key won't turn.
3. I have a terrible headache. I wish I could get rid of it.
4. I can't reach Fred. He's not at home. What should I do?

Have you tried changing the batteries?

Try _____ .

Have you _____ ?

Why don't you _____ ?

54.2 For each picture write a sentence with *need(s)* + one of the following verbs:

cut   empty   ~~wash~~   redecorate   tighten

1	2	3	4	5

1. This jacket is dirty. *It needs to be washed.* OR *It needs washing.*
2. The grass is very long. It _____ .
3. This room doesn't look very nice. _____
4. The screws are loose. _____
5. The garbage can is full. _____

54.3 Put the verbs into the correct form.

1. a) I was very tired. I tried *to keep* _____ (keep) my eyes open, but I couldn't.
   b) I rang the doorbell, but there was no answer. Then I tried _____ (knock) on the door, but there was still no answer.
   c) We tried _____ (put) the fire out, but we were unsuccessful. We had to call the fire department.
   d) Sue needed to borrow some money. She tried _____ (ask) Jerry, but he was short of money, too.
   e) I tried _____ (reach) the shelf, but I wasn't tall enough.
   f) Please leave me alone. I'm trying _____ (concentrate).
2. a) I need a change. I need _____ (go) away for a while.
   b) She isn't able to take care of herself. She needs _____ (take) care of.
   c) The windows are dirty. They need _____ (wash).
   d) You don't need _____ (iron) that shirt. It doesn't need _____ (iron).
3. a) They were talking very loudly. I couldn't help _____ (overhear) them.
   b) Can you help me _____ (get) dinner ready?
   c) He looks so funny. Whenever I see him, I can't help _____ (laugh).
   d) The nice weather helped _____ (make) it a very pleasant vacation.

Verb + -ing or to . . . (3) (like / would like, etc.)

A

| like   love   hate   can't bear   can't stand |

After these verbs you can use **to** . . . *(infinitive)* or **-ing**.

We normally use **-ing** *(not* **to** . . .) for a situation that already exists or existed. For example:
- I live in Vancouver now. I **like living** there. *(not* I like to live there)
- Do you **like being** a student? (You are a student now.)
- That office was horrible. I **hated working** there. (I worked there and hated it.)

In other situations, you can use **to** . . . or **-ing**. **To** . . . is more usual:
- I **like to get** up early.   *or*   I **like getting** up early.
- Ann **hates to fly.**   *or*   Ann **hates flying.**
- I **love to meet** people.   *or*   I **love meeting** people.
- I don't **like** friends **to call** me at work.   *or*   I don't **like** friends **calling** me at work.
- She **can't bear to be** alone.   *or*   She **can't bear being** alone.

B

After **enjoy** and **mind**, we use **-ing** *(not* to . . .):
- I **enjoy meeting** people. *(not* I enjoy to meet)
- Tom doesn't **mind working** at night. *(not* mind to work)

Compare:
- I **enjoy cooking.**
- I don't **mind cooking.**
- I **like to cook.** *or* I **like cooking.**

C

Would like / would love / would hate / would prefer are usually followed by **to** . . . *(infinitive):*
- I **would like to be** rich.
- **Would** you **like to come** to dinner on Friday?
- I'**d love** (= would love) **to be** able to travel around the world.
- **Would** you **prefer to have** dinner now or later?

Compare **I like** and **I would like**:
- I **like playing / to play** tennis. (= I enjoy it in general)
- I **would like to play** tennis today. (= I want to play today)

Note that **would mind** is followed by **-ing** *(not* to . . .):
- **Would** you **mind closing** the door, please?

D

You can also say "I would like **to have done** something" (= I regret now that I didn't or couldn't do something):
- It's too bad we didn't see Johnny when we were in Montreal. I **would like to have seen** him again.
- We'd **like to have gone** on vacation, but we didn't have enough money.

You can use the same structure after **would love / would hate / would prefer:**
- Poor Tom! I **would hate to have been** in his position.
- I'd **love to have gone** to the party, but it was impossible.

Exercises

55.1 Write sentences with *like + -ing*.

1. I'm a student. I like it.   *I like being a student.*
2. Ellen and Joel live in Atlanta. They like it. They _____ .
3. I used to work in a supermarket. I didn't like it very much.
   I _____ .
4. Ryan teaches biology. He likes it. He _____ .
5. Rachel is studying medicine. She likes it. She _____ .
6. Dan is famous. He doesn't like this. He _____ .

55.2 Write sentences about yourself. Say whether you like or don't like these activities.
Choose one of these verbs for each sentence:

   like / don't like   don't mind   enjoy   hate   love

1. (fly)   *I don't like to fly.* OR *I don't like flying.*
2. (play cards)   _____
3. (do the ironing)   _____
4. (go to museums)   _____
5. (lie on the beach all day)   _____

55.3 How would you feel about doing these jobs? Use one of these in your sentences:

   I'd like / I wouldn't like   I'd love   I'd hate   I wouldn't mind

1. (a teacher)   *I wouldn't like to be a teacher.*
2. (a dentist)   _____
3. (a hair stylist)   _____
4. (an airline pilot)   _____
5. (a tour guide)   _____

55.4 Write an appropriate verb in the correct form, *-ing* or *to . . .* Sometimes either form is
possible.

1. It's nice to be with other people, but sometimes I enjoy *being* _____ alone.
2. I'm not quite ready yet. Do you mind _____ a little longer?
3. When I was a child, I hated _____ to bed early.
4. I don't like _____ letters. I can never think what to write.
5. I need a new job. I can't stand _____ here anymore.
6. I would love _____ to your wedding, but I'm afraid I can't.
7. Caroline never wears a hat. She doesn't like _____ hats.
8. "Would you like _____ down?" "No, thanks. I'll stand."
9. I don't like _____ in this part of town. I want to live somewhere else.
10. Do you have a minute? I'd like _____ to you about something.
11. Robert misses his car when it's at the mechanic's. He can't stand _____
    without his car for even one day.

55.5 Write sentences like those in Section D. Use the verb in parentheses.

1. It's too bad I couldn't go to the wedding. (like) *I would like to have gone to the wedding.*
2. It's too bad I didn't see the program. (like) _____
3. I'm glad I didn't lose my watch. (hate) _____
4. It's too bad I didn't meet Ann. (love) _____
5. I'm glad I wasn't alone. (not / like) _____
6. It's a shame I couldn't travel by train. (prefer) _____

Prefer and would rather

Prefer to do and **prefer doing**

You can use **prefer to (do)** or **prefer -ing** to say what you prefer in general:

■ I don't like cities. I **prefer to live** in the country. *or* I **prefer living** in the country.

Study the differences in structure after **prefer.** We say:

	I prefer	something	to	something else.
	I prefer	**doing** something	to	**doing** something else.
but	I prefer	**to do** something	**rather than**	**(do)** something else.

■ I **prefer** this coat **to** the coat you were wearing yesterday.
■ I **prefer driving to traveling** by train.
but ■ I **prefer to drive rather than travel** by train.
■ Ann **prefers to live** in the country **rather than** in a city. *or* . . . **rather than live** in a city.

Would prefer (I'd prefer)

We use **would prefer** to say what somebody wants in a particular situation (not in general):

■ "**Would** you **prefer** tea or coffee?" "Coffee, please."

We say "**would prefer to do**" (*not* doing):

■ "Should we take the train?" "No, I**'d prefer to drive.**" (*not* I'd prefer driving)
■ I**'d prefer to stay** home tonight rather than go to the movies.

Would rather (I'd rather)

We use **would rather** + *base form* (**do/have/stay,** etc.). Compare:

■ "Should we take the train?" { "I**'d prefer to drive.**"
{ "I**'d rather drive.**" (*not* to drive)
■ "**Would** you **rather have** tea or coffee?" "Coffee, please."

The negative is "**I'd rather not** (do something)":

■ I'm tired. I**'d rather not go** out tonight, if you don't mind.
■ "Do you want to go out tonight?" "I**'d rather not.**"

We say "**would rather do** something **than do** something else":

■ I**'d rather stay** home **than go** to the movies.

I'd rather you **did** something

We say "**I'd rather** you **did** something" (*not* I'd rather you do). For example:

■ "I'll fix the car tomorrow, OK?" "I**'d rather** you **did** it today." (= I'd prefer this)
■ "Is it OK if Ben stays here?" "I**'d rather** he **came** with us." (*not* he comes)
■ Should I tell them the news, or **would you rather** they **didn't** know? (*not* don't know)

In this structure we use the *past* (**did/came,** etc.), but the meaning is not past. Compare:

■ I**'d rather make** dinner now.
but ■ I**'d rather you made** dinner now. (*not* I'd rather you make).

I'd rather you didn't (do something) = I'd prefer that you not do it:

■ I**'d rather you didn't tell** anyone what I said.
■ "Should I tell Stephanie?" "I**'d rather you didn't.**"

Prefer . . . to . . . Unit 132D

Exercises

56.1 Which do you prefer? Write sentences using *I prefer* (something) *to* (something else). Put the verb into the correct form where necessary.

1. (drive / travel by train) *I prefer driving to traveling by train.*
2. (tennis / soccer) I prefer _____.
3. (call people / write letters) I _____ to _____.
4. (go to the movies / watch videos at home)
   _____

Now rewrite sentences 3 and 4 using the structure *I prefer* (to do something) *rather than* (something else).

5. (1) *I prefer to drive rather than travel by train.*
6. (3) I prefer to _____.
7. (4) _____

56.2 Write sentences using *I'd prefer . . .* or *I'd rather . . .* + one of the following:

eat at home   ~~take a taxi~~   go alone   go for a swim   listen to some music   stand
think about it for a while   ~~wait till later~~

1. Shall we walk home? (prefer) *I'd prefer to take a taxi.*
2. Do you want to eat now? (rather) *I'd rather wait till later.*
3. Would you like to watch TV? (prefer) _____
4. What about a game of tennis? (rather) _____
5. Do you want to go to a restaurant? (prefer) _____
6. I think we should decide now. (rather) _____
7. Would you like to sit down? (rather) _____
8. Do you want me to come with you? (prefer) _____

Now write sentences using *than* or *rather than*.

9. (take a taxi / walk home)
   I'd prefer *to take a taxi rather than walk home*.
10. (go for a swim / play tennis)
    I'd rather _____.
11. (eat at home / go to a restaurant)
    I'd prefer _____.
12. (think about it for a while / decide now)
    I'd rather _____.

56.3 Complete the sentences using *would you rather I . . . ?*

1. Are you going to make dinner, or *would you rather I made it* ?
2. Are you going to tell Ann what happened, or would you rather _____ ?
3. Are you going to do the shopping, or _____ ?
4. Are you going to answer the phone, or _____ ?

56.4 Use your own ideas to complete these sentences.

1. "Should I tell Ann the news?" "No, I'd rather she *didn't* know."
2. Do you want me to go now, or would you rather I _____ here?
3. Do you want to go out tonight, or would you rather _____ home?
4. This is a private letter addressed to me. I'd rather you _____ read it.
5. I don't really like these shoes. I'd rather they _____ a different color.
6. "Do you mind if I turn on the radio?" "I'd rather you _____ . I'm trying to study."

Preposition (*in/for/about*, etc.) + *-ing*

If a *preposition* (**in/for/about**, etc.) is followed by a *verb*, the verb ends in **-ing**. For example:

preposition + *verb* (**-ing**)

Are you interested	**in**	**working**	for us?
I'm not very good	**at**	**learning**	languages.
She must be fed up	**with**	**studying.**	
What are the advantages	**of**	**having**	a car?
This knife is only	**for**	**cutting**	bread.
How	**about**	**playing**	tennis tomorrow?
I bought a new bicycle	**instead of**	**taking**	a vacation.
Carol went to work	**in spite of**	**feeling**	sick.

Note the use of the following prepositions + **-ing**:

before -ing and **after -ing**:
- **Before going** out, I called Sarah. (*not* Before to go out)
- What did you do **after finishing** school?

You can also say "**Before I went** out . . ." and ". . . **after you finished** school."

by -ing (to say how something happens):
- The burglars got into the house **by breaking** a window and **climbing** in.
- You can improve your English **by reading** more.

without -ing:
- I ran ten miles **without stopping.**
- They climbed through the window **without** anybody **seeing** them. (*or* . . . **without being** seen.)
- She needs to work **without** people **disturbing** her. (*or* . . . **without being** disturbed.)
- It's nice to take a vacation **without having** to worry about money.

To **-ing**

To is often part of an *infinitive* (**to do** / **to see**, etc.):
- We decided **to go** out.
- Would you like **to play** tennis?

But **to** is also a *preposition* (like **in/for/about/from**, etc.):
- We drove from Houston **to Chicago.**
- I prefer tea **to coffee.**
- Are you looking forward **to the weekend?**

If a preposition is followed by a verb, the verb ends in **-ing** (**in doing** / **about going**, etc.) – see Section A. So, when **to** is a preposition and it is followed by a verb, you must say **to -ing**:
- I prefer driving **to traveling** by train. (*not* to travel)
- Are you looking forward **to seeing** Ann again? (*not* looking forward to see)

For **be/get used to -ing**, see Unit 58.

Exercises

57.1 Complete the sentences so that they mean the same as the sentences in parentheses.

1. (Why is it useful to have a car?)
   What are the advantages of _having a car_ ?
2. (I don't intend to lend you any money.)
   I have no intention of _____ .
3. (Karen has a good memory for names.)
   Karen is good at _____ .
4. (Mark won't pass the exam. He has no chance.)
   Mark has no chance of _____ .
5. (Did you get into trouble because you were late?)
   Did you get into trouble for _____ ?
6. (We didn't eat at home. We went to a restaurant instead.)
   Instead of _____ .
7. (Tom thinks that working is better than doing nothing.)
   Tom prefers working to _____ .
8. (Our team played well, but we lost the game.)
   Our team lost the game in spite of _____ .

57.2 Complete the sentences using *by -ing*. Use one of the following (with the verb in the correct form):

borrow too much money ~~break a window~~ **drive too fast** **stand on a chair** **turn the key**

1. The burglars got into the house _by breaking a window_ .
2. I was able to reach the top shelf _____ .
3. You start the engine of a car _____ .
4. Kevin got himself into financial trouble _____ .
5. You can put people's lives in danger _____ .

57.3 Complete the sentences with an appropriate word. Use only one word each time.

1. I ran ten miles without _stopping_ .
2. He left the hotel without _____ his bill.
3. It's a nice morning. How about _____ for a walk?
4. I was surprised that she left without _____ good-bye to anyone.
5. Before _____ to bed, I like to have some hot cocoa.
6. We were able to translate the letter into English without _____ a dictionary.
7. It was a very long trip. I was very tired after _____ on a train for 36 hours.
8. I was annoyed because the decision was made without anybody _____ me.
9. After _____ the same job for ten years, I felt I needed a change.

57.4 For each situation, write a sentence with ... *(not) looking forward to.*

1. You are going on vacation next week. How do you feel about this?
   I'm looking forward to going on vacation.
2. Diane is a good friend of yours, and she is coming to visit you. So you will see her again soon. How do you feel about this? I'm _____ .
3. You are going to the dentist tomorrow. You don't like to go to the dentist. How do you feel about this? I'm not _____ .
4. Carol hates school, but she is graduating next summer. How does she feel about this?
   _____
5. You like tennis. You've arranged to play tennis tomorrow. How do you feel about this?
   _____

Be/get used to something (I'm used to . . .)

Study this example situation:

LISA

Lisa is an American who lives in Tokyo. When she first drove a car in Japan, she found it very difficult because she had to drive on the left instead of the right. Driving on the left was strange and difficult for her because:

She **wasn't used to it.**
She **wasn't used to driving** on the left.

But after a lot of practice, driving on the left became less strange. So:
She **got used to driving** on the left.

Now, it's no problem for Lisa:
She **is used to driving** on the left.

I'm used to something = it is not new or strange for me:

- Frank lives alone. He doesn't mind this because he has lived alone for 15 years. It is not strange for him. He **is used to it.** He **is used to living** alone.
- I bought some new shoes. They felt strange at first because I **wasn't used to them.**
- Our new apartment is on a very busy street. I suppose we'll **get used to the noise,** but for now it's very annoying.
- Diane has a new job. She has to get up much earlier now than before – at 6:30. She finds this difficult because she **isn't used to getting up** so early.
- Brenda's husband is often away. She doesn't mind. She **is used to him being** away.

After **be/get used** you cannot use the *infinitive* (**to do** / **to drive,** etc.). We say:
- She is used **to driving** on the left. (*not* she is used to drive)

When we say "**I am used to** something," **to** is a *preposition*, not part of the infinitive (see Unit 57C). So we say:
- Frank is **used to living** alone. (*not* Frank is used to live)
- Lisa had to get **used to driving** on the left. (*not* get used to drive)

Do not confuse **I am used to doing** and **I used to do:**

I am used to (doing) something = it isn't strange or new for me:
- I **am used to the weather** in this country.
- I **am used to driving** on the left because I've lived in Japan for a long time.

I used to do something = I did something regularly in the past but no longer do it (see Unit 17). You can use this structure only for the past, not for the present. The structure is **I used to do** (*not* I am used to do):
- I **used to drive** to work every day, but these days I usually ride my bike.
- We **used to live** in a small town, but now we live in Los Angeles.

Used to (do) Unit 17   *To -ing* Unit 57C

Exercises

58.1 Look again at the situation in Section A on the opposite page ("Lisa is an American . . ."). The following situations are similar. Complete the sentences using *used to*.

1. Juan is Spanish and went to live in Canada. In Spain he always had dinner late in the evening, but in Canada dinner was at 6:00. This was very early for him. When Juan first went to Canada, he _wasn't used to having_ dinner so early, but after a while he _____ it. Now he thinks it's normal. He _____ at 6:00.

2. Julia is a nurse. A year ago she started working nights. At first she found it hard and didn't like it. She _____ nights, and it took her a few months to _____ it. Now, after a year, she's quite happy. She _____ nights.

58.2 What do you say in these situations? Use *I'm (not) used to*.

1. You live alone. You don't mind this. You have always lived alone.
   Friend: Do you get a little lonely sometimes? *You:* No, _I'm used to living alone_ .

2. You sleep on the floor. You don't mind this. You have always slept on the floor.
   Friend: Wouldn't you prefer to sleep in a bed?
   You: No, I _____ .

3. You have to work hard. This is not a problem for you. You have always worked hard.
   Friend: You have to work very hard in your job, don't you?
   You: Yes, but I don't mind that. I _____ .

4. You usually go to bed early. Last night you went to bed very late (for you), and as a result you are very tired this morning.
   Friend: You look tired this morning.
   You: Yes, _____ .

58.3 Read the situation and complete the sentences using *used to*.

1. Some friends of yours have just moved into an apartment on a busy street. It is very noisy. They'll have to _get used to the noise_ .

2. Jack once went to the Middle East. It was very hard for him at first because of the heat. He wasn't _____ .

3. Sue moved from a big house to a much smaller one. She found it strange at first. She had to _____ in a much smaller house.

4. The children at school got a new teacher. She was different from the teacher before her, but this wasn't a problem for the children. The children soon _____ .

5. Some people from the United States are thinking of going to live in your city or country. What will they have to get used to? They will have to _____ .

58.4 Complete the sentences using only one word each time (see Section C).

1. Lisa had to get used to _driving_ on the left.
2. Tom used to _____ a lot of coffee. Now he prefers tea.
3. I feel very full after that meal. I'm not used to _____ so much.
4. I wouldn't like to share an office. I'm used to _____ my own office.
5. I used to _____ a car, but I sold it a few months ago.
6. When we were children, we used to _____ swimming every day.
7. There used to _____ a movie theater here, but it was torn down a few years ago.
8. I'm the boss here! I'm not used to _____ told what to do.

Verb + Preposition + -ing (succeed in -ing / accuse somebody of -ing, etc.)

A

Many verbs have the structure *verb + preposition* (**in/for/about**, etc.) *+ object*. For example:

verb + preposition + object

We **talked**	**about**	the problem.
You should **apologize**	**for**	what you said.

If the object is another verb, it ends in **-ing**:

verb + preposition + -ing (object)

We **talked**	**about**	**going** to South America.
She **apologized***	**for**	**not telling** the truth.

** We say "**apologize to** somebody **for**":*
- She **apologized to me** for not telling the truth. (*not* she apologized me)

Here are some more verbs with this structure:

succeed (in)	Have you **succeeded**	**in**	**finding** a job yet?
insist (on)	They **insisted**	**on**	**paying** for dinner.
think (of)	I'm **thinking**	**of**	**buying** a house.
dream (of)	I wouldn't **dream**	**of**	**asking** them for money.
approve (of)	She doesn't **approve**	**of**	**gambling**.
decide (against)	We have **decided**	**against**	**moving** to Chicago.
feel (like)	Do you **feel**	**like**	**going** out tonight?
look forward (to)	I'm **looking forward**	**to**	**meeting** her.

With some verbs, you can use the structure *verb + preposition + somebody + -ing*:
- She doesn't **approve of me** (*or* **my**) gambling.
- We are all **looking forward to Bob** (*or* **Bob's**) coming home.
- They **insisted on me** (*or* **my**) staying with them.

B

The following verbs can have the structure *verb + object + preposition + -ing*:

verb + object + preposition + -ing

congratulate (on)	I **congratulated**	Ann	**on**	**getting** a new job.
accuse (of)	They **accused**	me	**of**	**telling** lies.
suspect (of)	Nobody **suspected**	the man	**of**	**being** a spy.
prevent (from)	What **prevented**	him	**from**	**coming** to see us?
keep (from)	The noise **keeps**	me	**from**	**falling** asleep.
stop (from)	The police **stopped**	everyone	**from**	**leaving** the building.
thank (for)	I forgot to **thank**	them	**for**	**helping** me.
excuse (for)	**Excuse**	me	**for**	**not returning** your call.

Some of these verbs are often used in the *passive*. For example:
- They **were accused** of telling lies.
- The man **was suspected** of being a spy.
- We **were kept** from seeing Frank in the hospital.

Verb + to . . . Units 51–52   **Preposition + -ing** Unit 57   **Verb + Preposition** Units 128–132

Exercises

59.1 Complete each sentence using only one word.

1. Our neighbors apologized for *making* so much noise.
2. I feel lazy. I don't feel like _____ any work.
3. I wanted to go out alone, but Joe insisted on _____ with me.
4. I'm fed up with my job. I'm thinking of _____ something else.
5. We have decided against _____ a new car because we really can't afford it.
6. I hope you write to me soon. I'm looking forward to _____ from you.
7. The weather was extremely bad, and this kept us from _____ out.
8. The man who was arrested is suspected of _____ a false passport.
9. I think you should apologize to Sue for _____ so rude to her.
10. Some parents don't approve of their children _____ a lot of television.
11. I'm sorry I can't come to your party, but thank you for _____ me.

59.2 Complete the sentences using a preposition + one of the following verbs (in the correct form):

cause   escape   ~~go~~   help   interrupt   live   play   solve   spend   walk

1. Do you feel *like going* out tonight?
2. It took us a long time, but we finally succeeded _____ the problem.
3. I've always dreamed _____ in a small house by the sea.
4. The driver of the other car accused me _____ the accident.
5. There was a fence around the lawn to stop people _____ on the grass.
6. Excuse me _____ you, but may I ask you something?
7. Where are you thinking _____ your vacation this year?
8. The guards weren't able to prevent the prisoner _____ .
9. I wanted to cook the meal by myself, but Dave insisted _____ me.
10. I'm sorry we've had to cancel our tennis game tomorrow. I was really looking forward
    _____ .

59.3 Complete the sentences on the right.

1. YOU / KEVIN — It was nice of you to help me. Thanks very much.

   Kevin thanked *me for helping him* _____ .

2. ANN / TOM — I'll take you to the station. I insist.

   Tom insisted _____ _____ .

3. YOU / JIM — I hear you got married. Congratulations!

   Jim congratulated me _____ _____ .

4. SUE / MRS. BOND — It was nice of you to come to see me. Thank you.

   Mrs. Bond thanked _____ _____ .

5. YOU / AMY — I'm sorry I didn't phone you earlier.

   Amy apologized _____ _____ .

6. YOU / TRACY — You're selfish.

   Tracy accused _____ _____ .

Expressions + -ing

When these expressions are followed by a verb, the verb ends in **-ing**:

There's no point in . . . :
- **There's no point in having** a car if you never use it.
- **There was no point in waiting** any longer, so we left.

There's no use / It's no use . . . :
- There's nothing you can do about the situation, so **there's no use worrying** about it.
- *or* . . . **it's no use worrying** about it.

It's no good . . . :
- **It's no good trying** to persuade me. You won't succeed.

It's (not) worth . . . :
- I live only a short walk from here, so **it's not worth taking** a taxi.
- It was so late when we got home, **it wasn't worth going** to bed.

You can say "a movie is **worth seeing**," "a book is **worth reading**," etc.
- What was the movie like? Was it **worth seeing?**
- I don't think newspapers are **worth reading**.

Have trouble/difficulty -ing

We say "**have trouble/difficulty doing** something" (*not* to do):
- Did you **have** any **trouble getting** a visa?
- People often **have** great **trouble reading** my writing.
- I **had difficulty finding** a place to live. (*not* I had difficulty to find)

We use **-ing** after:

a waste of money / a waste of time (to . . . is also possible):
- That book was trash. It was a **waste of time reading** it. (*or* . . . **to read** it)
- It's a **waste of money buying** things you don't need. (*or* . . . **to buy** things you don't need)

spend/waste (time)
- He **spent hours trying** to repair the clock.
- I **waste** a lot of **time daydreaming**.

(be) busy
- She said she couldn't see me. She **was** too **busy doing** other things.

Go swimming / go fishing, etc.

We use **go -ing** for a number of activities (especially sports). For example, you can say:
go swimming / go sailing / go fishing / go hiking / go skiing / go jogging, etc.
We also say: **go shopping / go sightseeing**.
- I'd like to **go skiing**.
- When was the last time you **went shopping?**
- I've never **gone sailing**.

Exercises

60.1 Complete the sentences on the right.

1. Should we take a taxi home?
2. If you need help, why don't you ask Tom?
3. I don't really want to go out tonight.
4. Should I call Ann now?
5. Are you going to complain about what happened?
6. Do you ever read newspapers?

No, it isn't far. It's not worth _taking a taxi_ .
There's _____ .
He won't be able to help us.
Well, stay at home! There's no point
_____ if you don't want to.
No, don't waste your time _____ .
She won't be at home.
No, it's not worth _____ .
Nobody will do anything about it.
No. I think it's a waste _____ .

60.2 Make sentences with *worth -ing* or *not worth -ing*. Choose one of these verbs:

consider   keep   read   fix   ~~see~~   visit

1. The movie isn't very good. _It's not worth seeing._
2. It would cost too much to fix this watch. It's not worth _____ .
3. If you have time, you should go to the museum. It's worth _____ .
4. That's quite an interesting suggestion. _____ .
5. There's an interesting article in the paper today. _____ .
6. We can throw these old clothes away. They _____ .

60.3 Write sentences using *trouble* or *difficulty*.

1. I managed to get a visa, but it was difficult. _I had difficulty getting a visa._
2. I can't remember people's names. I have _____ .
3. Sarah managed to get a job without trouble.
   She had no _____ .
4. Do you think it's difficult to understand him?
   Do you have _____ ?
5. It won't be difficult to get a ticket for the concert.
   You won't have any _____ .

60.4 Complete the sentences. Use only one word each time.

1. It's a waste of money _buying_ things you don't need.
2. Every morning I spend about an hour _____ the newspaper.
3. There's no point in _____ for the job. I know I wouldn't get it.
4. "What's Karen doing?" "She's busy _____ letters."
5. I think you waste too much time _____ television.
6. Just stay calm. There's no point in _____ angry.
7. There's a beautiful view from that hill. It is worth _____ to the top.

60.5 Complete these sentences with one of the following (with the verb in the correct form):

go skiing   go shopping   go swimming   ~~go sailing~~   go riding

1. Robert lives by the ocean and he's got a boat, so he often _goes sailing_ .
2. There's plenty of snow in the mountains, so we'll be able to _____ .
3. It was a very hot day, so we _____ in the river.
4. Michelle has two horses. She often _____ .
5. The stores are closed now. It's too late to _____ .

To . . . , for . . . , and *so that* . . . (Purpose)

We use **to** . . . to say why somebody does something (= the purpose of an action):
- ■ "Why did you go out?" "**To mail** a letter."
- ■ A friend of mine called **to invite** me to a party.
- ■ We shouted **to warn** everybody of the danger.

We use **to** . . . to say why something exists or why somebody has/wants/needs something:
- ■ This fence is **to keep** people out of the yard.
- ■ The president has a team of bodyguards **to protect** him.
- ■ I need a bottle opener **to open** this bottle.

We use **to** . . . to say what can be done or must be done with something:
- ■ It's hard to find a place **to park** downtown. (= a place where you can park)
- ■ Would you like something **to eat?**
- ■ Do you have much work **to do?** (= work that you must do)
- ■ I get lonely if there's nobody **to talk to.**

We also use **money/time/chance/opportunity/energy/courage**, etc., **to do** (something):
- ■ They gave us some **money to buy** some food.
- ■ Do you have much **opportunity to practice** your English?
- ■ I need **a few days to think** about your proposal.

For . . . and **to** . . .

We use **for** + *noun*:
- ■ I'm going to Spain **for a vacation.**

- ■ What would you like **for dinner?**
- ■ Let's go to the cafe **for coffee.**

We use **to** + *verb*:
- ■ I'm going to Spain **to learn** Spanish. (*not* for learn, *not* for learning)
- ■ What would you like **to eat?** (*not* for eat)
- ■ Let's go to the cafe **to have** coffee.

Note that you can say "**for** somebody **to do** something":
- ■ There weren't any chairs **for us to sit on,** so we had to sit on the floor.

You can use **for -ing** to say what the general purpose of a thing is. **To** . . . is also possible:
- ■ This knife is only **for cutting** bread. (*or* **to cut** bread)

You can use **What** . . . **for?** to ask about purpose:
- ■ **What** is this switch **for?**
- ■ **What** did you do that **for?**

So that

Sometimes you have to use **so that** for purpose. We use **so that** (*not* to . . .):

1) when the purpose is negative (**so that** . . . **won't/wouldn't**):
   - ■ I hurried **so that** I **wouldn't** be late. (= because I didn't want to be late)
   - ■ Leave early **so that** you **won't** (*or* **don't**) miss the bus.

2) with **can** and **could** (**so that** . . . **can/could**):
   - ■ She's learning English **so that** she **can** study in Canada.
   - ■ We moved to the city **so that** we **could** visit our friends more often.

3) when one person does something **so that** another person does something else:
   - ■ **I** gave her my address **so that she** could contact me.
   - ■ **He** wore glasses and a fake beard **so that nobody** would recognize him.

Exercises

61.1 Use a sentence from Box A and a sentence from Box B to make a new sentence.

A
1. ~~I shouted.~~
2. I had to go to the bank.
3. I'm saving money.
4. I went into the hospital.
5. I'm wearing two sweaters.
6. I called the police.

B
I want to keep warm.
I wanted to report that my car had been stolen.
I want to go to Canada.
I had to have an operation.
I needed to get some money.
~~I wanted to warn people of the danger.~~

1. *I shouted to warn people of the danger.*
2. I had to go to the bank _____ .
3. I _____ .
4. _____
5. _____
6. _____

61.2 Complete these sentences using an appropriate verb.

1. The president has a team of bodyguards *to protect* _____ him.
2. I didn't have enough time _____ the newspaper today.
3. I came home by taxi. I didn't have the energy _____ .
4. "Would you like something _____ ?" "Yes, please. A cup of coffee."
5. We need a bag _____ these things in.
6. There will be a meeting next week _____ the problem.
7. I wish we had enough money _____ a new car.
8. I saw Kelly at the party, but we didn't have a chance _____ to each other.
9. I need some new clothes. I don't have anything nice _____ .
10. I can't do all this work alone. I need somebody _____ me.

61.3 Put in *to* or *for*.

1. I'm going to Mexico *for* _____ a vacation.
2. You need a lot of experience _____ this job.
3. You need a lot of experience _____ do this job.
4. We'll need more time _____ make a decision.
5. I went to the dentist _____ a checkup.
6. I had to put on my glasses _____ read the letter.
7. Do you wear glasses _____ reading?
8. I wish we had a yard _____ the children _____ play in.

61.4 Write sentences with *so that*.

1. I hurried. I didn't want to be late. *I hurried so that I wouldn't be late.*
2. We wore warm clothes. We didn't want to get cold.
   We wore _____ .
3. The man spoke very slowly. He wanted me to understand what he said.
   The man _____ .
4. Please arrive early. We want to be able to start the meeting on time.
   Please _____ .
5. She locked the door. She didn't want to be disturbed.
   _____
6. I slowed down. I wanted the car behind me to be able to pass.
   _____

Adjective + *to* . . .

A

Hard to understand, etc.

Compare sentences (a) and (b):

- Jim doesn't speak very clearly.

> (a) It is **hard to understand** him .
>
> (b) He is **hard to understand.**

Sentences (a) and (b) have the same meaning. But note that we say:

- He is **hard to understand.** (*not* He is hard to understand him)

You can use the structures in the box with:

difficult   easy   hard   impossible   dangerous   safe   expensive   cheap   nice   interesting
and a number of other *adjectives:*

- Do you think it is **safe to drink this water?**
  Do you think this water is **safe to drink?** (*not* to drink it)
- Your handwriting is awful. It is **impossible to read it.** (= to read your writing)
  Your handwriting is **impossible to read.** (*not* to read it)
- I like spending time with Jill. It's very **interesting to talk to her.**
  Jill is very **interesting to talk to.** (*not* to talk to her)

You can also use this structure with an *adjective + noun:*

- This is a **difficult question** (for me) **to answer.** (*not* to answer it)

B

It's nice of you to . . .

You can use this structure to say what you think of what somebody does:

- It was **nice of you to take** me to the airport. Thank you very much.

You can use many other adjectives in this way. For example:

careless   clever   considerate   foolish   generous   kind   mean   silly   stupid   unfair

- It's **foolish of Mary to quit** her job when she needs the money.
- I think it was very **unfair of him to criticize** me.

C

I'm sorry to . . .

You can use this structure to say how somebody reacts to something:

- I was **sorry to hear** that your father is sick.

You can use many other adjectives in this way. For example:

happy   glad   pleased   delighted   sad   disappointed
surprised   amazed   astonished   relieved

- Was Tom **surprised to see** you when you went to see him?
- We were **glad to get** your letter last week.

D

The **first** (person) **to know,** the **next** train **to arrive**

We use **to . . .** after the **first/second/third,** etc., and also after **the next, the last, the only:**

- If I have any more news, you will be **the first** (person) **to know.**
- **The next** plane **to arrive** at gate 4 will be Flight 268 from Bogotá.
- Everybody was late except me. I was **the only** one **to arrive** on time.

Exercises

62.1 Write these sentences in another way (see Section A).

1. It's hard to understand him. _He is hard to understand._
2. It's easy to use this machine. This machine is _____ .
3. It was very difficult to open the window. The window _____ .
4. It's impossible to translate some words. Some words _____ .
5. It's not safe to stand on that chair. That chair _____ .
6. It's expensive to maintain a car. A _____ .

62.2 Complete the second sentence using the adjective in parentheses. Use *a/an* + adjective
+ noun + *to . . .* , as in the example (see Section A).

1. I couldn't answer the question. (difficult) It was _a difficult question to answer_ .
2. Everybody makes that mistake. (easy) It's an _____ .
3. I like living in this place. (nice) It's a _____ .
4. We enjoyed watching the game. (good) It was _____ .

62.3 Make a new sentence beginning *It . . .* (see Section B). Use one of these adjectives each
time:

careless   considerate   ~~kind~~   nice

1. Sue offered to help me.
   It was kind of Sue to offer to help me.
2. You make the same mistake again and again.
   It _____ .
3. Don and Jenny invited me to stay with them.

   _____
4. John made a lot of noise when I was trying to sleep.
   It wasn't very _____ .

62.4 Use the following words to complete these sentences (see Section C):

glad/hear   ~~pleased/get~~   sorry/hear   surprised/see

1. We _were pleased to get_ your letter last week.
2. Thank you for your letter. I _____ that you're doing well.
3. We _____ Jennifer at the party. We didn't expect her to come.
4. I _____ that your mother is sick. I hope she gets well soon.

62.5 Complete the second sentence using the words in parentheses + *to . . .* (see Section D).

1. Nobody left before me. (the first)
   I was _the first person to leave_ .
2. Everybody else arrived before Paul. (the last)
   Paul was the _____ .
3. Jenny passed the exam. All the other students failed. (the only)
   Jenny was _____ .
4. I complained to the restaurant manager about the service. Another customer had
   already complained before me. (the second)
   I was _____ .
5. Neil Armstrong walked on the moon in 1969. Nobody had done this before him. (the first)
   Neil Armstrong was _____ .

To . . . (afraid to do) and
Preposition + *-ing (afraid of -ing)*

A
Afraid to do and **afraid of doing**

I am **afraid to do** something = I don't want to do it because it is dangerous or the result could be bad. We use **afraid to do** for things we do intentionally:

- A lot of people are **afraid to go** out at night. (= they don't want to go out because it is dangerous – so they don't go out)
- He was **afraid to tell** his parents about the broken window. (= he didn't want to tell them because he knew they would be angry)

I am **afraid of something happening** = it is possible that something bad will happen (for example, an accident). We do not use **afraid of -ing** for things we do intentionally:

- The sidewalk was icy, so we walked very carefully. We were **afraid of falling.** (= it was possible that we would fall)
- I don't like dogs. I'm always **afraid of being** bitten. (*not* afraid to be bitten)

So, you are **afraid to do** something because you are **afraid of something happening** as a result:

- I was **afraid to go** near the dog because I **was afraid of being** bitten.

B
Interested in doing and **interested to do**

I'm **interested in doing** something = I'm thinking of doing it, and I'd like to do it:

- I'm trying to sell my car, but nobody is **interested in buying** it. (*not* to buy)

We use **interested to** especially with **hear/see/know/read/learn**. I was **interested to hear** it = I heard it and it was interesting for me:

- I was **interested to hear** that Diane got a new job.
- Ask George for his opinion. I would be **interested to know** what he thinks.

This structure is the same as **surprised to / delighted to,** etc. (see Unit 62C):

- I was **surprised to hear** that Diane got a new job.

C
Sorry to do and **sorry for doing**

We usually say **sorry to . . .** to apologize when (or just before) we do something:

- I'm **sorry to bother** you, but I need to talk to you.

We use **sorry to hear/read,** etc., to show sympathy with somebody (see Unit 62C):

- I was **sorry to hear** that Jessica lost her job. (= I was sorry when I heard)

You can use **sorry for** (doing something) to apologize for something you did before:

- I'm **sorry for shouting** at you yesterday. (*not* sorry to shout)

You can also say:

- I'm **sorry I shouted** at you yesterday.

D
Note that we say:

I **want to** (do) / I'd **like to** (do)	*but*	I'm **thinking of** (doing) / I **dream of** (doing)
I **failed to** (do)	*but*	I **succeeded in** (doing)
I **allowed** them **to** (do)	*but*	I **stopped/prevented** them **from** (doing)

For examples, see Units 51–52 and 59.

Verb + Preposition + *-ing* Unit 59   **Adjective + Preposition** Units 126–127   *Sorry about/for* Unit 126D

Exercises

63.1 Read the situation and use the words in parentheses to make sentences.
Use *afraid to . . .* or *afraid of -ing.*

1. The streets aren't safe at night.
   (a lot of people / afraid / go / out) _A lot of people are afraid to go out._
2. I don't usually carry my passport with me.
   (I / afraid / lose / it) _____
3. The ocean was very rough.
   (we / afraid / go / swimming) _____
4. We rushed to the station.
   (we / afraid / miss / our train) _____
5. In the middle of the movie there was a particularly scary scene.
   (we / afraid / look) _____
6. The glasses were very full, so Rosa carried them very carefully.
   (she / afraid / spill / the drinks) _____
7. I didn't like the look of the food on my plate.
   a) (I / afraid / eat / it) _____
   b) (I / afraid / get / sick) _____

63.2 Complete the sentences using one of these verbs:

~~buy~~   get   go   hear   read   start

1. I'm trying to sell my car, but nobody is interested _in buying_____ it.
2. Julia is interested _____ her own business.
3. I was interested _____ your letter in the newspaper last week.
4. Bill wants to stay single. He's not interested _____ married.
5. Please tell me what you think. I'm always interested _____ your
   opinion.
6. There's a party tonight, but I'm not interested _____ .

63.3 Complete the sentences using the verb in parentheses.

1. I'm sorry _for shouting_____ at you yesterday. (shout)
2. Sorry _____ you, but do you have a pen I could borrow? (bother)
3. Sorry _____ late last night. I didn't realize what time it was. (be)
4. I'm sorry _____ what I said yesterday. I didn't really mean it. (say)
5. "I just got my exam results. I failed." "Oh? I'm sorry _____ that." (hear)

63.4 Complete the sentences using the verb in parentheses.

1. a) We wanted _to leave_____ the building. (leave)
   b) We weren't allowed _____ the building. (leave)
   c) We were prevented _____ the building. (leave)
2. a) Eric failed _____ the problem. (solve)
   b) Amy succeeded _____ the problem. (solve)
3. a) I'm thinking _____ away next week. (go)
   b) I'm hoping _____ away next week. (go)
   c) I'm looking forward _____ away next week. (go)
   d) I'd like _____ away next week. (go)
4. a) Lisa wanted _____ me lunch. (buy)
   b) Lisa promised _____ me lunch. (buy)
   c) Lisa insisted _____ me lunch. (buy)
   d) Lisa wouldn't dream _____ me lunch. (buy)

See somebody do and see somebody doing

A

Study this example situation:

Tom got into his car and drove away. You saw this.
You can say:

■ I saw Tom **get** into his car and **drive** away.

In this structure we use **get/drive/do,** etc. *(base form)*:

| Somebody **did** something | + | I saw this |

  I saw somebody **do** something.

Note that we do not use "to":

■ We saw them **go** out. *(not* to go*)*

YOU

B

Study this example situation:

Yesterday you saw Ann. She was waiting for a bus.
You can say:

■ I saw Ann **waiting** for a bus.

In this structure we use **-ing** (**waiting**):

| Somebody **was doing** something | + | I saw this |

  I saw somebody **doing** something.

C

Study the difference in meaning between the two structures:

1) I saw him **do** something = he **did** something *(simple past)*, and I saw this. I saw the complete action from beginning to end:

■ He **fell** off the wall. I saw this. → I saw him **fall** off the wall.
■ The accident **happened**. Did you see this? → Did you see the accident **happen**?

2) I saw him **doing** something = he **was doing** something *(past continuous)*, and I saw this. I saw him when he was in the middle of doing it. This does not mean I saw the complete action:

■ He **was walking** along the street.
I saw this when I drove past in my car. } → I saw him **walking** along the street.

Sometimes the difference is not important and you can use either form:

■ I've never seen her **dance**. *or* I've never seen her **dancing**.

D

We use these structures with **see** and **hear** and with a number of other verbs:

■ I didn't **hear** you **come** in. (= you **came** in but I didn't hear this)
■ Liz suddenly **felt** something **touch** her on the shoulder.
■ Did you **notice** anyone **go** out?

■ I could **hear** it **raining**. (= it **was raining** and I could hear it)
■ The missing boys were last **seen playing** near the river.
■ **Listen to** the birds **singing**!
■ Can you **smell** something **burning**?
■ I **found** Sue in my room **reading** my letters.

Exercises

64.1 Complete the answers to the questions.

1. Did anybody go out?	I don't think so. I didn't see _anybody go out_ .
2. Has Jill arrived yet?	Yes, I think I heard her _____ .
3. How do you know I took the money?	I know because I saw you _____ .
4. Did the doorbell ring?	I'm not sure. I didn't hear _____ .
5. Did I lock the door when I went out?	Yes, you did. I saw _____ .
6. How did the woman fall?	I don't know. I didn't see _____ .

64.2 In each of these situations you and a friend saw, heard, or smelled something. Look at the pictures and complete the sentences.

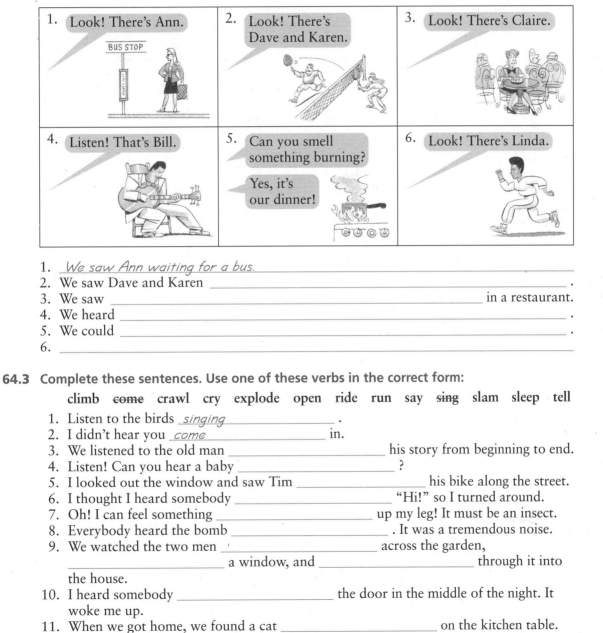

1. _We saw Ann waiting for a bus._
2. We saw Dave and Karen _____ .
3. We saw _____ in a restaurant.
4. We heard _____ .
5. We could _____ .
6. _____

64.3 Complete these sentences. Use one of these verbs in the correct form:

climb ~~come~~ crawl cry explode open ride run say ~~sing~~ slam sleep tell

1. Listen to the birds _singing_ .
2. I didn't hear you _come_ in.
3. We listened to the old man _____ his story from beginning to end.
4. Listen! Can you hear a baby _____ ?
5. I looked out the window and saw Tim _____ his bike along the street.
6. I thought I heard somebody _____ "Hi!" so I turned around.
7. Oh! I can feel something _____ up my leg! It must be an insect.
8. Everybody heard the bomb _____ . It was a tremendous noise.
9. We watched the two men _____ across the garden, _____ a window, and _____ through it into the house.
10. I heard somebody _____ the door in the middle of the night. It woke me up.
11. When we got home, we found a cat _____ on the kitchen table.

-ing Phrases (Feeling tired, I went to bed early.)

Study these situations:

Jim was playing tennis. He hurt his arm.
You can say:
- Jim hurt his arm **playing tennis.**

You were feeling tired. So you went to bed early.
You can say:
- **Feeling tired,** I went to bed early.

Playing tennis and **feeling tired** are **-ing** phrases.
If the **-ing** phrase is first (as in the second example), we write a comma (,) after it.

When two things happen at the same time, you can use **-ing** for one of the verbs:
- Carol is in the kitchen **making coffee.** (= she is in the kitchen and she is making coffee)
- A man ran out of the house **shouting.** (= he ran out of the house and he was shouting)
- Do something! Don't just stand there **doing nothing!**

We also use **-ing** when one action happens during another action. We use **-ing** for the longer action. The longer action is the second part of the sentence:
- Jim hurt his arm **playing tennis.** (= while he was playing)
- Did you cut yourself **shaving?** (= while you were shaving)

You can also use **-ing** after **while** or **when:**
- Jim hurt his arm **while playing** tennis.
- Be careful **when crossing** the road. (= when you are crossing)

When one action happens before another action, we use **having done** for the first action:
- **Having found** a hotel, we looked for someplace to have dinner.
- **Having finished** her work, she went home.

You can also say **after -ing:**
- **After finishing** her work, she went home.

If one short action follows another short action, you can use the simple **-ing** form (**doing** instead of **having done**) for the first action:
- **Taking** a key out of his pocket, he opened the door.

These structures are used more in written English than in spoken English.

You can use an **-ing** phrase to explain something or to say why somebody does something. The **-ing** phrase usually comes first:
- **Feeling tired,** I went to bed early. (= because I felt tired)
- **Being unemployed,** he doesn't have much money. (= because he is unemployed)
- **Not having a car,** she finds it difficult to get around. (= because she doesn't have a car)
- **Having** already **seen the movie** twice, I didn't want to go to the movies. (= because I had already seen it twice)

These structures are used more in written English than in spoken English.

Exercises

65.1 Join a sentence from Box A with one from Box B to make one sentence. Use an *-ing* phrase.

A
1. ~~Carol was in the kitchen.~~
2. Amy was sitting in an armchair.
3. Sarah went out.
4. Linda was in London for two years.
5. Mary walked around the town.

B
She looked at the sights and took photographs.
She said she would be back in an hour.
She was reading a book.
~~She was making coffee.~~
She worked as a teacher.

1. *Carol was in the kitchen making coffee.*
2. Amy was sitting _____ .
3. Sarah _____ .
4. _____
5. _____

65.2 Make one sentence from two using an *-ing* phrase.
1. Jim was playing tennis. He hurt his arm. *Jim hurt his arm playing tennis.*
2. I was watching TV. I fell asleep. I _____ .
3. The man slipped. He was getting off a bus. The man _____ .
4. Margaret was driving to work yesterday. She had an accident.
   _____
5. Two kids got lost. They were hiking in the woods.
   _____

65.3 Make sentences that begin with *Having*.
1. She finished her work. Then she went home.
   Having finished her work, she went home.
2. We bought our tickets. Then we went into the theater.
   _____
3. They continued their trip after they'd had dinner.
   _____
4. After Lucy had done all her shopping, she stopped for a cup of coffee.
   _____

65.4 Make sentences beginning with *-ing* or *Not -ing* (like those in Section D). Sometimes you need to begin with *Having (done something)*.
1. I felt tired. So I went to bed early.
   Feeling tired, I went to bed early.
2. I thought they might be hungry. So I offered them something to eat.
   _____
3. She is a foreigner. So she needs a visa to stay in this country.
   _____
4. I didn't know his address. So I wasn't able to contact him.
   _____
5. Sarah has traveled a lot. So she knows a lot about other countries.
   _____
6. The man wasn't able to understand English. So he didn't know what I wanted.
   _____
7. We had spent nearly all our money. So we couldn't afford to stay in a hotel.
   _____

Countable and Uncountable Nouns (1)

A

A noun can be *countable* or *uncountable*. Compare:

Countable

- I eat **a banana** every day.
- I like **bananas**.

Banana is a countable noun.

A countable noun can be *singular* (**banana**) or *plural* (**bananas**).
Countable nouns are things we can count. So we can say "one banana," "two bananas," etc.

Examples of nouns that are usually countable:

- There's **a beach** near here.
- Ann was singing **a song**.
- Do you have **a ten-dollar bill?**
- It wasn't your fault. It was **an accident**.
- There are no **batteries** in the radio.
- We don't have enough **cups**.

Uncountable

- I eat **rice** every day.
- I like **rice**.

Rice is an uncountable noun.

An uncountable noun has only one form (**rice**).
Uncountable nouns are things we cannot count. We cannot say "one rice," "two rices," etc.

Examples of nouns that are usually uncountable:

- There's **sand** in my shoes.
- Ann was listening to (some) **music**.
- Do you have any **money?**
- It wasn't your fault. It was bad **luck**.
- There is no **electricity** in this house.
- We don't have enough **water**.

B

You can use **a/an** with singular countable nouns:

a beach   a student   an umbrella

You cannot use singular countable nouns alone (without **a/the/my**, etc.):

- I want **a banana**. (*not* I want banana)
- There's been **an accident**. (*not* There's been accident)

You can use plural countable nouns alone:

- I like **bananas**. (= bananas in general)
- **Accidents** can be prevented.

See also Unit 72.

You cannot normally use **a/an** with uncountable nouns. We do not say "a sand" or "a music." But you can often use **a . . . of:**
a bowl of rice   **a drop of** water
a piece of music   **a game of** tennis, etc.

You can use uncountable nouns alone (without **the/my/some**, etc.):

- I eat **rice** every day.
- There's **blood** on your shirt.
- Can you hear **music?**

See also Unit 72.

C

You can use **some** and **any** with plural countable nouns:

- We sang **some songs**.
- Did you buy **any apples?**

We use **many** and **few** with plural countable nouns:

- We didn't take **many photographs**.
- I have **a few jobs** to do.

You can use **some** and **any** with uncountable nouns:

- We listened to **some music**.
- Did you buy **any apple juice?**

We use **much** and **little** with uncountable nouns:

- We didn't do **much shopping**.
- I have **a little work** to do.

Exercises

66.1 Some of these sentences need *a/an*. Correct the sentences that are wrong.

1. Jim goes everywhere by bike. He doesn't have car. *a car*
2. Ann was listening to music when I arrived. *RIGHT*
3. We went to very nice restaurant last weekend. _____
4. I brush my teeth with toothpaste. _____
5. I use toothbrush to brush my teeth. _____
6. Can you tell me if there's bank near here? _____
7. My brother works for insurance company in Detroit. _____
8. I don't like violence. _____
9. Do you smell paint? _____
10. We need gas. I hope we come to gas station soon. _____
11. I wonder if you can help me. I have problem. _____
12. John has interview for job tomorrow. _____
13. Liz doesn't usually wear jewelry, but yesterday she was wearing necklace. _____

66.2 Complete the sentences using one of the following words. Use *a/an* where necessary.

~~accident~~   blood   coat   cookie   decision   electricity   key   letter   moment
~~music~~   question   sugar

1. It wasn't your fault. It was *an accident* .
2. Listen! Can you hear *music* ?
3. I couldn't get into the house because I didn't have _____ .
4. It's very warm today. Why are you wearing _____ ?
5. Do you take _____ in your coffee?
6. Are you hungry? Would you like _____ with your coffee?
7. Our lives would be very difficult without _____ .
8. I didn't call them. I wrote _____ instead.
9. The heart pumps _____ throughout the body.
10. Excuse me, but can I ask you _____ ?
11. I'm not ready yet. Can you wait _____ , please?
12. We can't delay much longer. We have to make _____ soon.

66.3 Complete the sentences using one of the following words. Sometimes the word needs to be plural (*-s*). Use *a/an* if necessary.

country   day   friend   language   letter   line   meat   patience   people
~~picture~~   space   umbrella

1. I had my camera, but I didn't take many *pictures* .
2. There are seven _____ in a week.
3. A vegetarian is a person who doesn't eat _____ .
4. Outside the movie theater there was _____ of people waiting to see the movie.
5. I'm not very good at writing _____ .
6. Last night I went out with some _____ of mine.
7. There were very few _____ in the stores today. They were almost empty.
8. I think it's going to rain. Do you have _____ I can borrow?
9. George always wants things quickly. He has no _____ .
10. Do you speak any foreign _____ ?
11. Jane travels a lot. She has been to many _____ .
12. Our apartment is very small. We don't have much _____ .

Countable and Uncountable Nouns (2)

A

Many nouns can be used as *countable* or *uncountable* nouns, usually with a difference in meaning. Compare:

Countable	*Uncountable*
■ Did you hear **a noise** just now? (= a particular noise)	■ I can't work here. There's too much **noise.** (*not* too many noises)
■ I bought **a paper** to read. (= a newspaper)	■ I need some **paper** to write on. (= material for writing on)
■ There's **a hair** in my soup! (= one single hair)	■ You've got very long **hair.** (*not* hairs) (= all the hair on your head)
■ You can stay with us. We have **a** spare **room.** (= a room in a house)	■ You can't sit here. There isn't any **room.** (= space)
■ I had some interesting **experiences** while I was away. (= things that happened to me)	■ They offered me the job because I had a lot of **experience.** (*not* experiences)
■ Enjoy your vacation. Have **a** good **time!**	■ I can't wait. I don't have **time.**
■ I'd like **a coffee**, please. (= a cup of coffee)	■ I like **coffee.** (= in general)

B

There are some nouns that are usually uncountable in English but often countable in other languages. For example:

advice	bread	furniture	luggage	progress	weather
baggage	chaos	information	news	scenery	work
behavior	damage	luck	permission	traffic	

These nouns are usually uncountable, so:
1) you cannot use **a/an** with them (you cannot say "a bread," "an advice," etc.) and
2) they are not usually plural (we do not say "breads," "advices," etc.):
   - I'm going to buy **some bread.** *or* . . . **a loaf of bread.** (*not* a bread)
   - Enjoy your vacation! I hope you have good **weather.** (*not* a good weather)
   - Where are you going to put all your **furniture?** (*not* furnitures)

News is uncountable, not plural:
   - The **news was** very depressing. (*not* The news were)

Travel *(noun)* means *traveling in general.* You cannot say "a travel" to mean *a trip:*
   - We had **a** very good **trip.** (*not* a good travel)

Compare these countable and uncountable nouns:

Countable	*Uncountable*
■ I'm looking for **a job.**	■ I'm looking for **work.** (*not* a work)
■ What **a** beautiful **view!**	■ What beautiful **scenery!**
■ It's **a** nice **day** today.	■ It's nice **weather** today.
■ We had a lot of **bags** and **suitcases.**	■ We had a lot of **luggage.** (*not* luggages)
■ These **chairs** are mine.	■ This **furniture** is mine.
■ It was **a** good **suggestion.**	■ It was good **advice.**

Exercises

67.1 **Which of the underlined parts of these sentences is correct?**

1. "Did you hear ~~noise~~ / a noise just now?" "No, I didn't hear anything." (*a noise* is correct)
2. a) If you want to know the news, you can read paper / a paper.
   b) I want to write some letters, but I don't have a paper / any paper to write on.
3. a) I thought there was somebody in the house because there was light / a light on inside.
   b) Light / A light comes from the sun.
4. a) I was in a hurry this morning. I didn't have time / a time for breakfast.
   b) "Did you have a good vacation?" "Yes, we had wonderful time / a wonderful time."
5. Sue was very helpful. She gave us some very useful advice / advices.
6. We had very good weather / a very good weather while we were in Toronto.
7. We were very unfortunate. We had bad luck / a bad luck.
8. It's very difficult to find a work / job at the moment.
9. Our travel / trip from London to Istanbul by train was very tiring.
10. When the fire alarm rang, there was total chaos / a total chaos.
11. I had to buy a / some bread because I wanted to make some sandwiches.
12. Bad news don't / doesn't make people happy.
13. Your hair is / Your hairs are too long. You should have it / them cut.
14. The damage / The damages caused by the storm will cost a lot to repair.

67.2 **Complete the sentences using these words. Sometimes you need the plural (-s).**

chair experience experience furniture hair information job ~~luggage~~
permission progress work

1. I didn't have much *luggage* – just two small bags.
2. They'll tell you all you want to know. They'll give you plenty of
   _____ .
3. There is room for everybody to sit down. There are plenty of _____ .
4. We have no _____ – not even a bed or a table.
5. "What does Alan look like?" "He's got a long beard and very short
   _____ ."
6. Carla's English is better than it was. She's made _____ .
7. George is unemployed. He's looking for a _____ .
8. George is unemployed. He's looking for _____ .
9. If you want to leave work early, you have to ask for _____ .
10. I don't think Ann will get the job. She doesn't have enough _____ .
11. Rita has done many interesting things. She should write a book about her
    _____ .

67.3 **What do you say in these situations? Complete the sentences using words from Section B.**

1. Your friends have just arrived at the station. You can't see any suitcases or bags.
   You ask them: Do *you have any luggage* ?
2. You go into the tourist office. You want to know about places to see in the city.
   You say: I'd like _____ .
3. You are a student at school. You want your teacher to advise you about which courses
   to take. You say: Can you give me _____ ?
4. You want to watch the news on TV, but you don't know what time it is on.
   You ask your friend: What time _____ ?
5. You are standing on the top of a mountain. You can see a very long way. It's beautiful.
   You say: It _____ , isn't it?
6. You look out of the window. The weather is horrible: cold, wet, and windy.
   You say to your friend: What _____ !

Countable Nouns With *a/an* and *some*

A

Countable nouns can be *singular* or *plural*:

a dog	a child	the evening	this party	an umbrella
dogs	some children	the evenings	these parties	two umbrellas

B

Before singular countable nouns you can use **a/an**:
- Good-bye! Have **a** nice **evening.**
- Do you need **an umbrella?**

You cannot use singular countable nouns alone (without **a/the/my**, etc.):
- She never wears **a hat.** (*not* She never wears hat)
- Be careful of **the dog.** (*not* Be careful of dog)
- I've got **a headache.**

C

We use **a/an** . . . to say what kind of thing or person something/somebody is:
- A dog is **an animal.**
- I'm **an optimist.**
- Tim's father is **a doctor.**
- Are you **a good driver?**
- Jill is **a really nice person.**
- What **a pretty dress!**

We say that somebody has **a** long **nose** / **a** nice **face** / **a** strong **heart**, etc.:
- Jack has **a** long **nose.** (*not* the long nose)

In sentences like these, we use plural nouns alone (*not* with **some**):
- Dogs are **animals.**
- Most of my friends are **students.**
- Jill's parents are really nice **people.**
- What awful **shoes!**
- Jack has blue **eyes.** (*not* the blue eyes)

Remember to use **a/an** when you say what somebody's job is:
- Sandra is **a nurse.** (*not* Sandra is nurse)
- Would you like to be **an English teacher?**

D

You can use **some** with plural countable nouns. We use **some** in two ways:

1) **Some** = a number of / a few of / a pair of:
- I've seen **some** good **movies** recently. (*not* I've seen good movies recently)
- **Some friends** of mine are coming to stay this weekend.
- I need **some** new **sunglasses.** (= a new pair of sunglasses)

Do not use **some** when you are talking about things in general (see also Unit 72):
- I love **bananas.** (*not* some bananas)
- My aunt is a writer. She writes **books.** (*not* some books)

Sometimes you can make sentences with or without **some** (with no difference in meaning):
- There are (**some**) eggs in the refrigerator if you're hungry.

2) **Some** = some, but not all:
- **Some children** learn very quickly. (but not all children)
- **Some police officers** in Britain carry guns, but most of them don't.

Exercises

68.1 **What are these things? Try and find out if you don't know.**

1. an ant? _It's an insect._
2. ants and bees? _They're insects._
3. a cauliflower? _____
4. chess? _____
5. a violin, a trumpet, and a flute?
   _____
6. a skyscraper? _____
7. Earth, Mars, Venus, and Jupiter?
   _____
8. a tulip? _____
9. the Rhine, the Nile, and the
   Mississippi? _____
10. a pigeon, an eagle, and a crow?
    _____

Who were these people?

11. Beethoven? _He was a composer._
12. Shakespeare? _____
13. Albert Einstein? _____
14. George Washington, Abraham Lincoln, and John Kennedy? _____
15. Marilyn Monroe? _____
16. Elvis Presley and John Lennon? _____
17. Van Gogh, Renoir, and Picasso? _____

68.2 **Read about what these people do, and then say what their jobs are. Choose one of these jobs:**

> driving instructor   interpreter   journalist   ~~nurse~~   pilot   plumber
> travel agent   waiter

1. Sarah takes care of patients in the hospital. _She's a nurse._
2. Robert works in a restaurant. He brings the food to the tables.
   He _____.
3. Mary arranges people's trips for them. She _____.
4. Ron works for an airline. He flies airplanes. _____
5. Linda teaches people how to drive. _____
6. Dave installs and repairs water pipes. _____
7. Jenny writes articles for a newspaper. _____
8. John translates what people are saying from one language into another so that they can understand each other. _____

68.3 **Put in *a/an* or *some* where necessary. If no word is necessary, leave the space empty (–).**

1. I've seen _some_ good movies recently.
2. What's wrong with you? Have you got _a_ headache?
3. I know a lot of people. Most of them are ___—___ students.
4. When I was _____ child, I used to be very shy.
5. Would you like to be _____ actor?
6. Do you collect _____ stamps?
7. What _____ beautiful garden!
8. _____ birds, for example the penguin, cannot fly.
9. I've been walking for three hours. I have _____ sore feet.
10. I don't feel very well this morning. I have _____ sore throat.
11. It's too bad we don't have _____ camera. I'd like to take _____ picture of that house.
12. Those are _____ nice shoes. Where did you get them?
13. You need _____ visa to visit _____ countries, but not all of them.
14. Jane is _____ teacher. Her parents were _____ teachers, too.
15. Do you like going to _____ concerts?
16. I don't believe him. He's _____ liar. He's always telling _____ lies.

A/an and the

Study this example:

> I had **a** sandwich and **an** apple for lunch.
>
> **The** sandwich wasn't very good, but **the** apple was delicious.

 JOHN KAREN

← John says "**a** sandwich" and "**an** apple" because this is the first time he talks about them.

← John now says "**the** sandwich" and "**the** apple" because Karen knows which sandwich and which apple he means – **the** sandwich and **the** apple he had for lunch.

Compare **a** and **the** in these examples:

- **A** man and **a** woman were sitting across from me. **The** man was American, but I think **the** woman was British.
- When we were on vacation, we stayed at **a** hotel. Sometimes we had dinner at **the** hotel, and sometimes we went to **a** restaurant.

We use **the** when we are thinking of one particular thing. Compare **a/an** and **the**:

- Tom sat down on **a** chair. (perhaps one of many chairs in the room)

but Tom sat down on **the** chair **nearest the door.** (a particular chair)

- Ann is looking for **a** job. (not a particular job)

but Did Ann get **the** job **she applied for?** (a particular job)

- Do you have **a** car? (not a particular car)

but I washed **the** car yesterday. (= my car)

See also Units 68 and 70A.

We use **the** when it is clear in the situation which thing or person we mean. For example, in a room we talk about **the light / the floor / the ceiling / the door / the carpet,** etc.:

- Can you turn off **the light,** please? (= the light in this room)
- I took a taxi to **the station.** (= the station in that town)
- I'd like to speak to **the manager,** please. (= the manager of this store, etc.)

In the same way, we say (go to) **the bank / the post office:**

- I have to go to **the bank,** and then I'm going to **the post office** to get some stamps. (The speaker is usually thinking of a particular bank or post office.)

Also: **the doctor / the dentist / the hospital:**

- Carol isn't feeling very well. She went to **the doctor.** (= her usual doctor)
- Two people were taken to **the hospital** after the accident.

Compare **a:**

- Is there **a** bank near here?
- My sister is **a** doctor.

We say "once **a** week / three times **a** day / $1.20 **a** pound," etc.:

- "How often do you go to the movies?" "About once **a** month."
- "How much are those potatoes?" "A dollar **a** pound."
- She works eight hours **a** day, six days **a** week.

Exercises

69.1 Put in *a/an* or *the*.

1. This morning I bought __*a*__ newspaper and _____ magazine. _____ newspaper is in my briefcase, but I don't know where I put _____ magazine.
2. I saw _____ accident this morning. _____ car crashed into _____ tree. _____ driver of _____ car wasn't hurt, but _____ car was badly damaged.
3. There are two cars parked outside: _____ blue one and _____ gray one. _____ blue one belongs to my neighbors; I don't know who _____ owner of _____ gray one is.
4. My friends live in _____ old house in _____ small town. There is _____ beautiful garden behind _____ house. I would like to have _____ garden like that.

69.2 Put in *a/an* or *the*.

1. a) This house is very nice. Does it have __*a*__ yard?
   b) It's a beautiful day. Let's sit in _____ yard.
   c) I like living in this house, but it's too bad that _____ yard is so small.
2. a) Can you recommend _____ good restaurant?
   b) We had dinner in _____ very nice restaurant.
   c) We had dinner in _____ most expensive restaurant in town.
3. a) She has _____ French name, but in fact she's English, not French.
   b) What's _____ name of that man we met yesterday?
   c) We stayed at a very nice hotel. I wish I could remember _____ name!
4. a) There isn't _____ airport near where I live. _____ nearest airport is 70 miles away.
   b) Our plane was delayed. We had to wait at _____ airport for three hours.
   c) Excuse me, please. Can you tell me how to get to _____ airport?
5. a) "Are you going away next week?" "No, _____ week after next."
   b) I'm going away for _____ week in September.
   c) George has a part-time job. He works three mornings _____ week.

69.3 Put in *a/an* or *the* where necessary.

1. Would you like ∧apple?   __*an apple*_____
2. How often do you go to dentist?   _____
3. Could you close door, please?   _____
4. I'm sorry. I didn't mean to do that. It was mistake.   _____
5. Excuse me, where is bus station, please?   _____
6. I have problem. Can you help me?   _____
7. I'm just going to post office. I won't be long.   _____
8. There were no chairs, so we had to sit on floor.   _____
9. Are you finished with book I lent you?   _____
10. My sister has just gotten job in bank in Atlanta.   _____
11. There's supermarket on corner near my house.   _____

69.4 Answer these questions about yourself. Where possible, use the structure in Section D (*once a week / three times a day*, etc.).

1. How often do you go to the movies? __*Three or four times a year.*_____
2. How often do you take a vacation? _____
3. What's the usual speed limit on highways in your country? _____
4. How much does it cost to rent a car in your country? _____
5. How much sleep do you need? _____
6. How often do you go out at night? _____
7. How much television do you watch (on average)? _____

The (1)

A

We use **the . . .** when there is only one of something:
- What is **the** longest river in **the** world? (There is only one longest river.)
- **The** earth goes around **the** sun, and **the** moon goes around **the** earth.
- I'm going away at **the** end of this month.

Don't forget **the:**
- Paris is **the** capital of France. (*not* Paris is capital of)

But we use **a/an** to say what kind of thing something is (see Unit 68C). Compare **the** and **a:**
- **The** sun is **a** star. (= one of many stars)
- **The** hotel we stayed at was **a** very nice hotel.

B

We say **the sky / the sea / the ocean / the ground / the country / the environment:**
- We looked up at all the stars in **the sky.** (*not* in sky)
- Would you like to live in **the country?** (= not in a city)
- We must do more to protect **the environment.** (= the natural world around us)

Note that we say **space** (without **the**) when we mean "space in the universe":
- There are millions of stars in **space.** (*not* in the space)

but ■ I tried to park my car, but **the space** was too small.

C

We use **the** before **same** (= **the same**):
- Your sweater is **the same** color as mine. (*not* is same color)
- These two pictures are **the same.** (*not* are same)

D

We say (go to) **the movies / the theater:**
- I often go to **the movies,** but I haven't been to **the theater** for ages.

We usually say **the radio,** but **television** (*without* the):
- I often listen to **the radio.**
- I often watch **television.**
- We heard the news on **the radio.**
- We watched the news on **television.**

but ■ Can you turn off **the television,** please? (= the television set)

Compare **a:**
- There isn't **a theater** in this town.
- I'm going to buy **a** new **radio / television** (= television set).

E

Breakfast   lunch   dinner
We do not normally use **the** with the names of meals (**breakfast/lunch,** etc.):
- What did you have for **breakfast?**
- We had **lunch** at a very nice restaurant.
- What time is **dinner?**

But we use **a** if there is an adjective before **breakfast/lunch,** etc.:
- We had **a** very **nice lunch.** (*not* we had very nice lunch)

F

Room 126, Gate 10, etc.
We do not use **the** before *noun* + *number*. For example, we say:
- Our plane leaves from **Gate 10.** (*not* the Gate 10)
- (*in a store*) Do you have these shoes in **size 11?** (*not* the size 11)

In the same way, we say **Room 126** (in a hotel), **page 29** (of a book), **Section A,** etc.

Exercises

70.1 Put in *the* or *a/an* where necessary. If no word is necessary, leave the space empty *(–)*.

1. *A:* Where did you have ___—___ lunch? *B:* We went to __*a*__ restaurant.
2. *A:* Where's _____ nearest drugstore? *B:* There's one on _____ next block.
3. *A:* Do you often listen to _____ radio? *B:* No. In fact, I don't have _____ radio.
4. *A:* Did you have _____ nice vacation?
   B: Yes, it was _____ best vacation I've ever had.
5. *A:* Would you like to travel in _____ outer space?
   B: Yes, I'd love to go to _____ moon.
6. *A:* Do you go to _____ movies very often?
   B: No, not very often. But I watch a lot of movies on _____ television.
7. *A:* It was _____ nice day yesterday, wasn't it?
   B: Yes, it was beautiful. We went for a walk by _____ ocean.
8. *A:* What did you have for _____ breakfast this morning?
   B: Nothing. I never eat _____ breakfast.
9. *A:* Can you tell me where _____ Room 225 is, please?
   B: It's on _____ second floor.
10. *A:* We spent all our money because we stayed at _____ most expensive hotel in town.
    B: Why didn't you stay at _____ cheaper hotel?

70.2 Put in *the* where necessary. If you don't need *the*, leave the space empty *(–)*.

1. I haven't been to __*the*__ movies for ages.
2. I lay down on _____ ground and looked up at _____ sky.
3. Sarah spends most of her free time watching _____ TV.
4. _____ TV was on, but nobody was watching it.
5. Have you had _____ dinner yet?
6. Lisa and I arrived at _____ same time.
7. You'll find _____ information you need at _____ top of _____ page 15.

70.3 Put in *the* or *a/an* where necessary. (See Unit 69 for *a/an* and *the*.)

1. Sun is star.   *The sun, a star*
2. Moon goes around earth every 27 days.   _____
3. What is highest mountain in world?   _____
4. I'm fed up with doing same thing every day. _____
5. It was very hot day. It was hottest day of year. _____
6. I don't usually have lunch, but I always eat   _____
   good breakfast.
7. If you live in foreign country, you should try _____
   and learn language.
8. Next train to San Diego leaves from Platform 8. _____

70.4 Complete the sentences using one of the following. Use *the* if necessary.

~~breakfast~~   dinner   gate   Gate 21   movies   question 8   sea

1. I didn't have time for __*breakfast*__ this morning because I was in a hurry.
2. "I'm going to _____ tonight." "Really? What are you going to see?"
3. There was no wind, so _____ was very calm.
4. "Are you going out this evening?" "Yes, after _____."
5. The test wasn't too hard, but I couldn't answer _____.
6. Oh, _____ is open. I must have forgotten to close it.
7. *(airport announcement)* Flight 123 to Tokyo is now boarding at _____.

The (2) (school / the school)

Compare **school** and **the school**:

Claudia is ten years old. Every day she goes to **school**. She's at **school** now. **School** begins at 9:00 and finishes at 3:00.

When we say a child goes to **school** or is in **school** (as a student), we are not necessarily thinking of a particular school. We are thinking of **school** as a general idea.

Today Claudia's mother wants to speak to her daughter's teacher. So she has gone to **the school** to see her. She's at **the school** now.

Claudia's mother is not a student. She is not "in school," she doesn't "go to school." But if she wants to see Claudia's teacher, she goes to **the school** (= Claudia's school, a particular school).

We use **prison/jail, college,** and **church** in a similar way. We do not use **the** when we are thinking of the general idea of these places and what they are used for. Compare:

- Ken's brother is in **prison/jail** for robbery. (He is a prisoner. We are not thinking of a particular prison.)
- When I finish **high school,** I want to go to **college.**
- Mrs. Kelly goes to **church** every Sunday. (= to a religious service)

- Ken went to **the prison / the jail** to visit his brother. (He went as a visitor, not as a prisoner.)
- Dan is a student at **the college** where I used to work. (= a particular college)
- The workers went to **the church** to repair the roof. (not for a religious service)

With most other places, you need **the.** For example, **the hospital / the bank / the station.** See Units 69C and 70D.

Bed   work   home

We say **go to bed / be in bed,** etc. (*not* the bed):
- It's time to go to **bed** now.
- This morning I had breakfast in **bed.**
but - I sat down on **the bed.** (= a particular piece of furniture)

We say **go to work / be at work / start work / finish work,** etc. (*not* the work):
- Ann didn't go to **work** yesterday.
- What time do you usually finish **work?**

We also say **go home / come home / get home / be (at) home,** etc.:
- It's late. Let's go **home.**
- Will you be (at) **home** tomorrow afternoon?

We say **go to sea / be at sea** (*without* the) when the meaning is *go/be on a voyage:*
- Keith is a sailor. He spends most of his life at **sea.**
but - I'd like to live near **the sea.**
- It can be dangerous to swim in **the sea.**

Exercises

71.1 Complete the sentences using a preposition (*to/at/in,* etc.) + one of these words. You can use the words more than once.

bed   college   home   prison   school   work

1. When Julie finishes high school, she wants to study economics *in college* .
2. In Mexico, children from the age of seven have to go _____ .
3. Mark didn't go out last night. He stayed _____ .
4. I'll have to hurry. I don't want to be late _____ .
5. There is a lot of traffic in the morning when everybody is going _____ .
6. Bill never gets up before 9:00. It's 8:30 now, so he is still _____ .
7. If you commit a serious crime, you could be sent _____ .

71.2 Complete the sentences with the word given (*school,* etc.). Use *the* where necessary.

1. **school**
   a) Every semester parents are invited to *the school* to meet the teachers.
   b) Why aren't your children in *school* today? Are they sick?
   c) When he was younger, Ted hated _____ .
   d) What time does _____ usually start in your country?
   e) *A:* How do your children get home from _____ ? By bus?
      B: No, they walk. _____ isn't very far away.
   f) What kind of work does Jenny want to do when she finishes _____ ?
   g) There were some people waiting outside _____ to meet their children.

2. **college**
   a) In your country, do many people go to _____ ?
   b) The Smiths have four children in _____ at the same time.
   c) This is only a small town, but _____ is one of the best in the country.

3. **church**
   a) John's mother is a regular churchgoer. She goes to _____ every Sunday.
   b) John himself doesn't go to _____ .
   c) John went to _____ to take some pictures of the building.

4. **prison**
   a) In many places people are in _____ because of their political beliefs.
   b) The other day the fire department was called to _____ to put out a fire.
   c) The judge decided to fine the man $500 instead of sending him to _____ .

5. **home/work/bed**
   a) I like to read in _____ before I go to sleep.
   b) It's nice to travel, but there's no place like _____ !
   c) Should we meet after _____ tomorrow?
   d) If I'm feeling tired, I go to _____ early.
   e) What time do you usually start _____ in the morning?
   f) The economic situation is very bad. Many people are out of _____ .

6. **sea**
   a) There's a nice view from the window. You can see _____ .
   b) It was a long voyage. We were at _____ for four weeks.
   c) I love swimming in _____ .

The (3) (children / the children)

A

When we are talking about things or people in general, we do not use **the**:

- I'm afraid of **dogs.** (*not* the dogs)
  (**dogs** = dogs in general, not a particular group of dogs)
- **Doctors** are paid more than **teachers.**
- Do you collect **stamps?**
- **Crime** is a problem in most big cities. (*not* the crime)
- **Life** has changed a lot in the last 30 years. (*not* the life)
- Do you often listen to **classical music?** (*not* the classical music)
- Do you like **Chinese food / French cheese / Swiss chocolate?**
- My favorite sport is **football/skiing/running.** (*not* the football / the skiing, etc.)
- My favorite subject in school was **history/physics/English.**

We say **most** people / **most** books / **most** cars, etc. (*not* the most – see also Unit 85A):

- **Most people** like George. (*not* the most people)

B

We use **the** when we mean particular things or people. Compare:

In general (without **the**)	*Particular people or things* (with **the**)
- **Children** learn a lot from playing. (= children in general)	- We took **the children** to the zoo. (= a particular group, perhaps the speaker's own children)
- I often listen to **music.**	- The movie wasn't very good, but I liked **the music.** (= the music in the movie)
- All **cars** have wheels.	- All **the cars** in this parking lot belong to people who work here.
- **Sugar** isn't very good for you.	- Can you pass **the sugar,** please? (= the sugar on the table)
- Do **Americans** drink much tea? (= Americans in general)	- Do **the Americans** you know drink tea? (= only the Americans you know, not Americans in general)

C

The difference between "something in general" and "something in particular" is not always very clear. Compare these sentences:

In general (without **the**)	*Particular people or things* (with **the**)
- I like working with **people.** (= people in general)	
- I like working with **people who are lively.** (not all people, but "people who are lively" is still a general idea)	- I like **the people I work with.** (= a particular group of people)
- Do you like **coffee?** (= coffee in general)	
- Do you like **strong black coffee?** (not all coffee, but "strong black coffee" is still a general idea)	- Did you like **the coffee we had after dinner last night?** (= particular coffee)

Exercises

72.1 Choose four of these things and write whether you like or dislike them:

baseball	boxing	cats	fast-food restaurants	~~hot weather~~
math	opera	rock music	small children	zoos

Begin your sentences with:

I like . . . / I don't like . . .   I don't mind . . .
I love . . . / I hate . . .   I'm interested in . . . / I'm not interested in . . .

1. _I don't like hot weather very much._
2. _____
3. _____
4. _____
5. _____

72.2 Complete the sentences using one of the following. Use *the* where necessary.

~~(the) basketball~~	(the) **grass**	(the) **history**	(the) **hotels**
~~(the) information~~	(the) **lies**	(the) **meat**	(the) **patience**
(the) **people**	(the) **questions**	(the) **spiders**	(the) **water**

1. My favorite sport is _basketball_ .
2. _The information_ we were given wasn't correct.
3. Many people are afraid of _____ .
4. A vegetarian is somebody who doesn't eat _____ .
5. The test wasn't very hard. I answered all _____ easily.
6. Do you know _____ who live next door?
7. _____ is the study of the past.
8. Brian always tells the truth. He never tells _____ .
9. We couldn't find anywhere to stay downtown. All _____ were full.
10. _____ in the pool didn't look very clean, so we didn't go swimming.
11. Don't sit on _____ . It's wet from the rain.
12. You need _____ to teach young children.

72.3 Choose the correct form, with or without *the*.

1. I'm afraid of <u>dogs / the dogs</u>. (*dogs* is correct)
2. Can you pass <u>salt</u> / the salt, please? (*the salt* is correct)
3. <u>Apples / The apples</u> are good for you.
4. Look at <u>apples / the apples</u> on that tree! They're very big.
5. <u>Women / The women</u> live longer than <u>men / the men</u>.
6. We had a very nice meal. <u>Vegetables / The vegetables</u> were especially good.
7. <u>Life / The life</u> is strange sometimes. Some very odd things happen.
8. I like <u>skiing / the skiing</u>, but I'm not very good at it.
9. Who are <u>people / the people</u> in this photograph?
10. What makes <u>people / the people</u> violent? What causes <u>aggression / the aggression</u>?
11. <u>All books / All the books</u> on the top shelf belong to me.
12. Don't stay in that hotel. It's very noisy, and <u>beds / the beds</u> are very uncomfortable.
13. A pacifist is somebody who is against <u>war / the war</u>.
14. <u>First World War / The First World War</u> lasted from 1914 until 1918.
15. Ron and Brenda got married, but <u>marriage / the marriage</u> didn't last very long.
16. <u>Most people / The most people</u> believe that <u>marriage / the marriage</u> and <u>family life / the family life</u> are the foundation of <u>society / the society</u>.

The (4) (*the giraffe / the telephone / the piano, etc.; the + Adjective*)

A

Study these sentences:
- **The giraffe** is the tallest of all animals.
- **The bicycle** is an excellent means of transportation.
- When was **the telephone** invented?
- **The dollar** is the currency (= the money) of the United States.

In these examples, **the . . .** does not mean one particular thing. **The giraffe** = one particular type of animal, not one particular giraffe. We use **the** (+ *singular countable noun*) in this way to talk about a type of animal, machine, etc.

In the same way we use **the** for musical instruments:
- Can you play **the** guitar?
- **The** piano is my favorite instrument.

Compare **a**:
- I'd like to have **a guitar.**
- We saw **a giraffe** at the zoo.

B

The + *adjective*

We use **the +** *adjective* (without a noun) to talk about groups of people, especially:

the young	the old	the elderly	
the rich	the poor	the unemployed	the homeless
the sick	the disabled	the injured	the dead

The young = young people, **the rich** = rich people, etc.:
- Do you think **the rich** should pay more taxes to help **the poor**?
- **The homeless** need more help from the government.

These expressions are always *plural* in meaning. You cannot say "a young" or "an unemployed."

You must say **a young man / an unemployed woman,** etc.

Note also that we say **the poor** (*not* the poors) / **the young** (*not* the youngs), etc.

C

The + *nationality*

You can use **the** with some nationality adjectives to mean "the people of that country":
- **The French** are famous for their food. (= the people of France)

In the same way you can say:
the Dutch   the Spanish   the British   the English   the Irish

Note that **the French / the English,** etc., are plural in meaning. We do not say "a French / an English." We say **a Frenchman / an Englishwoman,** etc.

You can also use **the +** nationality words ending in -ese (**the Chinese / the Sudanese,** etc.):
- **The Chinese** invented printing.

These words can also be singular (**a Japanese / a Sudanese / a Vietnamese**).
Also: the Swiss / a Swiss (plural or singular)

With other nationalities, the plural noun ends in -s. For example:
a Mexican → Mexicans   an Italian → Italians   a Thai → Thais

With these words (**Mexicans,** etc.), we do not normally use **the** to talk about the people in general (see Unit 72).

Exercises

73.1 Answer the questions by choosing the right answer from the box. Don't forget *the.* Use a dictionary if necessary.

1 animals	2 birds	3 inventions	4 currencies
tiger elephant rabbit cheetah ~~giraffe~~ kangaroo	eagle penguin swan owl parrot robin	telephone wheel telescope cell phone helicopter typewriter	dollar peso euro rupee won yen

1. a) Which of the animals is the tallest? *the giraffe*
   b) Which animal can run the fastest? _____
   c) Which of these animals is found in Australia? _____
2. a) Which of these birds has a long neck? _____
   b) Which of these birds cannot fly? _____
   c) Which bird flies at night? _____
3. a) Which of these inventions is the oldest? _____
   b) Which one is the most recent? _____
   c) Which one is especially important for astronomy? _____
4. a) What is the currency of India? _____
   b) What is the currency of Portugal? _____
   c) What is the currency of your country? _____

73.2 Put in *the* or *a* where necessary. If the sentence is already complete, leave an empty space (–).

1. When was *the* telephone invented?
2. Can you play _____ musical instrument?
3. Jill plays _____ violin in an orchestra.
4. There was _____ piano in the corner of the room.
5. Can you play _____ piano?
6. The basic unit of our society is _____ family.
7. Michael comes from _____ large family.
8. When was _____ paper first made?
9. _____ computer has changed the way we live.

73.3 Complete these sentences using *the* + one of these adjectives:

injured poor rich sick unemployed ~~young~~

1. *The young*_____ have the future in their hands.
2. Ambulances arrived at the scene of the accident and took _____ to the hospital.
3. Life is all right if you have a job, but things are not so easy for _____ .
4. Julie has been a nurse all her life. She has spent her life caring for _____ .
5. In England there is an old story about a man called Robin Hood. It is said that he took money from _____ and gave it to _____ .

73.4 What do you call the people of these countries?

	one person (*a/an . . .*)	the people in general
1. Canada?	*a Canadian*	*Canadians*
2. Germany?	_____	_____
3. France?	_____	_____
4. Russia?	_____	_____
5. China?	_____	_____
6. Brazil?	_____	_____
7. Japan?	_____	_____
8. *and your country?*	_____	_____

Names With and Without *the* (1)

A We do not use **the** with names of people (Ann, Ann Taylor, etc.). In the same way, we do not normally use **the** with names of places. For example:

continents	Africa (*not* the Africa), Asia, South America
countries and states	France (*not* the France), Japan, Brazil, Texas
islands	Bermuda, Sicily, Vancouver Island
cities, towns, etc.	Cairo, New York, Bangkok
mountains	Everest, Kilimanjaro, Fuji

But we use **the** in names with **Republic, Kingdom, States,** etc.:
  the Dominican **Republic**   the United **Kingdom** (the UK)
  the Czech **Republic**   the United **States** of America (the USA)

Compare:
■ We visited **Canada** and the **United States.**

B When we use **Mr./Mrs./Captain/Doctor,** etc. + a name, we do not use **the.** We say:
  Mr. Johnson / **Doctor** Johnson / **Captain** Johnson / **President** Johnson, etc. (*not* the . . .)
  Uncle Robert / **Aunt** Jane / **Saint** Catherine / **Princess** Anne, etc. (*not* the . . .)

Compare:
■ We called **the doctor** *but* We called **Doctor Johnson.** (*not* the Doctor Johnson)

We use **mount** (= mountain) and **lake** in the same way (*without* the):
  Mount Everest (*not* the . . .)   **Mount** McKinley   **Lake** Superior   **Lake** Titicaca
  ■ They live near **the lake.** *but* They live near **Lake Superior.** (*without* the)

C We use **the** with the names of oceans, seas, rivers, and canals (see also Unit 75B):
  the Atlantic (Ocean)   the Amazon (River)   the Nile
  the Indian Ocean   the Red Sea   the English Channel (between
  the Caribbean (Sea)   the Suez Canal   France and Britain)

D We use **the** with *plural* names of people and places:

people	the Mitchells (= the Mitchell family), the Johnsons
countries	the Netherlands, the Philippines, the United States
groups of islands	the Canaries / the Canary Islands, the Bahamas, the Hawaiian Islands
mountain ranges	the Rocky Mountains / the Rockies, the Andes, the Alps

E North/northern, etc.

We say: **the north** (of Mexico)   *but*   **northern** Mexico (*without* the)
        the southeast (of Canada)   *but*   **southeastern** Canada

Compare:
■ Sweden is in **northern** Europe; Spain is in **the south.**

Also: **the** Middle East   **the** Far East

You can also use **north/south,** etc. + a place name (*without* the):
  North America   **West** Africa   **southeast** Texas

Exercises

74.1 Put in *the* where necessary. Leave a space (–) if the sentence is already complete.

1. Who is _____—_____ Doctor Johnson?
2. I was sick, so I went to see _____ doctor.
3. _____ president is the most powerful person in _____ United States.
4. _____ President Kennedy was assassinated in 1963.
5. Do you know _____ Wilsons? They're a very nice couple.
6. Do you know _____ Professor Brown's phone number?

74.2 Some of these sentences are correct, but some need *the* (perhaps more than once). Correct the sentences where necessary.

1. Everest was first climbed in 1953.   *RIGHT*
2. Jacksonville is in north of Florida.   *the north of Florida*
3. Africa is much larger than Europe.   _____
4. Last year I visited Mexico and United States.   _____
5. South of India is warmer than north.   _____
6. Portugal is in western Europe.   _____
7. Jim has traveled a lot in Middle East.   _____
8. Chicago is on Lake Michigan.   _____
9. Next year we are going skiing in Swiss Alps.   _____
10. The highest mountain in Africa is Kilimanjaro.   _____
11. United Kingdom consists of Great Britain
    and Northern Ireland.   _____
12. Seychelles are a group of islands in Indian Ocean.   _____
13. Hudson River flows into Atlantic Ocean.   _____

74.3 Here are some geography questions. Choose the right answer from one of the boxes and write *the* if necessary. You do not need all the names in the boxes. Use an atlas if necessary.

continents	countries	oceans and seas	mountains	rivers and canals	
Africa	Canada	Atlantic Ocean	Alps	Amazon	Rhine
Asia	Denmark	Indian Ocean	Andes	Nile	Volga
Australia	Indonesia	Pacific Ocean	Himalayas	Thames	
Europe	Sweden	Black Sea	Rockies	Mississippi	
North America	Thailand	Mediterranean Sea	Urals	Suez Canal	
South America	United States	Red Sea		Panama Canal	

1. What do you have to cross to travel from Europe to America? *the Atlantic Ocean*
2. Where is Argentina? _____
3. What is the longest river in Africa? _____
4. Of which country is Stockholm the capital? _____
5. Of which country is Washington, D.C., the capital? _____
6. What is the name of the mountain range in the west of North America? _____
7. What is the name of the sea between Africa and Europe? _____
8. What is the smallest continent in the world? _____
9. What is the name of the ocean between North America and Asia? _____
10. What is the name of the ocean between Africa and Australia? _____
11. What river flows through London? _____
12. What river flows through Memphis and New Orleans? _____
13. Of which country is Bangkok the capital? _____
14. What joins the Atlantic and Pacific Oceans? _____
15. What is the longest river in South America? _____

Names With and Without *the* (2)

A

Names without **the**

We do not use **the** with names of most streets/roads/squares/parks, etc.:

Union **Street** (*not* the . . .)	Fifth **Avenue**	Central **Park**
Wilshire **Boulevard**	**Broadway**	Times **Square**

Many names (especially names of important buildings and institutions) are two words:

Kennedy Airport   **Cambridge University**

The first word is usually the name of a person (Kennedy) or a place (Cambridge). We do not usually use **the** with names like these. Some more examples:

Penn Station (*not* the . . .)	**Boston University**	**Carnegie Hall**
Lincoln Center	**Buckingham Palace**	

But we say **the White House** and **the Royal Palace** because "white" and "royal" are not names like "Kennedy" and "Cambridge." This is only a general rule and there are exceptions.

B

Most other names (of places, buildings, etc.) have names with **the**:

the	Hilton	Hotel
	National	Theater
	Sahara	Desert
	Atlantic	Ocean

These places usually have names with **the**:

hotels / restaurants	the Sheraton **Hotel**, the Bombay **Restaurant**, the Holiday Inn (hotel)
theaters / movie theaters	the Shubert **Theater**, the Cineplex Odeon
museums / galleries	the Metropolitan **Museum**, the National **Gallery**
other buildings / bridges	the Empire State **Building**, the Golden Gate **Bridge**, the White **House**
oceans / seas / canals	the Indian **Ocean**, the Mediterranean **Sea**, the Suez **Canal**

Also:

newspapers	the Washington **Post**, the Financial **Times**
organizations (but see also Section D)	the European **Union**, the Red Cross

Sometimes we leave out the noun: **the Hilton** (Hotel), **the Sahara** (Desert)
Sometimes the name is only **the** + *noun*: **the Vatican** (in Rome), **the Pentagon** (in Washington, D.C.)

Names with **of** usually have **the**. For example:

the Bank of Montreal	the Tower of London	the Museum of Modern Art
the Houses of Congress	the Great Wall of China	the Tropic of Capricorn
the Gulf of Mexico	the University of Michigan	

C

Many stores, restaurants, hotels, banks, etc., are named after the people who started them. These names end in -**'s** or -**s**. We do not use **the** with these names:

Lloyds Bank (*not* the Lloyds Bank)	**McDonalds**
Macy's (department store)	**Harrah's** (casino)

Churches are often named after saints:

St. John's Church (*not* the St. John's Church)   **St. Patrick's Cathedral**

D

Names of companies, airlines, etc., are usually without **the**:

Fiat (*not* the Fiat)   **Sony**   **Kodak**   **United Airlines**   **IBM**

Exercises

75.1 Use the map to answer the questions in the way shown. Write the name of the place and the street it is on. On maps we do not normally use *the*. In your sentences, use *the* if necessary.

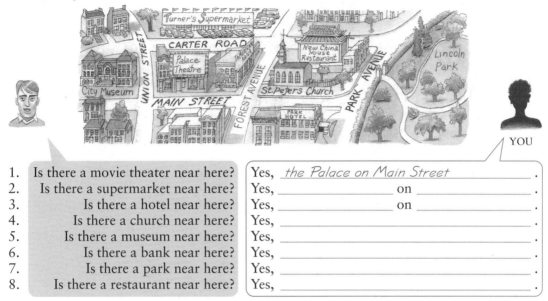

1. Is there a movie theater near here? | Yes, *the Palace on Main Street* .
2. Is there a supermarket near here? | Yes, _____ on _____ .
3. Is there a hotel near here? | Yes, _____ on _____ .
4. Is there a church near here? | Yes, _____ .
5. Is there a museum near here? | Yes, _____ .
6. Is there a bank near here? | Yes, _____ .
7. Is there a park near here? | Yes, _____ .
8. Is there a restaurant near here? | Yes, _____ .

75.2 Where are these streets and buildings? Choose from the box. Use *the* where necessary.

| Acropolis | Broadway | Buckingham Palace | Eiffel Tower |
| Sunset Boulevard | ~~Times Square~~ | Vatican | White House |

1. *Times Square* is in New York.
2. _____ is in Paris.
3. _____ is in Rome.
4. _____ is in London.
5. _____ is in Hollywood.
6. _____ is in Washington, D.C.
7. _____ is in Athens.
8. _____ is in New York.

75.3 Choose the correct form, with or without *the*.

1. Have you been to British Museum / the British Museum? (*the British Museum* is correct)
2. The biggest park in New York is Central Park / the Central Park.
3. My favorite park in London is St. James's Park / the St. James's Park.
4. Ramada Inn / The Ramada Inn is on Main Street / the Main Street.
5. We flew to Mexico City from O'Hare Airport / the O'Hare Airport in Chicago.
6. Frank is a student at McGill University / the McGill University.
7. If you're looking for some new clothes, I would recommend Harrison's Department Store / the Harrison's Department Store.
8. Statue of Liberty / The Statue of Liberty is at the entrance to New York harbor / the New York harbor.
9. You should go to Whitney Museum / the Whitney Museum. There are some wonderful paintings there.
10. John works for IBM / the IBM now. He used to work for General Electric / the General Electric.
11. "Which movie theater are you going to tonight?" "Classic / The Classic."
12. I'd like to go to China and see Great Wall / the Great Wall.
13. Which newspaper should I buy – Independent / the Independent or Herald / the Herald?
14. This book is published by Cambridge University Press / the Cambridge University Press.

UNIT 76

Singular and Plural

A

Sometimes we use a *plural* noun for one thing that has two parts. For example:

| pants *(two legs)* *also* jeans/slacks/shorts/trousers | pajamas *(top and bottom)* | glasses | binoculars | scissors |

These words are plural, so they take a plural verb:
- My **pants are** too long. (*not* is too long)

You can also use **a pair of** + these words:
- Those **are** nice **jeans**.   *or*   That's a nice **pair of jeans**. (*not* a nice jeans)
- I need **some** new **glasses**.   *or*   I need a new **pair of glasses**.

B

Some nouns end in -ics but are not usually plural. For example:
economics   electronics   gymnastics   mathematics   physics   politics
- **Gymnastics** is my favorite sport.

News is not plural (see Unit 67B):
- What time **is the news** on television? (*not* are the news)

Some words ending in -s can be singular or plural. For example:

means	**a means** of transportation	**many means** of transportation
series	a television **series**	**two** television **series**
species	a **species** of bird	**200 species** of birds

C

We always use a plural verb with **police**:
- The **police have** arrested a friend of mine. (*not* The police has)
- Do you think the **police are** well paid?

Note that a person in the police is **a police officer / a policewoman / a policeman** (*not* a police).

D

We do not often use the plural of **person** (persons). We normally use **people** (a plural word):
- He's **a** nice **person.** *but* They are nice **people.**
- Many **people don't** have enough to eat. (*not* doesn't have)

E

We think of a sum of money, a period of time, a distance, etc., as *one* thing. So we use a singular verb:
- **Twenty thousand dollars** (= it) **was** stolen in the robbery. (*not* were stolen)
- **Three years** (= it) **is** a long time to be without a job. (*not* Three years are)
- **Six miles is** a long way to walk every day.

Exercises

76.1 Complete the sentences using a word from Section A or B. Sometimes you need *a* or *some*.

1. My eyes aren't very good. I need _glasses_ .
2. This plant is _a_ very rare _species_ .
3. Soccer players don't wear pants when they play. They wear _____ .
4. The bicycle is _____ of transportation.
5. The bicycle and the car are _____ of transportation.
6. I want to cut this piece of material. I need _____ .
7. Ann is going to write _____ of articles for her local newspaper.
8. There are a lot of American TV _____ shown throughout the world.
9. While we were out walking, we saw 25 different _____ of birds.

76.2 In each example the words on the left are connected with an activity (for example, a sport or an academic subject). Write the name of the activity. The beginning of the word is given.

1. calculate   algebra   equation   m _athematics_
2. government   election   parliament   p _____
3. finance   trade   employment   e _____
4. light   heat   gravity   ph _____
5. handstand   somersault parallel bars   gy _____
6. computer   silicon chip video games   el _____

76.3 Choose the correct form of the verb, singular or plural.

1. Gymnastics <u>is</u> / ~~are~~ my favorite sport. (*is* is correct)
2. The pants you bought for me <u>doesn't / don't</u> fit me.
3. The police <u>want / wants</u> to interview two men about the robbery last week.
4. Physics <u>was / were</u> my best subject in school.
5. Can I borrow your scissors? Mine <u>isn't / aren't</u> sharp enough.
6. Fortunately, the news <u>wasn't / weren't</u> as bad as we expected.
7. Three days <u>isn't / aren't</u> long enough for a good vacation.
8. I can't find my binoculars. Do you know where <u>it is / they are</u>?
9. Do you think the people <u>is / are</u> happy with the government?
10. <u>Does / Do</u> the police know how the accident happened?
11. I don't like very hot weather. Ninety degrees <u>is / are</u> too hot for me.

76.4 Most of these sentences are wrong. Correct them where necessary.

1. Susan was wearing a black jeans.   _wearing black jeans_
2. I like Matt and Jill. They're very nice persons. _____
3. I need more money than that. Ten dollars are   _____
   not enough.   _____
4. I'm going to buy a new pajama.   _____
5. Many people has given up smoking.   _____
6. Three days wasn't long enough to see all the   _____
   sights in Toronto.   _____
7. There was a police standing at the corner   _____
   of the street.   _____
8. Has the police arrived yet?   _____
9. This scissors is not very sharp.   _____

Noun + Noun (*a tennis ball / a headache*, etc.)

A

We often use two nouns together (*noun + noun*) to mean one thing/person/idea, etc. For example:

a **tennis ball**   a **bank manager**   a **car accident**   **income tax**   the **water temperature**

The first noun is like an *adjective* – it tells us what kind of thing/person/idea, etc. For example:

a **tennis ball** = a ball used to play tennis
a **car accident** = an accident that happens while driving in a car
income tax = tax that you pay on your income
a **Boston doctor** = a doctor from Boston
the **water temperature** = the temperature of the water (in an ocean, a lake, etc.)

So you can say:

a **television** camera   a **television** program   a **television** studio   a **television** producer
(all of these different things or people have to do with television)
language **problems**   marriage **problems**   health **problems**   work **problems**
(all of these are different kinds of problems)

Compare:

garden vegetables (= vegetables that are grown in a garden)
a **vegetable garden** (= a garden where vegetables are grown)

Often the first word ends in **-ing**. Usually these are things used for doing something. For example:

a **frying** pan (a pan for frying)   a **washing** machine   a **swimming** pool   a **dining** room

Sometimes there are more than two nouns together:

- I waited at the **hotel reception desk**.
- We watched the **World Swimming Championships** on television.
- Everyone is talking about the **government corruption scandal**.

B

When nouns are together like this, sometimes we write them as one word and sometimes as two separate words. For example:

a **headache**   **toothpaste**   a **weekend**   a **swimming pool**   **pea soup**

There are no clear rules for this. If you are not sure, it is usually better to write two words.

C

Note the difference between:

a **wineglass** (the glass may be empty) and a **glass of wine** (= a glass with wine in it)
a **toolbox** (the box may be empty) and a **box of tools** (= a box full of tools)

D

When we use *noun + noun*, the first noun is like an adjective. It is normally *singular*, but the meaning is often *plural*. For example, a **bookstore** is a **store** where you can buy **books**, and an **apple tree** is a **tree** that has **apples**. In the same way we say:

a **three-hour** trip (*not* a three-hours trip)   two **14-year**-old girls (*not* years)
a **ten-dollar** bill (*not* dollars)   a **three-page** letter (*not* pages)
a **four-week** English course (*not* weeks)

Compare:

- It was **a three-hour** trip.   *but*   The trip took three **hours**.

For the structure "I need eight hours' sleep a night," see Unit 78E.

-'s and of . . .   **Unit 78**

Exercises

77.1 **What do we call these things and people? Use the structure noun + noun.**

1. A ticket for a concert is _a concert ticket_ .
2. A magazine about computers is _____ .
3. Pictures taken on your vacation are your _____ .
4. Chocolate made with milk is _____ .
5. Somebody whose job is to inspect factories is _____ .
6. A lawyer from Vancouver is _____ .
7. The results of your exams are your _____ .
8. A race for horses is _____ .
9. A horse that runs in races is _____ .
10. The carpet in the dining room is _____ .
11. A scandal involving an oil company is _____ .
12. A question that has two parts is _____ .
13. A girl who is seven years old is _____ .
14. A building with five stories is _____ .

77.2 **Answer the questions using two of the following words each time:**

| ~~accident~~ | belt | ~~car~~ | card | credit | editor | forecast |
| newspaper | number | room | seat | store | weather | window |

1. This can be caused by bad driving.   a _car accident_
2. If you're staying at a hotel, you need to remember this.   your _____
3. You should wear this when you're in a car.   a _____
4. You can often use this to pay for things instead of cash.   a _____
5. If you want to know if it's going to rain, you can read or listen to this.   the _____
6. This person is a top journalist.   a _____
7. You might stop to look in this when you're walking along a street.   a _____

77.3 **Complete the sentences using one of the following:**

| 15 minute(s) | 60 minute(s) | two hour(s) | five day(s) | two year(s) | 500 year(s) |
| six mile(s) | six mile(s) | 20 dollar(s) | five course(s) | ~~ten page(s)~~ | ~~450 page(s)~~ |

Sometimes you need the singular (*day/page*, etc.) and sometimes the plural (*days/pages*, etc.).

1. It's a very long book. There are _450 pages_ .
2. A few days ago I received a _ten-page_ letter from Julia.
3. I didn't have any change. I only had a _____ bill.
4. At work I usually have a _____ coffee break in the morning.
5. There are _____ in an hour.
6. It's only a _____ flight from London to Madrid.
7. It was a big meal. There were _____ .
8. Mary has just started a new job. She has a _____ contract.
9. The oldest building in the city is the _____-old castle.
10. I work _____ a week. I'm off on Saturday and Sunday.
11. We went for a _____ walk in the country.
12. We went for a long walk in the country. We walked _____ .

-'s (the girl's name) and of . . . (the name of the book)

We normally use -'s for people or animals (**Karen's** . . . / **the horse's** . . . , etc.):

Karen's eyes   **the manager's** office   **the horse's** tail   **Mr. Evans's** daughter

- Where is **the manager's** office? (*not* the office of the manager)
- What color are **Karen's** eyes? (*not* the eyes of Karen)
- What is **Karen's brother's** name?

Note that you can use -'s without a noun after it:

- This isn't my book. It's **my brother's.** (= my brother's book)

We do not always use -'s for people. For example, we would use of . . . in this sentence:

- What is the name **of the man who lent us the money?** ("the man who lent us the money" is too long to be followed by -'s)

Note that we say **a woman's hat** (= a hat for a woman), **a boy's name** (= a name for a boy), **a bird's egg** (= an egg laid by a bird), etc.

For things, ideas, etc., we normally use of (. . . of the book / . . . of the cafe, etc.):

the door **of the garage** (*not* the garage's door)   the name **of the book**   the owner **of the cafe**

Sometimes you can use the structure *noun + noun* (see Unit 77):

the **garage door**   the **cafe owner**

We normally use **of** with **the beginning / the end / the top / the bottom / the front / the back,** etc.:

the beginning of the month   **the back of** the car (*not* the car back)

You can usually use either -'s or of . . . for an organization (= a group of people). So you can say:

the government's decision   *or*   the decision **of the government**
the company's success   *or*   the success **of the company**

It is also possible to use -'s for places. So you can say:

the city's new theater   **the world's** population   **Brazil's** largest city

After a *singular* noun we use -'s:

my **sister's** room (= her room – one sister)   **Mr. Carter's** house

After a *plural* noun (**sisters/friends,** etc.) we put ' (an *apostrophe*) after the s:

my **sisters'** room (= their room – two or more sisters)
the **Carters'** house (Mr. and Mrs. Carter)

If a plural noun does not end in -s (for example, **men/women/children/people**), we use -'s:

the **men's** changing room   a **children's** book (= a book for children)

Note that you can use -'s after more than one noun:

Jack and Jill's wedding   **Mr. and Mrs. Carter's** house

You can also use -'s with time expressions (**yesterday / next week,** etc.):

- Do you still have **yesterday's** newspaper?
- **Next week's** meeting has been canceled.

In the same way, you can say **today's / tomorrow's / this evening's / Monday's,** etc.

We also use -'s (or -s' with plural words) with periods of time:

- I have **a week's** vacation starting on Monday.
- Sally needs eight **hours'** sleep a night.
- Brenda got to work 15 minutes late but lost **an hour's** pay.

Exercises

78.1 In some of these sentences, it would be more natural to use -'s or -'. Change the underlined parts where necessary.

1. Who is <u>the owner of this restuarant</u>? *OK*
2. Where are <u>the children of Chris</u>? *Chris's children*
3. Is this <u>the umbrella of your friend</u>?
4. Write your name at <u>the top of the page</u>.
5. I've never met <u>the daughter of Charles</u>.
6. Have you met <u>the son of Mary and Dan</u>?
7. We don't know <u>the cause of the problem</u>.
8. Do we still have the <u>newspaper of yesterday</u>?
9. What's <u>the name of this street</u>?
10. What is <u>the cost of a new computer</u>?
11. <u>The friends of your children</u> are here.
12. <u>The garden of our neighbors</u> is very nice.
13. I work on <u>the ground floor of the building</u>.
14. <u>The hair of Bill</u> is very long.
15. I couldn't go to <u>the party of Catherine</u>.
16. Today is <u>the birthday of my father</u>.
17. Have you seen <u>the car of the parents of Mike</u>?
18. We went to <u>the wedding of the best friend of Helen</u>.

78.2 What is another way of saying these things? Use -'s.

1. a hat for a woman *a woman's hat*
2. a name for a boy
3. clothes for children
4. a school for girls
5. a nest for a bird
6. a magazine for women

78.3 Read each sentence and write a new sentence beginning with the underlined words.

1. The meeting <u>tomorrow</u> has been canceled.
   Tomorrow's meeting has been canceled.
2. The storm <u>last week</u> caused a lot of damage.
   Last
3. The only movie theater in <u>town</u> has closed down.
   The
4. Exports from <u>Japan</u> to the United States have fallen recently.

5. Tourism is the main industry in <u>the region</u>.

78.4 Read the situation and complete the sentences. Use the word in parentheses.

1. I bought groceries at the supermarket last night. They will last us for a week.
   I bought *a week's groceries* at the supermarket last night. (groceries)
2. Kim got a new car. It cost the same as her salary for a year.
   Kim's new car cost her _____ . (salary)
3. Jim lost his job. His company gave him extra money equal to his pay for four weeks.
   Jim got _____ when he lost his job. (pay)
4. I haven't been able to rest all day. I haven't rested for even a minute.
   I haven't had _____ all day. (rest)
5. I went to bed at midnight and woke up at 5 A.M.
   I only had _____ last night. (sleep)

Myself/yourself/themselves, etc.

A

Study this example:

Steve cut **himself** while he was shaving this morning.

We use **myself/yourself/himself**, etc. *(reflexive pronouns)* when the *subject* and *object* are the same:

subject → Steve cut himself . ← *object*

The reflexive pronouns are:

singular:	**myself**	**yourself** *(one person)*	**himself/herself/itself**
plural:	**ourselves**	**yourselves** *(more than one person)*	**themselves**

- I don't want you to pay for me. I'll pay for **myself**. (*not* I'll pay for me)
- Julie had a great vacation. **She** enjoyed **herself** very much.
- *(said to one person)* Do **you** sometimes talk to **yourself**?
- *(said to more than one person)* If **you** want more to eat, help **yourselves**.

Compare:

- It's not our fault. **You** can't blame **us**.
- It's our own fault. **We** should blame **ourselves**.

Note that we do not use **myself/yourself**, etc., after **bring/take something with . . .** :

- It might rain. I'll **take** an umbrella **with me**. (*not* with myself)

B

We do not use **myself**, etc., after **concentrate/feel/relax/meet**:

- You have to try and **concentrate**. (*not* concentrate yourself)
- "Do you **feel** nervous?" "Yes, I can't **relax**."
- What time should we **meet**? (*not* meet ourselves, *not* meet us)

C

Study the difference between **-selves** and **each other**:

- Tom and Ann stood in front of the mirror and looked at **themselves**. (= Tom and Ann looked at Tom and Ann.)

but - Tom looked at Ann; Ann looked at Tom. They looked at **each other**.

 THEMSELVES

 EACH OTHER

You can use **one another** instead of **each other**:

- How long have you and Bill known **one another**? (*or* known **each other**)
- Sue and Ann don't like **each other**. (*or* don't like **one another**)

D

We also use **myself/yourself**, etc., in another way. For example:

- "Who repaired your bicycle for you?" "Nobody. I repaired it **myself**."

I repaired it **myself** = I repaired it, not anybody else. Here, **myself** is used to emphasize I (it makes it stronger). Some more examples:

- I'm not going to do it for you. **You** can do it **yourself**.
- **Let's** paint the house **ourselves**. It will be much cheaper.
- **The movie itself** wasn't very good, but I liked the music.
- I don't think Sue will get the job. **Sue herself** doesn't think she'll get it. (*or* Sue doesn't think she'll get it **herself**.)

By myself / by yourself, etc. **Unit 80C**

Exercises

79.1 Complete each sentence using *myself/yourself*, etc., with one of these verbs in the
correct form: blame burn ~~cut~~ enjoy express hurt put

1. Steve _cut himself_____ while he was shaving this morning.
2. Bill fell down some steps, but fortunately he didn't _____ badly.
3. It isn't her fault. She really shouldn't _____ .
4. Please try and understand how I feel. _____ in my position.
5. They had a great time. They really _____ .
6. Be careful! That pan is very hot. Don't _____ .
7. Sometimes I can't say exactly what I mean. I wish I could _____
    better.

79.2 Put in *myself/yourself*, etc., or *me/you/us*, etc.

1. Julie had a great vacation. She enjoyed _herself_____ .
2. It's not my fault. You can't blame _____ .
3. What I did was wrong. I'm ashamed of _____ .
4. We've got a problem. I hope you can help _____ .
5. "Can I have another cookie?" "Of course. Help _____ !"
6. Take some money with _____ in case you need it.
7. Don't worry about Tom and me. We can take care of _____ .
8. I gave them a key to our house so that they could let _____ in.
9. When they come to visit us, they always bring their dog with _____ .

79.3 Complete these sentences. Use *myself/yourself*, etc., only where necessary. Use one of
these verbs in the correct form: concentrate defend dry ~~feel~~ meet relax

1. I was sick yesterday, but I _feel_____ much better today.
2. She climbed out of the swimming pool and _____ with a towel.
3. I tried to study, but I just couldn't _____ .
4. If somebody attacks you, you need to be able to _____ .
5. I'm going out with Chris tonight. We're _____ at the movies at 7:30.
6. You're always rushing around. Why don't you sit down and _____ ?

79.4 Complete the sentences with *-selves* or *each other.*

1. How long have you and Bill known _each other_____ ?
2. If people work too hard, they can make _____ sick.
3. I need you and you need me. We need _____ .
4. In the U.S. friends often give _____ presents at Christmas.
5. Some people are very selfish. They think only of _____ .
6. We couldn't get back into the house. We had locked _____ out.
7. They've had an argument. They're not speaking to _____ at the moment.
8. We'd never met before, so we introduced _____ to _____ .

79.5 Complete the answers to the questions using *myself/yourself/itself*, etc.

1.	Who repaired the bicycle for you?	Nobody. I _repaired it myself_____ .
2.	Did Brian have his hair cut by a barber?	No, he cut _____ .
3.	Do you want me to mail that letter for you?	No, I'll _____ .
4.	Who told you that Linda was getting married?	Linda _____ .
5.	Can you call John for me?	Why can't you _____ ?

A friend of mine   My own house   By myself

A

A friend of mine / a friend of Tom's, etc.

We say "a friend **of mine/yours/his/hers/ours/theirs**":
- I'm going to a wedding on Saturday. **A friend of mine** is getting married. (*not* a friend of me)
- We went on a trip with **some friends of ours.** (*not* some friends of us)
- Michael had an argument with **a neighbor of his.**
- That was **a good idea of yours** to go swimming this afternoon.

In the same way, we say "a friend **of Tom's / of my sister's,**" etc.:
- It was **a good idea of Tom's** to go swimming.
- That woman over there is **a friend of my sister's.**

B

My own . . . / your own . . . , etc.

We use **my/your/his/her/its/our/their** before **own:**
  my own house   **your own** car   **her own** room
(*not* an own house, an own car, etc.)

My own . . . / your own . . . , etc. = something that is only mine/yours, etc., not shared or borrowed:
- I don't want to share a room with anybody. I want **my own room.**
- Vicky and George would like to have **their own house.** (*not* an own house)
- It's a shame that the apartment doesn't have **its own parking space.**
- It's **my own fault** that I don't have any money. I buy too many things I don't need.
- Why do you want to borrow my car? Why don't you use **your own?** (= your own car)

You can also use **. . . own . . .** to say that you do something yourself instead of somebody else doing it for you. For example:
- Bill usually cuts **his own** hair.
  (= he cuts it himself; he doesn't go to a barber)
- I'd like to have a garden so that I could grow **my own** vegetables.
  (= grow them myself instead of buying them in stores)

Bill usually cuts his own hair.

On my own / on your own, etc. means independently:
- Are your children living **on their own?** (= living in their own place and supporting themselves)
- Michelle traveled around Japan **on her own.** (= nobody helped her)
- I can do that job **on my own.** (= I don't need anyone's help)

C

By myself / by yourself, etc.

By myself / by yourself / by themselves, etc. = alone, without other people:
- "Did you go to Hawaii **by yourself?**" "No, I went with a friend."
- Jack was sitting **by himself** in a corner of the cafe.
- Student drivers are not allowed to drive **by themselves.**

By myself is not exactly the same as **on my own:**
- I live **by myself.** (= I live alone.)
- He lives **on his own** with a roommate. (= independently, but not alone)

Exercises

80.1 Rewrite these sentences using the structure in Section A (*a friend of mine,* etc.).

1. I am writing to <u>one of my friends</u>. I'm writing to <u>*a friend of mine*</u>   .
2. We met <u>one of your relatives</u>. We met a _____ .
3. Jason borrowed <u>one of my books</u>. Jason _____ .
4. Ann invited <u>some of her friends</u> to her place. Ann _____ .
5. We had dinner with <u>one of our neighbors</u>. _____
6. I took a trip with <u>two of my friends</u>. _____
7. Is that man <u>one of your friends</u>? _____
8. I met <u>one of Amy's friends</u> at the party. _____

80.2 Complete the sentences using *my own / your own,* etc. + one of the following:

business   government   ideas   money   private jet   ~~room~~   TV

1. I don't want to share a room. I want <u>*my own room*</u>   .
2. I don't watch TV with the rest of the family. I have _____
   in my room.
3. Sue doesn't need to borrow money from me. She has _____ .
4. Julia is fed up with working for other people. She wants to start _____
   _____ .
5. Jason is extremely rich. He has _____ .
6. You can give him advice, but he won't listen. He's got _____ .
7. The U.S. Virgin Islands is a group of islands in the Caribbean Sea. It is a United States
   territory, but it has _____ .

80.3 Complete the sentences using *my own / your own,* etc.

1. Why do you want to borrow my car? Why don't you <u>*use your own car*</u>   ?
2. How can you blame me? It's not my fault. It's _____ .
3. He's always using my ideas. Why can't he use _____ ?
4. Please don't worry about my problems. You've got _____ .
5. I can't make her decisions for her. She has to make _____ .

80.4 Complete the sentences using *my own / your own,* etc. Choose one of these verbs:

bake   ~~cut~~   make   write

1. Brian never goes to the barber. He usually <u>*cuts his own hair*</u>   .
2. Mary doesn't buy many clothes. She usually _____ .
3. Paul is a singer. He sings songs written by other people, but he also
   _____ .
4. We don't often buy bread from a bakery. We _____ .

80.5 Complete the sentences using *by myself / by himself,* etc.

1. Did you go to Hawaii <u>*by yourself*</u>   ?
2. The box was too heavy for me to lift _____ .
3. "Who was Tom with when you saw him?" "Nobody. He was _____ ."
4. Very young children should not go swimming _____ .
5. I don't think she knows many people. When I see her, she is always _____ .
6. Do you like working with other people, or do you prefer working _____ ?
7. We had no help painting the apartment. We did it completely _____ .

There . . . and *It . . .*

A

There and it

There's a new restaurant on Main Street.

Yes, I know. I went there last night. It's very good.

We use **there** when we talk about something for the first time, to say that it exists:

- **There's** a new restaurant on Main Street. (*not* A new restaurant is on Main Street)
- The trip took a long time. **There was** a lot of traffic. (*not* It was a lot of traffic)
- Things are more expensive now. **There has been** a big increase in the cost of living.

It = a particular thing, place, fact, situation, etc. (but see also Section C):

- We went to the new restaurant. **It's** very good. (it = the restaurant)
- I wasn't expecting them to come. **It** (= that they came) was a complete surprise.

Compare **there** and **it**:

- I don't like this town. **There's** nothing to do here. **It's** a boring place.

Note that **there** can also mean *to/at/in that place*:

- The new restaurant is very good. I went **there** (= to the restaurant) last night.
- When we got to the party, there were already a lot of people **there** (= at the party).

B

You can say **there will be, there must be, there used to be**, etc.:

- **Will there be** many people at the party?
- "Is there a flight to Miami this evening?" "**There might be.** I'll call the airport."
- If people drove more carefully, **there wouldn't be** so many accidents.

You can also say **there must have been, there should have been**, etc.:

- **There was** a light on. **There must have been** somebody at home.

Compare **there** and **it**:

- They live on a busy street. **There must be** a lot of noise from the traffic.
  They live on a busy main street. **It must be** very noisy.
- **There used to be** a movie theater on Main Street, but it closed a few years ago.
  That building is now a supermarket. **It used to be** a movie theater.

You can also say **there is sure/certain/likely to be** something:

- **There is sure to be** a flight to Miami this evening.

C

We also use **it** in sentences like this:

- **It's** dangerous to walk in the street. (It = to walk in the street)

It is unusual to say "To walk in the street is dangerous." Normally we begin with **It**:

- **It** didn't take us long to get here. (It = to get here)
- **It's** too bad (that) Sandra can't come to the party. (It = that Sandra can't come)
- Let's go. **It's** not worth waiting any longer. (It = waiting any longer)

We use **it** to talk about distance, time, and weather:

- **It's** a long way from here to the airport.
- What day is **it** today?
- **It's** been a long time since I last saw you.
- **It** was windy. (*but* There was a cold wind.)

It's worth / It's no use / There's no point Unit 60A   *There is + -ing/-ed* Unit 94D

Exercises

81.1 Put in *there is/was* or *it is/was.* Some sentences are questions
(*is there . . . ? / is it . . . ?* etc.) and some are negative (*isn't/wasn't*).

1. The trip took a long time. *There was* _____ a lot of traffic.
2. What's the new restaurant like? *Is it* _____ good?
3. "_____ a bookstore near here?" "Yes, _____ one on Hill Street."
4. When we got to the movie theater, _____ a line outside.
   _____ a very long line, so we decided not to wait.
5. I couldn't see anything. _____ completely dark.
6. _____ trouble at the soccer game last night. They had to call the police.
7. How far _____ from Hong Kong to Taipei?
8. _____ Keith's birthday yesterday. We had a party.
9. _____ too windy to play tennis this morning. Let's play tomorrow instead.
10. I wanted to visit the museum, but _____ enough time.
11. "_____ time to leave?" "Yes, _____ almost midnight."
12. A few days ago _____ a storm. _____ a lot of damage.
13. _____ anything on TV, so I turned it off.
14. _____ an accident on Main Street, but _____ very serious.

81.2 Read the first sentence, and then write a sentence beginning with *There . . .*

1. The roads were busy today. There *was a lot of traffic* _____ .
2. This soup is very salty. There _____ in the soup.
3. The box was empty. _____ in the box.
4. The movie was very violent. _____
5. The shopping mall was very crowded. _____

81.3 Complete the sentences. Use *there will be / there would be,* etc. Choose from:

will   **might**   ~~**would**~~   **wouldn't**   **should**   **used to**   **(be) going to**

1. If people drove more carefully, *there would be* _____ fewer accidents.
2. "Do we have any eggs?" "I'm not sure. _____ some in the fridge."
3. I think everything will be OK. I don't think _____ any problems.
4. Look at the sky. _____ a storm.
5. "Is there a school in this village?" "Not now. _____ one, but it closed."
6. People drive too fast on this road. I think _____ a speed limit.
7. If people weren't aggressive, _____ any wars.

81.4 Are these sentences right or wrong? Change *it* to *there* where necessary.

1. They live on a busy road. It must be a lot of noise.   *There must be* _____
2. Last winter it was very cold, and it was a lot of snow.   _____
3. I wish it was warmer. I hate cold weather.   _____
4. It used to be a church here, but it was torn down.   _____
5. Why was she so unfriendly? It must have been a reason.   _____
6. It's a long way from my house to the nearest store.   _____
7. "Where can we park the car?" "Don't worry. It's sure
   to be a parking lot somewhere."   _____
8. After the lecture it will be an opportunity to ask
   questions.   _____
9. I like the place where I live, but it would be nicer to
   live by the ocean.   _____
10. I was told that it would be somebody to meet me at
    the airport, but it wasn't anybody.   _____

UNIT 82

Some and any

A

In general we use **some** (also **somebody/someone/something**) in positive sentences and **any** (also **anybody,** etc.) in negative sentences (but see also Sections C and D). Compare:

some	any
■ We bought **some** flowers.	■ We didn't buy **any** flowers.
■ He's busy. He's got **some** work to do.	■ He's lazy. He **never** does **any** work.
■ There's **somebody** at the door.	■ There isn't **anybody** at the door.
■ I'm hungry. I want **something** to eat.	■ I'm not hungry. I don't want **anything** to eat.

We use **any** in the following sentences because the meaning is negative:
- ■ She went out **without any** money. (= She didn't take any money with her.)
- ■ He **refused** to eat **anything**. (= He didn't eat anything.)
- ■ **Hardly anybody** passed the examination. (= almost nobody passed)

B

In most questions we use **any**:
- ■ Do you have **any** luggage?
- ■ Has **anyone** seen my bag?

But we use **some** in questions when we expect the answer to be "yes":
- ■ What's wrong? Do you have **something** in your eye? (It seems like you have something in your eye, and I expect you to answer "yes.")

We use **some** in questions when we offer or ask for things:
- ■ Would you like **something** to eat?
- ■ Can I have **some** sugar, please?

C

We often use **any** after **if**:
- ■ **If** there are **any** letters for me, can you forward them to this address?
- ■ Let me know **if** you need **anything**.

The following sentences have the idea of **if**:
- ■ I'm sorry for **any** trouble I've caused. (= if I have caused any trouble)
- ■ **Anyone** who wants to take the exam should give me their name today. (= if there is anyone)

D

We also use **any** with the meaning "it doesn't matter which":
- ■ You can catch **any** bus. They all go downtown. (= it doesn't matter which bus you catch)
- ■ "Sing a song." "Which song should I sing?" "**Any** song. I don't care."
- ■ Come and see me **anytime** you want.
- ■ "Let's go out somewhere." "Where shall we go?" "**Anywhere**. It doesn't matter."
- ■ We left the door unlocked. **Anybody** could have come in.

Compare **something** and **anything**:
- ■ *A:* I'm hungry. I want **something** to eat.
  B: What would you like?
  A: I don't care. **Anything**. (= something, but it doesn't matter what)

E

Somebody/someone/anybody/anyone are *singular* words:
- ■ **Someone is** here to see you.

But we often use **they/them/their** after these words:
- ■ **Someone** has forgotten **their** umbrella. (= his or her umbrella)
- ■ If **anybody** wants to leave early, **they** can. (= he or she can)

No/none/any Unit 83   *Some of. . . / any of. . .* Unit 85   *Hardly any* Unit 98C

Exercises

82.1 Complete the sentences with *some* or *any*.

1. We didn't buy _any_ flowers.
2. I'm going out tonight with _____ friends of mine.
3. "Have you seen _____ good movies recently?" "No, I haven't been to the movies for ages."
4. I didn't have _____ money, so I had to borrow _____ .
5. Can I have _____ milk in my coffee, please?
6. I was too tired to do _____ work.
7. You can cash these traveler's checks at _____ bank.
8. Can you give me _____ information about places of interest in this area?
9. With the special tourist bus pass, you can travel on _____ bus you like.
10. If there are _____ words you don't understand, use a dictionary.

82.2 Complete the sentences with *some* or *any* + body/one/thing/where.

1. I was too surprised to say _anything_ .
2. There's _____ at the door. Can you go and see who it is?
3. Does _____ mind if I open the window?
4. I wasn't feeling hungry, so I didn't eat _____ .
5. You must be hungry. Would you like _____ to eat?
6. Quick, let's go! There's _____ coming, and I don't want _____ to see us.
7. Sarah was upset about _____ and refused to talk to _____ .
8. This machine is very easy to use. _____ can learn to use it in a very short time.
9. There was hardly _____ on the beach. It was almost deserted.
10. "Do you live _____ near Jim?" "No, he lives in another part of town."
11. "Where do you want to go on vacation?" "Let's go _____ warm and sunny."
12. They stay at home all the time. They never seem to go _____ .
13. I'm going out. If _____ calls while I'm out, tell them I'll be back at 11:30.
14. Why are you looking under the bed? Have you lost _____ ?
15. _____ who saw the accident should contact the police.
16. Sue is very secretive. She never tells _____ _____ . *(2 words)*

82.3 Complete the sentences. Use *any* + noun or *anybody/anyone/anything/anywhere*.

1. Which bus do I have to catch?	_Any bus._ They all go downtown.
2. Which day should I come?	It doesn't matter. _____
3. What do you want to eat?	_____ I don't care. Whatever you have.
4. Where should I sit?	It's up to you. You can sit _____ you like.
5. What kind of job are you looking for?	_____ It doesn't matter.
6. What time should I call tomorrow?	_____ I'll be home all day.
7. Who should I invite to the party?	I don't care. _____ you like.
8. Which newspaper should I buy?	_____ Whatever they have at the store.

No/none/any   Nothing/nobody, etc.

A   No and none

We use **no** + *noun*. **No** = **not a** or **not any**:
- We had to walk home because there was **no bus**. (= there wasn't **a** bus)
- I can't talk to you now. I have **no time**. (= I don't have **any** time)
- There were **no stores** open. (= There weren't **any** stores open.)

You can use **no** + *noun* at the beginning of a sentence:
- The plane was late. **No** reason was given for the delay.

We use **none** without a noun:
- "How much money do you have?" "**None.**" (= no money)
- All the tickets have been sold. There are **none** left. (= no tickets left)

Or we use **none of**:
- This money is all yours. **None of it** is mine.

After **none of** + *plural* (**none of the students**, **none of them**, etc.), the verb can be *plural* or *singular*:
- None of the **stores were** (*or* **was**) open.

B   Nothing   nobody / no one   nowhere

You can use these negative words at the beginning of a sentence or alone (as answers to questions):
- **Nobody** came to visit me while I was in the hospital.
- "What happened?" "**Nothing.**"
- "Where are you going?" "**Nowhere.** I'm staying here."

You can also use these words after a verb, especially after **be** and **have**:
- The house is empty. There's **no one** living there.
- We **had nothing** to eat.

Nothing/nobody, etc. = **not** + **anything/anybody**, etc.:
- I didn't say **anything**. (= I said **nothing**.)
- She didn't tell **anybody** about her plans. (= she told **nobody**)
- The station isn't **anywhere** near here. (= is **nowhere** near here)

When you use **nothing/nobody**, etc., do not use a negative verb (isn't, didn't, etc.):
- I **said nothing**. (*not* I didn't say nothing)
- **Nobody tells** me anything. (*not* Nobody doesn't tell)

C

We also use **any/anything/anybody**, etc. (*without* not), to mean "it doesn't matter which/what/who" (see Unit 82D). Compare **no-** and **any-**:
- There was **no** bus, so we walked home.
  You can catch **any** bus. They all go downtown. (= it doesn't matter which)
- "What do you want to eat?" "**Nothing.** I'm not hungry."
  I'm so hungry, I could eat **anything**. (= it doesn't matter what)
- The exam was extremely difficult. **Nobody** passed. (= everybody failed)
  The exam was very easy. **Anybody** could have passed. (= it doesn't matter who)

D

After **nobody / no one** you can use **they/them/their** (see also Unit 82E):
- **Nobody** called, did **they**? (= did he or she)
- The party was a disaster. **No one** enjoyed **themselves**. (= himself or herself)
- **No one** in the class did **their** homework. (= his or her homework)

Exercises

83.1 Complete these sentences with *no, none,* or *any.*

1. It was a holiday, so there were _no_ stores open.
2. I don't have _any_ money. Can you lend me some?
3. I couldn't make an omelette because there were _____ eggs.
4. I couldn't make an omelette because there weren't _____ eggs.
5. "How many eggs do we have?" "_____ . Should I go and buy some?"
6. We took a few pictures, but _____ of them were very good.
7. What a stupid thing to do! _____ intelligent person would do something like that.
8. I'll try and answer _____ questions you ask me.
9. I couldn't answer _____ of the questions they asked me.
10. We canceled the party because _____ of the people we invited were able to come.

83.2 Answer these questions using *none / nobody / no one / nothing / nowhere.*

1.	What did you do?	_Nothing._
2.	Where are you going?	_____
3.	How much luggage do you have?	_____
4.	How many children do they have?	_____
5.	Who were you talking to?	_____
6.	What do you want?	_____

Now answer the same questions using complete sentences with
any/anybody/anyone/anything/anywhere.

7. (1) _I didn't do anything._
8. (2) I _____ .
9. (3) _____
10. (4) _____
11. (5) _____
12. (6) _____

83.3 Complete these sentences with *no* or *any* + *body/one/thing/where.*

1. I don't want _anything_ to drink. I'm not thirsty.
2. The bus was completely empty. There was _____ on it.
3. "Where did you go for vacation?" "_____ . I stayed at home."
4. I went to the mall, but I didn't buy _____ .
5. "What did you buy?" "_____ . I couldn't find _____
   I wanted."
6. The town was still the same when I returned years later. _____ had
   changed.
7. Have you seen my watch? I've looked all over the house, but I can't find it
   _____ .
8. There was complete silence in the room. _____ said _____ .

83.4 Choose the right word.

1. She didn't tell ~~nobody~~ / anybody about her plans. (*anybody* is correct)
2. The accident looked serious, but fortunately no one / anyone was injured.
3. I looked out the window, but I couldn't see nobody / anybody.
4. My job is very easy. Nobody / Anybody could do it.
5. "What's in that box?" "Nothing. / Anything. It's empty."
6. The situation is uncertain. Nothing / Anything could happen.
7. I don't know nothing / anything about economics.

Much, many, little, few, a lot, plenty

A

We use **much** and **little** with *uncountable* nouns:

   much time   **much** luck   **little** energy   **little** money

We use **many** and **few** with *plural* nouns:

   many friends   **many** people   **few** cars   **few** countries

B

We use **a lot of / lots of / plenty of** with both uncountable and plural nouns:

   a lot of luck   **lots of** time   **plenty of** money
   a lot of friends   **lots of** people   **plenty of** ideas

Plenty = more than enough:

-   There's no need to hurry. We've got **plenty of** time.

C

Much is unusual in positive sentences (especially in spoken English). So we say:

-   We did**n't** spend **much** money. (negative)
-   Does he go out **much**? (question)

but
-   We spent **a lot of** money. (*not* We spent much money)
-   He goes out **a lot**. (*not* He goes out much)

We use **many, a lot (of)**, and **lots of** in all kinds of sentences:

-   Many people drive too fast.   *or*   **A lot of / Lots of** people drive too fast.
-   Do you know **many** people?   *or*   Do you know **a lot of / lots of** people?
-   He doesn't go out **a lot**.   *or*   He doesn't go out **much**.

D

Little and **few** (*without* a) are negative ideas (= not much / not many):

-   We had to make a quick decision. There was **little** time to think.
    (= not much time; not enough time)
-   Dave has **few** friends at the company now that Jason and Bruce have quit.
    (= not many friends; not enough friends)

We often say **very little** and **very few**:

-   There was **very little** time to think.
-   Dave has **very few** friends at the company.

A little and **a few** are more positive. **A little** = some, or a small amount:

-   Let's go and get something to drink. We've got **a little** time before the train leaves.
    (**a little time** = some time; enough time to have a drink)
-   "Do you speak English?" "**A little**." (so we can talk a bit)

A few = some, a small number:

-   I enjoy my life here. I have **a few** friends, and we get together pretty often. (a few
    friends = not many, but enough to have a good time)
-   "When was the last time you saw Claire?" "**A few** days ago." (= some days ago)

Compare:

-   He spoke **little** English, so it was hard to communicate with him.
    He spoke **a little** English, so we were able to communicate with him.
-   She's lucky. She has **few** problems. (= not many problems)
    Things are not going so well for her. She has **a few** problems. (= some problems)

Note that **only a little** and **only a few** have a negative meaning:

-   We have to hurry. We **only** have **a little** time.
-   The town was very small. There were **only a few** houses.

Countable and Uncountable Nouns Units 66–67   *Much (of) / many (of)* Unit 85

Exercises

84.1 In some of these sentences *much* is incorrect or unnatural. Change *much* to *many* or
a lot (of) where necessary.

1. We didn't spend much money.   *RIGHT*
2. Sue drinks much tea.   *a lot of tea*
3. Jim always puts much salt on his food.   _____
4. We'll have to hurry. We haven't got much time.   _____
5. Did it cost much to fix the car?   _____
6. It cost much to fix the car.   _____
7. I don't know much people in this town.   _____
8. I use the phone much at work.   _____

84.2 Complete the sentences using *plenty (of)* + one of the following:

> hotels   money   room   things to wear   ~~time~~   to learn

1. There's no need to hurry. _We've got plenty of time._
2. He doesn't have any financial problems. He has _____ .
3. Come and sit with us. There's _____ .
4. She knows a lot, but she still has _____ .
5. I'm sure we'll find a place to stay. There _____ .
6. She doesn't need to buy a new dress for the party. She has _____ .

84.3 Put in *much/many/few/little.*

1. He isn't very popular. He has very _few_ friends.
2. Ann is very busy these days. She has very _____ free time.
3. Did you take _____ pictures when you were on vacation?
4. I'm not very busy today. I don't have _____ to do.
5. Most of the town is modern. There are _____ old buildings.
6. The weather has been very dry recently. We've had very _____ rain.

84.4 Put in *a* where necessary.

1. She's lucky. She has <u>few problems</u>.   *RIGHT*
2. Things are not going so well for her. She has <u>few problems</u>.   *a few problems*
3. Can you lend me <u>few dollars</u>?   _____
4. I can't give you a decision yet. I need <u>little time</u> to think.   _____
5. There was <u>little traffic</u>, so the trip didn't take very long.   _____
6. It was a surprise that he won the match. <u>Few people</u>   _____
   expected him to win.
7. I don't know much Spanish – <u>only few words</u>.   _____

84.5 Put in *little / a little / few / a few.*

1. We have to hurry. We have _little_ time.
2. Listen carefully. I'm going to give you _____ advice.
3. Do you mind if I ask you _____ questions?
4. This town is not a very interesting place to visit, so _____ tourists
   come here.
5. I don't think Jill would be a good teacher. She has _____ patience.
6. "Would you like cream in your coffee?" "Yes, please. _____"
7. This is a very boring place to live. There's _____ to do.
8. "Have you ever been to Paris?" "Yes, I've been there _____ times."

All / all of, most / most of, no / none of, etc.

| all | most | some | any | much/many | little/few |

A

You can use the words in the box (and also **no**) with a noun (**some food / few books**, etc.):
- **All cars** have wheels.
- I don't go out very often. I stay home **most days.**
- **Some cars** can go faster than others.
- **Many people** drive too fast.
- *(on a sign)* **NO CARS** (= no cars allowed)

You cannot say "all of cars," "most of people," etc. (see also Section B):
- **Some people** are very unfriendly. (*not* some of people)

Note that we say **most** (*not* the most):
- **Most tourists** don't visit this part of town. (*not* the most tourists)

B

Some of . . . / most of . . . / none of . . . , etc.

You can use the words in the box (also **none** and **half**) with **of**. We use **some of / most of / none of**, etc., + **the/this/that/these/those/my**, etc. For example:
- **Some of the** people I work with are very friendly.
- **None of this** money is mine.
- Have you read **any of these** books?
- I was sick yesterday. I spent **most of the** day in bed.

You don't need **of** after **all** or **half**. So you can say:
- **All** my friends live in Los Angeles.   *or*   **All of** my friends . . .
- **Half** this money is mine.   *or*   **Half of** this money . . .

Compare these sentences:
- **All flowers** are beautiful. (= all flowers in general)
  All (of) the flowers in this garden are beautiful. (= a particular group of flowers)
- **Most problems** have a solution. (= most problems in general)
  We were able to solve **most of the problems we had.** (= a particular group of problems)

C

You can use **all of / some of / none of**, etc. + **it/us/you/them:**
- "How many of these people do you know?" "**None of them.**" / "**A few of them.**"
- Do **any of you** want to come to a party tonight?
- "Do you like this music?" "**Some of it. Not all of it.**"

Before **it/us/you/them** you need **of** after **all** and **half** (**all of, half of**):
    all of us (*not* all us)   **half of them** (*not* half them)

D

You can use the words in the box (and also **none**) alone, without a noun:
- **Some cars** have four doors, and **some** have two.
- A few of the shops were open, but **most** (of them) were closed.
- **Half** (of) this money is mine, and **half** (of it) is yours. (*not* the half)

Exercises

85.1 Put in *of* where necessary. Leave an empty space *(–)* if the sentence is already complete.

1. All —— cars have wheels.
2. None *of* this money is mine.
3. Some _____ movies are very violent.
4. Some _____ the movies I've seen recently have been very violent.
5. Joe never goes to museums. He says that all _____ museums are boring.
6. I think some _____ people watch too much television.
7. Are any _____ those letters for me?
8. Maria has lived in New York most _____ her life.
9. Jim has lived in Chicago all _____ his life.
10. Most days I get up before 7 o'clock.

85.2 Choose from the list and complete the sentences. Use *of* (*some of / most of,* etc.) where necessary.

accidents	her friends	my dinner	the buildings
birds	her opinions	my spare time	the population
~~cars~~	large cities	my teammates	~~these books~~

1. I haven't read many *of these books* .
2. All *cars* _____ have wheels.
3. I spend much _____ gardening.
4. Many _____ are caused by bad driving.
5. It's a historic town. Many _____ are over 400 years old.
6. When she got married she kept it a secret. She didn't tell any

   _____ .
7. Not many people live in the north of the country. Most
   _____ lives in the south.
8. Not all _____ can fly. For example the penguin can't fly.
9. Our team played badly and lost the game. None _____ played well.
10. Julia and I have very different ideas. I don't agree with many _____ .
11. New York, like most _____ has a traffic problem.
12. I had no appetite. I could only eat half _____ .

85.3 Use your own ideas to complete the sentences.

1. The building was damaged in the explosion. All the *the windows* _____ were broken.
2. We had a relaxing vacation. We spent most of _____ on the beach.
3. I went to the movies by myself. None of _____ wanted to come.
4. The test was difficult. I could only answer half _____ .
5. Some of _____ you took at the wedding were very good.
6. "Have you spent all _____ I gave you?" "No there's still some left."

85.4 Complete the sentences. Use *all of / some of / none of* + *it/them/us* (*all of it / some of them,* etc.).

1. These books are all Jane's. *None of them* belong to me.
2. "How many of these books have you read?" "_____ . Every one."
3. We all got wet in the rain because _____ had an umbrella.
4. Some of this money is yours, and _____ is mine.
5. I asked some people for directions, but _____ were able to help me.
6. She invented the whole story from beginning to end. _____ was true.
7. Not all the tourists in the group were American. _____ were Japanese.
8. I watched most of the movie, but not _____ .

Both / both of, neither / neither of, either / either of

A

We use **both/neither/either** for two things. You can use these words with a noun (**both books, neither book,** etc.).

For example, you are talking about two restaurants:
- **Both restaurants** are very good. (*not* the both restaurants)
- **Neither restaurant** is expensive.
- We can go to **either restaurant**. I don't care. (= one or the other, it doesn't matter which one)

B

Both of / neither of / either of

We use **both of / neither of / either of** + **the/these/my/Tom's** . . . , etc. So we say **both of the** restaurants, **both of those** restaurants, etc., but not "both of restaurants":
- **Both of these** restaurants are very good.
- **Neither of the** restaurants we went to was (*or* were) expensive.
- I haven't been to **either of those** restaurants. (= I haven't been to one or the other)

You don't need **of** after **both.** So you can say:
- **Both** my parents are from Michigan. *or* **Both of** my parents . . .

You can use **both of / neither of / either of** + **us/you/them:**
- *(talking to two people)* Can **either of you** speak Spanish?
- I asked two people the way to the station, but **neither of them** knew.

You must say "both **of**" before **us/you/them** (**of** is necessary):
- **Both of us** were very tired. (*not* Both us were . . .)

After **neither of,** a *singular* or a *plural* verb is possible:
- **Neither of** the children **wants** (*or* **want**) to go to bed.

C

You can also use **both/neither/either** alone:
- I couldn't decide which of the two shirts to buy. I liked **both.** (*or* I liked **both of** them.)
- "Is your friend British or American?" "**Neither.** She's Australian."
- "Do you want tea or coffee?" "**Either.** I don't care."

D

You can say:

both . . . and . . . :	■ **Both** Ann **and** Tom were late.
	■ I was **both** tired **and** hungry when I got home.
neither . . . nor . . . :	■ **Neither** Liz **nor** Robin came to the party.
	■ She said she would contact me, but she **neither** wrote **nor** called.
either . . . or . . . :	■ I'm not sure where he's from. He's **either** Spanish **or** Italian.
	■ **Either** you apologize, **or** I'll never speak to you again.

E

Compare **either/neither/both** (two things) and **any/none/all** (more than two):

■ There are **two** good hotels in the town. You can stay at **either** of them.	■ There are **many** good hotels in the town. You can stay at **any** of them.
■ We tried **two** hotels. **Neither** of them had any rooms. / **Both** of them were full.	■ We tried **a lot of** hotels. **None** of them had any rooms. / **All** of them were full.

Neither do I / I don't either Unit 48C   *Both of whom / neither of which* Unit 93B   *Both* Unit 106C

Exercises

86.1 Complete the sentences with *both/neither/either*.

1. "Do you want tea or coffee?" " _Either._ It really doesn't matter."
2. "What's today's date – the 18th or the 19th?" " _____ . It's the 20th."
3. A: Where did you go for your vacation – Florida or Puerto Rico?
   B: We went to _____ . A week in Florida and a week in Puerto Rico.
4. "When should I call you, morning or afternoon?" " _____ . I'll be home all day."
5. "Where's Kate? Is she at work or at home?" " _____ . She's out of town."

86.2 Complete the sentences with *both/neither/either*. Use *of* where necessary.

1. _Both_ my parents are from Michigan.
2. To get downtown, you can take the city streets or you can take the freeway. You can go _____ way.
3. I tried to call George twice, but _____ times he was out.
4. _____ Tom's parents is American. His father is Polish, and his mother is Italian.
5. I saw an accident this morning. One car drove into the back of another. Fortunately _____ driver was injured, but _____ cars were badly damaged.
6. I have two sisters and a brother. My brother is working, but _____ my sisters are still in school.

86.3 Complete the sentences with *both/neither/either of + us/them*.

1. I asked two people the way to the airport, but _neither of them_ could help me.
2. I was invited to two parties last week, but I didn't go to _____ .
3. There were two windows in the room. It was very warm, so I opened _____ .
4. Sarah and I play tennis together regularly, but _____ can play very well.
5. I tried two bookstores for the book I wanted, but _____ had it.

86.4 Write sentences with *both . . . and . . . / neither . . . nor . . . / either . . . or . . . .*

1. She didn't write, and she didn't call. _She neither wrote nor called._
2. Jim is on vacation, and so is Carol. _____
3. Brian doesn't smoke, and he doesn't drink. _____
4. It was a very boring movie. It was very long, too.
   The movie _____ .
5. Is that man's name Richard? Or is it Robert? It's one of the two.
   That man's name _____ .
6. I don't have the time to go on vacation. And I don't have the money.
   I have _____ .
7. We can leave today, or we can leave tomorrow – whichever you prefer.
   We _____ .

86.5 Complete the sentences with *neither/either/none/any*.

1. We tried a lot of hotels, but _none_ of them had any rooms.
2. I took two books with me on vacation, but I didn't read _____ of them.
3. I took five books with me on vacation, but I didn't read _____ of them.
4. There are a few stores in the next block, but _____ of them sell newspapers.
5. You can call me at _____ time during the evening. I'm always at home.
6. I can meet you on the 6th or the 7th. Would _____ of those days be convenient for you?
7. John and I couldn't get into the house because _____ of us had a key.
8. A few letters came this morning, but _____ of them were for me.

All, every, and whole

A

All and **everybody/everyone**

We do not normally use **all** to mean **everybody/everyone**:

- **Everybody** enjoyed the party. (*not* All enjoyed)

But note that we say **all of us/you/them**, not "everybody of . . .":

- **All of us** enjoyed the party. (*not* everybody of us)

B

All and **everything**

Sometimes you can use **all** or **everything**:

- I'll do **all** I can to help. *or* I'll do **everything** I can to help.

You can say **all I can / all you need**, etc., but we do not normally use **all** alone:

- He thinks he knows **everything**. (*not* he knows all)
- Our vacation was a disaster. **Everything** went wrong. (*not* All went wrong)

We use **all** in the expression **all about**:

- They told us **all about** their vacation.

We also use **all** (*not* everything) to mean *the only thing(s)*:

- **All** I've eaten today is a sandwich. (= the only thing I've eaten today)

C

Every/everybody/everyone/everything are *singular* words, so we use a *singular* verb:

- **Every seat** in the theater **was** taken.   ■ **Everyone has** arrived. (*not* have arrived)

But we often use **they/them/their** after **everybody/everyone**:

- **Everybody** said **they** enjoyed **themselves**. (= he or she enjoyed himself or herself)

D

Whole

Whole = complete, entire. Most often we use **whole** with singular nouns:

- Did you read the **whole book?** (= all of the book, not just a part of it)
- She has lived her **whole life** in Chile.
- Jack was so hungry, he ate a **whole package** of cookies. (= a complete package)

We do not normally use **whole** with *uncountable* nouns. We say:

- I've spent **all the money** you gave me. (*not* the whole money)

E

Every/all/whole with time words

We use **every** to say how often something happens. So we say **every day / every Monday / every ten minutes / every three weeks**, etc.:

- When we were on vacation, we went to the beach **every day**. (*not* all days)
- The bus service is very good. There's a bus **every ten minutes**.
- Ann gets paid **every two weeks**.

All day / the whole day = the complete day from beginning to end:

- We spent **all day / the whole day** on the beach.
- He was very quiet. He didn't say a word **all night / the whole night**.

Note that we say **all day** (*not* all the day), **all week** (*not* all the week), etc.

Compare **all the time** and **every time**:

- They never go out. They are at home **all the time**. (= always)
- **Every time** I see you, you look different. (= each time, on every occasion)

Exercises

87.1 Complete these sentences with *all, everything,* or *everybody/everyone.*

1. It was a good party. *Everyone* _____ enjoyed it.
2. *All* _____ I've eaten today is a sandwich.
3. _____ has their faults. Nobody is perfect.
4. Nothing has changed. _____ is the same as it was.
5. Kate told me _____ about her new job. It sounds very interesting.
6. Can _____ write their names on a piece of paper, please?
7. Why are you always thinking about money? Money isn't _____ .
8. I didn't have much money with me. _____ I had was ten dollars.
9. When the fire alarm rang, _____ left the building immediately.
10. We all did well on the exam. _____ in our class passed.
11. We all did well on the exam. _____ of us passed.
12. Why are you so lazy? Why do you expect me to do _____ for you?

87.2 Write sentences with *whole.*

1. I read the book from beginning to end. *I read the whole book.*
2. Everyone on the team played well. The _____ .
3. Paul opened a box of chocolates. When he finished eating, there were no chocolates left in the box. He ate _____ .
4. The police came to the house. They were looking for something. They searched everywhere, in every room. They _____ .
5. Everyone in Dave and Kelly's family plays tennis. Dave and Kelly play, and so do all their children. The _____ .
6. Ann worked from early in the morning until late at night.
   Ann _____ .
7. Jack and Lisa went on vacation to the beach for a week. It rained from the beginning of the week to the end. It _____ .

Now write sentences 6 and 7 again using *all* instead of *whole.*

8. (6) Ann _____ .
9. (7) _____

87.3 Complete these sentences using *every* with one of the following:

   five minutes   ~~ten minutes~~   **four hours**   **six months**   **four years**

1. The bus service is very good. There's a bus *every ten minutes* .
2. Tom is sick. He has some medicine. He has to take it _____ .
3. The Olympic Games take place _____ .
4. We live near a busy airport. A plane flies over our house _____ .
5. It's a good idea to have a checkup with the dentist _____ .

87.4 Which is the correct alternative?

1. I spent ~~the whole money~~ / all the money you gave me. (*all the money* is correct)
2. Sue works every day / all days except Sunday.
3. I'm tired. I've been working hard all the day / all day.
4. It was a terrible fire. Whole building / The whole building was destroyed.
5. I've been trying to call her, but every time / all the time I call, the line is busy.
6. I don't like the weather here. It rains every time / all the time.
7. When I was on vacation, all my luggage / my whole luggage was stolen.

Each and *every*

Each and **every** are similar in meaning. Often it is possible to use **each** or **every**:

- **Each** time (*or* **every** time) I see you, you look different.

But **each** and **every** are not exactly the same. Study the difference:

We use **each** when we think of things separately, one by one.	We use **every** when we think of things as a group. The meaning is similar to **all**.

■ Study **each sentence** carefully.
   (= study the sentences one by one)
	■ **Every sentence** must have a verb.
	   (= all sentences in general)

each = **✗** + **✗** + **✗** + **✗**	every = 
Each is more usual for a small number:	**Every** is more usual for a large number:
■ There were four books on the table. **Each book** was a different color. ■ *(in a card game)* At the beginning of the game, **each player** has three cards.	■ Carol loves reading. She has read **every book** in the library. (= all the books) ■ I would like to visit **every country** in the world. (= all the countries)

Each (*but not* every) can be used for two things:

- In a soccer game, **each team** has 11 players. (*not* every team)

We use **every** (*not* each) to say how often something happens:

- "How often do you go shopping?" "**Every day.**" (*not* each day)
- There's a bus **every ten minutes**.

Compare the structures we use with **each** and **every**:

You can use **each** with a noun:
   each book   **each student**
	You can use **every** with a noun:
	   every book **every student**

You can use **each** alone (without a noun): ■ None of the rooms were the same. **Each** was different. (= each room)	You can say **every one** (*but not* every alone): ■ "Have you read all these books?" "Yes, **every one.**"
Or you can use **each one**: ■ **Each one** was different.	
You can say **each of** (**the/these . . .** , etc.):	You can say **every one of . . .** :
■ Read **each of these** sentences carefully. ■ **Each of the** books is a different color. ■ **Each of them** is a different color.	■ I've read **every one of those** books. (*not* every of those books) ■ I've read **every one of them**.

You can also use **each** in the middle or at the end of a sentence. For example:

- The students were **each** given a book. (= Each student was given a book.)
- These oranges cost 50 cents **each**.

Everyone and **every one**

Everyone (one word) is only for people (= everybody). **Every one** (two words) is for things or people and is similar to **each one** (see Section B):

- **Everyone** enjoyed the party. (= Everybody . . .)
- He is invited to lots of parties, and he goes to **every one**. (= to every party)

Each other **Unit 79C**   ***All and every*** **Unit 87**

Exercises

88.1 Look at the pictures and complete the sentences with *each* or *every*.

1	2	3	4
		2.5 / 2.5 / 2.5 / 2.5	

5	6	7	8
	TRAINS TO THE CITY		GAMES PLAYED 24 WON 24 LOST 0

1. *Each* player has three cards.
2. Chris has read *every* book in the library.
3. _____ side of a square is the same length.
4. _____ seat in the theater was taken.
5. _____ apartment has a balcony.
6. There's a train to the city _____ hour.
7. She was wearing five rings – one on _____ finger.
8. Our soccer team has been very successful. We've won _____ game this season.

88.2 Put in *each/every/everyone*.

1. There were four books on the table. *Each* book was a different color.
2. It was a great party. *Everyone* enjoyed it.
3. _____ parent worries about their children.
4. In a game of tennis there are two or four players. _____ player has a racquet.
5. Nicole plays volleyball _____ Thursday evening.
6. As soon as _____ had arrived, we began the meeting.
7. I understood most of what they said, but not _____ word.
8. The book is divided into five parts, and _____ of these has three sections.
9. I get paid _____ two weeks.
10. We had a great weekend. I enjoyed _____ minute of it.
11. I tried to call her two or three times, but _____ time there was no reply.
12. She's very popular. _____ likes her.
13. Seat belts in cars save lives. _____ driver should wear one.
14. *(from an exam)* Answer all five questions. Write your answer to _____ question on a separate sheet of paper.

88.3 Complete the sentences using *each*.

1. The price of one of those oranges is 50 cents. Those *oranges are 50 cents each* .
2. I had ten dollars and so did Sonia. Sonia and I _____ .
3. One of those postcards costs 40 cents. Those _____ .
4. The hotel was expensive. I paid $195 and so did you. We _____ .

Relative Clauses (1) – Clauses With *who/that/which*

A

Look at this example sentence:

The woman who lives next door is a doctor.
└─ *relative clause* ─┘

A *clause* is a part of a sentence. A *relative clause* tells us which person or thing (or what kind of person or thing) the speaker means:

- The woman **who lives next door . . .** ("who lives next door" tells us which woman)
- People **who live in London . . .** ("who live in London" tells us what kind of people)

We use **who** in a relative clause when we are talking about people (not things). We use **who** instead of **he/she/they:**

the woman – she lives next door – is a doctor
↓
→ The woman **who** lives next door is a doctor.

we know a lot of people – they live in London
↓
→ We know a lot of people **who** live in London.

- An architect is someone **who designs buildings.**
- What was the name of the man **who lent you the money?**
- Anyone **who is interested in the job** must apply before next Friday.

You can also use **that** (instead of **who**):

- The man **that lives next door** is very friendly.

But sometimes you must use **who** (*not* that) for people – see Unit 92.

B

When we are talking about things, we use **that** or **which** (*not* who) in a relative clause:

where is the cheese? – it was in the refrigerator
↓
→ Where is the cheese $\left\{ \begin{array}{l} \text{that} \\ \text{which} \end{array} \right\}$ was in the refrigerator?

- I don't like stories **that have unhappy endings.** (*or* stories **which** have)
- Barbara works for a company **that makes washing machines.**
  (*or* a company **which** makes)
- The machine **that broke down** has now been repaired.
  (*or* The machine **which** broke down)

That is more usual than **which.** But sometimes you must use **which** (*not* that) – see Unit 92.

C

You cannot use **what** in sentences like these:

- Everything **that happened** was my fault. (*not* Everything what happened)

What = the thing(s) that:

- **What** happened was my fault. (= the thing that happened)

Exercises

89.1 In this exercise you have to explain what some words mean. Choose the right meaning from the box and then write a sentence with *who.* Use a dictionary if necessary.

he/she	steals from a store ~~designs buildings~~ doesn't believe in God is not brave	he/she	buys something from a store pays rent to live in a house or an apartment breaks into a house to steal things

1. (an architect) *An architect is someone who designs buildings.*
2. (a burglar) A burglar is someone _____ .
3. (a customer) _____
4. (a shoplifter) _____
5. (a coward) _____
6. (an atheist) _____
7. (a tenant) _____

89.2 Make one sentence from two. Use *who/that/which.*

1. A girl was injured in the accident. She is now in the hospital.
   The girl who was injured in the accident is now in the hospital.
2. A man answered the phone. He told me you were away.
   The man _____ .
3. A waitress served us. She was very impolite and impatient.
   The _____ .
4. A building was destroyed in the fire. It has now been rebuilt.
   _____
5. Some people were arrested. They have now been released.
   The _____ .
6. A bus goes to the airport. It runs every half hour.
   _____

89.3 Complete the sentences. Choose the most appropriate ending from the box and make it into a relative clause.

he invented the telephone	~~it makes washing machines~~
she runs away from home	it gives you the meanings of words
they are never on time	it won the race
they stole my car	it can support life
they were on the wall	it cannot be explained

1. Barbara works for a company *that makes washing machines* .
2. The book is about a girl _____ .
3. What was the name of the horse _____ ?
4. The police have caught the men _____ .
5. Alexander Graham Bell was the man _____ .
6. What happened to the pictures _____ ?
7. A mystery is something _____ .
8. A dictionary is a book _____ .
9. I don't like people _____ .
10. It seems that Earth is the only planet _____ .

UNIT 90

Relative Clauses (2) – Clauses With or Without *who/that/which*

A

Look again at these example sentences from Unit 89:

- The woman who **lives next door** is a doctor. (*or* The woman **that** lives)

    The woman lives next door.   who (= the woman) is the *subject*

- Where is the cheese **that** **was in the refrigerator**? (*or* the cheese **which** was)

    The cheese was in the refrigerator.   **that** (= the cheese) is the *subject*

You must use **who/that/which** when it is the subject of the relative clause. You cannot say
"The woman lives next door is a doctor" or "Where is the cheese was in the refrigerator?"

B

Sometimes **who/that/which** is the *object* of the verb. For example:

- The woman who **I wanted to see** was away on vacation.

    I wanted to see the woman .   who (= the woman) is the *object*
                                    I is the *subject*

- Have you found the keys **(that)** **you lost?**

    You lost the keys .   **that** (= the keys) is the *object*
                          you is the *subject*

When **who/that/which** is the object, you can leave it out. So you can say:
- **The woman I wanted to see** was away.   *or* The woman **who** I wanted to see . . .
- Have you found **the keys you lost?**   *or* . . . the keys **that** you lost?
- **The dress Ann bought** doesn't fit her very well. *or* The dress **that** Ann bought . . .
- Is there anything **I can do?**   *or* . . . anything **that** I can do?

C

Notice the position of prepositions (**in/at/with,** etc.) in relative clauses:

> do you know the woman? – Tom is talking to her
>
> → Do you know the woman (**who/that**) **Tom is talking** to ?
>
> the bed – I slept in it last night – wasn't very comfortable
>
> → The bed (**that/which**) I slept in **last night** wasn't very comfortable.

- Are these the keys (**that/which**) **you were looking for?**
- The woman (**who/that**) **he fell in love with** left him after a few weeks.
- The man (**who/that**) **I was sitting next to on the plane** talked all the time.

In all these examples, you can leave out **who/that/which.**

D

You cannot use **what** in sentences like these:
- Everything (**that**) **they said** was true. (*not* Everything what they said)
- I gave her all the money (**that**) **I had.** (*not* all the money what I had)

What = the thing(s) that:
- Did you hear **what they said?** (= the things that they said)

Exercises

90.1 In some of these sentences you don't need *who* or *that*. If you don't need these words, put them in parentheses like this: *(who) (that).*

1. The woman **who** lives next door is a doctor. (*who* is necessary in this sentence)
2. Have you found the keys (**that**) you lost? (in this sentence you don't need *that*)
3. The people **who** we met at the party were very friendly.
4. The people **who** work in the office are very friendly.
5. The people **who** I talked to were very friendly.
6. What have you done with the money **that** I gave you?
7. What happened to the money **that** was on the table? Did you take it?
8. It was an awful movie. It was the worst movie **that** I've ever seen.
9. It was an awful experience. It was the worst thing **that** has ever happened to me.

90.2 Complete these sentences with a relative clause. Use the sentences in the box to make your relative clauses.

Ann is wearing a dress	you're going to see a movie	we wanted to visit a museum
~~you lost some keys~~	you had to do some work	I invited some people to the party

1. Have you found the keys *you lost* _____ ?
2. I like the dress _____ .
3. The museum _____ was closed when we got there.
4. What's the name of the movie _____ ?
5. Some of the people _____ couldn't come.
6. Have you finished the work _____ ?

90.3 Complete these sentences using a relative clause with a preposition.

we went to a party last night	you can rely on Brian	we were invited to a wedding
I work with a number of people	I applied for a job	you told me about a hotel
~~you were looking for some keys~~	I saw you with a man	

1. Are these the keys *you were looking for* ?
2. Unfortunately, we couldn't go to the wedding _____ .
3. I enjoy my job. I like the people _____ .
4. What's the name of that hotel _____ ?
5. The party _____ wasn't very much fun.
6. I didn't get the job _____ .
7. Brian is a good person to know. He's somebody _____ .
8. Who was that man _____ in the restaurant?

90.4 Put in *that* or *what*. If the sentence is complete with or without *that*, write *(that)* in parentheses.

1. I gave her all the money *(that)* _____ I had.
2. They give their children everything _____ they want.
3. Tell me _____ you want, and I'll try to get it for you.
4. Why do you blame me for everything _____ goes wrong?
5. I won't be able to do much, but I'll do the best _____ I can.
6. I can only lend you ten dollars. It's all _____ I've got.
7. I don't agree with _____ you've just said.
8. I don't trust him. I don't believe anything _____ he says.

Relative Clauses (3) – *whose/whom/where*

A   Whose

We use **whose** in *relative clauses* instead of **his/her/their**:

> we saw some people – their car had broken down
>
> → We saw some people **whose car had broken down.**

We use **whose** mostly for people:

- A widow is a woman **whose husband is dead.** (**her** husband is dead)
- I met someone **whose brother I went to school with.** (I went to school with **his/her** brother)

Compare **who** and **whose**:

- I met a man **who** knows you. (**he** knows you)
- I met a man **whose sister** knows you. (**his sister** knows you)

B   Whom

Whom is possible instead of **who** when it is the *object* of the *verb* in the relative clause (see Unit 90B):

- The woman **whom I wanted to see** was away on vacation. (I wanted to see **her**)

You can also use **whom** with a preposition (**to whom / from whom / with whom,** etc.):

- The woman **with whom he fell in love** left him after a few weeks. (he fell in love **with her**)

But we do not often use **whom** in spoken English. We usually prefer **who** or **that**, or nothing (see Unit 90). So we usually say:

- The man **I saw** . . . *or* The man **who/that** I saw . . .

For **whom**, see also Units 92–93.

C   Where

You can use **where** in a relative clause to talk about a place:

> the hotel – we stayed there – wasn't very clean
>
> → The hotel **where we stayed** wasn't very clean.

- I recently went back to the town **where I was born.** (*or* . . . the town **I was born in** *or* . . . the town **that** I was born in)
- I would like to live in a country **where there is plenty of sunshine.**

D

We say: **the day / the year / the time** (etc.) { something happens *or*
                                                   that something happens

- Do you still remember **the day (that) we first met?**
- **The last time (that) I saw her,** she looked fine.
- I haven't seen them since **the year (that) they got married.**

E

We say: **the reason** { something happens *or*
                         that/why something happens

- **The reason I'm calling you** is to invite you to a party.
  (*or* The reason **that** I'm calling . . . / The reason **why** I'm calling . . .)

Exercises

91.1 You met these people at a party:

1	My mother writes detective stories.	2	My wife is an English teacher.	3	I own a restaurant.

4	My ambition is to climb Mt. Everest.	5	We just got married.	6	My parents used to work in a circus.

Later you tell a friend about these people. Complete the sentences using *who* or *whose*.

1. I met somebody *whose mother writes detective stories* .
2. I met a man _____ .
3. I met a woman _____ .
4. I met somebody _____ .
5. I met a couple _____ .
6. I met somebody _____ .

91.2 Complete the sentences. Use the sentences in the box to make relative clauses with *where*.

I can buy some postcards there	I was born there
Ann bought a dress there	we can have a really good meal there
John is staying there	we had the car repaired there

1. I recently went back to the town *where I was born* .
2. Do you know a restaurant _____ ?
3. Is there someplace near here _____ ?
4. I can't remember the name of the garage _____ .
5. Do you know the name of the hotel _____ ?
6. Ann bought a dress that didn't fit her, so she took it back to the store

   _____ .

91.3 Complete each sentence using *who/whom/whose/where*.

1. What's the name of the man *whose* car you borrowed?
2. A cemetery is a place _____ people are buried.
3. A pacifist is a person _____ believes that all wars are wrong.
4. An orphan is a child _____ parents are dead.
5. The place _____ we spent our vacation was really beautiful.
6. This school is only for children _____ first language is not English.
7. I don't know the name of the woman to _____ I spoke on the phone.

91.4 Use your own ideas to complete these sentences. They are like the sentences in Sections D and E.

1. I'll always remember the day *I first met you* .
2. I'll never forget the time _____ .
3. The reason _____ was that I didn't know your address.
4. Unfortunately, I wasn't at home the evening _____ .
5. The reason _____ is that they don't need one.

183

Relative Clauses (4) – "Extra Information" Clauses (1)

There are two types of *relative clauses*. In these examples, the relative clauses are underlined:

Type 1

- The woman <u>who lives next door</u> is a doctor.
- Barbara works for a company <u>that makes washing machines</u>.
- We stayed at the hotel <u>(that) Ann recommended to us</u>.

In these examples, the relative clause tells you which person or thing (or what kind of person or thing) the speaker means:

"The woman **who lives next door**" tells us *which* woman.
"A company **that makes washing machines**" tells us *what kind of* company.
"The hotel **(that) Ann recommended**" tells us *which* hotel.

We do not use commas (,) with these clauses:

- People <u>who come from</u> Texas love football.

Type 2

- My brother Jim, <u>who lives in Houston</u>, is a doctor.
- Brad told me about his new job, <u>which he's enjoying very much</u>.
- We stayed at the Grand Hotel, <u>which Ann recommended to us</u>.

In these examples, the relative clauses do not tell you which person or thing the speaker means. We already know which thing or person is meant: "My brother Jim," "Brad's new job," and "the Grand Hotel."

The relative clauses in these sentences give us *extra information* about the person or thing.

We use commas (,) with these clauses:

- My English teacher, <u>who comes from Texas</u>, loves computers.

In both types of relative clauses, we use **who** for people and **which** for things. But:

Type 1
You can use **that**:

- Do you know anyone **who/that** speaks French and Italian?
- Barbara works for a company **that/which** makes washing machines.

You can leave out **that/who/which** when it is the object (see Unit 90):

- We stayed at the hotel (**that/which**) Ann recommended.
- This morning I met somebody (**who/that**) I hadn't seen for ages.

Whom is unusual in this type of clause.

Type 2
You cannot use **that**:

- John, **who** (*not* that) speaks French and Italian, works as a tourist guide.
- Brad told me about his new job, **which** (*not* that) he's enjoying very much.

You cannot leave out **who** or **which**:

- We stayed at the Grand Hotel, **which** Ann recommended to us.

You can use **whom** (when it is the object):

- This morning I met Diane, **whom** (*or* who) I hadn't seen for ages.

In both types of relative clause you can use **whose** and **where**:

- We met some people **whose** car had broken down.
- What's the name of the place **where** you spent your vacation?

- Amy, **whose** car had broken down, was in a very bad mood.
- Mrs. Bond is going to spend a few weeks in Sweden, **where** her daughter lives.

Relative Clauses (Type 1) Units 89–91   Relative Clauses (Type 2) Unit 93

Exercises

92.1 Make one sentence from two. Use the sentence in parentheses to make a relative clause (Type 2). You will need to use *who(m)/whose/which/where.*

1. Ann is very friendly. (She lives next door.)
   Ann, who lives next door, is very friendly.
2. We stayed at the Grand Hotel. (Ann recommended it to us.)
   We stayed at the Grand Hotel, which Ann recommended to us.
3. We went to Sandra's party. (We enjoyed it very much.)
   We went to Sandra's party, _____.
4. I went to see the doctor. (He told me to rest for a few days.)
   _____
5. John is one of my closest friends. (I have known him for a very long time.)
   John, _____.
6. Sheila is away from home a lot. (Her job involves a lot of traveling.)
   _____
7. The new stadium will be opened next month. (It can hold 90,000 people.)
   The _____.
8. Alaska is the largest state in the United States. (My brother lives there.)
   _____

92.2 Read the information and complete the sentences. Use a relative clause of Type 1 or Type 2. Use commas (,) where necessary.

1. There's a woman living next door. She's a doctor.
   The woman *who lives next door is a doctor*.
2. I have a brother named Jim. He lives in Houston. He's a doctor.
   My brother Jim, *who lives in Houston, is a doctor*.
3. There was a strike at the car factory. It lasted ten days. It is now over.
   The strike at the car factory _____.
4. I was looking for a book this morning. I've found it now.
   I've found _____.
5. London was once the largest city in the world, but the population is now decreasing.
   The population of London _____.
6. A job was advertised. A lot of people applied for it. Few of them had the necessary qualifications. Few of _____.
7. Amanda has a son. She showed me a picture of him. He's a police officer.
   Amanda showed me _____.

92.3 In some of these sentences you can use *that* or *which;* in others, only *which* is possible. Cross out *that* if only *which* is possible. Also, put commas (,) where necessary.

1. Jane works for a company ✓that / ✓which makes shoes. (both possible, no commas)
2. Brad told me about his new job , ~~that~~ / which he's enjoying very much. (only *which* is possible; comma necessary)
3. My office that / which is on the second floor of the building is very small.
4. The office that / which I'm using at the moment is very small.
5. She told me her address that / which I wrote down on a piece of paper.
6. There are some words that / which are very difficult to translate.
7. The sun that / which is one of millions of stars in the universe provides us with heat and light.

Relative Clauses (5) – "Extra Information" Clauses (2)

A

Prepositions + **whom/which**

In "extra information" clauses (see Unit 92 – Type 2), you can use a *preposition* before **whom** (for people) and **which** (for things). So you can say:

to whom / with whom / about which / for which, etc.:

- ■ Mr. Carter, **to whom** I spoke on the phone last night, is very interested in our plan.
- ■ Fortunately we had a map, **without which** we would have gotten lost.

In spoken English we often keep the preposition after the verb in the relative clause. When we do this, we normally use **who** (*not* whom) for people:

- ■ This is Mr. Carter, **who** I was telling you **about.**
- ■ Yesterday we visited the City Museum, **which** I'd never been **to** before.

B

All of / most of, etc. + **whom/which**

Study these examples:

> Mary has three brothers. All of them are married. *(2 sentences)*
>
> → Mary has three brothers, **all of whom** are married. *(1 sentence)*
>
> They asked me a lot of questions. I couldn't answer most of them . *(2 sentences)*
>
> → They asked me a lot of questions, **most of which** I couldn't answer. *(1 sentence)*

In the same way you can say:

none of / neither of / any of / either of
some of / many of / much of / (a) few of } + **whom** (people)
both of / half of / each of / one of / two of (etc.) } + **which** (things)

- ■ Tom tried on three jackets, **none of which** fit him.
- ■ Two men, **neither of whom** I had ever seen before, came into my office.
- ■ They have three cars, **two of which** they never use.
- ■ Sue has a lot of friends, **many of whom** she went to school with.

C

Which

Study this example:

> Jim passed his driving test. This surprised everybody. *(2 sentences)*
>
> Jim passed his driving test, **which** surprised everybody. *(1 sentence)*
> ———— *relative clause* ————

In this example, **which** = the fact that he passed his driving test. You must use **which** (*not* what) in sentences like these:

- ■ Sheila couldn't come to the party, **which** was a shame. (*not* . . . what was a shame)
- ■ The weather was very good, **which** we hadn't expected. (*not* . . . what we hadn't expected)

For **what,** see also Units 89C and 90D.

All of / none of, etc. Unit 85   *Both of,* etc. Unit 86   **Relative Clauses** Units 89–92

Exercises

93.1 Make two sentences from one. Use the sentence in parentheses to make the relative clause.

1. Mr. Carter is very interested in our plan. (I spoke to him on the phone last night.)
   Mr. Carter, to whom I spoke on the phone last night, is very interested in our plan.
2. This is a picture of our friends. (We went on vacation with these friends.)
   This is a picture _____.
3. The wedding took place last Friday. (Only members of the family were invited to it.)
   The wedding, _____.
4. Sheila finally arrived. (We had been waiting for her.)
   _____
5. My room has a very large window. (You can see the whole lake.)
   _____

93.2 Write sentences with *all of / most of*, etc. + *whom/which*.

1. Mary has three brothers. (All of her brothers are married.)
   Mary has three brothers, all of whom are married.
2. We were given a lot of information. (Most of the information was useless.)
   We were given _____.
3. There were a lot of people at the party. (I had met only a few of these people before.)
   _____
4. I sent her two letters. (She has received neither of these letters.)
   _____
5. Ten people applied for the job. (None of these people were suitable.)
   _____
6. Kate has two cars. (She hardly ever uses one of them.)
   _____
7. Mike won $50,000. (He gave half of this to his parents.)
   _____
8. Julia has two sisters. (Both of her sisters are teachers.)
   _____

93.3 Join a sentence from Box A with a sentence from Box B to make a new sentence. Use *which*.

A	B
1. ~~Lauren couldn't come to the party.~~	This was very nice of her.
2. Jill doesn't have a phone.	This means we can't take our trip tomorrow.
3. Neil has passed his exams.	This makes it difficult to contact her.
4. Our flight was delayed.	This makes it difficult to sleep.
5. Ann offered to let me stay at her house.	~~This was a shame.~~
6. The street I live on is very noisy at night.	This is good news.
7. Our car has broken down.	This meant we had to wait four hours at the airport.

1. Lauren couldn't come to the party, *which was a shame* _____.
2. Jill doesn't _____.
3. _____
4. _____
5. _____
6. _____
7. _____

-ing and -ed Phrases (the woman talking to Tom, the boy injured in the accident)

A

Study these examples:

Do you know the woman **talking to Tom** ?
└ -ing *phrase* ┘

TOM

the woman
talking to Tom

The boy **injured in the accident** was taken to the hospital.
└──── -ed *phrase* ────┘

the boy injured
in the accident

B

We use -ing phrases to say what somebody (or something) is/was doing at a particular time:

- Do you know the woman **talking to Tom?** (the woman **is talking** to Tom)
- Police **investigating the crime** are looking for three men. (police **are investigating**)
- Who were those people **waiting outside?** (they **were waiting**)
- I was awakened by a bell **ringing.** (a bell **was ringing**)

When you are talking about *things* (and sometimes people), you can use an -ing phrase to say what something does all the time, not just at a particular time. For example:

- The road **connecting the two towns** is very narrow. (the road **connects** the two towns)
- I have a large bedroom **overlooking the garden.** (the bedroom **overlooks** the garden)
- Can you think of the name of a flower **beginning with "t"?** (the name **begins** with "t")

C

-ed phrases have a *passive* meaning:

- The boy **injured in the accident** was taken to the hospital. (the boy **was injured** in the accident)
- Some of the people **invited to the party** can't come. (they **have been invited**)

Injured and **invited** are *past participles*. Note that many past participles are irregular and do not end in -ed (**made, bought, stolen,** etc.):

- Most of the goods **made in this factory** are exported. (the goods **are made . . .**)
- The police never found the money **stolen in the robbery.** (the money **was stolen**)

You can use **left** in this way, with the meaning *not used, still there:*

- We've spent almost all our money. We only have a little **left.**

For irregular past participles, see Appendix 1.

D

We often use -ing and -ed phrases after **there is / there was,** etc.:

- There were some children **swimming in the river.**
- Is there anybody **waiting?**
- There was a big red car **parked outside the house.**

See/hear somebody *doing* something Unit 64   *-ing* Phrases Unit 65   *There (is)* Unit 81

Exercises

94.1 Make one sentence from two. Use the information in parentheses to make an *-ing* phrase. The *-ing* phrase sometimes goes in the middle of the new sentence, and sometimes goes at the end.

1. I was awakened by a bell. (The bell was ringing.)
   I was awakened by a bell ringing.
2. I didn't talk much to the man. (The man was sitting next to me on the plane.)
   _____
3. The taxi broke down. (The taxi was taking us to the airport.)
   _____
4. At the end of the street there is a path. (The path leads to the river.)
   _____
5. A new factory has just opened in town. (The factory employs 500 people.)
   _____

94.2 Make one sentence from two, beginning as shown. Each time make an *-ed* phrase.

1. A boy was injured in the accident. He was taken to the hospital.
   The boy injured in the accident was taken to the hospital.
2. A number of suggestions were made at the meeting. Most of them were not very practical.
   Most of the suggestions _____ .
3. Some paintings were stolen from the museum. They haven't been found yet.
   The _____ .
4. A man was arrested by the police. What was his name?
   What was the name _____ ?

94.3 Complete the sentences using one of the following verbs in the correct form:

blow   drive   ~~invite~~   live   name   offer   read   ~~ring~~   sell   sit

1. I was awakened by a bell *ringing* .
2. A lot of the people *invited* to the party cannot come.
3. Life must be very unpleasant for people _____ near busy airports.
4. A few days after the interview, I received a letter _____ me the job.
5. Somebody _____ Jack phoned while you were out.
6. There was a tree _____ down in the storm last night.
7. The waiting room was empty except for a young man _____ by the window _____ a magazine.
8. Look! The man _____ the red car almost hit the person _____ newspapers on the street corner.

94.4 Use the words in parentheses to make sentences using *there is / there was*, etc.

1. That house is empty. (no one / live / in it) *There's no one living in it.*
2. The accident wasn't serious. (nobody / injure) *There was nobody injured.*
3. I can hear footsteps. (someone / come)
   There _____ .
4. The train was full. (a lot of people / travel)
   _____
5. We were the only guests at the hotel. (nobody else / stay there)
   _____
6. The piece of paper was blank. (nothing / write / on it)
   _____
7. The school offers English courses in the evening. (a course / begin / next Monday)
   _____

Adjectives Ending in *-ing* and *-ed* (*boring/bored*, etc.)

A

There are many *adjectives* ending in **-ing** and **-ed**: for example, **boring** and **bored**.

bored

boring

Jane has been doing the same job for a very long time. Every day she does exactly the same thing again and again. She doesn't like it anymore and wants to do something different.

Jane's job is **boring**.

Jane is **bored** (with her job).

Somebody is **bored** if something (or somebody else) is **boring**. Or, if something is **boring**, it makes you **bored**. So:

- Jane is **bored** because her job is **boring**.
- Jane's job is **boring**, so Jane is **bored**. (*not* Jane is boring)

If a person is **boring**, this means that they make other people **bored**:

- George always talks about the same things. He's really **boring**.

B

Compare adjectives ending in **-ing** and **-ed**:

■ My job is	boring. interesting. tiring. satisfying. depressing. (etc.)	■ I'm **bored** with my job. ■ I'm not **interested** in my job anymore. ■ I'm always **tired** when I get home after work. ■ I'm not **satisfied** with my job. ■ My job makes me **depressed**. (etc.)
The **-ing** adjective tells you about the job.		The **-ed** adjective tells you how somebody feels (about the job).

Compare these examples:

interesting
- Julia thinks politics is very **interesting**.
- Did you meet anyone **interesting** at the party?

surprising
- It was quite **surprising** that he passed the exam.

disappointing
- The movie was **disappointing**. We expected it to be much better.

shocking
- The news was **shocking**.

interested
- Julia is very **interested** in politics. (*not* interesting in politics)
- Are you **interested** in buying a car? I'm trying to sell mine.

surprised
- Everybody was **surprised** that he passed the exam.

disappointed
- We were **disappointed** in the movie. We expected it to be much better.

shocked
- I was **shocked** when I heard the news.

Exercises

95.1 **Complete the sentences for each situation. Use the word in parentheses + -ing or -ed.**

1. The movie wasn't as good as we had expected. (disappoint-)
   a) The movie was _disappointing_ .
   b) We were _disappointed_ in the film.
2. Diana teaches young children. It's a very hard job, but she enjoys it. (exhaust-)
   a) She enjoys her job, but it's often _____ .
   b) At the end of a day's work, she is often _____ .
3. It's been raining all day. I hate this weather. (depress-)
   a) This weather is _____ .
   b) This weather makes me _____ .
   c) It's silly to get _____ because of the weather.
4. Claire is going to Mexico next month. She has never been there before. (excit-)
   a) It will be an _____ experience for her.
   b) Going to new places is always _____ .
   c) She is really _____ about going to Mexico.

95.2 **Choose the correct word.**

1. I was ~~disappointing~~ / disappointed in the movie. I had expected it to be better.
   (*disappointed* is correct)
2. Are you interesting / interested in soccer?
3. The soccer game was quite exciting / excited. I had a great time.
4. It's sometimes embarrassing / embarrassed when you have to ask people for money.
5. Do you get embarrassing / embarrassed easily?
6. I had never expected to get the job. I was really amazing / amazed when it was offered to me.
7. She has learned really fast. She has made astonishing / astonished progress.
8. I didn't find the situation funny. I was not amusing / amused.
9. It was a really terrifying / terrified experience. Everybody was very shocking / shocked.
10. Why do you always look so boring / bored? Is your life really so boring / bored?
11. He's one of the most boring / bored people I've ever met. He never stops talking and he never says anything interesting / interested.

95.3 **Complete the sentences by choosing a word from the box.**

amusing / amused	confusing / confused	exhausting / exhausted
annoying / annoyed	disgusting / disgusted	interesting / interested
boring / bored	exciting / excited	surprising / surprised

1. He works very hard. It's not _surprising_ that he's always tired.
2. I don't have anything to do. I'm _____ .
3. The teacher's explanation was _____ . Most of the students didn't understand it.
4. The kitchen hadn't been cleaned for ages. It was really _____ .
5. You don't have to get _____ just because I'm a few minutes late.
6. The lecture was _____ . I fell asleep.
7. I asked Emily if she wanted to go out with us, but she wasn't _____ .
8. I've been working very hard all day, and now I'm _____ .
9. I'm starting a new job next week. I'm very _____ about it.
10. Tom is good at telling funny stories. He can be very _____ .
11. Liz is a very _____ person. She knows a lot, she's traveled a lot, and she's done lots of different things.

Adjectives: Word Order (a nice new house)
Adjectives after Verbs (You look tired)

A

Sometimes we use two or more *adjectives* together:

- My brother lives in a **nice new** house.
- There was a **beautiful large round wooden** table in the kitchen.

Adjectives like **new/large/round/wooden** are *fact* adjectives. They give us factual information about age, size, color, etc.

Adjectives like **nice/beautiful** are *opinion* adjectives. They tell us what somebody thinks of something or somebody.

Opinion adjectives usually go before fact adjectives.

	opinion	fact	
a	nice	long	summer vacation
an	interesting	young	man
	delicious	hot	vegetable soup
a	beautiful	large round wooden	table

B

Sometimes we use two or more fact adjectives. Very often (but not always) we put fact adjectives in this order:

1 how big?	→	2 how old?	→	3 what color?	→	4 where from?	→	5 what is it made of?	———————→	NOUN

a **tall young** man (1 → 2)　　　　　　　　a **large wooden** table (1 → 5)
big blue eyes (1 → 3)　　　　　　　　　　an **old Russian** song (2 → 4)
a **small black plastic** bag (1 → 3 → 5)　　an **old white cotton** shirt (2 → 3 → 5)

Adjectives of size and length (**big/small/tall/short/long**, etc.) usually go before adjectives of shape and width (**round/fat/thin/slim/wide**, etc.):

a **large round** table　　　a **tall thin** girl　　　a **long narrow** street

When there are two or more color adjectives, we use **and**:

a **black and white** dress　　　a **red, white, and green** flag
but a **long black** dress (*not* a long and black dress)

C

We use adjectives after **be/get/become/seem**:

- **Be careful!**
- As the movie went on, it **became** more and more **boring**.
- Your friend **seems** very **nice**.
- I'm **tired** and I'm **getting hungry**.

We also use adjectives to say how somebody/something looks, feels, sounds, tastes, or smells:

- You **look tired**. / I **feel tired**. / She **sounds tired**.
- The dinner **smells good**.
- This milk **tastes strange**.

But to say how somebody does something, you must use an *adverb* (see Units 97–98):

- Drive **carefully!** (*not* Drive careful)
- Susan plays the piano very **well**. (*not* plays . . . very good)

Exercises

96.1 Put the adjectives in parentheses in the correct position.

1. a beautiful table (wooden / round)   *a beautiful round wooden table*
2. an unusual ring (gold)
3. a new sweater (nice)
4. a new sweater (green)
5. an old house (beautiful)
6. black gloves (leather)
7. an American movie (old)
8. a long face (thin)
9. big clouds (black)
10. a sunny day (lovely)
11. an ugly dress (yellow)
12. a wide avenue (long)
13. a red car (old / little)
14. a metal box (black / small)
15. a big cat (fat / black)
16. a little country inn (old / charming)
17. long hair (black / beautiful)
18. an old painting (interesting / Japanese)
19. an enormous umbrella (red / yellow)

96.2 Complete each sentence with a verb (in the correct form) from Box A and an adjective from Box B.

A	feel	look	~~seem~~
	smell	sound	taste

B	awful	fine	interesting
	nice	~~upset~~	wet

1. Ann _seemed upset_ this morning. Do you know what was wrong?
2. I can't eat this. I just tried it, and it _____ .
3. I was sick yesterday, but I _____ today.
4. What beautiful flowers! They _____ too.
5. You _____ . Have you been out in the rain?
6. Jim was telling me about his new job. It _____ very _____ – much better than his old job.

96.3 Choose the correct word.

1. This milk tastes _strange_ . (strange / strangely)
2. I always feel _____ when the sun is shining. (happy / happily)
3. The children were playing _____ in the yard. (happy / happily)
4. The man became _____ when the manager of the restaurant asked him to leave. (violent / violently)
5. You look _____ ! Are you all right? (terrible / terribly)
6. There's no point in doing a job if you don't do it _____ . (good / well)
7. This soup tastes _____ . (good / well)
8. Hurry up! You're always so _____ . (slow / slowly)

Adjectives and Adverbs (1) *(quick/quickly)*

A

Look at these examples:

- Our vacation was too short – the time passed very **quickly**.
- The driver of the car was **seriously** injured in the accident.

Quickly and **seriously** are *adverbs*. Many adverbs are made from an *adjective* + **-ly**:

adjective:	quick	serious	careful	quiet	heavy	bad
adverb:	quickly	seriously	carefully	quietly	heavily	badly

For spelling, see Appendix 6.

Not all words ending in **-ly** are adverbs. Some *adjectives* end in **-ly** too, for example:

friendly   lively   elderly   lonely   silly   lovely

B

Adjective or *adverb?*

Adjectives (**quick/careful**, etc.) tell us about a *noun*. We use adjectives before nouns and after some verbs, especially **be**:

- Tom **is a careful driver**. (*not* a carefully driver)
- We didn't go out because of the **heavy rain**.
- Please **be quiet**.
- I was disappointed that my test results **were** so **bad**.

We also use adjectives after the verbs **look/feel/sound**, etc. (see Unit 96C):

- Why do you always **look** so **serious**?

Compare:

- She speaks perfect English
  adjective + noun

Compare these sentences with **look**:

- Tom **looked sad** when I saw him. (= he seemed sad; his expression was sad)

Adverbs (**quickly/carefully**, etc.) tell us about a *verb*. An adverb tells us how somebody does something or how something happens:

- Tom **drove carefully** along the narrow road. (*not* drove careful)
- We didn't go out because it was **raining heavily**. (*not* raining heavy)
- Please **speak quietly**. (*not* speak quiet)
- I was disappointed that I **did** so **badly** on the test. (*not* did so bad)

- Why don't you ever **take** me **seriously**?

- She speaks English perfectly .
  verb + object + adverb

- Tom **looked** at me **sadly**. (= he looked at me in a sad way)

C

We also use adverbs before adjectives and other adverbs. For example:

reasonably cheap	*(adverb + adjective)*
terribly sorry	*(adverb + adjective)*
incredibly quickly	*(adverb + adverb)*

- It's a **reasonably cheap** restaurant, and the food is **extremely good**.
- Oh, I'm **terribly sorry**. I didn't mean to push you. (*not* terrible sorry)
- Maria learns languages **incredibly quickly**.
- The test was **surprisingly easy**.

You can also use an adverb before a *past participle* (**injured/organized/written**, etc.):

- Two people were **seriously injured** in the accident. (*not* serious injured)
- The meeting was very **badly organized**.

Exercises

97.1 Complete the sentences with adverbs. The first letters of each adverb are given.

1. We didn't go out because it was raining h _eavily_____ .
2. Our team lost the game because we played very ba_____ .
3. I had no trouble finding a place to live. I found an apartment quite ea_____ .
4. We had to wait for a long time, but we didn't complain. We waited pat_____ .
5. Nobody knew Steve was coming to see us. He arrived unex_____ .
6. Mike stays in shape by playing tennis reg_____ .

97.2 Put in the right word.

1. The driver of the car was _seriously_____ injured. (serious / seriously)
2. I think you behaved very _____ . (selfish / selfishly)
3. Kelly is _____ upset about losing her job. (terrible / terribly)
4. There was a _____ change in the weather. (sudden / suddenly)
5. Everybody at the party was _____ dressed. (colorful / colorfully)
6. Linda likes wearing _____ clothes. (colorful / colorfully)
7. She fell and hurt herself quite _____ . (bad / badly)
8. These pants started coming apart after I wore them only once. They're
   _____ made. (bad / badly)
9. Don't go up that ladder. It doesn't look _____ . (safe / safely)
10. He looked at me _____ when I interrupted him. (angry / angrily)

97.3 Complete each sentence using a word from the box. Sometimes you need the adjective
(*careful*, etc.) and sometimes the adverb (*carefully*, etc.).

careful(ly)	complete(ly)	continuous(ly)	financial(ly)	fluent(ly)
happy/happily	nervous(ly)	perfect(ly)	~~quick(ly)~~	special(ly)

1. Our vacation was too short. The time passed very _quickly_____ .
2. Tom doesn't take risks when he's driving. He's always _____ .
3. Sue works _____ . She never seems to stop.
4. Amy and Eric are very _____ married.
5. Nicole's English is very _____ , even though she makes lots of mistakes.
6. I cooked this meal _____ for you, so I hope you like it.
7. Everything was very quiet. There was _____ silence.
8. I tried on the shoes, and they fit me _____ .
9. Do you usually feel _____ before exams?
10. I'd like to buy a car, but it's _____ impossible for me at the moment.

97.4 Choose two words (one from each box) to complete each sentence.

absolutely	~~reasonably~~	unnecessarily
badly	seriously	unusually
completely	slightly	

changed	enormous	planned
~~cheap~~	ill	quiet
damaged	long	

1. I thought the restaurant would be expensive, but it was _reasonably cheap_____ .
2. Jeff's mother is _____ in the hospital.
3. What a big house. It's _____ .
4. It wasn't a serious accident. The car was only _____ .
5. The children are normally very lively but they're _____ today.
6. When I returned home after 20 years, everything had _____ .
7. The movie was _____ . It could have been much shorter.
8. A lot went wrong during our vacation because it was _____ .

Adjectives and Adverbs (2) (well/fast/late, hard/hardly)

A

Good/well

Good is an *adjective*. The *adverb* is **well**:

- Your **English** is **good**. *but* You **speak** English **well**.
- Susan is a **good pianist**. *but* Susan **plays** the piano **well**.

We use **well** (*not* good) with *past participles* (**dressed/known**, etc.):

  well dressed   **well known**   **well educated**   **well paid**

B

Fast/hard/late

These words are both adjectives and adverbs:

adjective	*adverb*
Jack is a very **fast runner**.	Jack can **run** very **fast**.
Ann is a **hard worker**.	Ann **works hard**. (*not* works hardly)
The **train** was **late**.	I **got up late** this morning.

Lately = recently:

- Have you seen Tom **lately**?

C

Hardly

Hardly = very little, almost not at all. Study these examples:

- Sarah wasn't very friendly to me at the party. She **hardly** spoke to me.
  (= she spoke to me very little, almost not at all)
- George and June want to get married, but they've only known each other for a few days. I don't think they should get married yet. They **hardly** know each other. (= they know each other very little)

Hard and **hardly** are completely different. Compare:

- He tried **hard** to find a job, but he had no luck. (= he tried a lot, with a lot of effort)
- I'm not surprised he didn't find a job. He **hardly** tried to find one. (= he tried very little)

We often use **hardly + any/anybody/anyone/anything/anywhere**:

- *A:* How much money have you got?
  B: **Hardly any.** (= very little, almost none)
- I'll have to go shopping. We **hardly** have **any** food.
- The exam results were very bad. **Hardly anybody** in our class passed. (= very few students passed)
- She **hardly** ate **anything**. She wasn't feeling hungry.
  (= she ate very little, almost nothing)

Note the position of **hardly**. You can say:

- She **hardly** ate **anything**. *or* She ate **hardly anything**.
- We **hardly** have **any** food. *or* We have **hardly any** food.

I **can hardly** do something = it's almost impossible for me to do it:

- Your writing is terrible. I **can hardly** read it.
  (= it is almost impossible for me to read it)
- My leg was hurting me. I **could hardly** walk.

We hardly have any food.

Hardly ever = almost never:

- I'm almost always at home at night. I **hardly ever** go out.

Exercises

98.1 Put in *good* or *well*.

1. I play tennis, but I'm not very ___good___ .
2. Your exam results were _____ .
3. You did very _____ on your exam.
4. The weather was very _____ while we were on vacation.
5. I didn't sleep _____ last night.
6. Jason speaks Spanish very _____ .
7. Jason's Spanish is very _____ .
8. Our new business is going very _____ at the moment.
9. I like your jacket. It looks _____ on you.
10. I've met her a few times, but I don't know her _____ .

98.2 Complete these sentences using *well* + one of the following words:

balanced ~~behaved~~ **dressed** **informed** **kept** **known** **paid**

1. The children were very good. They were _well behaved_____ .
2. I'm surprised you haven't heard of her. She is quite _____ .
3. Our neighbors' yard is neat and clean. It is very _____ .
4. You should eat different types of food. Your diet should be _____ .
5. Ann knows a lot about many things. She is quite _____ .
6. His clothes were wrinkled and dirty. He wasn't very _____ .
7. Jill has a lot of responsibility in her job, but she isn't very _____ .

98.3 Are the underlined words right or wrong? Correct the ones that are wrong.

1. I'm tired because I've been working <u>hardly</u>.   _hard_____
2. I tried <u>hard</u> to remember her name, but I couldn't.   _____
3. This coat is practically unused. I've <u>hardly</u> worn it. _____
4. She's a good tennis player. She hits the ball <u>hardly</u>. _____
5. Don't walk so <u>fast</u>! I can't keep up with you.   _____
6. Why are you walking so <u>slow</u>? Are you tired?   _____

98.4 Complete these sentences with *hardly* + one of the following verbs in the correct form:

change **hear** ~~know~~ **recognize** **say** **sleep** **speak**

1. Scott and Amy have only met once before. They _hardly know_____ each other.
2. You're speaking very quietly. I can _____ you.
3. I'm very tired this morning. I _____ last night.
4. We were so shocked when we heard the news, we could _____ .
5. Kate was very quiet tonight. She _____ a word.
6. You look almost the same now as you looked 15 years ago. You've _____ .
7. I met Dave a few days ago. I hadn't seen him for a long time, and he looks very different now. I _____ him.

98.5 Complete these sentences with *hardly* + *any/anybody/anything/anywhere/ever*.

1. I'll have to go shopping. We have _hardly any_____ food.
2. It was nice driving this morning. There was _____ traffic.
3. "Do you know much about computers?" "No, _____ ."
4. The hotel was almost empty. There was _____ staying there.
5. I listen to the radio a lot, but I _____ watch television.
6. Our new boss isn't very popular. _____ likes her.
7. We used to be good friends, but we _____ see each other now.
8. I hate this town. There's _____ to do and _____ to go.

So and such

A

Compare **so** and **such**:

We use **so** + *adjective/adverb*:
    so stupid   **so** quick
    so nice   **so** quickly

■ I didn't enjoy the book. The story was **so stupid.**
■ I like Tom and Ann. They are **so nice.**

We use **such** + *noun*:
    such a story   **such** people

We also use **such** + *adjective* + *noun*:
    such a stupid story   **such** nice people

■ I didn't like the book. It was **such** a stupid **story.** (*not* a so stupid story)
■ I like Tom and Ann. They are **such nice people.** (*not* so nice people)

Note that we say **such a . . . :**
■ It's **such a big house.** (*not* a such big house)

B

So and **such** make the meaning of an adjective (or adverb) stronger:

■ It's a beautiful day, isn't it? It's **so warm.** (= really warm)
■ He's hard to understand because he speaks **so quickly.**

You can use **so . . . that . . . :**
■ The book was **so good that** I couldn't put it down.
■ I was **so tired that** I fell asleep in the armchair.

You can leave out **that:**
■ I was **so tired** (that) I fell asleep.

■ We enjoyed our vacation. We had **such a good time.** (= a really good time)

You can use **such . . . that . . . :**
■ It was **such a good book that** I couldn't put it down.
■ It was **such nice weather that** we spent the whole day at the beach.

You can leave out **that:**
■ It was **such nice weather** (that) we . . .

C

We also use **so** and **such** to mean "like this":

■ I was surprised to find out that the house was built 100 years ago. I didn't realize it was **so old.** (= as old as it is)
■ I'm tired because I got up at 6:00. I don't usually get up **so early.**

■ I didn't realize it was **such an old house.**
■ The house was so messy. I've never seen **such a mess.** (= a mess like this)

D

We say **so long** *but* **such a long time:**

■ I haven't seen her for **so long** I've forgotten what she looks like.

so far *but* **such a long way:**
■ I didn't know it was **so far.**

so much, so many *but* **such a lot of:**
■ Why did you buy **so much** food?

■ I haven't seen her for **such a long time.** (*not* so long time)

■ I didn't know it was **such a long way.**

■ Why did you buy **such a lot of** food?

Not so . . . as Unit 103A   ***Such as*** Unit 113A

Exercises

99.1 Put in *so*, *such*, or *such a(n)*.

1. He's hard to understand because he speaks _so_ quickly.
2. I like Tom and Ann. They're _such_ nice people.
3. It was a great vacation. We had _such a_ good time.
4. I was surprised that he looked _____ good after his recent illness.
5. Everything is _____ expensive these days, isn't it?
6. The weather is beautiful, isn't it? I didn't expect it to be _____ nice day.
7. I have to go. I didn't realize it was _____ late.
8. He always looks good. He wears _____ nice clothes.
9. It was _____ exciting movie that I couldn't go to sleep when I got home.
10. I couldn't believe the news. It was _____ shock.
11. I think she works too hard. She looks _____ tired all the time.
12. The food at the hotel was _____ awful. I've never eaten _____ awful food.
13. They've got _____ much money, they don't know what to do with it.
14. I didn't realize you lived _____ long way from downtown.
15. I can't decide what to do. It's _____ problem.

99.2 Make one sentence from two. Use *so* or *such*.

1. ~~She worked hard.~~   You could hear it from miles away.
2. ~~It was a beautiful day.~~   You would think it was her native language.
3. I was tired.   We spent the whole day indoors.
4. We had a good time on vacation. ~~She made herself sick.~~
5. She speaks English well.   I couldn't keep my eyes open.
6. I've got a lot to do.   I didn't eat anything else for the rest of the day.
7. The music was loud.   ~~We decided to go to the beach.~~
8. I had a big breakfast.   I don't know where to begin.
9. It was terrible weather.   We didn't want to come home.

1. _She worked so hard (that) she made herself sick._
2. _It was such a beautiful day (that) we decided to go to the beach._
3. I was _____ .
4. _____
5. _____
6. _____
7. _____
8. _____
9. _____

99.3 Use your own ideas to complete these pairs of sentences.

1. a) We enjoyed our vacation. It was so _relaxing_ .
   b) We enjoyed our vacation. We had such _a good time_ .
2. a) I don't like New York very much. It's so _____ .
   b) I don't like New York very much. It's such _____ .
3. a) I like Ann. She's so _____ .
   b) I like Ann. She's such _____ .
4. a) I wouldn't want to be a teacher. It's so _____ .
   b) I wouldn't want to be a teacher. It's such _____ .
5. a) It's great to see you again! I haven't seen you for so _____ .
   b) It's great to see you again! I haven't seen you for such _____ .

Enough and too

A

The position of **enough**

Enough goes after adjectives and adverbs:

- He didn't get the job because he wasn't **experienced enough**. (*not* enough experienced)
- You won't pass the exam if you don't study **hard enough**.
- They can get married. They're **old enough**.

Compare **too** (**too hard** / **too old**, etc.):

- You never stop working. You work **too hard**. (= more than is necessary)

Enough usually goes *before* nouns:

- He didn't get the job because he didn't have **enough experience**. (*not* experience enough)
- Do you have **enough money?** I can lend you some if you don't.
- Some of us had to sit on the floor because there weren't **enough chairs**.

You can also use **enough** alone (without a noun):

- I'll lend you some money if you don't have **enough**.

Compare **too much / too many**:

- We can't take a vacation. It costs **too much** (money).
- There are **too many** people and not enough chairs.

B

We say "**enough/too . . . for** somebody/something":

- I have **enough money for a vacation**, but I don't have enough time.
- He wasn't experienced **enough for the job**.
- This shirt is **too big for me**. I need a smaller size.

But we usually say "**enough/too . . . to do** something" (*not* for doing). So we say:
enough money to buy something, **too young to do** something, etc.

For example:

- Do you have **enough money to take** a vacation right now? (*not* for taking)
- He wasn't **experienced enough to do** the job.
- She's not **old enough to get** married. *or* She's **too young to get** married.
- Let's get a taxi. It's **too far to walk** home from here.
- There weren't **enough chairs** for everyone **to sit down**.
- They spoke **too quickly** for us **to understand**.

C

We say:

- The food was very hot. We couldn't eat **it**.
and The food was so hot that we couldn't eat **it**.
but The food was **too hot to eat**. (*without* it)

Some more examples like this:

- The wallet was **too big to put** in my pocket.
  (*not* too big to put it)
- These boxes are **too heavy to carry**.
  (*not* too heavy to carry them)
- The water wasn't **clean enough to swim** in.

***To . . . and for . . . (Purpose)* Unit 61   *Adjective + to . . . (difficult to understand*, etc.) Unit 62A**

Exercises

100.1 Complete these sentences using *enough* with one of the following adjectives or nouns:

> adjectives: big ~~old~~ qualified warm well
> nouns: cups milk money room time

1. She shouldn't get married yet. She's not _old enough_____ .
2. I'd like to buy a car, but I don't have _____ .
3. Do you have _____ in your coffee, or would you like some more?
4. Are you _____ ? Or should I turn up the heat?
5. It's only a small car. There isn't _____ for all of you.
6. Steve didn't feel _____ to go to work this morning.
7. I didn't answer all the questions on the test. I didn't have _____ .
8. Do you think I am _____ to apply for the job?
9. Try this jacket on and see if it's _____ for you.
10. There weren't _____ for everybody to have coffee at the same time.

100.2 Complete the answers to the questions. Use *too* or *enough* with the word in parentheses.

1.	Is she going to get married?	(old) No, she's not _old enough to get married_____ .
2.	I need to talk to you about something.	(busy) Sorry, but I'm _____ _____ to you now.
3.	Why don't we sit outside?	(warm) It's not _____ _____ outside.
4.	Would you like to be a politician?	(shy) No, I'm _____ _____ a politician.
5.	Do you want to play tennis today?	(energy) No, I don't have _____ _____ tennis today.
6.	Did you hear what he was saying?	(far away) No, we were _____ _____ what he was saying.
7.	Can he read a newspaper in English?	(English) No, he doesn't know _____ _____ a newspaper.

100.3 Make one sentence from two. Complete the new sentence using *too* or *enough.*

1. We couldn't eat the food. It was too hot.
   The food was _too hot to eat_____ .
2. I can't drink this coffee. It's too hot.
   This coffee is _____ .
3. Nobody could move the piano. It was too heavy.
   The piano _____ .
4. I don't wear this coat in the winter. It isn't warm enough.
   This coat _____ .
5. I can't explain the situation. It is too complicated.
   The situation _____ .
6. Three people can't sit on this sofa. It isn't wide enough.
   This sofa _____ .
7. We couldn't climb over the wall. It was too high.
   The wall _____ .
8. You can't see some things without a microscope. They are too small.
   Some _____ .

Comparison (1) – *cheaper, more expensive*, etc.

A

Look at these examples:

> Should I drive or take the train?
>> You should drive. It's **cheaper**.
>> Don't take the train. It's **more expensive**.
>
> **Cheaper** and **more expensive** are *comparative forms*.

After comparatives you can use **than** (see also Unit 103):
- It's **cheaper** to drive **than** to take the train.
- Taking the train is **more expensive than** driving.

B

The comparative form is -**er** or **more** . . . :

We use -**er** for short words (one syllable):

cheap → cheaper   fast → faster
large → larger   thin → thinner

We also use -**er** for two-syllable words that end in -**y** (-**y** → -**ier**):
lucky → luckier   early → earlier
easy → easier   pretty → prettier
For spelling, see Appendix 5.

- You're **older** than me.
- The exam was easy – **easier** than we expected.
- Can you walk a little **faster**?
- I'd like to have a **bigger** car.
- Last night I went to bed **earlier** than usual.

We use **more** . . . for longer words (two syllables or more):
more serious   **more often**
more expensive   **more comfortable**

We use **more** . . . for *adverbs* that end in -**ly**:

more slowly   **more seriously**
more quietly   **more carefully**

- You're **more patient** than me.
- The exam was difficult – **more difficult** than we expected.
- Can you walk a little **more slowly**?
- I'd like to have a **more reliable** car.
- I don't play tennis much these days. I used to play **more often**.

You can use -**er** or **more** . . . with some *two-syllable adjectives*, especially:
quiet   clever   narrow   shallow   simple
- It's too noisy here. Can we go somewhere **quieter** / **more quiet**?

C

These adjectives and adverbs have irregular comparative forms:

good/well → better:
- The yard looks **better** since you cleaned it up.
- I know him **well** – probably **better** than anybody else does.

bad/badly → worse:
- "Is your headache better?" "No, it's **worse**."
- He did very badly on the exam – **worse** than expected.

far → farther *or* **further**:
- It's a long walk from here to the station – **farther** than I thought. (*or* **further** than . . .)

Comparison Units 102–103   **Superlatives (*the longest / the most enjoyable*, etc.)** Unit 104

Exercises

101.1 Complete the sentences using a comparative form (*older / more important,* etc.).

1. It's too noisy here. Can we go somewhere *quieter* OR *more quiet* _____ ?
2. This coffee is very weak. I like it a little _____ .
3. The hotel was surprisingly big. I expected it to be _____ .
4. The hotel was surprisingly cheap. I expected it to be _____ .
5. My job is kind of boring sometimes. I'd like to do something _____ .
6. I was surprised how easy it was to use the computer. I thought it would be
   _____ .
7. Your work isn't very good. I'm sure you can do _____ .
8. Don't worry. The situation isn't so bad. It could be _____ .
9. You're talking very loudly. Can you speak _____ ?
10. You hardly ever call me. Why don't you call me _____ ?
11. You're standing too close to the camera. Can you move a little _____
    away?
12. You were a little depressed yesterday, but you look _____ today.

101.2 Complete the sentences using the comparative form of one of the following words. Use *than* where necessary.

big	crowded	~~early~~	easily	high	important
interested	peaceful	~~reliable~~	serious	simple	thin

1. I was feeling tired last night, so I went to bed *earlier than* _____ usual.
2. I'd like to have a *more reliable* _____ car. Mine keeps breaking down.
3. Unfortunately, her illness was _____ we thought at first.
4. You look _____ . Have you lost weight?
5. I want a _____ apartment. We don't have enough space here.
6. He doesn't study very hard. He's _____ in having a good time.
7. Health and happiness are _____ money.
8. The instructions were very complicated. They could have been _____ .
9. There were a lot of people on the bus. It was _____ usual.
10. I like living in the country. It's _____ living in a city.
11. You'll find your way around the city _____ if you have
    a good map.
12. In some parts of the country, prices are _____ in others.

101.3 Read the situations and complete the sentences. Use a comparative form (*-er* or *more . . .*).

1. Yesterday the temperature was 28 degrees. Today it's only 20 degrees.
   It's *colder today than it was yesterday* _____ .
2. The trip takes four hours by car and five hours by train.
   It takes _____ .
3. Dave and I went for a run. I ran five miles. Dave stopped after three miles.
   I ran _____ .
4. Chris and Joe both did poorly on the exam. Chris got a C, and Joe got only a C–.
   Joe did _____ .
5. I expected my friends to arrive at about 4:00. Instead they arrived at 2:30.
   My friends _____ .
6. You can go by bus or by train. The buses run every 30 minutes. The trains run every hour.
   The buses _____ .
7. We were very busy at work today. We're not usually as busy as that.
   We _____ .

Comparison (2)

A

Before *comparatives* you can use:

much   a lot   a little   slightly (= a little)   **far** (= a lot)

- Let's drive. It's **much cheaper.** (*or* It's **a lot cheaper.**)
- The train is **a lot more expensive.** (*or* **much more expensive**)
- Could you speak **a little more slowly?**
- This bag is **slightly heavier** than the other one.
- Her illness was **far more serious** than we thought at first. (*or* **much more serious** *or* **a lot more serious**)

B

You can use **any** or **no** + a comparative (**any longer / no bigger,** etc.):

- I've waited long enough. I'm not waiting **any longer.** (= not even a little longer)
- We expected their house to be very big, but it's **no bigger** than ours. (*or* it **isn't any bigger** than ours)
- Yesterday you said you felt sick. Do you feel **any better** today?
- This hotel is better than the other one, and it's **no more expensive.**

C

Harder and harder / more and more / more and more difficult, etc.

We repeat comparatives like this (**. . . and . . .**) to say that something is changing continuously:

- It's becoming **harder and harder** to find a job.
- It's becoming **more and more difficult** to find a job.
- Your English is improving. It's getting **better and better.**
- **More and more** people are learning English these days.

D

The . . . the better

Study these examples:

- "What time should we leave?" "**The sooner the better.**" (= as soon as possible)
- "What size box do you want?" "**The bigger the better.**" (= as big as possible)
- When you're traveling, **the less** luggage you have to carry **the better.** (= It is best to have as little luggage as possible.)

We also use **the . . . the . . .** (with two comparatives) to say that one thing depends on another thing:

- **The warmer** the weather, **the better** I feel. (= If the weather is warmer, I feel better.)
- **The sooner** we leave, **the sooner** we will get there.
- **The younger** you are, **the easier** it is to learn.
- **The more expensive** the hotel, **the better** the service.
- **The more** electricity you use, **the higher** your bill will be.
- **The more** I thought about the plan, **the less** I liked it.

E

Older and elder

The comparative of **old** is **older:**

- Tom looks **older** than he really is.

You can use **elder** (*or* **older**) when you talk about people in a family:

- My **elder sister** is a doctor. (*or* My older sister . . .)

We say "**elder sister**," but we do not say that somebody is elder:

- My sister is **older** than I am. (*not* elder than I am)

Exercises

102.1 Use the words in parentheses to complete the sentences. Use *much / a bit*, etc. + a comparative form. Use *than* where necessary.

1. Her illness was <u>*much more serious than*</u> we thought at first. (much / serious)
2. This bag is too small. I need something _____ . (much / big)
3. I'm afraid the problem is _____ it seems. (much / complicated)
4. You looked depressed this morning, but you look _____ now. (a little / happy)
5. I enjoyed our visit to the museum. It was _____ I expected. (far / interesting)
6. You're driving too fast. Could you drive _____ ? (a little / slowly)
7. It's _____ to learn a foreign language in the country where it is spoken. (a lot / easy)
8. I thought she was younger than I am, but in fact she's _____ . (slightly / old)

102.2 Complete the sentences using *any/no* + a comparative. Use *than* where necessary.

1. I'm tired of waiting. I'm not waiting <u>*any longer*</u> .
2. I'm sorry I'm late, but I couldn't get here _____ .
3. This store isn't expensive. The prices are _____ anywhere else.
4. I need to stop for a rest. I can't walk _____ .
5. The traffic isn't particularly bad today. It's _____ usual.

102.3 Complete the sentences using the structure in Section C.

1. It's becoming <u>*harder and harder*</u> to find a job. (hard)
2. That hole in your sweater is getting _____ . (big)
3. My bags seemed to get _____ as I carried them. (heavy)
4. As I waited for my interview, I became _____ . (nervous)
5. As the day went on, the weather got _____ . (bad)
6. Health care is becoming _____ . (expensive)
7. Since she has been in Canada, her English has gotten _____ . (good)
8. As the conversation went on, he became _____ . (talkative)

102.4 These sentences are like those in Section D. Use the words in parentheses (in the correct form) to complete the sentences.

1. I like warm weather. The warmer the weather, <u>*the better I feel*</u> . (feel)
2. I didn't really like him when we first met.
   But the more I got to know him, _____ . (like)
3. If you're in business, you want to make a profit.
   The more goods you sell, _____ . (profit)
4. It's hard to concentrate when you're tired.
   The more tired you are, _____ . (hard)
5. She had to wait a very long time.
   The longer she waited, _____ . (impatient / become)

102.5 Which is correct, *older* or *elder*? Or both of them?

1. My <u>older / elder</u> sister is a doctor. (*older* and *elder* are both correct)
2. I'm surprised Diane is only 25. I thought she was <u>older / elder</u>.
3. Ann's younger brother is still in school. Her <u>older / elder</u> brother is a pilot.
4. Martin is <u>older / elder</u> than his brother.

Comparison (3) – *as . . . as / than*

Study this example situation:

SARAH   ERIC   DAVID

Sarah, Eric, and David are all millionaires. They are all very rich.
Sarah has $10 million, Eric has $8 million, and David has $2 million. So:

Eric is rich.
He is **richer than** David.
But he **isn't as rich as** Sarah. (= Sarah is **richer than** he is.)

Some more examples of **not as . . . (as)**:
- Tom **isn't as old as** he looks. (= he looks older than he is)
- The shopping mall **wasn't as crowded as** usual. (= it is usually more crowded)
- Jenny **didn't** do **as well** on the exam **as** she had hoped. (= she had hoped to do better)
- "The weather is better today, isn't it?" "Yes, it's **not as cold.**" (= yesterday was colder)
- I **don't** know **as many** people **as** you do. (= you know more people)

You can also say "**not so . . . (as)**":
- It's not warm, but it **isn't so cold as** yesterday. (= it isn't as cold as yesterday)

Less . . . (than) is similar to **not as . . . (as)**:
- I spent **less money than** you. (= I didn't spend as much money as you)
- The shopping mall was **less crowded than** usual. (= it wasn't as crowded as usual)

You can use **as . . . as** (*but not* so . . . as) in positive sentences and questions:
- I'm sorry I'm late. I got here **as fast as** I could.
- There's plenty of food. You can have **as much as** you want.
- Let's walk. It's just **as quick as** taking the bus.
- Can you send me the money **as soon as** possible, please?

Also: **twice as . . . as, three times as . . . as,** etc.:
- Gas is **twice as expensive as** it was a few years ago.
- Their house is about **three times as big as** ours.

We say **the same as** (*not* the same like):
- Ann's salary is **the same as** mine. *or* Ann makes **the same** salary **as** me.
- Tom is **the same** age **as** Brian.
- "What would you like to drink?" "I'll have **the same as** you."

We usually say:
- You are older **than me.** (*not* than I)
- He isn't as popular **as her.** (*not* as she)

After **than/as** it is more usual to say **me/him/her/them/us** when there is no verb. Compare:
- You are taller **than I am.**   *but*   You are taller **than me.**
- They have more money **than we do.**   *but*   They have more money **than us.**
- I can't run as fast **as he can.**   *but*   I can't run as fast **as him.**

Exercises

103.1 Complete the sentences using *as . . . as.*

1. I'm pretty tall, but you are taller. I'm not *as tall as you*   .
2. My salary is high, but yours is higher. My salary isn't _____.
3. You know a little bit about cars, but I know more.
   You don't _____.
4. I still feel a little tired, but I felt a lot more tired yesterday.
   I don't _____.
5. They've lived here quite a while, but we've lived here longer.
   They haven't _____.
6. I was a little nervous before the interview, but usually I'm a lot more nervous.
   I wasn't _____.

103.2 Rewrite these sentences so that they have the same meaning.

1. Jack is younger than he looks. Jack isn't *as old as he looks*   .
2. I didn't spend as much money as you. You *spent more money than me*   .
3. The station was nearer than I thought. The station wasn't _____.
4. I go out less than I used to. I don't _____.
5. Her hair isn't as long as it used to be. She used to _____.
6. I know them better than you do. You don't _____.
7. There were fewer people at this meeting than at the last one.
   There weren't _____.

103.3 Complete the sentences using *as . . . as.* Choose one of the following:

   bad   comfortable   experienced   ~~fast~~   long   often   soon   well

1. I'm sorry I'm late. I got here *as fast as* _____ I could.
2. It was a hard question. I answered it _____ I could.
3. "How long can I stay with you?" "You can stay _____ you like."
4. I need the information quickly, so please let me know _____ possible.
5. I like to stay in shape, so I go swimming _____ I can.

   In the following sentences use *just as . . . as.*

6. I'm going to sleep on the floor. It's _____ sleeping in that
   hard bed.
7. Why did he get the job rather than me? I'm _____ him.
8. At first I thought he was nice, but he's really _____
   everybody else.

103.4 Write sentences using *the same as.*

1. Sally and Kate are both 22 years old. Sally is *the same age as Kate*   .
2. You and I both have dark brown hair. Your hair _____.
3. I arrived at 10:25 and so did you. I _____.
4. My birthday is April 5. Tom's birthday is April 5, too. My _____.

103.5 Complete the sentences with *than . . .* or *as . . .*

1. I can't reach as high as you. You are taller *than me*   .
2. He doesn't know much. I know more _____.
3. I don't work particularly hard. Most people work as hard _____.
4. We were very surprised. Nobody was more surprised _____.
5. She's not a very good player. I'm a better player _____.
6. They've been very lucky. I wish we were as lucky _____.

Superlatives – *the longest / the most enjoyable*, etc.

A

Study these examples:
- What is **the longest** river in the world?
- What is **the most enjoyable** vacation you've ever had?

Longest and **most enjoyable** are *superlative* forms.

B

The superlative form is **-est** or **most** .... In general, we use **-est** for short words and **most** ... for longer words. (The rules are the same as those for the *comparative* – see Unit 101.)

long → longest	hot → hottest	easy → easiest	hard → hardest
but most famous	most boring	most difficult	most expensive

These *adjectives* are irregular:
good → **best**   bad → **worst**   far → **farthest/furthest**

For spelling, see Appendix 5.

C

We normally use **the** before a superlative (**the longest / the most famous**, etc.):
- Yesterday was **the hottest** day of the year.
- That movie was really boring. It was **the most boring** movie I've ever seen.
- She is a really nice person – one of **the nicest** people I know.
- Why does he always come to see me at **the worst** possible moment?

Compare:
- This hotel is **the cheapest** in town. (*superlative*)
- This hotel is **cheaper** than all the others in town. (*comparative*)

D

Oldest and **eldest**

The superlative of **old** is **oldest**:
- That church is **the oldest** building in the town. (*not* the eldest)

You can use **eldest** or **oldest** to talk about people in a family:
- My **eldest** son is 13 years old. (*or* My **oldest** son)
- Are you **the eldest** in your family? (*or* **the oldest**)

E

After superlatives we use **in** with places (towns, buildings, etc.):
- What is the longest river **in the world**? (*not* of the world)
- We had a great room. It was one of the nicest **in the hotel**. (*not* of the hotel)

We also use **in** for organizations and groups of people (a class, a company, etc.):
- Who is the best student **in the class**? (*not* of the class)

We normally use **of** for a period of time:
- What was the happiest day **of your life**?
- Yesterday was the hottest day **of the year**.

F

We often use the *present perfect* (**I have done**) after a superlative (see also Unit 8A):
- What's **the best** movie you've ever seen?
- That was **the most delicious** meal I've had in a long time.

Comparison (*cheaper / more expensive*, etc.) Units 101–103   *Elder* Unit 102E

Exercises

104.1 Complete the sentences. Use a superlative (*-est* or *most . . .*) + a preposition.

1. It's a very nice room. It's _the nicest room in_ _____ the hotel.
2. It's a very cheap restaurant. It's _____ the town.
3. It was a very happy day. It was _____ my life.
4. She's a very intelligent student. She _____ the class.
5. It's a very valuable painting. It _____ the gallery.
6. Spring is a very busy time for me. It _____ the year.

In the following sentences use *one of* + a superlative + a preposition.

7. It's a very nice room. It _is one of the nicest rooms in_ _____ the hotel.
8. He's a very rich man. He's one _____ the world.
9. It's a very old house. It _____ our street.
10. It's a very good college. It _____ the state.
11. It was a very bad experience. It _____ my life.
12. He's a very dangerous criminal. He _____ the country.

104.2 Complete the sentences. Use a superlative (*-est* or *most . . .*) or a comparative
(*-er* or *more . . .*).

1. We stayed at _the cheapest_ _____ hotel in town. (cheap)
2. Our hotel was _cheaper_ _____ than all the others in the town. (cheap)
3. The United States is very large, but Canada is _____ . (large)
4. What's _____ river in the world? (long)
5. He was a little depressed yesterday, but he looks _____ today. (happy)
6. It was an awful day. It was _____ day of my life. (bad)
7. What is _____ sport in your country? (popular)
8. Everest is _____ mountain in the world. It is _____
   than any other mountain. (high)
9. We had a great vacation. It was one of _____ vacations we've
   ever had. (enjoyable)
10. I prefer this chair to the other one. It's _____ . (comfortable)
11. What's _____ way of getting from here to the bus station? (quick)
12. Mr. and Mrs. Brown have three daughters. _____ is 14 years old. (old)

104.3 What do you say in these situations? Use a superlative + *. . . ever . . .* Use the words
given in parentheses (in the correct form).

1. You've just been to the movies. The movie was extremely boring. You tell your friend:
   (boring / movie / see) That's _the most boring movie I've ever seen_ _____ .
2. Your friend has just told you a joke, which you think is very funny. You say:
   (funny / joke / hear) That's _____ .
3. You're drinking coffee with a friend. It's really good coffee. You say:
   (good / coffee / taste) This _____ .
4. You are talking to a friend about Mary. Mary is very patient. You tell your friend about
   her: (patient / person / meet) She _____ .
5. You have just run ten miles. You've never run farther than this. You say to your friend:
   (far / run) That _____ .
6. You decided to quit your job. Now you think this was a bad mistake. You say to your
   friend: (bad / mistake / make) It _____ .
7. Your friend meets a lot of people, some of them famous. You ask your friend:
   (famous / person / meet) Who _____ ?

Word Order (1) – Verb + Object; Place and Time

A

Verb + object

The *verb* and the *object* of the verb usually go together. We do not usually put other words between them:

	verb +	*object*	
I	like	children	very much. (*not* I like very much children)
Did you	see	your friends	yesterday?
Ann often	plays	tennis.	

Study these examples. Notice how the verb and the object go together each time:

- Do you clean the house every weekend? (*not* Do you clean every weekend the house?)
- Everybody enjoyed the party very much. (*not* Everybody enjoyed very much the party)
- Our guide spoke English fluently. (*not* spoke fluently English)
- I not only lost all my money – I also lost my passport . (*not* I lost also my passport)
- At the end of the street, you'll see a supermarket on your left. (*not* see on your left a supermarket)

B

Place and *time*

Usually the verb and the place (where?) go together:
go home   live in a city   walk to work

If the verb has an object, the place comes after the *verb + object*:
take somebody home   meet a friend in the street

Time (when? / how often? / how long?) usually goes after *place*:

	place +	*time*
Tom walks	to work	every morning. (*not* Tom walks every morning to work)
She has been	in Canada	since April.
We arrived	at the airport	early.

Study these examples. Notice how *time* goes after *place*:

- I'm going to Paris on Monday . (*not* I'm going on Monday to Paris)
- They have lived in the same house for a long time .
- Don't be late. Make sure you're here by 8:00 .
- Sarah gave me a ride home after the party .
- You really shouldn't go to bed so late .

It is often possible to put time at the beginning of the sentence:
- **On Monday** I'm going to Paris.
- **Every morning** Tom walks to work.

Some time words (for example, **always/never/often**) usually go with the verb in the middle of the sentence. See Unit 106.

Word Order in Questions Units 46–47   **Adjectives: Word Order** Unit 96   **Word Order (2)** Unit 106

Exercises

105.1 Is the word order right or wrong? Correct the sentences that are wrong.

1. Everybody enjoyed the party very much.   _RIGHT_
2. Tom walks every morning to work.   _Tom walks to work every morning._
3. Jim doesn't like very much soccer.   _____
4. I drink three or four cups of coffee every morning.   _____
5. I ate quickly my dinner and went out.   _____
6. Are you going to invite to the party a lot of people?   _____
7. I called Tom immediately after hearing the news.   _____
8. Did you go late to bed last night?   _____
9. Did you learn a lot of things at school today?   _____
10. I met on my way home a friend of mine.   _____

105.2 Put the parts of the sentence in the right order.

1. (the party / very much / everybody enjoyed) _Everybody enjoyed the party very much._
2. (we won / easily / the game) _____
3. (quietly / the door / I closed) _____
4. (Diane / quite well / speaks / Chinese) _____
5. (Tim / all the time / TV / watches) _____
6. (again / please don't ask / that question)

   _____
7. (soccer / every weekend / does Ken play?)

   _____
8. (some money / I borrowed / from a friend of mine)

   _____

105.3 Complete the sentences. Put the parts in the right order.

1. (for a long time / have lived / in the same house)
   They _have lived in the same house for a long time_ .
2. (to the bank / every Friday / go) I _____ .
3. (home / did you come / so late) Why _____ ?
4. (her car / drives / every day / to work)
   Ann _____ .
5. (been / recently / to the movies) I haven't _____ .
6. (at the top of the page / your name / write)
   Please _____ .
7. (her name / after a few minutes / remembered)
   I _____ .
8. (around the town / all morning / walked)
   We _____ .
9. (on Saturday night / didn't see you / at the party)
   I _____ .
10. (some interesting books / found / in the library)
    We _____ .
11. (the children / yesterday / to the zoo / took)
    Sally _____ .
12. (across from the park / a new hotel / are building)
    They _____ .

Word Order (2) – Adverbs with the Verb

A

Some *adverbs* (for example, **always/also/probably**) go with the *verb* in the middle of a sentence:
- Tom **always drives** to work.
- We were feeling very tired, and we **were also** hungry.
- Your car **has probably** been stolen.

B

Study these rules for the position of adverbs in the middle of a sentence. (They are only general rules, so there are exceptions.):

1) If the verb is one word (**goes/fell/cooked**, etc.), the adverb usually goes *before* the verb:

	adverb	*verb*	
Tom	**always**	**drives**	to work.
I	**almost**	**fell**	as I was going down the stairs.

- I cleaned the house and **also cooked** dinner. (*not* cooked also)
- Lucy **hardly ever watches** television and **rarely reads** newspapers.

Note that these adverbs (**always/often/also**, etc.) go before **have to**:
- We **always have to** wait a long time for the bus. (*not* We have always to wait)

2) But adverbs go after **am/is/are/was/were**:
- We were feeling very tired, and we **were also** hungry.
- Why are you always late? You**'re never** on time.
- The traffic **isn't usually** as bad as it was this morning.

3) If the verb is two or more words (**can remember / doesn't smoke / has been stolen**, etc.), the adverb goes *after the first verb* (**can/doesn't/has**, etc.):

	verb 1	*adverb*	*verb 2*	
I	**can**	**never**	**remember**	his name.
Ann	**doesn't**	**usually**	**complain.**	
Are you		**definitely**	**going**	to the party tomorrow?
Your car	**has**	**probably**	**been**	stolen.

- My parents **have always lived** in Chicago.
- Jack can't cook. He **can't even boil** an egg.
- The house **was only built** a year ago, and it's **already falling** down.

Note that **probably** goes before the negative. So we say:
- I **probably won't** see you. *or* I will **probably not** see you. (*but not* I won't probably)

C

We also use **all** and **both** in these positions:
- We **all felt** sick after the meal. (*not* We felt all sick)
- My parents **are both** teachers. (*not* My parents both are teachers)
- Sarah and Jane **have both applied** for the job.
- We **are all going** out this evening.

D

Sometimes we use **is/will/did**, etc., instead of repeating part of a sentence (see Unit 48A).
Note the position of **always/never**, etc., in these sentences:
- He always says he won't be late, but he **always is**. (= he is always late)
- I've never done it, and I **never will**. (= I will never do it)

We usually put **always/never**, etc., before the verb in sentences like these.

Exercises

106.1 Is the word order in the underlined parts of these sentences right or wrong? Correct the ones that are wrong.

1. <u>Tom drives always</u> to work.   *Tom always drives*
2. I cleaned the house and <u>also cooked</u> dinner.   *RIGHT*
3. <u>I have usually</u> a shower when I get up.   _____
4. <u>We soon found</u> the solution to the problem.   _____
5. <u>Steve gets hardly ever</u> angry.   _____
6. I did some shopping, and <u>I went also</u> to the bank.   _____
7. <u>Jane has always to hurry</u> in the morning because she gets up so late.   _____
8. <u>We all were</u> tired, so <u>we all fell</u> asleep.   _____
9. <u>She always says</u> she'll call me, but <u>she never does</u>.   _____

106.2 Rewrite the sentences to include the word in parentheses.

1. Ann doesn't drink tea. (usually) *Ann doesn't usually drink tea.*
2. We were on vacation. (all) _____
3. We were staying at the same hotel. (all) _____
4. We enjoyed ourselves. (all) _____
5. Catherine is very generous. (always) _____
6. I don't have to work on Saturdays. (usually)

   _____
7. Do you watch TV in the evenings? (always)

   _____
8. Josh is studying Spanish. He is studying Japanese. (also)
   Josh is studying Spanish. He _____ .
9. That hotel is very expensive. (probably) _____
10. It costs a lot to stay there. (probably) _____

106.3 Complete the sentences. Use the words in parentheses in the correct order.

1. I *can never remember* her name. (remember / never / can)
2. I _____ sugar in my coffee. (take / usually)
3. I _____ hungry when I get home from work. (am / usually)
4. "Where's Jim?" "He _____ home early." (gone / has / probably)
5. Mark and Diane _____ in Texas. (both / were / born)
6. Liz is a good pianist. She _____ very well. (sing / also / can)
7. Our cat _____ under the table. (always / sleeps)
8. They live on the same street as me, but I _____ to them. (never / have / spoken)
9. My eyesight isn't very good. I _____ with glasses. (read / can / only)
10. I _____ early tomorrow. (probably / leaving / will / be)
11. I _____ able to come to the party. (probably / be / won't)
12. It's hard to get in touch with Sue. She _____ at home when I call her. (is / hardly ever)
13. We _____ in the same place. We haven't moved. (still / are / living)
14. If we hadn't taken the same train, we _____ each other. (never / met / would / have)
15. "Are you tired?" "Yes, I _____ at this time of day." (am / always)

UNIT 107

Still, yet, and *already*
Anymore / any longer / no longer

A Still

We use **still** to say that a situation or action is continuing. It hasn't changed or stopped:

- It's 10:00 and Tom is **still** in bed.
- When I went to bed, Jane was **still** working.
- Do you **still** want to go to the party, or have you changed your mind?

Still usually goes in the middle of the sentence with the verb. See Unit 106.

B Anymore / any longer / no longer

We use **not . . . anymore** or **not . . . any longer** to say that a situation has changed. **Anymore** and **any longer** go at the end of a sentence:

- Ann doesn't work here **anymore** (*or* **any longer**). She left last month.
- We used to be good friends, but we aren't **anymore** (*or* **any longer**).

You can also use **no longer. No longer** goes in the middle of the sentence:

- Ann **no longer** works here.

Note that we do not normally use **no more** in this way:

- We are **no longer** friends. (*not* We are no more friends)

Compare **still** and **not . . . anymore:**

- Sheila **still** works here, but Ann doesn't work here **anymore.**

C Yet

Yet = until now. We use **yet** mainly in negative sentences (I haven't finished **yet**) and questions (Have you finished **yet**?). **Yet** shows that the speaker is expecting something to happen. **Yet** usually goes at the end of a sentence:

- It's 10:00 and Tom hasn't gotten up **yet.**
- I'm hungry. Is dinner ready **yet**?
- We don't know where we're going for our vacation **yet.**

Compare **yet** and **still:**

- Jack lost his job a year ago and is **still** unemployed.
  Jack lost his job a year ago and hasn't found another job **yet.**
- Is it **still** raining?
  Has it stopped raining **yet**?

Still is also possible in negative sentences (before the negative):

- She said she would be here an hour ago, and she **still** hasn't come.

This is similar to "she hasn't come **yet**." But **still . . . not** shows a stronger feeling of surprise or impatience. Compare:

- I wrote to him last week. He hasn't replied **yet.** (but I expect he will reply soon)
- I wrote to him months ago, and he **still** hasn't replied. (he should have replied before now)

D Already

We use **already** to say that something happened sooner than expected. **Already** goes in the middle of a sentence (see Unit 106) or at the end:

- "When is Sue going on vacation?" "She has **already** gone." (= sooner than you expected)
- Should I tell Liz the news, or does she **already** know?
- I've just had lunch, and I'm hungry **already.**

Present Perfect + *already/yet* **Unit 7C   Word Order (2) Unit 106**

Exercises

107.1 Compare what Paul said a few years ago with what he says now. Some things are the same as before, and some things have changed.

Paul a few years ago

I travel a lot.
I work in a gym.
I write poems.
I want to be a teacher.
I'm interested in politics.
I'm single.
I go fishing a lot.

Paul now

I travel a lot.
I work in a hospital.
I gave up writing poems.
I want to be a teacher.
I'm not interested in politics.
I'm single.
I haven't been fishing for years.

Write sentences about Paul using *still* and *not . . . anymore*.

1. (travel) *He still travels a lot.*
2. (gym) *He doesn't work in a gym anymore.*
3. (poems) He _____ .
4. (teacher) _____
5. (politics) _____
6. (single) _____
7. (fishing) _____
8. (beard) _____

Now write three sentences about Paul using *no longer*.

9. *He no longer works in a gym.*
10. He _____ .
11. _____
12. _____

107.2 For each sentence (with *still*) write a sentence with a similar meaning using *not . . . yet* + one of the following verbs:

> decide   finish   leave   ~~stop~~   take off   wake up

1. It's still raining. *It hasn't stopped raining yet.*
2. George is still here. He _____ .
3. They're still eating dinner. They _____ .
4. The children are still asleep. _____
5. I'm still wondering what to do. _____
6. The plane is still waiting on the runway. _____

107.3 Put *still, yet, already,* or *anymore* in the underlined sentence (or part of a sentence). Study the examples carefully.

1. Jack lost his job a year ago, and <u>he is unemployed</u>. *he is still unemployed*
2. Do you want me to tell Liz the news, or <u>does she know</u>? *does she already know*
3. I'm hungry. <u>Is dinner ready</u>? *Is dinner ready yet?*
4. I was hungry earlier, but <u>I'm not hungry</u>. *I'm not hungry anymore*
5. Can we wait a few minutes? <u>I don't want to go out</u>. _____
6. Jill used to work at the airport, but <u>she doesn't work there</u>. _____
7. I used to live in Tokyo. <u>I have a lot of friends there</u>. _____
8. "Should I introduce you to Jim?" "You don't have to. <u>We've met</u>." _____
9. <u>Do you live in the same house</u>, or have you moved? _____
10. Would you like to eat with us, or <u>have you eaten</u>? _____
11. "Where's John?" "<u>He isn't here</u>. He'll be here soon." _____
12. Tim said he would be here at 8:30. It's 9:00 now, and <u>he isn't here</u>. _____
13. Do you want to join the club, or <u>are you a member</u>? _____
14. It happened a long time ago, but <u>I can remember it very clearly</u>. _____
15. I've put on weight. <u>These pants don't fit me</u>. _____

A

Study this example situation:

Tina loves watching television.
She has a lot of television sets.
She has a TV set in every room of
the house – **even** the bathroom.

We use **even** to say that something
is unusual or surprising. It is unusual
to have a TV set in the bathroom.

Some more examples:

- These pictures aren't very good. **Even I** could take better pictures than these. (and I'm certainly not a good photographer)
- He always wears a coat – **even in hot weather.**
- Nobody would lend her the money – **not even her best friend.** *or* **Not even her best friend** would lend her the money.

B

Very often we use **even** with the verb in the middle of a sentence (see Unit 106):

- Sue has traveled all over the world. She has **even** been to the Antarctic. (It's especially unusual to go to the Antarctic, so she must have traveled a lot.)
- They are very rich. They **even** have their own private jet.

Study these examples with **not even**:

- I can't cook. I **can't even** boil an egg. (and boiling an egg is very easy)
- They weren't very friendly to us. They **didn't even** say hello.
- Jenny is in great shape. She's just run five miles, and she's **not even** out of breath.

C

You can use **even** + *a comparative* (**cheaper / more expensive**, etc.):

- I got up very early, but John got up **even earlier.**
- I knew I didn't have much money, but I have **even less** than I thought.
- We were surprised to get a letter from her. We were **even more surprised** when she came to see us a few days later.

D

Even though / even when / even if

You can use **even** + **though/when/if** to join sentences. Note that you cannot use **even** alone in the following examples:

- **Even though** she can't drive, she has bought a car. (*not* Even she can't drive)
- He never shouts, **even when** he's angry.
- I'll probably see you tomorrow. But **even if** I don't see you tomorrow, I'm sure we'll see each other before the weekend. (*not* even I don't see you)

Compare **even if** and **if**:

- We're going to the beach tomorrow. It doesn't matter what the weather is like. We're going to the beach **even if** it's raining.
- We hope to go to the beach tomorrow, but we won't go **if** it's raining.

Exercises

108.1 Julie, Sarah, and Amanda are three friends who went on vacation together. Use the information given about them to complete the sentences using *even* or *not even*.

Julie	Sarah	Amanda
is usually happy is usually on time likes getting up early is very interested in art	is usually miserable usually hates hotels doesn't have a camera doesn't particularly like art	likes taking pictures is almost always late loves staying at hotels isn't good at getting up early

1. They stayed at a hotel. Everybody liked it, *even Sarah* .
2. They arranged to meet. They all arrived on time, _____.
3. They went to an art gallery. Nobody enjoyed it, _____.
4. Yesterday they had to get up early. They all managed to do this, _____.
5. They were together yesterday. They were all in a good mood, _____.
6. None of them took any pictures, _____.

108.2 Make sentences with *even*. Use the words in parentheses.

1. She has been all over the world. (the Antarctic) *She has even been to the Antarctic.*
2. She has to work every day. (on Sundays) _____
3. They painted the whole room. (the floor)
   They _____.
4. You could hear the noise from a long way away. (from the next street)
   You _____.

In the following sentences you have to use *not even*.

5. They didn't say anything to us. (hello) *They didn't even say hello.*
6. I can't remember anything about her. (her name)
   I _____.
7. There isn't anything to do in this town. (a movie theater)
   _____
8. He didn't tell anybody where he was going. (his wife)
   _____

108.3 Complete these sentences using *even* + a comparative.

1. It was very hot yesterday, but today it's *even hotter* .
2. The church is 500 years old, but the house next to it is _____.
3. That's a good idea, but I've got an _____ one.
4. The first question was difficult to answer. The second one was _____.
5. I did very badly on the test, but most of my friends did _____.
6. Neither of us were hungry. I ate very little, and my friend ate _____.

108.4 Put in *if*, *even*, *even if*, or *even though*.

1. *Even though* she can't drive, she has bought a car.
2. The bus leaves in five minutes, but we can still catch it _____ we run.
3. The bus leaves in two minutes. We won't catch it now _____ we run.
4. His Spanish isn't very good – _____ after three years in Mexico.
5. His Spanish isn't very good, _____ he's lived in Mexico for three years.
6. _____ with the heat on, it was very cold in the house.
7. _____ I was very tired, I couldn't sleep.
8. I won't forgive them for what they said, _____ they apologize.

Although / though / even though
In spite of / despite

A

Study this example situation:

Last year Jack and Jill spent their vacation at the beach.
It rained a lot, but they enjoyed themselves.
You can say:
Although it rained a lot, they enjoyed themselves.
(= It rained a lot, but they . . .)
or
In spite of } **the rain,** they enjoyed themselves.
Despite

B

After **although** we use a *subject + verb*:
- **Although it rained** a lot, we enjoyed our vacation.
- I didn't get the job **although I was** extremely qualified.

Compare the meaning of **although** and **because**:
- We went out **although** it was raining.
- We didn't go out **because** it was raining.

C

After **in spite of** or **despite**, we use a *noun*, a *pronoun* (**this/that/what**, etc.), or **-ing**:
- **In spite of the rain,** we enjoyed our vacation.
- I didn't get the job **in spite of being** extremely qualified.
- She felt sick, but **in spite of this** she went to work.
- **In spite of what** I said yesterday, I still love you.

Despite is the same as **in spite of**. Note that we say **in spite of** but **despite** (*without* of):
- She felt sick, but **despite this** she went to work. (*not* despite of this)

You can say **in spite of the fact (that)** and **despite the fact (that)**:
- I didn't get the job { **in spite of the fact** (that) / **despite the fact** (that) } I was extremely qualified.

Compare **in spite of** and **because of**:
- We went out **in spite of the rain.** (*or* despite the rain)
- We didn't go out **because of the rain.**

D

Compare **although** and **in spite of** / **despite**:
- **Although** the traffic was bad, } I arrived on time. (*not* In spite of the traffic was bad)
  In spite of the traffic,
- I couldn't sleep { **although I was** very tired. / **despite being** very tired. } (*not* despite I was tired)

E

Sometimes we use **though** instead of **although**:
- I didn't get the job **though** I had all the necessary qualifications.

In spoken English we often use **though** at the end of a sentence:
- The house isn't very nice. I like the garden **though**. (= but I like the garden)
- I see him every day. I've never spoken to him **though**. (= but I've never spoken to him)

Even though (*not* **even** alone) is a stronger form of **although**:
- **Even though** I was really tired, I couldn't sleep. (*not* Even I was really tired)

Exercises

109.1 Complete the sentences. Use *although* + a sentence from the box.

I didn't speak the language	~~he has a very important job~~
I had never seen her before	we don't like them very much
it was pretty cold	the heat was on
I'd met her twice before	we've known each other for a long time

1. _Although he has a very important job_____ , he isn't particularly well paid.
2. _____ , I recognized her from a picture.
3. She wasn't wearing a coat _____ .
4. We thought we'd better invite them to the party _____ .
5. _____ , I managed to make myself understood.
6. _____ , the room wasn't very warm.
7. I didn't recognize her _____ .
8. We're not very good friends _____ .

109.2. Complete the sentences with *although / in spite of / because / because of.*

1. _Although_____ it rained a lot, we enjoyed our vacation.
2. a) _____ all our careful plans, a lot of things went wrong.
   b) _____ we had planned everything carefully, a lot of things went wrong.
3. a) I went home early _____ I was feeling sick.
   b) I went to work the next day _____ I was still feeling sick.
4. a) She only accepted the job _____ the salary, which was very high.
   b) She accepted the job _____ the salary, which was rather low.
5. a) I managed to get to sleep _____ there was a lot of noise.
   b) I couldn't get to sleep _____ the noise.

Use your own ideas to complete the following sentences:

6. a) He passed the exam although _____ .
   b) He passed the exam because _____ .
7. a) I didn't eat anything although _____ .
   b) I didn't eat anything in spite of _____ .

109.3. Make one sentence from two. Use the word(s) in parentheses in your sentences.

1. I couldn't sleep. I was tired. (despite) _I couldn't sleep despite being tired._
2. They have very little money. They are happy. (in spite of)
   In spite of _____ .
3. My foot was injured. I managed to walk to the nearest town. (although)

   _____
4. We live on the same street. We hardly ever see each other. (despite)

   _____
5. I got very wet in the rain. I had an umbrella. (even though)

   _____

109.4. Use the words in parentheses to make a sentence with *though* at the end.

1. The house isn't very nice. (like / garden) _I like the garden though._
2. It's pretty warm. (a little windy) _____
3. We didn't like the food. (ate) _____
4. Liz is very nice. (don't like / husband) I _____ .

In case

Study this example situation:

Jeff is a soccer referee. He always wears two watches during a game because it is possible that one watch will stop.

He wears two watches **in case** one of them stops.

In case one of them stops = because it is possible one of them will stop.

Some more examples of **in case**:

- Ann might call tonight. I don't want to go out **in case** she calls. (= because it is possible she will call)
- I'll draw a map for you **in case** you can't find our house. (= because it is possible you won't be able to find it)

We use **just in case** for a smaller possibility:

- I don't think it will rain, but I'll take an umbrella **just in case**. (= **just in case** it rains)

Do not use **will** after **in case**. Use the present tense with a future meaning (see also Unit 24):

- I don't want to go out tonight **in case** Ann **calls**. (*not* in case Ann will call)

In case is not the same as **if**. We use **in case** to say *why* somebody does (or doesn't do) something. You do something now **in case** something happens later. Compare:

in case	if
■ We'll buy some more food **in case** Tom comes. (= Perhaps Tom will come; we'll buy some more food now, whether he comes or not; then we'll *already* have the food *if* he comes.)	■ We'll buy some more food **if** Tom comes. (= Perhaps Tom will come; if he comes, we'll buy some more food; if he doesn't come, we won't buy any more food.)
■ I'll give you my phone number **in case** you need to contact me.	■ You can call me at the hotel **if** you need to contact me.

You can use **in case** (+ *past*) to say why somebody did something:

- We bought some more food **in case** Tom **came**. (= because it was possible that Tom would come)
- I drew a map for Sarah **in case** she **couldn't** find the house.
- We rang the bell again **in case** they **hadn't** heard it the first time.

In case of . . . is not the same as **in case**. **In case of . . .** = if there is . . . (especially on signs, etc.):

- **In case of fire,** please leave the building as quickly as possible. (= if there is a fire)
- **In case of emergency,** telephone this number. (= if there is an emergency)

Exercises

110.1 Barbara is going for a long walk in the country. She is going to take these things with her:

~~some chocolate~~   a map   an umbrella   her camera   some water   a towel

She has decided to take these things because:

maybe she'll want to go for a swim	it's possible she'll get lost	~~she might get hungry~~
she might want to take some pictures	perhaps she'll get thirsty	maybe it will rain

Write sentences with *in case* saying why Barbara has decided to take these things with her.

1. *She's going to take some chocolate in case she gets hungry.* _____
2. She's going to take a map in case _____ .
3. She's going to _____ .
4. _____
5. _____
6. _____

110.2 What do you say in these situations? Use *in case.*

1. It's possible that Mary will need to contact you, so you give her your phone number.
   You say: Here's my phone number _____ .
2. A friend of yours is going away for a long time. Maybe you won't see her again before
   she goes, so you decide to say good-bye now.
   You say: I'll say _____ .
3. You are shopping in a supermarket with a friend. You think you have everything you need,
   but perhaps you've forgotten something. Your friend has the list. You ask him to check it.
   You say: Can you _____ ?

110.3 Write sentences with *in case.*

1. There was a possibility that Ann would call. So I didn't go out.
   I didn't go out in case Ann called. _____
2. I thought my parents might be worried about me. So I called them.
   I called _____ .
3. I wrote a letter to Jane, but I didn't get a reply. So I wrote to her again because I
   thought that perhaps she hadn't gotten my first letter.
   I _____ .
4. I met some people when I was on vacation in France. They said they might come to
   New York one day. I live in New York, so I gave them my address.
   I _____ .

110.4 Put in *in case* or *if.*

1. Ann might call this evening. I don't want to go out _*in case*_ she calls.
2. You should tell the police _*if*_ your bicycle is stolen.
3. I hope you'll come to Chicago sometime. _____ you come, you can stay with us.
4. This letter is for Susan. Can you give it to her _____ you see her?
5. Write your name and address on your bag _____ you lose it.
6. Go to the Lost and Found office _____ you lose your bag.
7. The burglar alarm will ring _____ somebody tries to break into the house.
8. I've just painted the door. I'll put a WET PAINT sign next to it _____
   somebody doesn't realize the paint is still wet.
9. I was advised to get insurance _____ I needed medical treatment while I was
   abroad.

Unless *As long as* and *provided/providing*

Unless
Study this example situation:

> MEADOWS COUNTRY CLUB MEMBERS ONLY
>
> The club is for members only.
> You can't play tennis there **unless you are a member**.
> This means:
> You can't play tennis there except if you are a member *or*
> You can play tennis there only if you are a member.
> **Unless** = except if

Some more examples of **unless**:
- ■ I'll see you tomorrow **unless I have to work late**. (= except if I have to work late)
- ■ Don't tell Sue what I said **unless she asks you**. (= except if she asks you)
- ■ "Should I tell Sue what you said?" "**Not unless she asks you**." (= only if she asks you)
- ■ I don't like fish. I wouldn't eat it **unless I was extremely hungry**. (= except if I was/were extremely hungry)

We often use **unless** in warnings:
- ■ We'll be late **unless we hurry**. (= except if we hurry)
- ■ **Unless you work much harder**, you won't pass the exam.
- ■ I was told I wouldn't pass the exam **unless I worked harder**.

Instead of **unless**, it is often possible to say **if . . . not**:
- ■ Don't tell Sue what I said **if she doesn't ask you**.
- ■ We'll be late **if we don't hurry**.

As long as, etc.

as long as / so long as
provided (that) / providing (that) } All these expressions mean "if" or "on condition that."

For example:
- ■ You can use my car { **as long as** / **so long as** } you drive carefully.

  (= You can use my car, but you must drive carefully – this is a condition.)

- ■ Traveling by car is convenient { **provided (that)** / **providing (that)** } you have somewhere to park.

  (= but only if you have somewhere to park)

- ■ **Providing (that)** / **Provided (that)** } she studies hard, she'll pass her exams.

  (= She must study hard – if she does this, she will pass.)

When you are talking about the future, do not use **will** after **unless / as long as / so long as / provided / providing**. Use a *present* tense (see also Unit 24):
- ■ We'll be late **unless we hurry**. (*not* unless we will hurry)
- ■ **Providing she studies** hard, she will pass the exam. (*not* Providing she will study)

Exercises

111.1 Write a new sentence with the same meaning. Use *unless* in your sentence.

1. You need to work a lot harder, or you won't pass the exam.
   You won't pass the exam unless you work a lot harder.
2. Listen carefully, or you won't know what to do.
   You won't know what to do _____ .
3. She has to apologize to me, or I'll never speak to her again.
   I'll _____ .
4. You have to speak very slowly, or he won't be able to understand you.

   _____
5. The company has to offer me more money, or I'm going to look for another job.

   _____

111.2 Write a new sentence with the same meaning. Use *unless* in your sentence.

1. You are allowed into the club only if you're a member.
   You aren't allowed into the club unless you're a member.
2. I'm going to the party only if you go, too.
   I'm not going _____ .
3. The dog will attack you only if you move suddenly.

   _____
4. He'll speak to you only if you ask him a question.

   _____
5. The doctor will see you today only if it's an emergency.

   _____

111.3 Choose the correct word or expression for each sentence.

1. You can use my car ~~unless~~ / as long as you drive carefully. (*as long as* is correct)
2. I'm playing tennis tomorrow unless / providing it rains.
3. I'm playing tennis tomorrow unless / providing it doesn't rain.
4. I don't mind if you come in late unless / as long as you come in quietly.
5. I'm going now unless / provided you want me to stay.
6. I don't watch TV unless / as long as I have nothing else to do.
7. Children are allowed to use the swimming pool unless / provided they are with an adult.
8. Unless / Provided they are with an adult, children are not allowed to use the swimming pool.
9. We can sit here in the corner unless / as long as you'd rather sit over there by the window.
10. *A:* Our vacation cost a lot of money.
    B: Did it? Well, that doesn't matter unless / as long as you enjoyed yourselves.

111.4 Use your own ideas to complete these sentences.

1. We'll be late unless *we hurry* .
2. I like hot weather unless _____ .
3. I like hot weather provided _____ .
4. Kate reads a newspaper every day as long as _____ .
5. I don't mind walking home so long as _____ .
6. I like to walk to work in the morning unless _____ .
7. We can meet tomorrow unless _____ .
8. You can borrow the money providing _____ .
9. You won't achieve anything unless _____ .

As (Time and Reason)

A

As (time)

You can use **as** when two things happen at the same time:
- ■ I watched her **as** she opened the letter. (**I watched** and **she opened** at the same time.)
- ■ **As** they walked along the street, they looked in the store windows.

Or you can say that something happened **as** you were doing something else (= in the middle of doing something else):
- ■ Jill slipped **as** she was getting off the bus.
- ■ The thief was seen **as** he was climbing over the wall.

In these examples **as** is similar to **while**.
For the *past continuous* (**was getting / were going,** etc.), see Unit 6.

Often we use **as** when two short actions happen at the same time:
- ■ We all waved good-bye to Liz **as** she drove away in her car.
  (**we waved** and **she drove** away at the same time)
- ■ Turn off the light **as** you go out, please.

But we also use **as** when two things change together over a
longer period of time:
- ■ **As** the day went on, the weather got worse.
- ■ I began to enjoy the job more **as** I got used to it.

You can also use **just as** (= exactly at that moment):
- ■ **Just as** I sat down, the phone rang.
- ■ I had to leave **just as** the conversation was getting interesting.

We use **as** only if two things happen at the same time. Use **when** (*not* as) if one thing happens
after another:
- ■ **When** I got home, I took a bath. (= not as I got home, but after I got home)
- ■ **As** I walked into the room, the phone started ringing. (= at the same time)

B

As (reason)

As sometimes means "because":
- ■ **As** it was a national holiday, all the banks were closed. (= because it was a national
  holiday)
- ■ We watched TV all evening **as** we had nothing better to do.

Note that we also use **since** in this way:
- ■ **Since** it was a national holiday, all the banks were closed.

C

We use **as** (time) with actions and happenings (see Section A):
- ■ I watched her **as** she read the letter.

When we use **as** with a situation (not an action), the meaning is usually **because**:
- ■ **As** I was asleep, I didn't hear the bell. (= because I was asleep)
- ■ **As** they live near us, we see them quite often. (= because they live near us)

Compare **while** or **when**:
- ■ The bell rang **while** (*or* **when**) I was asleep. (*not* as I was asleep)
- ■ They got married **when** (*or* **while**) they were living in London. (*not* as they were living)

Exercises

112.1 Use *as* to join a sentence from Box A with one from Box B.

A
1. ~~we all waved good-bye to Liz~~
2. we all smiled
3. I burned myself
4. the crowd cheered
5. a dog ran out in front of the car

B
we were driving along the road
I was taking a hot dish out of the oven
~~she drove away in her car~~
we posed for the photograph
the two teams ran onto the field

1. *We all waved good-bye to Liz as she drove away in her car.*
2. _____
3. _____
4. _____
5. _____

112.2 Put in *as* or *when*. Sometimes you can use either *as* or *when*.

1. Maria got married *when* she was 23.
2. My camera was stolen _____ I was on vacation.
3. He dropped the glass _____ he was taking it out of the cupboard.
4. _____ I finished high school, I went into the army.
5. The train slowed down _____ it approached the station.
6. I used to live near the ocean _____ I was a child.

112.3 What does *as* mean in these sentences?

	because	at the same time as
1. As they live near us, we see them pretty often.	✓	
2. Jill slipped as she was getting off the bus.		✓
3. As I was tired, I went to bed early.		
4. Unfortunately, as I was parking the car, I hit the car behind me.		
5. As we climbed the hill, we got more and more tired.		
6. We decided to go out to eat as we had no food at home.		
7. As we don't use the car very often, we've decided to sell it.		

Now rewrite the sentences where *as* means *because*. Use *since*.

8. *Since they live near us, we see them pretty often.*
9. _____
10. _____
11. _____

112.4 Use your own ideas to complete these sentences.

1. I saw you as _____.
2. It began to rain just as _____.
3. As I didn't have enough money for a taxi, _____.
4. Just as I took the photograph, _____.

Like and *as*

A

Like = similar to, the same as:
- What a beautiful house! It's **like** a palace. (*not* as a palace)
- "What does Sandra do?" "She's a teacher, **like** me." (*not* as me)
- Be careful! The floor has been polished. It's **like** walking on ice. (*not* as walking)
- We heard a noise **like** a baby crying. (*not* as a baby crying)

In these sentences, **like** is a *preposition*. So it is followed by a *noun* (**like a palace**), a *pronoun* (**like me**), or **-ing** (**like walking**). You cannot use **as** in these sentences.

Sometimes **like** = "for example." You can also use **such as**:
- Some sports, **like** race-car driving, can be dangerous. *or* Some sports, **such as** race-car driving, can be dangerous.

B

We use **as** (= in the same way) before a *subject + verb*:
- I didn't move anything. I left everything **as I found** it. (= the way I found it)
- You should have done it **as I showed** you. (= the way I showed you)

You can also use **like** in these sentences, especially in informal speech:
- I left everything **like** I found it.

Compare **like** and **as**:
- You should have done it **like** this. (*not* as this)
- You should have done it **as** I showed you *or* . . . **like** I showed you.

Note that we say **as usual / as always**:
- You're late **as usual**.

C

Sometimes **as** (+ *subject + verb*) has other meanings. For example, after **do**:
- Please **do as** I say. (= do what I say)
- They **did as** they promised. (= they did what they promised)

We also say **as you know / as I was saying / as she expected / as I thought**, etc.:
- **As you know**, it's Tom's birthday next week. (= you know it's his birthday)
- Ann failed her driving test, **as she expected**. (= she expected this)

You can also say **like I was saying / like I said**, but generally **like** is not used in the other expressions (**as you know**, etc.).

D

As can also be a *preposition*, but the meaning is different from **like**. Compare:

Brenda Casey is the manager of a company. **As the manager,** she has to make many important decisions. (**As the manager** = in her position as the manager)	Mary Stone is the assistant manager. **Like the manager** (Brenda Casey), she also has to make important decisions. (**Like the manager** = similar to the manager)

As (preposition) = in the position of, in the form of, etc.:
- A few years ago I worked **as a bus driver.** (*not* like a bus driver)
- We've got a garage, but we don't have a car, so we use the garage **as a workshop**.
- Many English words (for example, "work" and "rain") can be used **as verbs or nouns**.
- New York is all right **as a place to visit**, but I wouldn't like to live there.
- The news of her death came **as a great shock**.

As . . . as Unit 103   *The same as* Unit 103C   *As (Time and Reason)* Unit 112   *As if* Unit 114

Exercises

113.1 Put in *like* or *as* (see Sections A–C). Sometimes either word is possible.

1. It's raining again. I hate weather _like_ this.
2. Jane failed her driving test _as_ she expected.
3. Do you think Carol looks _____ her mother?
4. He really gets on my nerves. I can't stand people _____ him.
5. Why didn't you do it _____ I told you to do it?
6. "What does Bill do?" "He's a student, _____ most of his friends."
7. _____ I said yesterday, I'm thinking of changing my job.
8. Tom's idea seemed to be a good one, so we did _____ he suggested.
9. It's a difficult problem. I never know what to do in situations _____ this.
10. I'll phone you tomorrow _____ usual, OK?
11. This tea is awful. It tastes _____ water.
12. Suddenly there was a terrible noise. It was _____ a bomb exploding.
13. She's a very good swimmer. She swims _____ a fish.
14. We saw Keith last night. He was very cheerful, _____ always.

113.2 Complete the sentences using *like* or *as* + one of the following (see Sections A and D):

| a beginner | blocks of ice | ~~a palace~~ | a birthday present |
| a child | a church | winter | a tour guide |

1. This house is beautiful. It's _like a palace_ .
2. Margaret once had a part-time job _____ .
3. My feet are really cold. They're _____ .
4. I've been learning Spanish for a few years, but I still speak _____ .
5. I wonder what that building with the tower is. It looks _____ .
6. My brother gave me this watch _____ a long time ago.
7. It's very cold for the middle of summer. It's _____ .
8. He's 22 years old, but he sometimes behaves _____ .

113.3 Put in *like* or *as*. Sometimes either word is possible.

1. Your English is very fluent. I wish I could speak _like_ you.
2. Don't take my advice if you don't want to. You can do _____ you like.
3. You waste too much time doing things _____ sitting in cafes all day.
4. I wish I had a car _____ yours.
5. You don't need to change your clothes. You can go out _____ you are.
6. My neighbor's house is full of interesting things. It's _____ a museum.
7. I think I preferred this room _____ it was, before we decorated it.
8. When we asked Sue to help us, she agreed immediately, _____ I knew she would.
9. Sharon has been working _____ a waitress for the last two months.
10. While we were on vacation, we spent most of our time doing active things _____ sailing, water skiing, and swimming.
11. You're different from the other people I know. I don't know anyone _____ you.
12. We don't need all the bedrooms in the house, so we use one of them _____ a study.
13. _____ her father, Catherine has a very good voice.
14. The news that Sue and Jim were getting married came _____ a complete surprise to me.
15. At the moment I've got a temporary job in a bookstore. It's OK _____ a temporary job, but I wouldn't like to do it permanently.

As if, as though, and like

You can use **as if** to say how somebody or something **looks/sounds/feels,** etc.:

- That house **looks as if** it's going to fall down.
- Ann **sounded as if** she had a cold, didn't she?
- I've just come back from vacation, but I feel tired and depressed. I don't **feel as if** I've just had a vacation.

Compare:

- You **look tired.** (look + *adjective*)
- You **look as if you didn't sleep** last night. (look + **as if** + *subject* + *verb*)

You can use **as though** or **like** instead of **as if**:

- Ann sounded **as though** she had a cold. *or* Ann sounded **like** she had a cold.

You can also say:

$$\text{It} \begin{cases} \text{looks} \\ \text{sounds} \\ \text{smells} \end{cases} + \begin{cases} \text{like} \ldots \\ \text{as if} \ldots \\ \text{as though} \ldots \end{cases}$$

It sounds like they're having a party next door.

- Sandra is very late, isn't she? **It looks like** she isn't coming.
- We took an umbrella with us because **it looked as if** it was going to rain.
- Do you hear that music next door? **It sounds like** they're having a party.
- **It smells as though** someone has been smoking in here.

You can use **like / as if / as though** with other verbs to say how somebody does something:

- He **ran like** he was running for his life.
- After the interruption, the speaker **went on talking as if** nothing had happened.
- When I told them my plan, they **looked at me as though** I was crazy.

After **as if** we sometimes use the past when we are talking about the present. For example:

- I don't like Norma. She talks **as if** she **knew** everything.

The meaning is not past in this sentence. We use the past (as if she **knew**) because the idea is *not real*: Norma does *not* know everything. We use the past in the same way with **if** and **wish** (see Unit 36).

Some more examples:

- She's always asking me to do things for her – **as if I didn't have** enough to do. (I do have enough to do.)
- Harry's only 40. Why do you talk about him **as if he was** an old man? (He isn't an old man.)

When you use the past in this way, you can use **were** instead of **was**:

- Why do you talk about him **as if he were** (*or* **was**) an old man?
- They treat me **as if I were** (*or* **was**) their own son. (I'm not their son.)

Like and **as though** are not usually used in this type of sentence.

Look/sound, **etc. + Adjective** Unit 96C   *Like* **and** *as* Unit 113

Exercises

114.1 Choose from the box to complete the sentences. Use *as if* or *like*.

he hadn't eaten for a week	she was enjoying it	she had hurt her leg
he meant what he was saying	~~he needs a good rest~~	she didn't want to come

1. Mark looks very tired. He looks *as if he needs a good rest* .
2. Sue was having trouble walking. She looked _____ .
3. I don't think he was joking. He looked _____ .
4. Peter was extremely hungry and ate his dinner very quickly.
   He ate _____ .
5. Carol had a bored expression on her face during the concert.
   She didn't look _____ .
6. I called Ellen and invited her to the party, but she wasn't very enthusiastic about it.
   She sounded _____ .

114.2 What do you say in these situations? Use *You look / You sound / I feel + as if . . .*
Use the words in parentheses to make your sentence.

1. You meet Bill. He has a black eye and some bandages on his face.
   You say to him: *You look as if you've been in a fight.* (be / a fight)
2. Christine comes into the room. She looks absolutely terrified. You say to her:
   What's the matter? You _____ . (see / a ghost)
3. Sarah is talking to you on the phone about her new job and she sounds very happy
   about it. You say to her: _____ (enjoy / it)
4. You have just run one mile. You are absolutely exhausted.
   You say to a friend: I _____ . (run / a marathon)

114.3 Make sentences beginning *It looks like . . . / It sounds like . . .*

you had a good time	there's been an accident	they're having an argument
it's going to rain	~~she isn't coming~~	we'll have to walk

1. Sandra said she would be here an hour ago. You say: *It looks like she isn't coming.*
2. The sky is full of black clouds.
   You say: It _____ .
3. You hear two people shouting at each other next door.
   You say: _____
4. You see an ambulance, some police officers, and two damaged cars on the side of the road.
   You say: _____
5. You and a friend have just missed the last bus home.
   You say: _____
6. Sue and Dave have just been telling you about all the interesting things they did while
   they were on vacation.
   You say: _____

114.4 These sentences are like the ones in Section D. Complete each sentence using *as if*.

1. Brian is a terrible driver. He drives *as if he were* the only driver on the road.
2. I'm 20 years old, so please don't talk to me _____ a child.
3. Steve has only met Maria once, but he talks about her _____
   a close friend.
4. It was a long time ago that we first met, but I remember it _____
   yesterday.

229

For, during, and *while*

A

For and **during**

We use **for** + a period of time to say how long something goes on.
For example:

for two hours   **for a week**   **for ages**

- We watched television **for two hours** last night.
- Ann is going away **for a week** in September.
- Where have you been? I've been waiting **for ages.**
- Are you going away **for the weekend?**

We use **during** + *noun* to say when something happens (*not* how long).
For example:

during the movie   **during our vacation**   **during the night**

- I fell asleep **during the movie.**
- We met a lot of nice people **during our vacation.**
- The ground is wet. It must have rained **during the night.**

With a "time" word (for example, **the morning / the afternoon / the summer**), you can usually say **in** or **during:**

- It must have rained **in the night.** (*or* . . . **during the night.**)
- I'll call you sometime **during the afternoon.** (*or* . . . **in the afternoon.**)

You cannot use **during** to say how long something goes on:

- It rained **for three days** without stopping. (*not* during three days)

Compare **during** and **for:**

- I fell asleep **during the movie.** I was asleep **for half an hour.**

B

During and **while**

Compare:

We use **during** + *noun:*	We use **while** + *subject* + *verb:*
noun	*subject* + *verb*
■ I fell asleep **during** the movie .	■ I fell asleep **while** I was watching TV.
■ We met a lot of interesting people **during our vacation.**	■ We met a lot of interesting people **while we were** on vacation.
■ Robert suddenly began to feel sick **during the exam.**	■ Robert suddenly began to feel sick **while he was taking** the exam.

Some more examples of **while:**

- We saw Amanda **while we were waiting** for the bus.
- **While you were** out, there was a phone call for you.
- Tom read a book **while I watched** TV.

When you are talking about the future, use the *present* (*not* will) after **while:**

- I'll be in Toronto next week. I hope to see Tom **while I'm** there. (*not* while I will be there)
- What are you going to do **while** you **are waiting?** (*not* while you will be waiting)

See also Unit 24.

For* and *since Unit 12A   ***While -ing*** Unit 65B

Exercises

115.1 Put in *for* or *during.*

1. It rained *for* three days without stopping.
2. I fell asleep *during* the movie.
3. I went to the theater last night. I met Sue _____ the intermission.
4. Matt hasn't lived in the United States all his life. He lived in Brazil _____ four years.
5. Production at the factory was seriously affected _____ the strike.
6. I felt really sick last week. I could hardly eat anything _____ three days.
7. I waited for you _____ half an hour and decided that you weren't coming.
8. Sue was very angry with me. She didn't speak to me _____ a week.
9. We usually go out on weekends, but we don't often go out _____ the week.
10. Jack started a new job a few weeks ago. Before that he was out of work _____ six months.
11. I need a change. I think I'll go away _____ a few days.
12. The president gave a long speech. She spoke _____ two hours.
13. We were hungry when we arrived. We hadn't had anything to eat _____ the trip.
14. We were hungry when we arrived. We hadn't had anything to eat _____ eight hours.

115.2 Put in *during* or *while.*

1. We met a lot of people *while* we were on vacation.
2. We met a lot of people *during* our vacation.
3. I met Mike _____ I was shopping.
4. _____ we were in Paris, we stayed at a very comfortable hotel.
5. _____ our stay in Paris, we visited a lot of museums and galleries.
6. The phone rang three times _____ we were having dinner.
7. The phone rang three times _____ the night.
8. I had been away for many years. _____ that time, many things had changed.
9. What did they say about me _____ I was out of the room?
10. Carlos read a lot of books and magazines _____ he was sick.
11. I went out for dinner last night. Unfortunately, I began to feel sick _____ the meal and had to go home.
12. Please don't interrupt me _____ I'm speaking.
13. There were many interruptions _____ the president's speech.
14. We were hungry when we arrived. We hadn't had anything to eat _____ we were traveling.

115.3 Use your own ideas to complete these sentences.

1. I fell asleep while *I was watching TV* .
2. I fell asleep during *the movie* .
3. I hurt my arm while _____ .
4. Can you wait here while _____ ?
5. Most of the students looked bored during _____ .
6. I was asked a lot of questions during _____ .
7. Don't open the car door while _____ .
8. The lights suddenly went out during _____ .
9. It started to rain during _____ .
10. It started to rain while _____ .

By and *until* *By the time* . . .

A

By (+ a time) = "no later than":
- I mailed the letter today, so they should receive it **by Monday.** (= on or before Monday, no later than Monday)
- We'd better hurry. We have to be home **by 5:00.**
  (= at or before 5:00, no later than 5:00)
- Where's Sue? She should be here **by now.** (= now or before now – so she should have arrived already)

You cannot use **until** with this meaning:
- Tell me **by Friday** whether or not you can come to the party. (*not* Tell me until Friday)

*This cheese should be sold **by August 14.***

B

We use **until** (*or* **till**) to say how long a situation continues:
- "Should we go now?" "No, let's wait **until** (*or* **till**) it stops raining."
- I couldn't get up this morning. { I stayed in bed **until** half past ten.
  { I didn't get up **until** half past ten.

Compare **until** and **by:**

until	by
Something *continues* **until** a time in the future:	Something *happens* **by** a time in the future:
■ Fred **will be away until** Monday. (so he'll be back on Monday)	■ Fred **will be back by** Monday. (= he'll be back no later than Monday)
■ I'll be working **until** 11:30. (so I'll stop working at 11:30)	■ I'll have finished my work **by** 11:30. (I'll finish my work no later than 11:30)

C

You can say "**by the time** something happens." Study these examples:
- *(from a letter)* I'm flying to Mexico this evening. So **by the time you receive** this letter, I'll be in Mexico City. (= I will arrive in Mexico City between now and the time you receive this letter.)
- Hurry up! **By the time we get** to the theater, the play will already have started.

You can say "**by the time** something happened" (for the past):
- Jane's car broke down on the way to the party last night. **By the time she arrived,** most of the other guests had left. (= It took her a long time to get to the party, and most of the guests went home during this time.)
- I had a lot of work to do yesterday evening. I was very tired **by the time I finished.** (= It took me a long time to do the work, and I became more and more tired during this time.)
- We went to the theater last night. It took us a long time to find somewhere to park the car. **By the time we got** to the theater, the play had already started.

Also **by then** or **by that time:**
- Jane finally arrived at the party at midnight, but **by then** (*or* **by that time**), most of the guests had left.

Exercises

116.1 Make sentences with *by*.

1. I have to be home no later than 5:00. _I have to be home by 5:00._
2. I have to be at the airport no later than 10:30. I have to be at the airport _____ .
3. Let me know no later than Saturday whether you can come to the party.
   Let me know _____ .
4. Please make sure that you're here no later than 2:00.
   Please _____ .
5. If we leave now, we should arrive no later than lunchtime.

   _____

116.2 Put in *by* or *until*.

1. Fred has gone out of town. He'll be out of town _until_ Monday.
2. Sorry, but I have to go. I have to be home _by_ 5:00.
3. I've been offered a job. I haven't decided yet whether to accept it or not. I have to decide _____ Thursday.
4. I think I'll wait _____ Thursday before making a decision.
5. It's too late to go shopping. The stores are only open _____ 5:30. They'll be closed _____ now.
6. I'd better pay the phone bill. It has to be paid _____ tomorrow.
7. Don't pay the bill today. Wait _____ tomorrow.
8. *A:* Have you finished painting your house?
   B: Not yet. We hope to finish _____ the end of the week.
9. *A:* I'm going out now. I'll be back at 4:30. Will you still be here?
   B: I don't think so. I'll probably have left _____ then.
10. I'm moving into my new apartment next week. I'm staying with a friend _____ then.
11. I've got a lot of work to do. _____ the time I finish, it will be time to go to bed.
12. If you want to take the exam, you should register _____ April 3rd.

116.3 Use your own ideas to complete these sentences. Use *by* or *until*.

1. Fred is out of town at the moment. He'll be out of town _until Monday_ .
2. Fred is out of town at the moment. He'll be back _by Monday_ .
3. I'm going out. I won't be very long. Wait here _____ .
4. I'm going shopping. It's 4:30 now. I won't be very long. I'll be back _____ .
5. If you want to apply for the job, your application must be received _____ .
6. Last night I watched TV _____ .

116.4 Read the situations and complete the sentences using *By the time* . . .

1. Lisa was invited to a party, but she got there much later than she intended.
   By the time she got to the party, most of the other guests had left.
2. I was supposed to catch a train, but it took me longer than expected to get to the station.
   _____ , my train had already left.
3. I saw two men who looked as if they were trying to steal a car. I called the police, but it was some time before they arrived.
   _____ , the two men had disappeared.
4. A man escaped from prison last night. It was a long time before the guards discovered what had happened.
   _____ , the escaped prisoner was miles away.
5. I intended to go shopping after finishing my work. But I finished my work much later than expected.
   _____ , it was too late to go shopping.

At/on/in (Time)

Compare **at**, **on**, and **in**:

- They arrived **at 5:00.**
- They arrived **on Friday.**
- They arrived **in October.** / They arrived **in 1998.**

We use:

at for the time of day:	
at 5:00 at 11:45 at midnight at lunchtime at sunset	

on for days and dates:
on Friday / on Fridays   on March 12, 2002   on Christmas Day   on my birthday
also on the weekend, on weekends

in for longer periods (for example, months/years/seasons):
in October   in 1998   in the 18th century   in the past
in (the) winter   in the 1970s   in the Middle Ages   in the future

We also use **at** in these expressions:

at night	■ I don't like going out **at night.**
at Christmas / at Easter	■ Do you give each other presents **at Christmas?**
at the moment / at this time	■ Mr. Brown is busy **at the moment / at this time.**
at the same time	■ Liz and I arrived **at the same time.**

We say:

    in the morning(s)   **in the afternoon(s)**   **in the evening(s)**

- I'll see you **in the morning.**   ■ Do you work **in the evenings?**

but: **on Friday morning(s)**   **on Sunday afternoon(s)**   **on Monday evening(s)**

- I'll be at home **on Friday morning.**   ■ Do you usually go out **on Saturday evenings?**

We do not use **at/on/in** before **last/next/this/every:**

- I'll see you **next Friday.** (*not* on next Friday)
- They got married **last March.**

Note that we often leave out **on** before days and dates
(**Monday / Mondays / Monday morning / March 12th,** etc.):

- I'll see you (**on**) **Friday.**
- She works (**on**) **Saturday mornings.**
- They got married (**on**) **March 12th.**

In a few minutes / in six months, etc. = a time in the future:

- The train will be leaving **in a few minutes.** (= a few minutes from now)
- Jack has left town. He'll be back **in a week.** (= a week from now)
- She'll be here **in a moment.** (= a moment from now)

You can also say "**in six months' time,**" "**in a week's time,**" etc.:

- They're getting married **in six months' time.** (*or* . . . **in six months.**)

We also use **in . . .** to say how long it takes to do something:

- I learned to drive **in four weeks.** (= It took me four weeks to learn.)

On/in time, at/in the end Unit 118   *In/at/on* (Place) Units 119–121   *On/in/at* (Other Uses) Unit 123

Exercises

117.1 Complete the sentences. Each time use *at, on,* or *in* + one of the following:

the evening	about 20 minutes	~~1492~~	Sundays	the Middle Ages	11 seconds
the moment	July 21, 1969	night	the 1920s	the same time	

1. Columbus made his first voyage from Europe to America *in 1492* .
2. Most people in the United States do not work _____ .
3. If the sky is clear, you can see the stars _____ .
4. After working hard during the day, I like to relax _____ .
5. The first man walked on the moon _____ .
6. It's difficult to listen if everyone is speaking _____ .
7. Jazz became popular in the United States _____ .
8. I'm going out to the store. I'll be back _____ .
9. *(on the phone)* "Can I speak to Chris?" "I'm sorry, he's not here _____ ."
10. Many of Europe's great cathedrals were built _____ .
11. Bob is a very fast runner. He can run 100 meters _____ .

117.2 Put in *at, on,* or *in.*

1. Mozart was born in Salzburg *in* 1756.
2. "Have you seen Kate recently?" "Yes, I saw her _____ Tuesday."
3. The price of electricity is going up _____ October.
4. I've been invited to a wedding _____ February 14th.
5. Hurry up! We've got to go _____ five minutes.
6. I'm busy now, but I'll be with you _____ a moment.
7. Jenny's brother is an engineer, but he's out of work _____ the moment.
8. There are usually a lot of parties _____ New Year's Eve.
9. I hope the weather will be nice _____ the weekend.
10. _____ Saturday night I went to bed _____ 11:00.
11. I don't like driving _____ night.
12. We traveled overnight to Paris and arrived _____ 5:00 _____ the morning.
13. The course begins _____ January 7th and ends sometime _____ April.
14. It was a short book and easy to read. I read it _____ a day.
15. I might not be at home _____ Tuesday morning, but I'll be there _____ the afternoon.
16. The telephone and the doorbell rang _____ the same time.
17. Mary and Henry always go out for dinner _____ their anniversary.
18. Henry is 63. He'll be retiring from his job _____ two years' time.

117.3 Which is correct, (a), (b), or both of them?

1. a) I'll see you Friday.   b) I'll see you on Friday.   *BOTH*
2. a) I'll see you next Friday.   b) I'll see you on next Friday.   _____
3. a) Paul got married February.   b) Paul got married in February.   _____
4. a) Do you work every Saturday?   b) Do you work on every Saturday?   _____
5. a) They never go out Sunday evenings.   b) They never go out on Sunday evenings.   _____
6. a) We usually take a short vacation Christmas.   b) We usually take a short vacation at Christmas.   _____
7. a) What are you doing the weekend?   b) What are you doing on the weekend?   _____
8. a) Will you be here Tuesday?   b) Will you be here on Tuesday?   _____
9. a) I hope to go to Europe the summer.   b) I hope to go to Europe in the summer.   _____

On time / in time, at the end / in the end

On time / in time

On time = punctual, not late. If something happens **on time**, it happens at the time that was planned:

- The 11:45 train left **on time**. (= it left at 11:45)
- "I'll meet you at 7:30." "OK, but please be **on time**." (= don't be late, be there at 7:30)
- The conference was very well organized. Everything began and finished **on time**.

The opposite of **on time** is **late**:

- Be **on time**. Don't be **late**.

In time (for something / to do something) = soon enough:

- Will you be home **in time** for dinner? (= soon enough for dinner)
- I've sent Jill her birthday present. I hope it arrives **in time** (for her birthday). (= soon enough for her birthday)
- I'd better hurry. I want to get home **in time** to see the baseball game on TV. (= soon enough to see the baseball game)

The opposite of **in time** is **too late**:

- I got home **too late** to see the baseball game.

You can say **just in time** (= almost too late):

- We got to the station **just in time** to catch the train.

At the end and in the end

At the end of (something) = at the time when something ends. For example:

at the end of the month	at the end of January	at the end of the game
at the end of the movie	at the end of the course	at the end of the concert

- I'm going away **at the end of** January / **at the end of** the month.
- **At the end of** the concert, there was great applause.
- All the players shook hands **at the end of** the game.

You cannot say "in the end *of something*." So you cannot say "in the end of January" or "in the end of the concert."

The opposite of **at the end of** is **at the beginning of**:

at the beginning of January   at the beginning of the concert

In the end = finally

We use **in the end** when we say what the final result of a situation was:

- We had a lot of problems with our car. **In the end** we sold it and bought another one. (= finally we sold it)
- He got angrier and angrier. **In the end** he just walked out of the room.
- Jim couldn't decide where to go on vacation. He didn't go anywhere **in the end**.

The opposite of **in the end** is usually **at first**:

- **At first** we didn't like each other very much, but **in the end** we became good friends.

Exercises

118.1 Complete the sentences with *on time* or *in time*.

1. The bus was late this morning, but it's usually _on time_____ .
2. The movie was supposed to start at 8:30, but it didn't begin _____ .
3. I like to get up _____ to have a big breakfast before going to work.
4. We want to start the meeting _____ , so please don't be late.
5. I've just washed this shirt. I want to wear it this evening, so I hope it will dry
   _____ .
6. The train service isn't very good. The trains are rarely _____ .
7. I almost missed my flight this morning. I got to the airport just _____ .
8. I almost forgot that it was Joe's birthday. Fortunately, I remembered
   _____ .
9. Why aren't you ever _____ ? You always keep everybody waiting.

118.2 Complete the sentences using *at the end of* + one of the following:

   the course   ~~the game~~   the interview   the month   the race

1. All the players shook hands _at the end of the game_____ .
2. I usually get paid _____ .
3. The students had a party _____ .
4. Two of the runners collapsed _____ .
5. To my surprise, I was offered the job _____ .

118.3 Write sentences with *In the end* . . . Use the verb in parentheses.

1. We had a lot of problems with our car.
   (sell) _In the end we sold it._____
2. Judy got more and more fed up with her job.
   (resign) _____
3. I tried to learn Korean, but it was too hard for me.
   (give up) _____
4. We couldn't decide whether to go to the party or not.
   (not / go) _____

118.4 Put in *at* or *in*.

1. I'm going away _at_____ the end of the month.
2. It took me a long time to find a job. _____ the end I got a job in a hotel.
3. Are you going away _____ the beginning of August or _____ the end?
4. I couldn't decide what to buy Mary for her birthday. I didn't buy her anything _____
   the end.
5. We waited ages for a taxi. We gave up _____ the end and walked home.
6. I'll be moving to a new address _____ the end of September.
7. At first Sarah didn't want to go to the theater, but she came with us _____ the end.
8. I'm going away _____ the end of this week.
9. "I didn't know what to do." "Yes, you were in a difficult position. What did you do
   _____ the end?"

In/at/on (Place) (1)

A

In

in a room
in a building
in a box

in a garden
in a town / city
in a country

in a pool
in an ocean
in a river

- There's no one **in the room** / **in the building** / **in the garden**.
- What do you have **in your hand** / **in your mouth**?
- When we were **in Italy**, we spent a few days **in Venice**. (*not* at Venice)
- I have a friend who lives **in a small village in the mountains**.
- Look at those people swimming **in the pool** / **in the ocean** / **in the river**.
- What's the highest mountain **in the world**?

B

At

at the bus stop

at the door

at the intersection

at the traffic light

- Who is that man standing **at the bus stop** / **at the door** / **at the window**?
- Turn left **at the traffic light** / **at the intersection** / **at the church**.
- When you leave the hotel, please leave your key **at the front desk**.

C

On

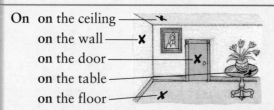

on the ceiling
on the wall
on the door
on the table
on the floor

on her cheek

on a page

on an island

- I sat **on the floor** / **on the ground** / **on the grass** / **on a chair** / **on the beach**.
- There's a red mark **on the wall** / **on your shirt** / **on your cheek**.
- Have you seen the notice **on the bulletin board** / **on the door**?
- You'll find the listings of TV programs **on page 7** (of the newspaper).

D

Compare **in** and **at**:
- There were a lot of people **in the store**. It was very crowded.

but ■ (*somebody giving directions*) Go along this road, then turn left **at the store**.

Compare **in** and **on**:
- There is some water **in the bottle**.

but ■ There is a label **on the bottle**.

Compare **at** and **on**:
- There is somebody **at the door**.
  Should I go and see who it is?

but ■ There is a sign **on the door**.
  It says "Do not disturb."

Exercises

119.1 Answer the questions about the pictures. Use *in*, *at*, or *on* with the words below the pictures.

1 (bottle)	2 (traffic light)	3 (arm)	4 (door)
5 (table)	6 (Paris)	7 (front desk)	8 (beach)

1. Where's the label? ___*on the bottle*___
2. Where is the car waiting? _____
3. Where's the butterfly? _____
4. a) Where's the sign? _____
   b) Where's the key? _____
5. Where is the woman sitting? _____
6. Where's the Eiffel Tower? _____
7. a) Where's the man standing? _____
   b) Where's the telephone? _____
8. Where are the children playing? _____

119.2 Complete the sentences. Use *in*, *at*, or *on* + one of the following:

the window	your coffee	the mountains	that tree
my guitar	~~the river~~	the island	the next gas station

1. Look at those people swimming ___*in the river*___ .
2. One of the strings _____ is broken.
3. There's something wrong with the car. We'd better stop _____ .
4. Would you like sugar _____ ?
5. The leaves _____ are a beautiful color.
6. Last year we had a wonderful ski trip _____ .
7. There's nobody living _____ . It's uninhabited.
8. He spends most of the day sitting _____ and looking outside.

119.3 Complete the sentences with *in*, *at*, or *on*.

1. There was a long line of people __*at*__ the bus stop.
2. I like that picture hanging _____ the wall _____ the kitchen.
3. There was an accident _____ the intersection this morning.
4. I wasn't sure whether I had come to the right office. There was no name _____ the door.
5. Look at those beautiful horses _____ that field!
6. You'll find the sports results _____ the back page of the newspaper.
7. I wouldn't like a job in an office. I couldn't spend the whole day sitting _____ a desk.
8. What's the tallest building _____ the world?
9. The man the police are looking for has a scar _____ his right cheek.
10. The main office of the company is _____ Tokyo.
11. Maria was wearing a silver ring _____ her little finger.

In/at/on (Place) (2)

A

We say:

> in a line / in a row
> in a photograph / in a picture / (look at yourself) in a mirror
> in a book / in a newspaper / in a magazine / in a letter (*but* on a page)

in a row

- When I go to the movies, I prefer to sit **in the front row.**
- Who is the woman **in that photograph?** (*not* on that photograph)
- Have you seen this article **in the paper?** (= newspaper)

We say **in the front / in the back** of a car, room, theater, group of people, etc.:

- I was **in the back** of the car when the accident happened.

in the front →

- Let's sit **in the front** (of the theater).

in the back →

- John was standing **in the back** of the crowd.

B

We say:

> on the left / on the right
> on the first floor / on the second floor, etc.
> on a map / on a menu / on a list
> on a farm / on a ranch
> on a street / on a river / on the coast
> on the way (to . . .)

Washington, D.C., is on the east coast of the United States on the Potomac River.

- In Britain they drive **on the left.**
- Our apartment is **on the second floor** of the building.
- Here's a shopping list. Don't buy anything that's not **on the list.**
- Have you ever worked **on a farm?** It's a lot like working **on a ranch.**
- I live **on Main Street.** My brother lives **on Elm.**
- We stopped at a small town **on the way** to Montreal.

We say **on the front / on the back** of a piece of paper, envelope, photograph, etc.:

- Write your name **on the back** of this piece of paper.

C

We say:

> at the top / at the bottom (of a page, a list, etc.)
> at the end (of a street, a road, etc.)

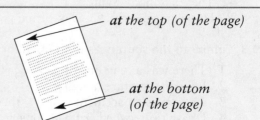

at the top (of the page)

- Write your name **at the top** of the page.
- Angela's house is **at the end** of the street.

at the bottom (of the page)

D

In/at/on the corner

We say "**in the corner** of a room," but "**at the corner** (*or* **on the corner**) of a street":

- The television is **in the corner** of the room.
- There is a public telephone **at/on the corner** of Charleston Street.

in the corner

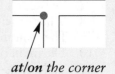

at/on the corner

Exercises

120.1 Answer the questions about the pictures. Use *in*, *at*, or *on* with the words below the pictures.

1 (back / car)	2 (second floor)	3 (corner)	4 (corner)	5 (end / line)
6 (mirror)	7 (top / stairs)	8 (last row)	9 (left / right)	10 (farm)

1. Where's the dog? _In the back of the car._
2. Sue lives in this building. Where's her apartment exactly? _____
3. Where is the woman standing? _____
4. Where is the man standing? _____
5. Where is Tom standing? _____
6. What's the man doing? He's looking _____ .
7. Where is the cat? _____
8. Tom is at the movies. Where is he sitting? _____
9. a) Where's the post office? _____
   b) And the bank? _____
10. Where does Kate work? _____

120.2 Complete the sentences. Use *in*, *at*, or *on* + one of the following:

the west coast	~~Third Avenue~~	the front row
the back of this card	the end of the street	the back of the class

1. My sister has an apartment _on Third Avenue_ .
2. We went to the theater last night. We had seats _____ .
3. _____ , there is a path leading to the river.
4. San Francisco is _____ of the United States.
5. I couldn't hear the teacher very well. She spoke quietly, and I was sitting

   _____ .
6. I don't have your phone number. Could you write it _____ ?

120.3 Complete the sentences with *in*, *at*, or *on*.

1. When I'm a passenger in a car, I prefer to sit _in_ the front.
2. If you walk to the end of the block, you'll see a small store _____ the corner.
3. Is Tom _____ this photograph? I can't find him.
4. My office is _____ the second floor. It's _____ the left as you come out of the elevator.
5. You will find the page number _____ the bottom of the page.
6. I usually buy a newspaper _____ the way to work in the morning.
7. *A:* Is there anything interesting _____ the paper today?
   B: Well, there's an unusual picture _____ the back page.
8. *(in a restaurant)* "Where should we sit?" "Over there, _____ the corner."
9. It's a very small town. You probably won't find it _____ your map.
10. Paris is _____ the Seine River.

In/at/on (Place) (3)

A

We say that somebody is **in bed**, **in prison/jail**, **in the hospital**:
- Mark isn't up yet. He's still **in bed**.
- Kay's mother is **in the hospital**.

We say that somebody is **at home / at work**:
- I'll be **at work** until 5:30, but I'll be **at home** all evening.

We can also say **be/stay home** (*without* at):
- You can stop by anytime. I'll **be home** all evening.

You can be **in** or **at school/college**. Use **at school/college** to say where someone is:
- Kim is not living at home. She's away **at college**.

But use **in school/college** to say what someone is doing:
- Amy works at a bank, and her brother is **in medical school**. (= he's studying medicine)
- Kevin has been **in college** for five years but still hasn't graduated. (= he's been a student)

B

We say that somebody is **at an event** (at a party / at a conference, etc.):
- Were there many people **at the party / at the meeting**?
- I saw Jack **at a baseball game / at a concert** last Saturday.

C

You can often use **in** or **at** with buildings. For example, you can eat **in a cafe** or **at a cafe**. We usually say **at** when we say where an event takes place (for example, a concert, a film, a meeting):
- We went to a concert **at Lincoln Center**.
- The meeting took place **at the company's main office**.
- The movie I want to see is showing **at the Odeon** (movie theater).

We say **at the station / at the airport**:
- Don't meet me **at the station**. I can get a taxi.

We say **at somebody's house**:
- I was **at Judy's house** last night. *or* I was **at Judy's** last night.

Also: **at the doctor's**, **at the hairdresser's**, etc.

We use **in** when we are thinking about the building itself:
- The rooms **in Judy's house** are very small. (*not* at Judy's house)
- I enjoyed the movie, but it was very cold **in the theater**. (*not* at the theater)

D

We normally use **in** with cities, towns, and villages:
- Tom's parents live **in St. Louis**. (*not* at St. Louis)
- The Louvre is a famous art museum **in Paris**. (*not* at Paris)

But you can use **at** or **in** when you think of the place as a point or station on a trip:
- Do you know if this train stops **at** (*or* **in**) Denver? (= at the Denver station)
- We stopped **at** (*or* **in**) a nice town on the way to Denver.

E

We usually say **on a bus / on a train / on a plane / on a ship** *but* **in a car / in a taxi**:
- **The bus** was very full. There were too many people **on it**.
- George arrived **in a taxi**.

We say **on a bicycle / on a motorcycle / on a horse**:
- Mary passed me **on her bicycle**.

For **by bus / by car / by bicycle**, etc., see Unit 124.

At school / in prison, etc. Unit 71   *In/at/on (Place)* Units 119–120   *To/at/in* Unit 122

Exercises

121.1 Complete the sentences about the pictures. Use *in, at,* or *on* with the words below the pictures.

1 AIRPORT CAR RENTALS (the airport)	2 DAVE (a train)	3 SUE conference (a conference)	4 MATT (the hospital)
5 JUDY (the hairdresser)	6 MARY (her bicycle)	7 (New York)	8 Ford Theater (the Ford Theater)

1. You can rent a car _at the airport_ .
2. Dave is _____ .
3. Sue is _____ .
4. Matt is _____ .
5. Judy is _____ .
6. I saw Mary _____ .
7. We spent a few days _____ .
8. We saw a play _____ .

121.2 Complete the sentences. Use *in, at,* or *on* + one of the following:

> **the airport**　**bed**　**the gym**　**the hospital**　**the plane**　**prison**　**school**　~~the station~~

1. My train arrives at 11:30. Can you meet me _at the station_ ?
2. I didn't feel too good when I woke up, so I stayed _____ .
3. Some people are _____ for crimes that they did not commit.
4. "What does your sister do? Does she have a job?" "No, she's still _____ ."
5. I play basketball _____ on Friday evenings.
6. A friend of mine was seriously injured in an accident yesterday. She's still _____ .
7. Our flight was delayed. We had to wait _____ for four hours.
8. I enjoyed the flight, but the food _____ wasn't very good.

121.3 Complete these sentences with *in, at,* or *on.*

1. I didn't see you _at_ the party on Saturday. Where were you?
2. It was a very slow train. It stopped _____ every station.
3. I don't know where my umbrella is. Maybe I left it _____ the bus.
4. Should we go _____ your car or mine?
5. The exhibition _____ the Museum of Modern Art closed on Saturday.
6. We stayed _____ a very nice hotel when we were _____ Amsterdam.
7. There were fifty rooms _____ the hotel.
8. Tom is sick. He wasn't _____ work today. He was _____ home _____ bed.
9. I wasn't in when you called. I was _____ my sister's house.
10. It's always too hot _____ my sister's house. The heat is always on too high.
11. I haven't seen Kate for some time. I last saw her _____ Dave's wedding.
12. Paul lives _____ Boston. He's a student _____ Boston University.

To/at/in/into

A

We say **go/come/travel to** a place or an event. For example:

go to South America	**go to** bed	**take** somebody **to** the hospital	
return to Italy	**go to** the bank	**come to** my house	TO → ▪
drive to the airport	**go to** a concert	**be sent to** prison	

- When are your friends **returning to Italy?** (*not* returning in Italy)
- After the accident three people were **taken to the hospital.**

In the same way we say **on my way to . . . / a trip to . . . / welcome to . . .** , etc.:
- **Welcome to** our country! (*not* Welcome in)

Compare **to** (for movement) and **in/at** (for position):
- They are **going to** France.   *but*   They **live in** France.
- Can you **come to** the party?   *but*   I'll **see you at** the party.

B

Been to

We usually say "I've **been to** a place":
- I've **been to Italy** four times, but I've never **been to Rome.**
- Ann **has** never **been to a football game** in her life.
- Jack has some money. He **has** just **been to the bank.**

C

Get and **arrive**

We say "**get to** a place":
- What time did they **get to London** / **get to work** / **get to the party** / **get to the hotel?**

But we say "**arrive in . . .** / **arrive at . . .**" (*not* arrive to).
We say "**arrive in** a country or town/city":
- When did they **arrive in Brazil** / **arrive in Rio de Janeiro?**

For other places (buildings, etc.) or events, we say **arrive at:**
- What time did they **arrive at the hotel** / **arrive at the party** / **arrive at work?**

D

Home

We do not say "to home." We say **go home** / **get home** / **arrive home**, etc. (no preposition):
- I'm tired. Let's **go home.** (*not* go to home)
- I met Caroline **on my way home.**

For **at home**, see Units 71C and 121A.

E

Into

Go into / **get into**, etc. = enter (a room / a building / a car, etc.):

INTO →

- She **got into the car** and drove away.
- A bird **flew into the kitchen** through the window.

We sometimes use **in** (instead of **into**):
- Don't wait outside. **Come in the house.** (*or* Come **into** the house.)

The opposite of **into** is **out of:**
- She **got out of** the car and **went into** a store.

Note that we usually say "**get on/off** a bus / a train / a plane":
- She **got off the bus** and I never saw her again.

Been to Unit 8A   ***In/at/on*** (Place) Units 119–121

Exercises

122.1 Put in *to/at/in/into* where necessary. If no preposition is necessary, leave an empty space *(–)*.

1. Three people were taken _*to*_ the hospital after the accident.
2. I met Kate on my way _*—*_ home.
3. We left our luggage _____ the station and went to find something to eat.
4. Should we take a taxi _____ the station, or should we walk?
5. I have to go _____ the bank today to change some money.
6. The Rhine River flows _____ the North Sea.
7. I'm tired. As soon as I get _____ home, I'm going _____ bed.
8. Marcel is French. He has just returned _____ France after two years _____ Brazil.
9. Are you going _____ Linda's party next week?
10. Carl was born _____ Chicago, but his family moved _____ New York when he was three. He still lives _____ New York.
11. Have you ever been _____ China?
12. I had lost my key, but I managed to climb _____ the house through a window.
13. We got stuck in a traffic jam on our way _____ the airport.
14. We had lunch _____ the airport while we were waiting for our plane.
15. Welcome _____ the Morgan Hotel. We hope you enjoy your stay here.

122.2 Have you been to these places? If so, how many times? Choose three of the places and write a sentence using *been to.*

~~Australia~~ **Hong Kong   Mexico   Paris   Thailand   Tokyo   Washington, D.C.**

1. (example answers) _I've never been to Australia. / I've been to Australia three times._
2. _____
3. _____
4. _____

122.3 Put in *to/at/in* where necessary. If no preposition is necessary, leave an empty space *(–)*.

1. What time does this train get _*to*_ Chicago?
2. What time does this train arrive _____ Chicago?
3. What time did you get _____ home last night?
4. What time do you usually arrive _____ work in the morning?
5. When we got _____ the theater, there was a long line outside.
6. I arrived _____ home feeling very tired.

122.4 Write sentences using *got + into / out of / on / off.*

1. You were walking home. A friend passed you in her car. She saw you, stopped, and offered you a ride. She opened the door. What did you do? _I got into the car._
2. You were waiting for the bus. At last your bus came. The doors opened. What did you do then? I _____ .
3. You drove home in your car. You arrived at your house and parked the car. What did you do then? _____
4. You were traveling by train to Chicago. When the train got to Chicago, what did you do?
   _____
5. You needed a taxi. After a few minutes a taxi stopped for you. You opened the door. What did you do then? _____
6. You were traveling by air. At the end of your flight, the plane landed at the airport and stopped. The doors were opened, and you took your bag and stood up. What did you do then? _____

On/in/at (Other Uses)

A

On vacation, etc.

We say (be/go) **on vacation / on business / on a trip / on a tour / on a cruise**, etc.:
- ■ Tom's away at the moment. He's **on vacation** in France. (*not* in vacation)
- ■ One day I'd like to go **on a world tour**.

Note that you can also say "go to a place **for a vacation / for my vacation / for vacation**":
- ■ Tom has gone to France **for a vacation**. (*or* for vacation)
- ■ Where are you going **for your vacation** next summer?

B

Other expressions with on

on television / on the radio:
- ■ I didn't watch the news **on television**, but I heard it **on the radio**.

on the phone/telephone:
- ■ I've never met her, but I've spoken to her **on the phone**.

(be/go) **on strike / on a diet**:
- ■ There are no trains today. The railroad workers are **on strike**.
- ■ I've put on a lot of weight. I'll have to go **on a diet**.

(be) **on fire**:
- ■ Look! That car is **on fire!**

on the whole (= in general):
- ■ Sometimes I have problems at work, but **on the whole** I enjoy my job.

on purpose (= intentionally):
- ■ I'm sorry. I didn't mean to annoy you. I didn't do it **on purpose**.

C

Expressions with in

in the rain / in the sun (= sunshine) / **in the shade / in the dark / in bad weather**, etc.:
- ■ We sat **in the shade**. It was too hot to sit **in the sun**.
- ■ Don't go out **in the rain**. Wait until it stops.

(write) **in ink / in pen / in pencil**:
- ■ When you take the exam, you're not allowed to write **in pencil**.

Also: **in words, in numbers, in capital letters**, etc.:
- ■ Please fill out the form **in capital letters**.

(pay) **in cash**:
- ■ I paid the bill **in cash**. *but* I paid **by check / by credit card**. (See Unit 124.)

(be/fall) **in love** (**with** somebody):
- ■ Have you ever been **in love with** anybody?

in my opinion (*or* your/his/our, etc.):
- ■ **In my opinion**, the movie wasn't very good.

D

At the age of . . . , etc.

We say: **at the age of . . . / at a speed of . . . / at a temperature of . . .** , etc. For example:
- ■ Jill graduated from school **at 17**. *or* . . . **at the age of 17**.
- ■ The train was traveling **at 120 miles an hour**. *or* . . . **at a speed of 120 miles an hour**.
- ■ Water boils **at 212 degrees Fahrenheit**. *or* . . . **at a temperature of 212 degrees Fahrenheit**.

Exercises

123.1 Complete the sentences using *on* + one of the following:

> business   a diet   ~~fire~~   purpose   strike   television   a tour   vacation   the whole

1. Look! That car is _on fire_____ ! Somebody call the fire department.
2. Workers at the factory have gone _____ for better pay and conditions.
3. Soon after we arrived, we were taken _____ of the city.
4. *A:* I'm going _____ next week.
   B: Really? Where? Somewhere nice?
5. I feel lazy this evening. Is there anything worth watching _____ ?
6. I'm sorry. It was an accident. I didn't do it _____ .
7. George has put on a lot of weight recently. I think he should go _____ .
8. Jane's job involves a lot of traveling. She often has to go away _____ .
9. *A:* How did your exams go?
   B: Well, there were some difficult questions, but _____ they were OK.

123.2 Complete the sentences using *in* + one of the following:

> capital letters   cash   ~~cold weather~~   love   my opinion   pencil   the shade

1. He likes to keep warm, so he doesn't go out much _in cold weather_____ .
2. Julie never uses a pen. She always writes _____ .
3. They fell _____ almost immediately and were married in a few weeks.
4. Please write your address clearly, preferably _____ .
5. I don't like the sun. I prefer to sit _____ .
6. Ann thought the restaurant was OK, but _____ it wasn't very good.
7. I hardly ever use a credit card or checks. I prefer to pay for things _____ .

123.3 Put in the correct preposition: *on, in, at,* or *for.*

1. Water boils _at_____ 212 degrees Fahrenheit.
2. When I was 14, I went _____ a trip to Mexico organized by my school.
3. I wouldn't like his job. He spends most of his time talking _____ the phone.
4. Julia's grandmother died recently _____ the age of 79.
5. Can you turn the light on, please? I don't want to sit _____ the dark.
6. We didn't go _____ vacation last year. We stayed at home.
7. I'm going to Miami _____ a short vacation next month.
8. I won't be here next week. I'll be _____ vacation.
9. He got married _____ 17, which is rather young to get married.
10. There was an interesting program _____ the radio this morning.
11. _____ my opinion, violent movies should not be shown _____ TV.
12. I wouldn't like to go _____ a cruise. I think I'd get bored.
13. I can't eat much. I'm supposed to be _____ a diet.
14. In the United States, young people usually start high school _____ the age of fourteen.
15. There was panic when people realized that the building was _____ fire.
16. The Earth travels around the Sun _____ a speed of 64,000 miles an hour.
17. *A:* Did you enjoy your vacation?
    B: Not every minute, but _____ the whole, yes.
18. When you write a check, you have to write the amount _____ words and numbers.

A

We use **by** in many expressions to say how we do something. For example, you can:

    send something **by mail**   do something **by hand**

    pay **by check** / **by credit card** (*but* pay **in cash**)

or something can happen **by mistake** / **by accident** / **by chance** (*but* do something **on purpose**):

- Did you pay **by check** or **in cash**?
- We hadn't arranged to meet. We met **by chance**.

In these expressions we use **by** + *noun* without "a" or "the." We say **by chance** / **by check**, etc. (*not* by a chance / by a check).

B

In the same way we use **by** to say how somebody travels:

    by car / **by train** / **by plane** / **by boat** / **by ship** / **by bus** / **by bicycle**, etc.

    by road/ **by rail** / **by air** / **by sea** / **by subway**

- Liz usually goes to work **by bus**.
- Do you prefer to travel **by air** or **by train**?

But we say **on foot**:

- Did you come here **by car** or **on foot**?

You cannot use **by** with **my car** / **the train** / **a taxi**, etc. We use **by** + *noun* without "a/the/my," etc.:

    by car   *but*   **in my car** (*not* by my car)

    by train *but*   **on the train** (*not* by the train)

We use **in** for cars and taxis:

- They didn't come **in their car**. They came **in a taxi**.

We use **on** for bicycles and public transportation (buses, trains, etc.):

- We came **on the 6:45 train**.

C

We say that something is done **by somebody/something** (*passive* – see Units 39–41):

- Have you ever been bitten **by a dog**?
- The program was watched **by millions of people**.

Compare **by** and **with**:

- The door must have been opened **with a key**. (*not* by a key) (= somebody used a key to open it)
- The door must have been opened **by somebody** with a key.

We say: a play **by Shakespeare** / a painting **by Rembrandt** / a novel **by Tolstoy**, etc.

- Have you read any books **by Agatha Christie**?

D

By also means "next to / beside":

- Come and sit **by me**. (= beside me)
- "Where's the light switch?" "**By the door**."

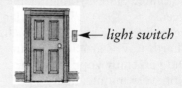
light switch

E

Note the following use of **by**:

- Claire's salary has just gone up from $2,000 a month to $2,200. So it has increased **by $200** / **by ten percent**.
- John and Roger ran a 100-meter race. Roger won **by about five meters**.

New salary —————— $2,200

increased by $200 ↑

Old salary —————— $2,000

Exercises

124.1 Complete the sentences using *by* + one of the following:

~~chance~~ chance check hand mistake satellite

1. We hadn't arranged to meet. We met *by chance* .
2. I didn't mean to take your umbrella. I took it _____ .
3. I didn't put the sweater in the washing machine. I washed it _____ .
4. If you haven't got any cash, you can pay _____ .
5. The two cities were connected _____ for a television program.
6. I never suspected anything. It was only _____ that I found out what had happened.

124.2 Put in *by*, *in*, or *on*.

1. Liz usually goes to work _*by*_ bus.
2. I saw Jane this morning. She was _____ the bus.
3. How did you get here? Did you come _____ train?
4. How did you get here? Did you come _____ the train?
5. I decided not to go _____ car. I went _____ my bike instead.
6. I didn't feel like walking home, so I came home _____ a taxi.
7. How long does it take to cross the Atlantic _____ boat.
8. Sorry we're late. We missed the bus, so we had to come _____ foot.

124.3 Write three sentences like the examples. Write about a book, a song, a painting, a movie, etc.

1. *War and Peace is a book by Tolstoy.*
2. *Romeo and Juliet is a play by Shakespeare.*
3. _____
4. _____
5. _____

124.4 Put in the correct preposition: *by*, *in*, *on*, or *with*.

1. Who is that man standing _*by*_ the window?
2. I managed to put the fire out _____ a fire extinguisher.
3. The plane was badly damaged _____ lightning.
4. These photographs were taken _____ a friend of mine.
5. These photographs were taken _____ a very good camera.
6. I don't mind going _____ car, but I don't want to go _____ your car.
7. Should we get a taxi, or should we go _____ foot?
8. What's that music? I know it's _____ Beethoven, but I can't remember the name of the piece.
9. There was a small table _____ the bed _____ a lamp and a clock _____ it.
10. Our team lost the game because of a mistake _____ one of our players.

124.5 Complete the sentences using *by*.

1. Karen's salary was $2,000 a month. Now it is $2,200.
   Her salary has increased *by $200 a month* .
2. The daily newspaper used to cost 50 cents. Starting today, it costs 60 cents.
   The price has gone up _____ .
3. There was an election. Amy got 25 votes and John got 23.
   Amy won _____ .
4. I went to Lauren's house to see her, but she had gone out five minutes before I arrived.
   I missed her _____ .

Noun + Preposition (*reason for, cause of,* etc.)

A

a **check FOR** (a sum of money):
- They sent me **a check for** $75.

a **demand** / a **need FOR** . . . :
- The company closed down because there wasn't enough **demand for** its product.
- There's no excuse for behavior like that. There's no **need for** it.

a **reason FOR** . . . :
- The train was late, but nobody knew the **reason for** the delay. (*not* reason of)

B

an **advantage** / a **disadvantage OF** . . . :
- The **advantage of** living alone is that you can do what you like.

But we usually say **there is an advantage in** (*or* **to**) doing something:
- **There are many advantages in** (*or* **to**) living alone.

a **cause OF** . . . :
- Nobody knows what the **cause of** the explosion was.

a **photograph** / a **picture** / a **map** / a **plan** / a **drawing OF** . . . :
- She showed me some **pictures of** her family.
- I had a **map of** the town, so I was able to find my way around.

C

an **increase** / a **decrease** / a **rise** / a **drop IN** (prices, etc.):
- There has been an **increase in** the number of traffic accidents recently.
- Last year was a bad year for the company. There was a big **drop in** sales.

D

damage TO . . . :
- The accident was my fault, so I had to pay for the **damage to** the other car.

an **invitation TO** . . . (a party / a wedding, etc.):
- Did you get an **invitation to** the party?

a **solution TO** (a problem) / a **key TO** (a door) / an **answer TO** (a question) / a **reply TO** (a letter) / a **reaction TO** . . . :
- Do you think we'll find a **solution to** the problem? (*not* a solution of the problem)
- I was surprised at her **reaction to** my suggestion.

an **attitude TOWARD** . . . :
- His **attitude toward** his job is very negative.

E

a **relationship** / a **connection** / **contact WITH** . . . :
- Do you have a good **relationship with** your parents?
- The police want to question a man in **connection with** the robbery.

but: a **relationship** / a **connection** / **contact** / a **difference BETWEEN** two things or people:
- The police believe that there is no **connection between** the two crimes.
- There are some **differences between** British and American English.

Exercises

125.1 Complete the second sentence so that it has the same meaning as the first.

1. What caused the explosion? What was the cause *of the explosion* ?
2. We're trying to solve the problem. We're trying to find a solution _____ .
3. Sue gets along well with her brother. Sue has a good relationship _____ .
4. Prices have gone up a lot. There has been a big increase _____ .
5. I don't know how to answer your question.
   I can't think of an answer _____ .
6. I don't think that a new road is necessary.
   I don't think there is any need _____ .
7. The number of people without jobs dropped last month.
   Last month there was a drop _____ .
8. Nobody wants to buy shoes like these anymore.
   There is no demand _____ .
9. In what way is your job different from mine?
   What is the difference _____ ?

125.2 Complete the sentences using one of the following nouns + the correct preposition.

cause connection contact damage invitation key ~~map~~ photographs reason reply

1. On the wall there were some pictures and a *map of* _____ the world.
2. Thank you for the _____ your party next week.
3. Since she left home two years ago, she has had little _____ her family.
4. I can't open this door. Do you have a _____ the other door?
5. The _____ the fire at the hotel last night is still unknown.
6. I wrote to Jim last week, but I still haven't received a _____ my letter.
7. The two companies are completely independent. There is no _____ them.
8. Jane showed me some old _____ the city as it looked 100 years ago.
9. Carol has decided to quit her job. I don't know the _____ her decision.
10. It wasn't a bad accident. The _____ the car wasn't serious.

125.3 Complete the sentences with the correct preposition.

1. There are some differences *between* British and American English.
2. If I give you the camera, can you take a picture _____ me?
3. Money isn't the solution _____ every problem.
4. When I opened the envelope, I was delighted to find a check _____ $500.
5. The advantage _____ having a car is that you don't have to rely on public transportation.
6. There are many advantages _____ being able to speak a foreign language.
7. When Paul left home, his attitude _____ his parents seemed to change.
8. Bill and I used to be good friends, but I don't have much contact _____ him now.
9. There has been a sharp rise _____ the cost of living in the past few years.
10. You've missed three classes this week. What's the reason _____ your poor attendance?
11. What was Ann's reaction _____ the news?
12. The company has rejected the workers' demands _____ an increase _____ pay.
13. What was the answer _____ question 3 on the test?
14. The fact that Kim was offered a job has no connection _____ the fact that her cousin is the managing director.

Adjective + Preposition (1)

A

It was **nice of** you to . . .

nice/kind/good/generous/polite/silly/stupid OF somebody (to do something):
- Thank you. It was very **nice/kind of** you to help me.
- It is **stupid of** her to go out without a coat in such cold weather.

but: (be) **nice/kind/good/generous/polite/friendly/cruel TO** somebody:
- They have always been very **nice/kind to** me. (*not* with me)

B

Adjective + **about/with/at**

mad/angry/furious/annoyed/upset ABOUT something:
- Max is really **angry about** what his brother said.

mad AT somebody
angry/furious AT/WITH somebody } **FOR** doing something
annoyed/upset WITH somebody
- Are you **mad at** me **for** being late?
- Pat's pretty **upset with** me **for** forgetting her birthday.

excited/worried/nervous/happy ABOUT something:
- Carol is **worried about** not having enough money.

pleased/satisfied/disappointed WITH something:
- Were you **disappointed with** your paycheck?

*Max is really angry about
what his brother said.*

C

Adjective + **at/by/with**

surprised/shocked/amazed/astonished AT/BY something:
- Everybody was **surprised at** (*or* **by**) the news.
- I hope you weren't **shocked by** (*or* **at**) what I said.

impressed WITH/BY somebody/something:
- I'm very **impressed with** (*or* **by**) her English. It's very good.

fed up / bored WITH something:
- I don't like my job anymore. I'm **fed up with** it. / I'm **bored with** it.

D

sorry about/for

sorry ABOUT something:
- I'm **sorry about** the noise last night.
  We were having a party.

I'm sorry about the noise last night.

but: **sorry FOR doing** something:
- I'm **sorry for shouting** at you yesterday.

You can also say "**I'm sorry I** (**did** something)":
- I'm **sorry I shouted** at you yesterday.

We say "**feel/be sorry FOR** somebody":
- I feel **sorry for** George. He has a lot of problems.

Exercises

126.1 Write sentences using the words in parentheses.

1.	I went out in the cold without a coat.	(silly) _That was silly of you._
2.	Sue offered to drive me to the airport.	(nice) That was _____ her.
3.	I needed money, and Sam gave me some.	(generous) That _____ _____ .
4.	Can I help you with your luggage?	(very kind) _____ _____ you.
5.	Kevin didn't thank me for the present.	(not very polite) _____ _____
6.	They've had an argument, and now they refuse to speak to each other.	(a little childish) _____ _____

126.2 Complete the sentences using one of the following adjectives + the correct preposition:

> annoyed annoyed astonished bored ~~excited~~ impressed kind sorry

1. We're all _excited about_ going on vacation next week.
2. Thank you for all your help. You've been very _____ me.
3. I wouldn't like to be in her position. I feel _____ her.
4. What have I done wrong? Why are you _____ me?
5. Why do you always get so _____ things that don't matter?
6. I wasn't very _____ the service in the restaurant. We had to wait ages for our food to come.
7. John isn't happy at college. He says he's _____ the classes he's taking.
8. I had never seen so many people before. I was _____ the crowds.

126.3 Put in the correct preposition.

1. I was very happy _with_ the present you gave me.
2. It was very nice _____ you to do my shopping for me. Thank you very much.
3. Why are you always so rude _____ your parents? Can't you be nice _____ them?
4. It was careless _____ you to leave the door unlocked when you went out.
5. We always have the same food every day. I'm fed up _____ it.
6. I can't understand people who are cruel _____ animals.
7. We enjoyed our vacation, but we were a little disappointed _____ the hotel.
8. I was surprised _____ the way he behaved. It was completely out of character.
9. I've been trying to learn Spanish, but I'm not very satisfied _____ my progress.
10. Linda doesn't look very well. I'm worried _____ her.
11. Are you angry _____ what happened?
12. I'm sorry _____ what I said. I hope you're not mad _____ me.
13. The people next door are furious _____ us _____ making so much noise last night.
14. Jill starts her new job next week. She's quite excited _____ it.
15. I'm sorry _____ the smell of paint in this room. I just painted it.
16. I was shocked _____ what I saw. I'd never seen anything like it before.
17. The man we interviewed for the job was intelligent, but we weren't very impressed _____ his appearance.
18. Are you still upset _____ what I said to you yesterday?
19. He said he was sorry _____ the situation, but there was nothing he could do.
20. I felt sorry _____ the children when we were on vacation. It rained every day, and they had to spend most of the time inside.

Adjective + Preposition (2)

A   *Adjective* + **of** (1)

afraid/frightened/terrified/scared OF . . . :
- ■ "Are you **afraid of** dogs?" "Yes, I'm **terrified of** them."

fond/proud/ashamed/jealous/envious OF . . . :
- ■ Why are you always so **jealous of** other people?

suspicious/critical/tolerant OF . . . :
- ■ He didn't trust me. He was **suspicious of** my intentions.

B   *Adjective* + **of** (2)

aware/conscious OF . . . :
- ■ "Did you know he was married?" "No, I wasn't **aware of** that."

capable/incapable OF . . . :
- ■ I'm sure you are **capable of** passing the examination.

full/short OF . . . :
- ■ The letter I wrote was **full of** mistakes. (*not* full with)
- ■ I'm a little **short of** money. Can you lend me some?

typical OF . . . :
- ■ He's late again. It's **typical of** him to keep everybody waiting.

tired/sick OF . . . :
- ■ Come on, let's go! I'm **tired of** waiting. (= I've had enough of waiting)

certain/sure OF *or* **ABOUT . . . :**
- ■ I think she's arriving tonight, but I'm not **sure of** that. (*or* **sure about** that)

C   *Adjective* + **at/to/from/in/on/with/for**

good/bad/excellent/hopeless AT . . . :
- ■ I'm not very **good at** repairing things. (*not* good in repairing things)

married/engaged TO . . . :
- ■ Linda is **married to** an American. (*not* married with)

but ■ Linda is married **with three children.** (= she is married and has three children)

similar TO . . . :
- ■ Your writing is **similar to** mine.

different FROM (*or* **THAN**) **. . . :**
- ■ The movie was **different from** (*or* **different than**) what I'd expected.

interested IN . . . :
- ■ Are you **interested in** art?

dependent ON . . . (*but* **independent OF . . .**):
- ■ I don't want to be **dependent on** anybody.

crowded WITH (people, etc.):
- ■ The city was **crowded with** tourists. (*but* **full of** tourists)

famous FOR . . . :
- ■ The Italian city of Florence is **famous for** its art treasures.

responsible FOR . . . :
- ■ Who was **responsible for** all that noise last night?

Preposition + *-ing* Unit 57   ***Afraid of / to . . .*** Unit 63A   **Adjective + Preposition (1)** Unit 126

Exercises

127.1 Complete the second sentence so that it has the same meaning as the first one.

1. There were lots of tourists in the city. The city was crowded _with tourists_ .
2. There was a lot of furniture in the room. The room was full _____ .
3. I'm not a very good tennis player. I'm not very good _____ .
4. I don't like sports very much. I'm not very fond _____ .
5. Catherine's husband is Russian. Catherine is married _____ .
6. We don't have enough time. We're a little short _____ .
7. My problem is not the same as yours. My problem is different _____ .
8. I don't trust Robert. I'm suspicious _____ .

127.2 Complete the sentences with one of the following adjectives + the correct preposition:

   afraid   different   interested   proud   responsible   similar   ~~sure~~

1. I think she's arriving tonight, but I'm not _sure of_ that.
2. Your camera is _____ mine, but it isn't exactly the same.
3. Don't worry. I'll take care of you. There's nothing to be _____ .
4. I never watch the news on TV. I'm not _____ it.
5. The editor is the person who is _____ what appears in a newspaper.
6. Mrs. Davis loves gardening. She's very _____ her garden and loves showing it to visitors.
7. I was surprised when I met her for the first time. She was _____ what I expected.

127.3 Put in the correct preposition.

1. The letter I wrote was full _of_ mistakes.
2. My hometown is not especially interesting. It's not famous _____ anything.
3. Kate is very fond _____ her younger brother.
4. I don't like climbing ladders. I'm afraid _____ heights.
5. You look bored. You don't seem interested _____ what I'm saying.
6. Did you know that Liz is engaged _____ a friend of mine?
7. I'm not ashamed _____ what I did. In fact I'm quite proud _____ it.
8. These days everybody is aware _____ the dangers of smoking.
9. The station platform was crowded _____ people waiting for the train.
10. She's much more successful than I am. Sometimes I feel a little jealous _____ her.
11. I'm tired _____ doing the same thing every day. I need a change.
12. Do you know anyone who might be interested _____ buying an old car?
13. She is a very honest person. I don't think she is capable _____ telling a lie.
14. We've got plenty to eat. The fridge is full _____ food.
15. Our house is similar _____ yours. Perhaps yours is a little larger.
16. John has no money of his own. He's totally dependent _____ his parents.
17. I'm not surprised she changed her mind at the last moment. That's typical _____ her.

127.4 Write sentences about yourself. Are you good at these things or not? Use:

   very good   **pretty good**   **not very good**   **hopeless**

1. (repairing things) _I'm not very good at repairing things._
2. (telling jokes) _____
3. (mathematics) _____
4. (remembering names) _____

Verb + Preposition (1) – *at* and *to*

Verb + at

look / have a look / take a look / stare / glance AT . . . :
- ■ Why are you **looking** at me like that?

laugh/smile AT . . . :
- ■ I look awful with this haircut. Everybody will **laugh** at me.

aim/point (something) AT . . . , shoot/fire (a gun) AT . . . (= in the direction of):
- ■ Don't **point** that knife at me. It's dangerous.
- ■ We saw someone with a gun **shooting** at birds, but he didn't hit any.

Verb + to

talk/speak TO (somebody) (with is also possible but less common):
- ■ Who was that man you were **talking to?**　■ Can I **speak to** Jane, please?

listen TO . . . :
- ■ We spent the evening **listening to** music. (*not* listening music)

invite somebody TO (a party / a wedding, etc.):
- ■ They only **invited** a few people **to** their wedding.

Some verbs can be followed by **at** or **to**, with a difference in meaning. For example:

shout AT somebody (when you are angry):
- ■ She got very angry and started **shouting at** me.

shout TO somebody (so that they can hear you):
- ■ She **shouted to** me from the other side of the street.

throw something AT somebody/something (in order to hit them):
- ■ Somebody **threw** an egg at the politician.

throw something TO somebody (for somebody to catch):
- ■ Julie shouted "Catch!" and **threw** the keys **to** me from the window.

Explain/describe/apologize

explain something (TO somebody):
- ■ Can you **explain** this word **to** me? (*not* explain me this word)

Also: **explain (to somebody) that/what/how/why . . . :**
- ■ I **explained to** them **what** I wanted them to do. (*not* I explained them)

Describe is similar:
- ■ Let me **describe to** you **what** I saw.

Note that we say "**apologize TO somebody (for . . .)**":
- ■ He **apologized to** me. (*not* He apologized me.)

but: **thank somebody (for something), ask somebody (for something):**
- ■ He **asked** me for money. (*not* He asked to me)

Exercises

128.1 Complete the sentences. Choose one of the following verbs in the correct form + the correct preposition:

explain   glance   invite   ~~laugh~~   listen   point   speak   throw   throw

1. I look awful with this haircut. Everybody will _laugh at_ me.
2. I don't understand what this means. Can you _____ it _____ me?
3. I _____ my watch to see what time it was.
4. We've been _____ the party, but unfortunately we can't go.
5. Please _____ me! I've got something important to tell you.
6. Don't _____ stones _____ the birds! It's mean.
7. If you don't want to eat that sandwich, _____ it _____ the birds. They'll eat it.
8. Sally and Kevin had an argument, and now they're not _____ each other.
9. Be careful with those scissors! Don't _____ them _____ me!

128.2 Put in *to* or *at*.

1. They only invited a few people _to_ their wedding.
2. Look _____ these flowers. Aren't they pretty?
3. Please don't shout _____ me! Try to calm down.
4. I saw Sue as I was riding along the road. I shouted _____ her, but she didn't hear me.
5. Don't listen _____ what he says. He doesn't know what he's talking about.
6. Can I speak _____ you for a moment? There's something I want to ask you.
7. Do you think I could have a look _____ your newspaper, please?
8. I'm a little lonely. I need somebody to talk _____ .
9. She was so angry she threw a book _____ me.
10. The woman sitting opposite me on the train kept staring _____ me.

128.3 You ask somebody to explain some things that you don't understand. Write sentences using *explain (something) to me* or *explain to me (how/what . . . , etc.).*

1. (I don't understand this word.) _Can you explain this word to me?_
2. (I don't understand what you mean.) _Can you explain to me what you mean?_
3. (I don't understand this question.)
   Can you explain _____ ?
4. (I don't understand the system.)
   Can _____ ?
5. (I don't understand how this machine works.)
   _____
6. (I don't understand what your problem is.)
   _____

128.4 Put in *to* where necessary. If the sentence is already complete, leave an empty space (–).

1. I know who she is, but I've never spoken _to_ her.
2. George won't be able to help you, so there's no point in asking ___—___ him.
3. I like to listen _____ the radio while I'm having breakfast.
4. I apologized _____ Nancy for the misunderstanding.
5. I thanked _____ everybody for all the help they had given me.
6. I explained _____ everybody what they had to do.
7. Mike described _____ me how the accident happened.
8. I'd like to ask _____ you some questions.

Verb + Preposition (2) – *about/for/of/after*

A

Verb + **about**

talk ABOUT / read ABOUT / tell somebody ABOUT . . . :
- We **talked about** a lot of things at the meeting.

We say "**have a discussion about** something" *but* "**discuss** something" (no preposition):
- We **discussed** a lot of things at the meeting. (*not* discussed about)

Also: **do** something **ABOUT** something (= do something to improve a bad situation):
- If you're worried about the problem, you should **do** something **about** it.

B

Care about, care for, and **take care of**

care ABOUT somebody/something (= think that somebody/something is important):
- He's very selfish. He doesn't **care about** other people.

We say "**care what/where/how,**" etc. (*without* about):
- You can do what you like. I don't **care what** you do.

care FOR somebody/something = like somebody or something (usually in questions and negative sentences):
- Would you **care for** a cup of coffee? (= Would you like . . . ?)
- I don't **care for** very hot weather. (= I don't like . . .)
- Amy doesn't **care for** Jason very much. (= She doesn't like . . .)

take care OF . . . (= look after):
- Have a nice holiday. **Take care of** yourself! (= Look after yourself.)

C

Verb + **for**

ask (somebody) **FOR . . . :**
- I wrote to the company **asking** them **for** more information about the job.
but - I **asked** her **a question.** / They **asked** me **the way** to the station. (no preposition)

apply (**TO** a person, a company, etc.) **FOR** (a job, etc.):
- I think you'd be good at this job. Why don't you **apply for** it?

wait FOR . . . / wait FOR something to happen:
- Don't **wait for** me. I'll see you later.
- I'm not going out yet. I'm **waiting for** the rain to stop.

search (a person / a place / a bag, etc.) **FOR . . . :**
- I've **searched** (the house) **for** my keys, but I still can't find them.

leave (a place) **FOR** (another place):
- I haven't seen her since she **left** (home) **for** work this morning. (*not* left to work)

D

Look for and **look after**

look FOR . . . (= search for, try to find):
- I've lost my keys. Can you help me **look for** them?

look AFTER . . . (= take care of):
- You can have a pet dog if you promise to **look after** it.

Verbs + *about/of* (*think / hear,* etc.) Unit 130   Other Verbs + *for* Unit 131B

Exercises

129.1 Put in the correct preposition. If no preposition is needed, leave the space empty (–).

1. I'm not going out yet. I'm waiting _for_ the rain to stop.
2. You're always asking me _____ money. Ask somebody else for a change.
3. I've applied _____ a job at the factory. I don't know if I'll get it.
4. I've applied _____ three colleges. I hope one of them accepts me!
5. I've searched everywhere _____ John, but I haven't been able to find him.
6. I don't want to talk _____ what happened last night. Let's forget it.
7. I don't want to discuss _____ what happened last night. Let's forget it.
8. We had an interesting discussion _____ the problem, but we didn't reach a decision.
9. We discussed _____ the problem, but we didn't reach a decision.
10. I don't want to go out yet. I'm waiting _____ the mail to arrive.
11. The roof of the house is in very bad condition. I think we ought to do something _____ it.
12. Tomorrow morning I have to catch a plane. I'm leaving my house _____ the airport at 7:30.

129.2 Complete the sentences with one of the following verbs in the correct form + preposition:

> apply   ask   do   leave   ~~search~~   take care   talk   wait

1. Police are _searching for_ the man who escaped from prison.
2. We're still _____ a reply to our letter. We haven't heard anything yet.
3. I think Ben likes his job, but he doesn't _____ it much.
4. When I finished my meal, I _____ the waiter _____ the check.
5. Maria is unemployed. She has _____ several jobs, but she hasn't had any luck.
6. If something is wrong, why don't you _____ something _____ it?
7. Linda's car is very old, but it's in excellent condition. She has really _____ it.
8. Diane is from Boston, but now she lives in Paris. She _____ Boston _____ Paris when she was 19.

129.3 Put in the correct preposition after *care*. If no preposition is needed, leave the space empty (–).

1. He's very selfish. He doesn't care _about_ other people.
2. Are you hungry? Would you care _____ something to eat?
3. She doesn't care _____ the exam. She doesn't care whether she passes or not.
4. Please let me borrow your camera. I promise I'll take good care _____ it.
5. "Do you like this coat?" "Not really. I don't care _____ the color."
6. Don't worry about the shopping. I'll take care _____ it.
7. I want to have a nice vacation. I don't care _____ the cost.
8. I want to have a nice vacation. I don't care _____ how much it costs.

129.4 Complete the sentences with *look for* or *look after*. Use the correct form of *look*.

1. I _looked for_ my keys, but I couldn't find them anywhere.
2. Jennifer is _____ a job. I hope she finds one soon.
3. Who _____ you when you were sick?
4. I'm _____ Elizabeth. Have you seen her?
5. All the parking meters were taken, so we had to _____ a parking garage.
6. A babysitter is somebody who _____ other people's children.

Verb + Preposition (3) – *about* and *of*

dream ABOUT . . . :
- ■ I **dreamed about** you last night. (when I was asleep)

dream OF being something / doing something (= imagine):
- ■ I often **dream of** being rich.
- ■ "Don't tell anyone what I said." "No, I wouldn't **dream of** it." (= I would never do it)

hear ABOUT . . . (= be told about something):
- ■ Did you **hear about** the fight in the restaurant on Saturday night?

hear OF . . . (= know that somebody/something exists):
- ■ "Who is Tom Hart?" "I have no idea. I've never **heard of** him." (*not* heard from him)

Also: hear FROM . . . (= receive a letter or phone call from somebody):
- ■ "Have you **heard from** Lisa lately?" "Yes, I got a letter from her a few days ago."

think ABOUT . . . and think OF . . .

When you **think ABOUT** something, you consider it, you concentrate your mind on it:
- ■ You look serious. What are you **thinking about?**
- ■ "Will you lend me the money?" "I'll **think about** it."

When you **think OF** something, the idea comes to your mind:
- ■ He told me his name, but I can't **think of** it now. (*not* think about it)
- ■ That's a good idea. Why didn't I **think of** that? (*not* think about that)

We also use **think of** when we ask or give an opinion:
- ■ "What did you **think of** the movie?" "I didn't **think** much **of** it." (= I didn't like it much)

For possible future actions, you can say **think of** or **think about** doing something:
- ■ My sister is **thinking of** (*or* **about**) going to Canada. (= she is considering it)

remind somebody ABOUT . . . (= tell somebody not to forget):
- ■ I'm glad you **reminded** me **about** the meeting. I had completely forgotten about it.

remind somebody OF . . . (= cause somebody to remember):
- ■ This house **reminds** me **of** the one I lived in when I was a child.
- ■ Look at this picture of Richard. Who does he **remind** you **of?**

complain (TO somebody) ABOUT . . . (= say that you are not satisfied):
- ■ We **complained to** the manager of the restaurant **about** the food.

complain OF a pain / an illness, etc. (= say that you have a pain, etc.):
- ■ We called the doctor because George was **complaining of** a pain in his stomach.

warn somebody ABOUT a person or thing that is dangerous, unusual, etc.:
- ■ I knew he was a strange person. I had been **warned about** him. (*not* warned of him)
- ■ Vicky **warned** us **about** the traffic. She said it would be bad.

warn somebody ABOUT/OF a danger, something bad that might happen:
- ■ Everybody has been **warned about/of** the dangers of smoking.

Remind/warn somebody to . . . **Unit 52B**

Exercises

130.1 Put in the correct preposition.

1. Did you hear _about_ what happened at the party on Saturday?
2. "I had a strange dream last night." "You did? What did you dream _____?"
3. Our neighbors complained _____ us _____ the noise we made last night.
4. Ken was complaining _____ pains in his chest, so he went to the doctor.
5. I love this music. It reminds me _____ a warm day in spring.
6. He loves his job. He thinks _____ his job all the time, he dreams _____ it, he talks _____ it, and I'm sick of hearing _____ it.
7. I tried to remember the name of the book, but I couldn't think _____ it.
8. Janet warned me _____ the water. She said it wasn't safe to drink.
9. We warned our children _____ the dangers of playing in the street.

130.2 Complete the sentences using one of the following verbs in the correct form + the correct preposition:

complain   dream   hear   remind   remind   ~~think~~   think   warn

1. That's a good idea. Why didn't I _think of_ that?
2. Bill is never satisfied. He is always _____ something.
3. I can't make a decision yet. I need time to _____ your proposal.
4. Before you go into the house, I should _____ you _____ the dog. He is very aggressive sometimes, so be careful.
5. She's not a well-known singer. Not many people have _____ her.
6. *A:* You wouldn't leave without telling me, would you?
   B: Of course not. I wouldn't _____ it.
7. I would have forgotten my appointment if Jane hadn't _____ me _____ it.
8. Do you see that man over there? Does he _____ you _____ anybody you know?

130.3 Complete the sentences using *hear* or *heard* + the correct preposition.

1. I've never _heard of_ Tom Hart. Who is he?
2. "Did you _____ the accident last night?" "Yes, Vicky told me."
3. Jill used to write to me quite often, but I haven't _____ her for ages now.
4. *A:* Have you _____ a writer called William Hudson?
   B: No, I don't think so. What sort of writer is he?
5. Thank you for your letter. It was good to _____ you again.
6. "Do you want to _____ our vacation?" "Not now. Tell me later."
7. I live in a very small town in Texas. You've probably never _____ it.

130.4 Complete the sentences using *think about* or *think of*. Use the correct form of *think*.

1. You look serious. What are you _thinking about_ ?
2. I like to have time to make decisions. I like to _____ things carefully.
3. I don't know what to get Ann for her birthday. Can you _____ anything?
4. What did you _____ the book I lent you? Did you like it?
5. We're _____ going out for dinner tonight. Would you like to come?
6. I don't really want to go out with Sam. I'll have to _____ an excuse.
7. Carol is very homesick. She's always _____ her family back home.
8. When I was offered the job, I didn't accept immediately. I went away and _____ it for a while. In the end I decided to take the job.
9. I don't _____ much _____ this coffee. It tastes like water.

Verb + Preposition (4) – *of/for/from/on*

A | Verb + of

accuse/suspect somebody **OF** . . . :
- Sue **accused** me **of** being selfish.
- Three students were **suspected of** cheating on the exam.

approve OF . . . :
- His parents don't **approve of** what he does, but they can't stop him.

die OF (an illness):
- "What did he **die of?**" "A heart attack."

consist OF . . . :
- We had an enormous meal. It **consisted of** seven courses.

B | Verb + for

pay FOR (something that you buy):
- I didn't have enough money to **pay for** the meal. (*not* pay the meal)

but: **pay** a bill / a fine / a tax / a fare / rent / a sum of money, etc. (no preposition):
- I didn't have enough money to **pay** my telephone bill.

thank/forgive somebody **FOR** . . . :
- I'll never **forgive** them **for** what they did.

apologize (**to** somebody) **FOR** . . . :
- When I realized I was wrong, I **apologized** (**to** them) **for** my mistake.

blame somebody/something **FOR** . . . :
- Everybody **blamed** me **for** the accident.

Also: somebody is **to blame for** . . . :
- Everybody said that I was **to blame for** the accident.

Also: **blame** something **ON** . . . :
- Everybody **blamed** the accident **on** me.

C | Verb + from

suffer FROM (an illness, etc.):
- The number of people **suffering from** heart disease has increased.

protect somebody/something **FROM** (*or* **AGAINST**) something:
- Sunscreen can **protect** you **from** the sun. (*or* . . . **against** the sun.)

D | Verb + on

depend / rely ON . . . :
- "What time will you get there?" "I don't know. It **depends on** the traffic."
- You can **rely on** Jill. She always keeps her promises.

You can use **depend + when/where/how,** etc. (question words), with or without **on:**
- "Are you going to buy it?" "It **depends how** much it is." (*or* depends **on** how much)

live ON (money/food):
- George's salary is very low. It isn't enough to **live on.**

congratulate (someone) **ON** . . . / **compliment** (somebody) **ON** . . . :
- I **congratulated** her **on** being admitted to law school.

Verb + Preposition + -*ing* Unit 59   **Other Verbs + *for*** Unit 129   **Other Verbs + *on*** Unit 132E

Exercises

131.1 Complete the second sentence so that it means the same as the first.

1. Sue said I was selfish. Sue accused me _of being selfish_____.
2. The misunderstanding was my fault, so I apologized.
   I apologized _____.
3. She won the tournament, so I congratulated her.
   I congratulated her _____.
4. He has enemies, but he has a bodyguard to protect him.
   He has a bodyguard to protect him _____.
5. There are 11 players on a soccer team.
   A soccer team consists _____.
6. She eats only bread and eggs.
   She lives _____.

Complete the second sentence using *for* or *on*. (These sentences all have the verb *blame*.)

7. Kay said that what happened was Jim's fault. Kay blamed Jim _for what happened_.
8. You always say everything is my fault.
   You always blame me _____.
9. Do you think the economic crisis is the fault of the government?
   Do you blame the government _____?
10. I think the increase in violent crime is because of television.
    I blame the increase in _____.

Now rewrite sentences 9 and 10 using *to blame for*.

11. Do you think the government _____?
12. I think that _____.

131.2 Complete the sentences using one of the following verbs in the correct form + the correct preposition:

   accuse   apologize   ~~approve~~   congratulate   depend   live   pay

1. His parents don't _approve of_____ what he does, but they can't stop him.
2. When you went to the theater with Paul, who _____ the tickets?
3. It's a terrible feeling when you are _____ something you didn't do.
4. "Are you playing tennis tomorrow?" "I hope so. It _____ the weather."
5. Things are very cheap there. You can _____ very little money.
6. When I saw Dave, I _____ him _____ passing his driving test.
7. You were very rude to Pat. Don't you think you should _____ her?

131.3 Put in the correct preposition. If no preposition is necessary, leave the space empty (–).

1. Three students were suspected _of_____ cheating on the exam.
2. Sally is often sick. She suffers _____ very bad headaches.
3. You know that you can rely _____ me if you ever need any help.
4. It is terrible that some people are dying _____ hunger while others eat too much.
5. Are you going to apologize _____ what you did?
6. The accident was my fault, so I had to pay _____ the repairs.
7. I didn't have enough money to pay _____ the bill.
8. I complimented her _____ her English. She spoke very fluently.
9. She doesn't have a job. She depends _____ her parents for money.
10. I don't know whether I'll go out tonight. It depends _____ how I feel.
11. They wore warm clothes to protect themselves _____ the cold.
12. Cake consists mainly _____ sugar, flour, and butter.

Verb + Preposition (5) – *in/into/with/to/on*

A

believe IN . . . :
- Do you **believe in** God? (= do you believe that God exists?)
- I **believe in** saying what I think. (= I believe it is right to say what I think)

specialize IN . . . :
- Helen is a lawyer. She **specializes in** corporate law.

succeed IN . . . :
- I hope you **succeed in** finding the job you want.

B

break INTO . . . :
- Our house was **broken into** a few days ago, but nothing was stolen.

crash/drive/bump/run INTO . . . :
- He lost control of the car and **crashed into** a wall.

divide/cut/split something INTO (two or more parts):
- The book is **divided into** three parts.
- **Cut** the meat **into** small pieces before frying it.

translate (a book, etc.) **FROM** one language **INTO** another:
- Ernest Hemingway's books have been **translated into** many languages.

C

collide WITH . . . :
- There was an accident this morning. A bus **collided with** a car. (*but* **crashed into**)

fill something WITH . . . (*but* **full of . . .** – see Unit 127B):
- Take this pot and **fill** it **with** water.

provide/supply somebody WITH . . . :
- The school **provides** all its students **with** books.

D

happen TO . . . :
- What **happened to** that gold watch you used to have? (= Where is it now?)

prefer one thing/person **TO** another:
- I **prefer** tea **to** coffee.

E

concentrate ON . . . :
- Don't look out the window. **Concentrate on** your work.

insist ON . . . :
- I wanted to go alone, but they **insisted on** coming with me.

spend (money) **ON . . . :**
- How much money do you **spend on** food each week?

Verb + Preposition + -*ing* Unit 59   **Other Verbs + *to*** Unit 128   **Other Verbs + *on*** Unit 131D

Exercises

132.1 Complete the second sentence so that it means the same as the first.

1. There was a collision between a bus and a car. A bus collided _with a car_____ .
2. I don't mind big cities, but I prefer small towns.
   I prefer _____ .
3. I got all the information I needed from Jill.
   Jill provided me _____ .
4. This morning I bought a pair of shoes that cost $60.
   This morning I spent _____ .

132.2 Complete the sentences using one of the following verbs in the correct form + the correct preposition:

> believe   concentrate   divide   drive   fill   happen   ~~insist~~   succeed

1. I wanted to go alone, but Sue _insisted on_____ coming with me.
2. I haven't seen Mike for ages. I wonder what has _____ him.
3. I was driving along when the car in front of me stopped suddenly. Unfortunately, I couldn't stop in time and _____ the back of it.
4. It's a very large house. It's _____ four apartments.
5. I don't _____ ghosts. I think people only imagine that they see them.
6. Steve gave me an empty bucket and told me to _____ it _____ water.
7. Don't try and do two things together. _____ one thing at a time.
8. It wasn't easy, but in the end we _____ finding a solution to the problem.

132.3 Put in the correct preposition.

1. The school provides all its students _with_____ books.
2. A strange thing happened _____ me a few days ago.
3. Mark decided to give up his job so that he could concentrate _____ his studies.
4. I don't believe _____ working very hard. It's not worth it.
5. My current job isn't wonderful, but I prefer it _____ what I did before.
6. I hope you succeed _____ getting what you want.
7. As I was going out of the room, I collided _____ somebody who was coming in.
8. There was an awful noise as the car crashed _____ a tree.
9. Jim is a photographer. He specializes _____ sports photography.
10. Do you spend much money _____ clothes?
11. The country is divided _____ six regions.
12. I prefer traveling by train _____ driving. It's much more pleasant.
13. Somebody broke _____ my car and stole the radio.
14. I was very cold, but Peter insisted _____ keeping the window open.
15. Some words are difficult to translate _____ one language _____ another.
16. What happened _____ the money I lent you? What did you spend it _____ ?
17. The teacher decided to split the class _____ four groups.
18. I filled the tank, but unfortunately I filled it _____ the wrong kind of gas.

132.4 Use your own ideas to complete these sentences. Use a preposition.

1. I wanted to go out alone, but my friend insisted _on coming with me_____ .
2. I spend lots of money _____ .
3. I saw the accident. The car crashed _____ .
4. Sarah prefers basketball _____ .
5. Shakespeare's plays have been translated _____ .

Phrasal Verbs (*get up / break down / fill in*, etc.)

We often use verbs with the following words:

in	on	up	away	around	about	over	by
out	off	down	back	through	along	forward	

So you can say **put out / get on / take off / run away**, etc. These verbs are *phrasal verbs*.

We often use **out/off/up**, etc., with verbs of movement. For example:

get on	■	The bus was full. We couldn't **get on**.
drive off	■	A woman got into the car and **drove off**.
come back	■	Sally is leaving tomorrow and **coming back** on Saturday.
turn around	■	When I touched him on the shoulder, he **turned around**.

But often the second word (**out/off/up**, etc.) gives a special meaning to the verb. For example:

break down	■	Sorry I'm late. The car **broke down**. (= the engine stopped working)
look out	■	**Look out!** There's a car coming. (= be careful)
take off	■	It was my first flight. I was nervous as the plane **took off**. (= went into the air)
get up	■	I was very tired this morning. I couldn't **get up**. (= get out of bed)
get by	■	My Japanese isn't very good, but it's enough to **get by**. (= to manage)

Sometimes a phrasal verb is followed by a *preposition*. For example:

phrasal verb   *preposition*

run away	from		■ Why did you **run away from** me?
keep up	with		■ You're walking too fast. I can't **keep up with** you.
look forward	to		■ Are you **looking forward to** your vacation?

Sometimes a phrasal verb has an *object*. Usually there are two possible positions for the object. So you can say:

            object   *object*

■ I **turned off** the light. *or* I **turned** the light **off**.

If the object is a *pronoun* (**it/them/me/him**, etc.), only one position is possible:

■ I **turned it off**. (*not* I turned off it)

Some more examples:

■ Could you { **fill out** this form? / **fill** this form **out**? }

but   They gave me a form and told me to **fill it out**. (*not* fill out it)

■ The police got into the house by { **breaking down** the door. / **breaking** the door **down**. }

but   The door wasn't locked. Why did the police **break it down**? (*not* break down it)

■ I think I'll { **throw away** these newspapers. / **throw** these newspapers **away**. }

but   Do you want these newspapers, or should I **throw them away**? (*not* throw away them)

■ Don't { **wake up** the baby. / **wake** the baby **up**. }

but   The baby is asleep. Don't **wake her up**. (*not* wake up her)

Exercises

133.1 Complete the sentences using one of these phrasal verbs in the correct form:

~~break down~~
clear up (= get better)
close down (= go out of business)
doze off (= fall asleep)

drop out (= stop taking part in something)
move in (= start living in a house, etc.)
show up (= appear/arrive)

1. Sorry I'm late. The car _broke down_ on the way here.
2. I arranged to meet Jane after work last night, but she didn't _____ .
3. "We've bought a new house." "Oh, you have? When are you _____ ?"
4. There used to be a store on the corner, but it _____ a year ago.
5. I ran in a marathon last week but _____ after 15 miles.
6. I was very sleepy. I was sitting in an armchair and _____ .
7. The weather is terrible outside, isn't it? I hope it _____ later.

133.2 Complete the sentences using a word from List A and a word from List B. You need to use some words more than once.

A: **along   away   back   forward   out   up**   B: **at   of   to   with**

1. You're walking too fast. I can't keep _up with_ you.
2. My vacation is almost over. Next week I'll be _____ work.
3. We've nearly run _____ money. We hardly have any left.
4. Martin isn't very happy in his job because he doesn't get _____ his boss.
5. I love to look _____ the stars in the sky at night.
6. Are you looking _____ the party next week?
7. There was a bank robbery last week. The robbers got _____ $30,000.

133.3 Complete the sentences using one of these verbs in the correct form + *it/them/her/you*:

cross out   give away   make up   see off (= see somebody leave)
~~fill out~~   **give back   show around   turn down** (= refuse)

1. They gave me a form and told me to _fill it out_ .
2. If you make a mistake on the form, just _____ .
3. The story she told you wasn't true. She _____ .
4. I don't like people who borrow things and don't _____ .
5. Kathy is going to Australia tomorrow. I'm going to the airport to _____ .
6. I had a lot of books that I didn't want to keep, so I _____ to a friend.
7. Would you like to see the factory? Would you like me to _____ ?
8. Sue was offered a job as a translator, but she _____ .

133.4 Complete the sentences. Use the word in parentheses (*away/up*, etc.) with one of the following:

~~that box~~   **your cigarette   a jacket   the television   a word   ~~it~~   it   them   him**

1. Don't throw _away that box / that box away_ . I want to keep it. (away)
2. "Do you want this box?" "No, you can throw _it away_ ." (away)
3. Shh! The children are asleep. Don't wake _____ . (up)
4. We can turn _____ . Nobody is watching it. (off)
5. Tom got very angry and started shouting. I tried to calm _____ . (down)
6. I tried _____ in the store, but I didn't buy it. (on)
7. Please put _____ . This is a no-smoking area. (out)
8. It was only a small fire. I was able to put _____ quite easily. (out)
9. You can look _____ in a dictionary if you don't know what it means. (up)

APPENDIX 1
Regular and Irregular Verbs

1.1 *Regular verbs*

If a verb is *regular*, the *simple past* and *past participle* end in **-ed**. For example:

base form *simple past* *past participle* }	clean	finish	use	paint	stop	carry
	cleaned	finished	used	painted	stopped	carried

For spelling rules, see Appendix 5.
For the simple past (I **cleaned** / they **finished** / she **carried**, etc.), see Unit 5.

We use the past participle to make the *perfect tenses* and for all the *passive* forms.
Perfect tenses (**have/has/had cleaned**):
- ■ I **have cleaned** my room. (*present perfect* – see Units 7–8)
- ■ They were still working. They **hadn't finished**. (*past perfect* – see Unit 14)

Passive (**is cleaned** / **was cleaned**, etc.):
- ■ He **was carried** out of the room. (*simple past passive*) } see Units 39–41
- ■ This gate **has** just **been painted**. (*present perfect passive*)

1.2 *Irregular verbs*

When the simple past / past participle do *not* end in **-ed** (for example, I **saw** / I **have seen**), the verb is *irregular*.

With some irregular verbs, the simple past and past participle are the same as the *base form*. For example, **hit**:
- ■ Don't **hit** me. *(base form)*
- ■ Somebody **hit** me as I came into the room. *(simple past)*
- ■ I've never **hit** anybody in my life. *(past participle – present perfect)*
- ■ George was **hit** on the head by a stone. *(past participle – passive)*

With other irregular verbs, the simple past is the same as the past participle (but different from the base form). For example, **tell → told**:
- ■ Can you **tell** me what to do? *(base form)*
- ■ She **told** me to come back the next day. *(simple past)*
- ■ Have you **told** anybody about your new job? *(past participle – present perfect)*
- ■ I was **told** to come back the next day. *(past participle – passive)*

With other irregular verbs, all three forms are different. For example, **wake → woke/woken**:
- ■ I'll **wake** you up. *(base form)*
- ■ I **woke** up in the middle of the night. *(simple past)*
- ■ The baby has **woken** up. *(past participle – present perfect)*
- ■ I was **woken** up by a loud noise. *(past participle – passive)*

1.3 List of irregular verbs

base form	*simple past*	*past participle*
be	was/were	been
beat	beat	beaten
become	became	become
begin	began	begun
bend	bent	bent
bet	bet	bet
bite	bit	bitten

base form	*simple past*	*past participle*
blow	blew	blown
break	broke	broken
bring	brought	brought
broadcast	broadcast	broadcast
build	built	built
burst	burst	burst
buy	bought	bought

base form	simple past	past participle
catch	caught	caught
choose	chose	chosen
come	came	come
cost	cost	cost
creep	crept	crept
cut	cut	cut
deal	dealt	dealt
dig	dug	dug
do	did	done
draw	drew	drawn
drink	drank	drunk
drive	drove	driven
eat	ate	eaten
fall	fell	fallen
feed	fed	fed
feel	felt	felt
fight	fought	fought
find	found	found
fit	fit	fit
flee	fled	fled
fly	flew	flown
forbid	forbade	forbidden
forget	forgot	forgotten
forgive	forgave	forgiven
freeze	froze	frozen
get	got	gotten
give	gave	given
go	went	gone
grow	grew	grown
hang	hung	hung
have	had	had
hear	heard	heard
hide	hid	hidden
hit	hit	hit
hold	held	held
hurt	hurt	hurt
keep	kept	kept
kneel	knelt	knelt
know	knew	known
lay	laid	laid
lead	led	led
leave	left	left
lend	lent	lent
let	let	let
lie	lay	lain
light	lit	lit
lose	lost	lost
make	made	made
mean	meant	meant
meet	met	met
pay	paid	paid
put	put	put

base form	simple past	past participle
quit	quit	quit
read	read*	read*
ride	rode	ridden
ring	rang	rung
rise	rose	risen
run	ran	run
say	said	said
see	saw	seen
seek	sought	sought
sell	sold	sold
send	sent	sent
set	set	set
sew	sewed	sewn/sewed
shake	shook	shaken
shoot	shot	shot
show	showed	shown/showed
shrink	shrank	shrunk
shut	shut	shut
sing	sang	sung
sink	sank	sunk
sit	sat	sat
sleep	slept	slept
slide	slid	slid
speak	spoke	spoken
spend	spent	spent
spit	spit/spat	spit/spat
split	split	split
spread	spread	spread
spring	sprang	sprung
stand	stood	stood
steal	stole	stolen
stick	stuck	stuck
sting	stung	stung
stink	stank	stunk
strike	struck	struck
swear	swore	sworn
sweep	swept	swept
swim	swam	swum
swing	swung	swung
take	took	taken
teach	taught	taught
tear	tore	torn
tell	told	told
think	thought	thought
throw	threw	thrown
understand	understood	understood
wake	woke	woken
wear	wore	worn
weep	wept	wept
win	won	won
write	wrote	written

*pronounced [rɛd]

Present and Past Tenses

	simple	continuous
present	**I do** *simple present* (Units 2–4) ■ Ann often **plays** tennis. ■ I **work** in a bank, but I **don't enjoy** it very much. ■ **Do** you **like** parties? ■ It **doesn't rain** much in the summer.	**I am doing** *present continuous* (Units 1, 3–4) ■ "Where's Ann?" "She's **playing** tennis." ■ Please don't bother me now. **I'm working** ■ Hello. **Are** you **enjoying** the party? ■ It **isn't raining** right now.
present perfect	**I have done** *present perfect simple* (Units 7–8, 10–13) ■ Ann **has played** tennis many times. ■ **I've lost** my key. **Have** you **seen** it anywhere? ■ How long **have** they **known** each other? ■ "Is it still raining?" "No, it **has stopped.**" ■ The house is dirty. We **haven't cleaned** it for weeks.	**I have been doing** *present perfect continuous* (Units 9–12) ■ Ann is very tired. She **has been playing** tennis. ■ You're out of breath. **Have** you **been running?** ■ How long **have** they been **studying** English? ■ It's still raining. It **has been raining** all day. ■ I **haven't been feeling** well lately. Maybe I should go to the doctor.
past	**I did** *simple past* (Units 5–6, 12–13) ■ Ann **played** tennis yesterday afternoon. ■ I **lost** my key a few days ago. ■ There was a movie on TV last night, but we **didn't watch** it. ■ What **did** you **do** when you finished work yesterday?	**I was doing** *past continuous* (Unit 6) ■ I saw Ann in the park yesterday. She **was playing** tennis. ■ I dropped my key when I **was trying** to open the door. ■ The TV was on, but we **weren't watching** it. ■ What **were** you **doing** at this time yesterday?
past perfect	**I had done** *past perfect* (Unit 14) ■ It wasn't her first game of tennis. She **had played** many times before. ■ I couldn't get into the house because I **had lost** my key. ■ The house was dirty because we **hadn't cleaned** it for weeks.	**I had been doing** *past perfect continuous* (Unit 15) ■ Ann was tired last night because she **had been playing** tennis in the afternoon. ■ Matt decided to go to the doctor because he **hadn't been feeling** well.

For the *passive*, see Units 39–41.

APPENDIX 3
The Future

3.1 List of future forms

■ I'm **leaving** tomorrow.	*present continuous*	(Unit 18A)
■ My train **leaves** at 9:30 tomorrow.	*simple present*	(Unit 18B)
■ I'm **going to leave** tomorrow.	**(be) going to**	(Units 19, 22)
■ I'll **leave** tomorrow.	**will**	(Units 20–22)
■ I'll **be leaving** tomorrow.	*future continuous*	(Unit 23)
■ I'll **have left** by this time tomorrow.	*future perfect*	(Unit 23D)
■ I hope to see you before **I leave** tomorrow.	*simple present*	(Unit 24C)

3.2 *Future actions*

We use the *present continuous* (**I'm doing**) for arrangements that have already been made:
- ■ **I'm leaving** tomorrow. I have my plane ticket.
- ■ "When **are** they **getting** married?" "Next month."

We use the *simple present* (**I leave** / it **leaves**, etc.) for schedules, programs, etc.:
- ■ My train **leaves** at 9:30 tomorrow. (according to the schedule)
- ■ What time **does** the movie **start?**

We use **(be) going to . . .** to say what somebody has already decided to do:
- ■ I've decided not to stay here any longer. **I'm going to leave** tomorrow. (*or* **I'm leaving** tomorrow.)
- ■ **Are** you **going to watch** the movie on TV tonight?

We use **will** (**'ll**) when we decide or agree to do something at the time of speaking:
- ■ *A:* I don't want you to stay here any longer.
  B: OK. **I'll leave** tomorrow. (B decides this at the time of speaking.)
- ■ That bag looks heavy. **I'll help** you with it.
- ■ I promise I **won't tell** anybody what happened. (**won't = will not**)

3.3 *Future happenings and situations*

We usually use **will** to talk about future happenings or situations (something **will happen**):
- ■ I don't think John is happy at work. I think he'**ll leave** soon.
- ■ By this time next year **I'll be** in Japan. Where **will** you **be?**

We use **(be) going to** when the situation *now* shows what is going to happen *in the future*:
- ■ Look at those black clouds. It'**s going to rain.** (You can see the clouds *now*.)

3.4 *Future continuous* and *future perfect*

Will be doing = will be in the middle of doing something:
- ■ This time next week I'll be on vacation. **I'll be lying** on a beach and **swimming** in the ocean.

We also use **will be -ing** for future actions (see Unit 23C):
- ■ What time **will** you **be leaving** tomorrow?

We use **will have** (**done**) to say that something will already be complete before a time in the future:
- ■ I won't be here at this time tomorrow. **I'll have** already **left.**

3.5 We use the present (*not* will) after **when/if/while/before**, etc. (see Unit 24):
- ■ I hope to see you **before I leave** tomorrow. (*not* before I will leave)
- ■ Please come and see us **when** you **are** in New York again. (*not* when you will be)
- ■ If we **don't hurry,** we'll be late.

APPENDIX 4
Short Forms (*I'm/you've/didn't,* etc.)

4.1 In spoken English we usually say **I'm/you've/didn't,** etc. *(short forms),* rather than **I am / you have / did not,** etc. We also use short forms in informal written English (for example, in letters to friends), but not in formal written English (for example, essays for school or business reports).

When we write short forms, we use an *apostrophe* (') for the missing letter(s):

I'm = I **am**   you've = you **have**   didn't = did **not**

4.2 List of short forms of auxiliary verbs

'm = am	I'm						
's = is *or* has		he's	she's	it's			
're = are					you're	we're	they're
've = have	I've				you've	we've	they've
'll = will	I'll	he'll	she'll		you'll	we'll	they'll
'd = would *or* had	I'd	he'd	she'd		you'd	we'd	they'd

's can be **is** or **has:**
- She's sick. (= She **is** sick.)
- She's gone away. (= She **has** gone away.)

but **let's** = let us:
- Let's go now. (= Let **us** go now.)

'd can be **would** or **had:**
- I'd see a doctor if I were you. (= I **would** see)
- I'd never seen her before. (= I **had** never seen)

We use some of these short forms (especially **'s**) after question words (**who/what,** etc.) and after **that/there/here:**

who's what's where's how's that's there's here's who'll there'll who'd
- **Who's** that woman over there? (= Who **is**)
- **What's** happened? (= What **has**)
- Do you think **there'll** be many people at the party? (= there **will**)

You can also use short forms (especially **'s**) after a noun:
- **John's** going out tonight. (= John **is**)
- **My friend's** just gotten married. (= My friend **has**)

You cannot use **'m / 's / 're / 've / 'll / 'd** at the *end* of a sentence (because the verb is stressed in this position):
- "Are you tired?" "Yes, I **am.**" (*not* Yes, I'm.)
- Do you know where she **is**? (*not* Do you know where she's?)

4.3 *Negative short forms*

isn't	(= is not)	don't	(= do not)	haven't	(= have not)
aren't	(= are not)	**doesn't**	(= does not)	**hasn't**	(= has not)
wasn't	(= was not)	**didn't**	(= did not)	**hadn't**	(= had not)
weren't	(= were not)				

| **can't** | (= cannot) | **won't** | (= will not) | | |
| **couldn't** | (= could not) | **wouldn't** | (= would not) | **shouldn't** | (= should not) |

Negative short forms for **is** and **are** can be:

he **isn't** / she **isn't** / it **isn't**   *or*   he's **not** / she's **not** / it's **not**
you **aren't** / we **aren't** / they **aren't**   *or*   you're **not** / we're **not** / they're **not**

APPENDIX 5
Spelling

5.1   Nouns, verbs, and adjectives can have the following endings:

noun + -s/es *(plural)*	books	ideas	matches
verb + -s/-es (after **he/she/it**)	works	enjoys	washes
verb + -ing	working	enjoying	washing
verb + -ed	worked	enjoyed	washed
adjective + -er *(comparative)*	cheaper	quicker	brighter
adjective + -est *(superlative)*	cheapest	quickest	brightest
adjective + -ly *(adverb)*	cheaply	quickly	brightly

When we use these endings, there are sometimes changes in spelling. These changes are listed below.

5.2   Nouns and verbs + -s/-es

The ending is -es when the word ends in -s, -ss, -sh, -ch, or -x:

bus/buses	miss/misses	wash/washes
match/matches	search/searches	box/boxes

Note also:

potato/potatoes	tomato/tomatoes
do/does	go/goes

5.3   Words ending in -y (baby, carry, easy, etc.)

If a word ends in a *consonant** + y (-by, -ry, -sy, -vy, etc.):

y changes to ie before the ending -s:

baby/babies	story/stories	country/countries	secretary/secretaries
hurry/hurries	study/studies	apply/applies	try/tries

y changes to i before the ending -ed:

hurry/hurried	study/studied	apply/applied	try/tried

y changes to i before the endings -er and -est:

easy/easier/easiest   heavy/heavier/heaviest   lucky/luckier/luckiest

y changes to i before the ending -ly:

easy/easily   heavy/heavily   temporary/temporarily

y does not change before -ing:
hurry**ing**   study**ing**   apply**ing**   try**ing**

y does not change if the word ends in a *vowel + y (-ay, -ey, -oy, -uy):**
play/plays/played   monkey/monkeys   enjoy/enjoys/enjoyed   buy/buys
An exception is: **day/daily**
Note also: **pay/paid   lay/laid   say/said**

5.4   Verbs ending in -ie (**die, lie, tie**)

If a verb ends in -ie, ie changes to y before the ending -ing:
die/dying   lie/lying   tie/tying

---

*a e i o u are *vowel* letters. The other letters (**b c d f g**, etc.) are *consonant* letters.

5.5 Words ending in -e (hope, dance, wide, etc.)
   Verbs

> If a verb ends in -e, we leave out e before the ending -ing:
>   hope/hoping   smile/smiling   dance/dancing   confuse/confusing
> Exceptions are: **be/being**
> *and* verbs ending in -ee: see/seeing   agree/agreeing

> If a verb ends in -e, we add -d for the *past* (of regular verbs):
>   hope/hoped   smile/smiled   dance/danced   confuse/confused

Adjectives and adverbs

> If an adjective ends in -e, we add -r and -st for the *comparative* and *superlative*:
>   wide/wider/widest   late/later/latest   large/larger/largest

> If an adjective ends in -e, we keep e before the adverb ending -ly:
>   polite/politely   extreme/extremely   absolute/absolutely

> If an adjective ends in -le (simple, terrible, etc.), we delete e and add y to form the adverb ending -ly:
>   simple/simply   terrible/terribly   reasonable/reasonably

5.6 Doubling consonants (**stop/stopping/stopped, wet/wetter/wettest**, etc.)

Sometimes a word ends in *vowel + consonant*. For example:
   stop   plan   wet   thin   slip   prefer   regret

Before the endings -ing/-ed/-er/-est, we double the consonant at the end. So **p → pp, n → nn,** etc. For example:

stop	p → pp	stopping	stopped	big	g → gg	bigger	biggest
plan	n → nn	planning	planned	wet	t → tt	wetter	wettest
rub	b → bb	rubbing	rubbed	thin	n → nn	thinner	thinnest

If the word has more than one syllable (**prefer, begin,** etc.), we double the consonant at the end only if the final syllable is stressed:
   preFER / preferring / preferred   perMIT / permitting / permitted
   reGRET / regretting / regretted   beGIN / beginning

If the final syllable is not stressed, we do not double the final consonant:
   VISit / visiting / visited   deVELop / developing / developed
   HAPpen / happening / happened   reMEMber / remembering / remembered

Note that:

> We do not double the final consonant if the word ends in two consonants (-rt, -lp, -ng, etc.):
>   start/starting/started   help/helping/helped   long/longer/longest

> We do not double the final consonant if there are two vowel letters before it (-oil, -eed, etc.):
>   boil/boiling/boiled   need/needing/needed   explain/explaining/explained
>   cheap/cheaper/cheapest   loud/louder/loudest   quiet/quieter/quietest

> We do not double y or w at the end of words. (At the end of words y and w are not consonants.)
>   stay/staying/stayed   grow/growing   new/newer/newest

APPENDIX 6
British English

There are a few grammatical differences between North American English and British English:

Unit	North American	British
7 A–C, 13A	The *present perfect* or the *simple past* can be used for an action in the past with a result now: ■ I've **lost** my key. **Have** you **seen** it? *or* I **lost** my key. **Did** you **see** it? ■ Sally isn't here. { She's **gone** out. / She **went** out. The *present perfect* or the *simple past* can be used with **just, already,** and **yet.** ■ I'm not hungry. { I've **just had** lunch. / I **just had** lunch. ■ *A:* What time is he leaving? ■ *B:* { He **has already left.** / He **already left.** ■ **Have** you **finished** your work **yet?** *or* **Did** you **finish** your work **yet?**	The present perfect (not usually the simple past) is used: ■ I've **lost** my key. **Have** you **seen** it? ■ Sally isn't here. She's **gone** out. Usually the present perfect is used with **just, already,** and **yet:** ■ I'm not hungry. I've **just had** lunch. ■ *A:* What time is he leaving? ■ *B:* He **has already left.** ■ **Have** you **finished** your work **yet?**
16B	North American speakers say: **take** a bath, **take** a shower, **take** a vacation, **take** a break	British speakers say: **have** a bath, **have** a shower, **have** a holiday, **have** a break
20D	**Will** is used with **I/we. Shall** is unusual: ■ I **will** be late tonight. **Should I . . . ?** and **should we . . . ?** are used to ask for advice, etc.: ■ Which way **should we** go?	**Will** or **shall** can be used with **I/we:** ■ I **will/shall** be late this evening. **Shall I . . . ?** and **shall we . . . ?** are used to ask for advice, etc.: ■ Which way **shall we** go?
27	North American speakers use **must not** to say they feel sure something is not true: ■ Their car isn't outside their house. They **must not** be at home. ■ She walked past me without speaking. She **must not** have seen me.	British speakers usually use **can't** in these situations: ■ Their car isn't outside their house. They **can't be** at home. ■ She walked past me without speaking. She **can't** have seen me.
32 A–B	After **demand, insist,** etc., the *subjunctive* is usually used: ■ I demanded that he **apologize.** ■ She suggested that I **buy** some new clothes.	British speakers also use the *simple past* and *simple present:* ■ I demanded that he **apologised.*** ■ I demand that he **apologises.** ■ She suggested that I **bought** some new clothes.
69C	North American speakers say "to/in **the** hospital": ■ Two people were injured and taken **to the hospital.**	British speakers usually say "to/in hospital" (*without* the): ■ Two people were injured and taken **to hospital.**

*Many verbs ending in **-ize** in North American English (apologize, organize, specialize, etc.) are spelled with **-ise** in British English (apologise, organise, specialise, etc.).

Unit	North American	British
118A	**on the weekend / on weekends:** ■ Will you be here **on the weekend?**	**at the weekend / at weekends:** ■ Will you be here **at the weekend?**
121B	**on a street:** ■ Do you live **on this street?**	**in a street:** ■ Do you live **in this street?**
128C	**different from** or **different than:** ■ It was **different from** (*or* **than**) what I'd expected.	**different from** or **different to:** ■ It was **different from** (*or* **to**) what I'd expected.

Appendix	North American	British
1.3	The following verbs are regular in North American English: **burn** → burned **dream** → dreamed **lean** → leaned **learn** → learned **smell** → smelled **spell** → spelled **spill** → spilled **spoil** → spoiled	In British English, these verbs can be regular or irregular: **burn** → burned *or* burnt **dream** → dreamed *or* dreamt **lean** → leaned *or* leant **learn** → learned *or* learnt **smell** → smelled *or* smelt **spell** → spelled *or* spelt **spill** → spilled *or* spilt **spoil** → spoiled *or* spoilt
	The past participle of **get** is **gotten:** ■ Your English has **gotten** much better. (= has become much better)	The past participle of **get** is **got:** ■ Your English has **got** much better.
	But **have got** (*not* gotten) is an alternative to **have:** ■ I've **got** two brothers. (= I have two brothers.)	**Have got** is a more usual alternative to **have:** ■ I've **got** two brothers.
5.6	Note the differences in spelling: travel → traveling, traveled cancel → canceling, canceled	travel → travelling, travelled cancel → cancelling, cancelled

Additional Exercises

Present and Past   Units 1–6, Appendix 2

1   Put the verb into the correct form: simple present *(I do)*, present continuous *(I am doing)*, simple past *(I did)*, or past continuous *(I was doing)*.

1. We can go out now. It _isn't raining_____ (not / rain) anymore.
2. Jane _was waiting_____ (wait) for me when I _arrived_____ (arrive).
3. I _____ (get) hungry. Let's have something to eat.
4. What _____ (you / do) in your spare time? Do you have any hobbies?
5. How fast _____ (the car / go) at the time of the accident?
6. Mary usually _____ (call) me on Fridays, but she _____ (not / call) last Friday.
7. *A:* When I last saw you, you _____ (think) of moving to a new apartment.
   B: That's right, but in the end I _____ (decide) to stay where I was.
8. What's that noise? What _____ (happen)?
9. It's usually dry here at this time of the year. It _____ (not / rain) much.
10. Last night the phone _____ (ring) three times while we _____ (have) dinner.
11. Linda was busy when we _____ (go) to see her yesterday. She _____ (study) for an exam. We _____ (not / want) to bother her, so we _____ (not / stay) very long.
12. When I first _____ (tell) Tom the news, he _____ (not / believe) me. He _____ (think) that I _____ (joke).

2 Choose the correct alternative.

1. Everything is going well. We ~~didn't have~~ / haven't had any problems so far. (*haven't had* is correct)
2. Lisa didn't go / hasn't gone to work yesterday. She wasn't feeling well.
3. Look! That man over there wears / is wearing the same sweater as you.
4. I wonder why Jim is / is being so nice to me today. He isn't usually like that.
5. Jane had a book open in front of her, but she didn't read / wasn't reading it.
6. I wasn't very busy. I didn't have / wasn't having much to do.
7. Mary wasn't happy in her new job at first, but she begins / is beginning to like it now.
8. After graduating from college, Tim found / has found it very difficult to get a job.
9. When Sue heard the news, she wasn't / hasn't been very happy.
10. This is a nice restaurant, isn't it? Is this the first time you are / you've been here?
11. I need a new job. I'm doing / I've been doing the same job for too long.
12. "Ann has gone out." "Oh, she has? What time did she go / has she gone?"
13. "You look tired." "Yes, I've played / I've been playing basketball."
14. Where are you coming / do you come from? Are you Australian?
15. I'd like to see Tina again. It's been a long time since I saw her / that I didn't see her.
16. Bob and Alice have been married since 20 years / for 20 years.

3 Complete the questions using an appropriate verb.

1. A: I'm looking for Paul. *Have you seen* _____ him?
   B: Yes, he was here a minute ago.
2. A: Why *did you go* _____ to bed so early last night?
   B: Because I was very tired.
3. A: Where _____ ?
   B: To the post office. I want to mail these letters. I'll be back in a few minutes.
4. A: _____ TV every night?
   B: No, only if there's a good program on.
5. A: Your house is very beautiful. How long _____ here?
   B: Nearly ten years.
6. A: How was your vacation? _____ a nice time?
   B: Yes, thanks. It was great.
7. A: _____ Julie recently?
   B: Yes, we had lunch together a few days ago.
8. A: Can you describe the woman you saw? What _____ ?
   B: A red sweater and black jeans.
9. A: I'm sorry to keep you waiting. _____ long?
   B: No, only about ten minutes.
10. A: How long _____ you to get to work in the morning?
    B: Usually about 45 minutes. It depends on the traffic.
11. A: _____ with that newspaper yet?
    B: No, I'm still reading it. I won't be long.
12. A: _____ to Mexico?
    B: No, never, but I went to Costa Rica a few years ago.

4 Use your own ideas to complete B's sentences.

1. A: What's the new restaurant like? Is it good?
   B: I have no idea. *I've never been* _____ there.
2. A: How well do you know Bill?
   B: Very well. We _____ since we were children.

3. *A:* Did you enjoy your vacation?
   B: Yes, it was fantastic. It's the best vacation _____ .
4. *A:* Is Brad still here?
   B: No, I'm afraid he isn't. _____ about ten minutes ago.
5. *A:* I like your suit. I haven't seen it before.
   B: It's new. It's the first time _____ .
6. *A:* How did you cut your knee?
   B: I slipped and fell while _____ tennis.
7. *A:* Do you ever go swimming?
   B: Not these days. I haven't _____ a long time.
8. *A:* How often do you go to the movies?
   B: Hardly ever. It's been almost a year _____ to the movies.
9. *A:* I bought some new shoes. Do you like them?
   B: Yes, they're very nice. Where _____ them?

Present and Past   Units 1–16, Appendix 2

5 Put the verb into the correct form: simple past *(I did)*, past continuous *(I was doing)*, past
perfect *(I had done)*, or past perfect continuous *(I had been doing)*.

1.

SARAH   STATION

Yesterday afternoon Sarah _went_____ (go) to the station to meet Paul.
When she _____ (get) there, Paul _____ (already /
wait) for her. His train _____ (arrive) early.

2. BILL

Hello.

When I got home, Bill _____ (lie) on the sofa. The TV was on, but he
_____ (not / watch) it. He _____ (fall) asleep and
_____ (snore) loudly. I _____ (turn) the TV off,
and just then he _____ (wake) up.

3.

Last night I _____ (just / go) to bed and _____
(read) a book when suddenly I _____ (hear) a noise. I
_____ (get) up to see what it was, but I _____
(not / see) anything, so I _____ (go) back to bed.

4.

Oh no! I forgot my passport!

Enjoy your flight!

Maria had to go to Tokyo last week, but she almost _____ (miss) the plane. She _____ (stand) in line at the check-in counter when she suddenly _____ (realize) that she _____ (leave) her passport at home. Fortunately, she doesn't live very far from the airport, so she _____ (have) time to take a taxi home to get it. She _____ (get) back to the airport just in time for her flight.

5.

Hello.

Did you have a good game?

Yes, great.

Come and have some iced tea.

I'm sorry, but . . .

I _____ (meet) Jeff and Amy yesterday as I _____ (walk) through the park. They _____ (be) at the Sports Center, where they _____ (play) tennis. They _____ (go) to a cafe for some iced tea and _____ (invite) me to join them, but I _____ (arrange) to meet a friend and _____ (not / have) time.

6 **Make sentences from the words in parentheses. Put the verb into the correct form: present perfect (*I have done*), present perfect continuous (*I have been doing*), past perfect (*I had done*), or past perfect continuous (*I had been doing*).**

1. Ann is sitting on the ground. She's out of breath.
   (she / run) *She has been running.*
2. Where's my bag? I left it under this chair.
   (somebody / take / it) _____
3. We were all surprised when Jenny and Alex got married last year.
   (they / only / know / each other / a few weeks) _____
4. It's still raining. I wish it would stop.
   (it / rain / all day) _____
5. Suddenly I woke up. I was confused and didn't know where I was.
   (I / dream) _____
6. I wasn't hungry at lunchtime, so I didn't have anything to eat.
   (I / have / a big breakfast) _____
7. Every year Bob and Alice spend a few days at the same hotel in Hawaii.
   (they / go / there for years) _____
8. I have a headache.
   (I / have / it / since I got up) _____
9. Next week Dave is going to run in a marathon.
   (he / train / very hard for it) _____

7 Put the verbs into the correct form.

Julie and Kevin are old friends. They meet by chance at the airport.

Julie: Hello, Kevin. (1) _____
(I / not / see) you for ages. How are you?

Kevin: I'm fine. How about you? (2) _____
(you / look) good.

Julie: Thanks. So, (3) _____ (you /
go) somewhere, or (4) _____
(you / meet) somebody's flight?

Kevin: (5) _____ (I / go) to New York for a business meeting.

Julie: Oh. (6) _____ (you / often / go) away on business?

Kevin: Fairly often, yes. And you? Where (7) _____ (you / go)?

Julie: Nowhere. (8) _____ (I / meet) a friend. Unfortunately,
her flight (9) _____ (be) delayed –
(10) _____ (I / wait) here for nearly an hour.

Kevin: How are your children?

Julie: They're all fine, thanks. The youngest (11) _____ (just
/ start) school.

Kevin: How (12) _____ (she / do)?
(13) _____ (she / like) it?

Julie: Yes, (14) _____ (she / think) it's great.

Kevin: (15) _____ (you / work) these days? The last time I
(16) _____ (speak) to you,
(17) _____ (you / work) in a travel agency.

Julie: That's right. Unfortunately, the company (18) _____ (go)
out of business a couple of months after (19) _____
(I / start) working there, so (20) _____ (I / lose) my job.

Kevin: And (21) _____ (you / not / have) a job since then?

Julie: Not a permanent job. (22) _____ (I / have) a few
temporary jobs. By the way, (23) _____ (you / see)
Mark recently?

Kevin: Mark? He's in Canada.

Julie: Really? How long (24) _____ (he / be) in Canada?

Kevin: About a year now. (25) _____ (I / see) him a few days
before (26) _____ (he / go).
(27) _____ (he / be) unemployed for months, so
(28) _____ (he / decide) to try his luck somewhere else.
(29) _____ (he / really / look forward) to going.

Julie: What (30) _____ (he / do) there?

Kevin: I have no idea. (31) _____ (I / not / hear) from him
since (32) _____ (he / leave). Anyway, I have to go –
my plane is boarding. It was really nice to see you again.

Julie: You, too. Bye. Have a good trip.

Kevin: Thanks. Bye.

8 Put the verb into the most appropriate form.

1. Who _____ (invent) the bicycle?
2. "Do you still have a headache?" "No, _____ (it / go)
away. I'm all right now."
3. I was the last one to leave the office. Everybody else _____
(go) home.

4. What _____ (you / do) last weekend?
   _____ (you / go) away for the weekend?
5. I like your car. How long _____ (you / have) it?
6. We decided not to go out because _____ (it / rain) pretty hard.
7. Jill is an experienced teacher. _____ (she / teach) for 15 years.
8. A few days ago _____ (I / see) a man at a party whose face
   _____ (be) very familiar. At first I couldn't think where
   _____ (I / see) him before. Then suddenly
   _____ (I / remember) who _____ (he / be).
9. _____ (you / hear) of Agatha Christie?
   _____ (she / be) a writer who _____
   (die) in 1976. _____ (she / write) more than 70 detective novels.
   _____ (you / read) any of them?
10. *A:* What _____ (this word / mean)?
    B: I don't know. _____ (I / never / see) it before. Look it
    up in the dictionary.
11. *A:* _____ (you / get) to the theater in time for the play last night?
    B: No, we were late. By the time we got there, _____
    (it / already / begin).
12. I went to John's room and _____ (knock) on the door, but there
    _____ (be) no answer. Either _____
    (he / go) out, or _____ (he / not / want) to see anyone.
13. Angela asked me how to use the photocopier. _____
    (she / never / use) it before, so _____ (she / not / know)
    what to do.
14. Mary _____ (go) for a swim after work yesterday.
    _____ (she / need) some exercise because
    _____ (she / sit) in an office all day in front of a computer.

Past Continuous and *used to*   Units 6 and 17

9 Complete the sentences using the past continuous *(was doing)* or *used to (do)*. Use the
verb in parentheses.

1. I haven't been to the movies for ages. We *used to go* _____ a lot. (go)
2. Ann didn't see me wave to her. She *was looking* _____ in the other
   direction. (look)
3. I _____ a lot, but I don't use my car very much these
   days. (drive)
4. I asked the driver to slow down. She _____ too fast.
   (drive)
5. Rosa and Jim met for the first time when they _____ at
   the same bank. (work)
6. When I was a child, I _____ a lot of bad dreams. (have)
7. When the phone rang, I _____ a shower. (take)
8. "Where were you yesterday afternoon?" "I _____
   volleyball." (play)
9. "Do you play any sports?" "Not these days. I _____
   volleyball." (play)
10. George looked very nice. He _____ a very nice suit.
    (wear)

10 What do you say to your friend in these situations? Use the words given in parentheses.
Use the present continuous *(I am doing)*, *going to (do)*, or *will (I'll)*.

1. You have made all your vacation plans. Your destination is Jamaica.
   Friend: Have you decided where you're going on vacation yet?
   You: Yes, *I'm going to Jamaica* _____ . (I / go)

2. You have made an appointment with the dentist for Friday morning.
   Friend: Do you want to get together on Friday morning?
   You: I can't on Friday. _____ (I / go)

3. You and some friends are planning a vacation in Mexico. You have decided to rent a car,
   but you haven't arranged this yet.
   Friend: How do you plan to travel around Mexico? By bus?
   You: No, _____ . (we / rent)

4. Your friend has two young children. She wants to go out tomorrow night. You offer to
   take care of the children.
   Friend: I want to go out tomorrow night, but I don't have a baby-sitter.
   You: That's no problem. _____ (I / take care)

5. You have already arranged to have lunch with Sue tomorrow.
   Friend: Are you free at lunchtime tomorrow?
   You: No, _____ . (have lunch)

6. You are in a restaurant. You and your friend are looking at the menu. You ask your
   friend if he/she has decided what to have.
   You: What _____ ? (you / have)
   Friend: I don't know. I can't make up my mind.

7. You and a friend are reading. It's getting dark, and your friend is having trouble reading.
   You decide to turn on the light.
   Friend: It's getting dark, isn't it? I'm having trouble reading.
   You: _____ (I / turn on)

8. You and a friend are reading. It's getting dark, and you decide to turn on the light. You
   stand up and walk toward the light switch.
   Friend: What are you doing?
   You: _____ (I / turn on)

11 Put the verb into the most appropriate form. Use a present tense (simple or continuous),
will (I'll), or *shall/should*.

Conversation 1 (in the morning)

Jenny: (1) *Are you doing* _____ (you / do) anything tomorrow night, Karen?
Karen: No, why?
Jenny: Well, do you feel like going to the movies? *Strangers on a Plane* is playing. I want to
        see it, but I don't want to go alone.
Karen: OK, (2) _____ (I / go) with you. What time
        (3) _____ (we / meet)?
Jenny: Well, the movie (4) _____ (begin) at 8:45, so
        (5) _____ (I / meet) you at about 8:30 outside the
        theater, OK?
Karen: Fine. (6) _____ (I / see) Mary later this evening.
        (7) _____ (I / ask) her if she wants to come, too?
Jenny: Yes, why don't you? (8) _____ (I / see) you tomorrow
        then. Bye.

Conversation 2 (later the same day)

Karen: Jenny and I (9) _____ (go) to the movies tomorrow
night to see *Strangers on a Plane*. Why don't you come with us?

Mary: I'd love to come. What time (10) _____ (the movie / begin)?

Karen: 8:45.

Mary: (11) _____ (you / meet) outside the theater?

Karen: Yes, at 8:30. Is that OK for you?

Mary: Yes, (12) _____ (I / be) there at 8:30.

12 **Put the verbs into the most appropriate form. Sometimes there is more than one
possibility.**

1. A has decided to learn a language.
   A: I've decided to try and learn a foreign language.
   B: You have? What language (1) *are you going to study* _____ (you / study)?
   A: Spanish.
   B: (2) _____ (you / take) a class?
   A: Yes, (3) _____ (it / start) next week.
   B: That's great. I'm sure (4) _____ (you / enjoy) it.
   A: I hope so. But I think (5) _____ (it / be) a lot of work.

2. A wants to know about B's vacation plans.
   A: I hear (1) _____ (you / go) on vacation soon.
   B: That's right. (2) _____ (we / go) to Brazil.
   A: I hope (3) _____ (you / have) a great time.
   B: Thanks. (4) _____ (I / send) you a postcard and
       (5) _____ (I / get) in touch with you when
       (6) _____ (I / get) back.

3. A invites B to a party.
   A: (1) _____ (I / have) a party next Saturday. Can you come?
   B: On Saturday? I'm not sure. Some friends of mine (2) _____
       (come) to stay with me next week, but I think (3) _____
       (they / leave) by Saturday. But if (4) _____ (they / be) still
       here, (5) _____ (I / not / be) able to come to the party.
   A: OK. Well, tell me as soon as (6) _____ (you / know).
   B: All right. (7) _____ (I / call) you during the week.

4. A and B are two secret agents arranging a meeting. They are talking on the phone.
   A: Well, what time (1) _____ (we / meet)?
   B: Come to the cafe by the station at 4:00.
       (2) _____ (I / wait) for you
       when (3) _____ (you / arrive).
       (4) _____ (I / sit) by the window,
       and (5) _____ (I / wear) a bright
       green sweater.
   A: OK. (6) _____ (Agent 307 /
       come), too?
   B: No, she can't be there.
   A: Oh. (7) _____ (I / bring) the
       documents?
   B: Yes. (8) _____ (I / explain)
       everything when (9) _____ (I / see)
       you. And don't be late.
   A: OK. (10) _____ (I / try) to be on time.

13 Put the verb into the correct form. Choose from the following:

> *present continuous* (**I am doing**)   **will ('ll) / won't**
> *simple present* (**I do**)   **will be doing**
> **going to** (**I'm going to do**)   **shall / should**

1. I'm a little hungry. I think _____ (I / have) something to eat.
2. Why are you putting on your coat? _____ (you / go) somewhere?
3. Look! That plane is flying toward the airport. _____ (it / land).
4. We have to do something soon, before _____ (it / be) too late.
5. I'm sorry you've decided to leave the company. _____ (I / miss) you when _____ (you / go).
6. Are you still watching that TV program? What time _____ (it / end)?
7. _____ (I / go) to Chicago next weekend for a wedding. My sister _____ (get) married.
8. I'm not ready yet. _____ (I / tell) you when _____ (I / be) ready. I promise _____ (I / not / be) very long.
9. *A:* Where are you going?
   B: To the hairdresser. _____ (I / have) my hair cut.
10. She was very rude to me. I refuse to speak to her again until _____ (she / apologize).
11. I wonder where _____ (we / live) ten years from now?
12. What do you plan to do when _____ (you / finish) college?

Modal Verbs (*can*/*must*/*would*, etc.)   Units 25–31

14 Make sentences from the words in parentheses.

1. Don't phone Ann now. (she might / have / lunch)
   She might be having lunch.
2. I ate too much. Now I feel sick. (I shouldn't / eat / so much)
   I shouldn't have eaten so much.
3. I wonder why Tom didn't phone me. (he must / forget)
   _____
4. Why did you go home so early? (you shouldn't / leave / so early)
   _____
5. You've signed the contract. (it / can't / change / now)
   _____
6. "What's Linda doing?" "I'm not sure." (she may / watch / television)
   _____
7. Lauren was standing outside the movie theater. (she must / wait / for somebody)
   _____
8. He was in prison at the time that the crime was committed, so (he couldn't / do / it).
   _____
9. Why weren't you here earlier? (you should / be / here earlier)
   _____
10. Why didn't you ask me to help you? (I would / help / you)
    _____
11. I'm surprised nobody told you that the road was dangerous. (you should / warn)
    _____
12. Brian was in a strange mood yesterday. (he might not / feel / very well)
    _____

15 Complete B's sentences using *can / could / might / must / should / would* + the verb in parentheses. In some sentences you need to use *have* (*must have done / should have done*, etc.). In some sentences you need the negative (*can't/couldn't*, etc.).

1. A: I'm hungry.
    B: But you've just had lunch. You _can't be_____ hungry already. (be)
2. A: I haven't seen our neighbors for ages.
    B: Me either. They _must have gone_____ away. (go)
3. A: What's the weather like? Is it raining?
    B: Not right now, but it _____ later. (rain)
4. A: Where has Julie gone?
    B: I'm not sure. She _____ to the bank. (go)
5. A: I didn't see you at John's party last week.
    B: No, I had to work that night, so I _____ . (go)
6. A: I saw you at John's party last week.
    B: No, you _____ me. I didn't go to John's party. (see)
7. A: What time will we get to Sue's house?
    B: Well, it's about a two-hour drive, so if we leave at 3:00, we
    _____ there by 5:00. (get)
8. A: When was the last time you saw Eric?
    B: Years ago. I _____ him if I saw him now. (recognize)
9. A: Did you hear the explosion?
    B: What explosion?
    A: There was a loud explosion a few minutes ago. You
    _____ it. (hear)
10. A: We weren't sure which way to go. We decided to turn right.
    B: You went the wrong way. You _____ left. (turn)

Conditionals

Units 24, 35–37

16 Put the verb into the correct form.

1. If you _found_____ a wallet in the street, what would you do with it? (find)
2. I have to hurry. My friend will be upset if I _'m not_____ on time. (not / be)
3. I didn't realize that Jeff was in the hospital. If I _had known_____ he was in the hospital, I would have gone to visit him. (know)
4. If the phone _____ , can you answer it? (ring)
5. I can't decide what to do. What would you do if you _____ in my position? (be)
6. A: What should we do tomorrow?
    B: Well, if it _____ a nice day, we can go to the beach. (be)
7. A: Let's go to the beach.
    B: No, it's too cold. If it _____ warmer, I wouldn't mind going to the beach. (be)
8. A: Did you go to the beach yesterday?
    B: No, it was too cold. If it _____ warmer, we would have gone. (be)
9. If you _____ enough money to go anywhere in the world, where would you go? (have)
10. I'm glad we had a map. I'm sure we would have gotten lost if we
    _____ one. (not / have)
11. The accident was your fault. If you _____ more carefully, it wouldn't have happened. (drive)
12. A: Why do you read newspapers?
    B: Well, if I _____ newspapers, I wouldn't know what was happening in the world. (not / read)

17 Complete the sentences in the way shown.

1. Liz is tired all the time. She shouldn't go to bed so late.
   If _Liz didn't go to bed so late, she wouldn't be tired all the time_ .
2. It's getting late. I don't think Ann will come to see us now.
   I'd be surprised if Ann _____ .
3. I'm sorry I disturbed you. I didn't know you were busy.
   If I'd known you were busy, I _____ .
4. The dog attacked you, but only because you provoked it.
   If _____ .
5. I don't want them to be upset, so I've decided not to tell them what happened.
   They _____ if _____ .
6. Unfortunately, I didn't have an umbrella, so I got very wet in the rain.
   I _____ if _____ .
7. Matt failed his driver's test last week. He was very nervous, and that's why he failed.
   If he _____ .

18 Use your own ideas to complete these sentences.

1. I'd go out tonight if _____ .
2. I'd have gone out last night if _____ .
3. If you hadn't reminded me, _____ .
4. We wouldn't have been late if _____ .
5. If I'd been able to get tickets, _____ .
6. Who would you phone if _____ ?
7. Cities would be nicer places if _____ .
8. If there were no television, _____ .

Wish   Units 36–38

19 Put the verb into the correct form.

1. I feel sick. I wish _I hadn't eaten_ so much cake. (I / not / eat)
2. I'm fed up with this rain. I wish _it would stop_ raining. (it / stop)
3. It's a difficult question. I wish _____ the answer. (I / know)
4. I should have listened to you. I wish _____ your advice.
   (I / take)
5. I wish _____ here. She'd be able to help us. (Ann / be)
6. Aren't they ready yet? I wish _____ . (they / hurry up)
7. It would be nice to stay here. I wish _____ to go now.
   (we / not / have)
8. When we were in Bangkok last year, we didn't have time to see all the things we wanted
   to see. I wish _____ more time. (we / have)
9. It's freezing today. I wish _____ so cold. I hate cold
   weather. (it / not / be)
10. What's her name again? I wish _____ remember her
    name. (I / can)
11. What I said was rude. I wish _____ anything. (I / not / say)
12. *(in a car)* You're driving too fast. I wish _____ .
    (you / slow down)
13. It was a terrible movie. I wish _____ to see it. (we / not / go)
14. You're always tired. I wish _____ to bed so late.
    (you / not / go)

20   Put the verb into the most appropriate passive form.

1. There's somebody behind us. I think we _are being followed_____ (follow).
2. A mystery is something that _can't be explained_____ (can't / explain).
3. We didn't play soccer yesterday. The match _____ (cancel).
4. The television _____ (repair). It's working again now.
5. The church tower _____ (restore). The work is almost finished.
6. "How old is the church?" "It _____ (believe) to be over 600 years old."
7. If I didn't do my job right, I _____ (would / fire).
8. *A:* I left some papers on the desk last night, and I can't find them now.
   B: They _____ (might / throw) away.
9. I learned to swim when I was very young. I _____ (teach) by my mother.
10. After _____ (arrest), I was taken to the police station.
11. "_____ (you / ever / arrest)?" "No, never."
12. *(TV news report)* Two people _____ (report) to _____ (injure) in an explosion at a factory in Miami early this morning.

21   Put the verb into the correct form, active or passive.

1. This house is very old. It _was built_____ (build) over 100 years ago.
2. My grandfather was a builder. He _built_____ (build) this house many years ago.
3. "Is your car still for sale?" "No, I _____ (sell) it."
4. "Is the house at the end of the street still for sale?"
   "No, it _____ (sell)."
5. Sometimes mistakes _____ (make). It's inevitable.
6. I wouldn't leave your car unlocked. It _____ (might / steal).
7. My bag has disappeared. It _____ (must / steal).
8. I can't find my hat. Somebody _____ (must / take) it by mistake.
9. It's a serious problem. I don't know how it _____ (can / solve).
10. We didn't leave early enough. We _____ (should / leave) earlier.
11. Every time I travel by plane, my flight _____ (delay).
12. A new bridge _____ (build) across the river. Work started last year, and the bridge _____ (expect) to open next year.

22   Read the newspaper reports and put the verbs into the most appropriate form.

1. **Fire at City Hall**
   City Hall (1) _was damaged_____ (damage) in a fire last night. The fire, which (2) _____ (discover) at about 9:00 P.M., spread very quickly. Nobody (3) _____ (injure), but two people had to (4) _____ (rescue) from the basement. A large number of documents (5) _____ (believe / destroy). It (6) _____ (not / know) how the fire started.

2. **Convenience Store Robbery**

A convenience store clerk (1) _____ (force) to hand over $500 yesterday after (2) _____ (threaten) by a man with a gun. The gunman escaped in a car that (3) _____ (steal) earlier in the day. The car (4) _____ (later / find) in a parking lot, where it (5) _____ (abandon). A man (6) _____ (arrest) in connection with the robbery and (7) _____ (still / question) by the police.

3. **Road Delays**

Repair work started yesterday on Route 22. The road (1) _____ (resurface), and there will be long delays. Drivers (2) _____ (ask) to use an alternative route if possible. The work (3) _____ (expect) to last two weeks. Next Sunday the road (4) _____ (close), and traffic (5) _____ (reroute).

4. **Accident**

A woman (1) _____ (take) to the hospital after her car collided with a truck on Route 309 yesterday. She (2) _____ (allow) to go home later that day after treatment. The road (3) _____ (block) for an hour after the accident, and traffic had to (4) _____ (reroute). A police inspector said afterward: "The woman was lucky. She could (5) _____ (kill)."

-ing and the Infinitive   Units 50–63

23 Put the verb into the correct form.

1. How old were you when you learned *to drive* _____ (drive) ?
2. I don't mind *walking* _____ (walk) home, but I'd rather *take* _____ (take) a taxi.
3. I can't make a decision. I keep _____ (change) my mind.
4. He had made his decision and refused _____ (change) his mind.
5. Why did you change your decision? What made you _____ (change) your mind?
6. It was a great vacation. I really enjoyed _____ (be) at the ocean again.
7. Did I really tell you I was unhappy? I don't remember _____ (say) that.
8. "Remember _____ (call) Tom tomorrow." "OK. I won't forget."
9. The water here isn't very good. I'd avoid _____ (drink) it if I were you.
10. I pretended _____ (be) interested in the conversation, but it was really very boring.
11. I got up and looked out of the window _____ (see) what the weather was like.
12. I have a friend who claims _____ (be) able to speak five languages.
13. I didn't like _____ (live) in my old apartment, so I decided _____ (move) .
14. Steve used _____ (be) a soccer player. He had to stop _____ (play) because of an injury.
15. After _____ (stop) by the police, the man admitted _____ (steal) the car but denied _____ (drive) 100 miles an hour.
16. *A:* How do you make this machine _____ (work) ?
    B: I'm not sure. Try _____ (press) that button and see what happens.

24 Make sentences from the words in parentheses.

1. I can't find the tickets. (I / seem / lose / them) *I seem to have lost them.*
2. I don't have far to go. (it / not / worth / take / a taxi) *It's not worth taking a taxi.*
3. Tim isn't very reliable. (he / tend / forget / things) _____
4. I've got a lot of luggage. (you / mind / help / me?) _____
5. There's nobody in the house. (everybody / seem / go out)

   _____

6. We don't like our apartment. (we / think / move) _____
7. The vase was very valuable. (I / afraid / touch / it) _____
8. Bill never carries much money with him. (he / afraid / robbed)

   _____

9. I wouldn't go to see that movie. (it / not / worth / see) _____
10. I'm very tired after that long walk. (I / not / used / walk / so far)

    _____

11. Beth is on vacation. I received a postcard from her yesterday. (she / seem / enjoy / herself)

    _____

12. Dave had lots of vacation pictures. (he / insist / show / them to me)

    _____

13. I don't want to clean my apartment. (I'd rather / somebody else / do / it)

    _____

25 Complete the second sentence so that the meaning is similar to the first.

1. I was surprised I passed the exam. I didn't expect *to pass the exam* .
2. Did you manage to solve the problem? Did you succeed *in solving the problem* ?
3. I don't read newspapers anymore. I've given up _____ .
4. I'd prefer not to go out tonight. I'd rather _____ .
5. He can't walk very well. He has trouble _____ .
6. Should I call you tonight? Do you want _____ ?
7. Nobody saw me come in. I came in without _____ .
8. They said I was a liar. I was accused _____ .
9. It will be good to see them again. I'm looking forward _____ .
10. What do you think I should do? What do you advise me _____ ?
11. It's too bad I couldn't go out with you. I'd like _____ .
12. I'm sorry that I didn't take your advice. I regret _____ .

Articles   Units 66–75

26 Put in *a/an* or *the* where necessary. Leave an empty space (–) if the sentence is already complete.

1. I don't usually like staying at __—__ hotels, but last summer we spent a few days at __a__ very nice hotel at __the__ beach.
2. _____ tennis is my favorite sport. I play once or twice _____ week if I can, but I'm not _____ very good player.
3. I won't be home for _____ dinner this evening. I'm meeting some friends after _____ work, and we're going to _____ movies.
4. _____ unemployment is very high right now, and it's very difficult for _____ people to find _____ work.
5. There was _____ accident as I was going _____ home last night. Two people were taken to _____ hospital. I think _____ most accidents are caused by _____ people driving too fast.
6. Carol is _____ economist. She used to work in _____ investment department of _____ Lloyds Bank. Now she works for _____ American bank in _____ United States.

7. A: What's _____ name of _____ hotel where you're staying?
   B: _____ Royal. It's on _____ West Street in _____ suburbs. It's near _____ airport.
8. I have two brothers. _____ older one is training to be _____ pilot with _____
   Western Airlines. _____ younger one is still in _____ high school. When he finishes
   _____ school, he hopes to go to _____ college to study _____ engineering.

Conjunctions   Units 24, 35, 109–114

27 **Choose the correct alternative.**

1. I'll try to be on time, but don't worry <u>if / when</u> I'm late. (*if* is correct)
2. Don't throw that bag away. <u>If / When</u> you don't want it, I'll take it.
3. Please report to the front desk <u>if / when</u> you arrive at the hotel.
4. We've arranged to play tennis tomorrow, but we won't play <u>if / when</u> it's raining.
5. Jennifer is in her last year at school. She still doesn't know what she's going to do
   <u>if / when</u> she graduates.
6. What would you do <u>if / when</u> you lost your keys?
7. I hope I'll be able to come to the party, but I'll let you know <u>if / unless</u> I can't.
8. I don't want to be disturbed, so don't phone me <u>if / unless</u> it's something important.
9. Please sign the contract <u>if / unless</u> you're happy with the conditions.
10. I like traveling by ship <u>as long as / unless</u> the sea isn't rough.
11. You might not remember the name of the hotel, so write it down <u>if / in case</u> you
    forget it.
12. It's not cold now, but take your coat with you <u>if / in case</u> it gets cold later.
13. Take your coat with you, and then you can put it on <u>if / in case</u> it gets cold later.
14. The television is always on, <u>even if / if</u> nobody is watching it.
15. <u>Even / Although</u> we played very well, we lost the baseball game.
16. <u>Despite / Although</u> we've known each other a long time, we're not very close friends.
17. "When did you finish school?" "<u>As / When</u> I was 18."
18. Ann will be surprised <u>when / as</u> she hears the news.

Prepositions (Time)   Units 12, 115–118

28 **Put in one of the following prepositions:**

> **at   on   in   for   since   during   by   until**

1. Jack has gone out of town. He'll be back _in_____ a week.
2. We're having a party _____ Saturday. Can you come?
3. I have an interview next week. It's _____ 9:30 _____ Tuesday morning.
4. Sue isn't usually here _____ weekends. She goes out of town.
5. The train service is very good. The trains are almost always _____ time.
6. It was a confusing situation. Many things were happening _____ the same time.
7. I couldn't decide whether or not to buy the sweater. _____ the end I decided not to.
8. The road is busy all the time, even _____ night.
9. I was woken up by a loud noise _____ the night.
10. I saw Helen _____ Friday, but I haven't seen her _____ then.
11. Brian has been doing the same job _____ five years.
12. Ann's birthday is _____ the end of March. I'm not sure which day it is.
13. We have some friends staying with us _____ the moment. They're staying
    _____ Friday.
14. If you're interested in applying for the job, your application must be received _____
    Friday.

29 Put in the missing preposition.

1. I'd love to be able to visit every country _in_ the world.
2. "Margaret White is my favorite author. Have you read anything _____ her?" "Yes, I've read all her books."
3. "Is there a bank near here?" "Yes, there's one _____ the end of this block."
4. Tim is out of town at the moment. He's _____ vacation.
5. You've got something _____ your cheek. Take a look _____ the mirror.
6. We went _____ a party _____ Kelly's house on Saturday.
7. Bombay is _____ the west coast of India.
8. Look at the leaves _____ that tree. They're a beautiful color.
9. "Have you ever been _____ Tokyo?" "No, I've never been _____ Japan."
10. Mozart died _____ Vienna in 1791 _____ the age of 35.
11. "Are you _____ this photograph?" "Yes, that's me, _____ the left."
12. We went _____ the theater last night. We had seats _____ the front row.
13. "Where's the light switch?" "It's _____ the wall _____ the door."
14. What time did you arrive _____ the party?
15. I couldn't decide what to eat. There was nothing _____ the menu that I liked.
16. We live _____ a high rise. Our apartment is _____ the fifteenth floor.
17. "What did you think of the movie?" "Some parts were a little boring, but _____ the whole I enjoyed it."
18. When you paid the hotel bill, did you pay _____ cash or _____ credit card?
19. "How did you get here? _____ the bus?" "No, _____ car."
20. *A:* I wonder what's _____ TV tonight. Do you have a newspaper?
    B: Yes, the TV listings are _____ the back page.

30 Put in the missing preposition.

1. The plan has been changed, but nobody seems to know the reason _for_ this.
2. Don't ask me to decide. I'm not very good _____ making decisions.
3. Some people say that Sue is unfriendly, but she's always very nice _____ me.
4. What do you think is the best solution _____ the problem?
5. There has been a big increase _____ the price of land recently.
6. He lives a pretty lonely life. He doesn't have much contact _____ other people.
7. Paula is a wonderful photographer. She likes taking pictures _____ people.
8. Jim got married _____ a woman he met when he was in college.
9. He's very brave. He's not afraid _____ anything.
10. I'm surprised _____ the amount of traffic today. I didn't think it would be so heavy.
11. Thank you for lending me the guidebook. It was full _____ useful information.
12. Please come in and sit down. I'm sorry _____ the mess.

31 Put in a preposition where necessary. If the sentence is already complete, leave an empty space *(–)*.

1. She works quite hard. You can't accuse her _of_ being lazy.
2. Who's going to look _____ your children while you're at work?
3. The problem is becoming serious. We have to discuss _____ it.

4. The problem is becoming serious. We have to do something _____ it.
5. I prefer this chair _____ the other one. It's more comfortable.
6. Josh asked _____ me _____ money again, but I didn't give him any.
7. The river divides the city _____ two parts.
8. "What do you think _____ the new manager?" "She's all right, I guess."
9. Can somebody please explain _____ me what I have to do?
10. "Do you like staying at hotels?" "It depends _____ the hotel."
11. "Have you ever been to Borla?" "No, I've never heard _____ it. Where is it?"
12. You remind me _____ somebody I knew a long time ago. You look just like her.
13. What's so funny? What are you laughing _____ ?
14. What have you done with all the money you had? What did you spend it _____ ?

Study Guide

This guide will help you decide which units you need to study. The sentences in the guide are grouped together (Present and Past, Articles and Nouns, etc.) in the same way as the units in the Contents (page iii).

Each sentence can be completed using one or more of the alternatives (A, B, C, etc.). There are between two and five alternatives each time. **In some sentences more than one alternative is possible.**

If you don't know or if you are not sure which alternatives are correct, then you probably need to study the unit(s) listed on the right. You will also find the correct sentence in this unit. (If two or three units are listed, you will find the correct sentence in the first one.)

There is an Answer Key to this study guide on page 333.

IF YOU ARE NOT SURE WHICH IS RIGHT	STUDY UNIT

Present and Past

1.1 "_____ this week?" "No, she's on vacation."
A. Is Sarah working   B. Does Sarah work   C. Does work Sarah
1, 3

1.2 I don't understand this sentence. What _____ ?
A. does mean this word   B. does this word mean   C. means this word
2, 46

1.3 In the summer John _____ tennis once or twice a week.
A. is playing usually   B. is usually playing   C. usually plays   D. plays usually
2, 3

1.4 How _____ now? Better than before?
A. you are feeling   B. do you feel   C. are you feeling
4

1.5 It was a boring weekend. _____ anything.
A. I didn't   B. I don't do   C. I didn't do
5

1.6 Matt _____ his hand while he was cooking dinner.
A. burned   B. was burning   C. has burned
6, 13

Present Perfect and Past

2.1 Kimberly isn't here. _____ out.
A. She goes   B. She went   C. She's gone
7

2.2 Everything is going well. We _____ any problems so far.
A. didn't have   B. don't have   C. haven't had
8

2.3 Sarah has lost her passport again. It's the second time this _____ .
A. has happened   B. happens   C. happened
8

2.4 You're out of breath. _____ ?
A. Are you running   B. Have you run   C. Have you been running
9

2.5 Where's the book I gave you? What _____ with it?
A. have you done   B. have you been doing   C. are you doing
10

2.6 We're good friends. We _____ each other since we were in high school.
A. know   B. have known   C. have been knowing   D. knew
11

2.7 Kelly has been working here _____ .
A. for six months   B. since six months   C. six months ago
12

2.8 It's been two years _____ Joe.
A. that I don't see   B. that I haven't seen   C. since I didn't see
D. since I last saw

12

2.9 What time _____ work yesterday?
A. did you finish   B. have you finished   C. are you finished   D. do you finish

13, 7

2.10 The Chinese _____ printing.
A. invented   B. have invented   C. had invented

13, 14

2.11 John _____ in New York for ten years. Now he lives in Los Angeles.
A. lived   B. has lived   C. has been living

13, 11

2.12 The man sitting next to me on the plane was very nervous. He _____ before.
A. hasn't flown   B. didn't fly   C. hadn't flown   D. wasn't flying

14

2.13 _____ a car when they were living in Miami?
A. Had they   B. Did they have   C. Were they having   D. Have they had

16

2.14 I _____ TV a lot, but I don't anymore.
A. was watching   B. was used to watch   C. used to watch

17, 107

Future

3.1 _____ tomorrow, so we can go somewhere.
A. I shall not work   B. I'm not working   C. I won't work

18, 20

3.2 That bag looks heavy. _____ you with it.
A. I'm helping   B. I help   C. I'll help

20

3.3 I think the weather _____ be nice later.
A. will   B. shall   C. is going to

22, 21

3.4 "Anna is in the hospital." "Yes, I know. _____ her tonight."
A. I visit   B. I'm going to visit   C. I'll visit

22, 19

3.5 We're late. The movie _____ by the time we get to the theater.
A. will already start   B. will be already started   C. will already have started

23

3.6 Don't worry _____ late tonight.
A. if I'm   B. when I'm   C. when I'll be   D. if I'll be

24

Modals

4.1 The fire spread through the building quickly, but everybody _____ .
A. was able to escape   B. managed to escape   C. could escape

25

4.2 The phone is ringing. It _____ be Alex.
A. might   B. can   C. could

26, 28

4.3 Why did you stay at a hotel when you went to New York? You _____
with Candice.
A. can stay   B. could stay   C. could have stayed

26

4.4 I've lost one of my gloves. I _____ it somewhere.
A. must drop   B. must have dropped   C. must be dropping
D. must have been dropping

27

4.5 Take an umbrella with you when you go out. It _____ rain later.
A. may   B. might   C. can   D. could

29, 28

4.6 What was wrong with you? Why _____ go to the hospital?
A. had you to   B. did you have to   C. must you

30

4.7 Sue isn't working tomorrow, so she _____ get up early.   30
A. don't have to   B. doesn't have to   C. mustn't

4.8 It was a great party last night. You _____ come. Why didn't you?   31
A. must have   B. should have   C. ought to   D. had to

4.9 Lisa _____ some new clothes.   32
A. suggested that Mary buy   B. suggested that Mary bought
C. suggested Mary to buy

4.10 I think all drivers _____ seat belts.   33
A. should wear   B. had better wear   C. had better to wear

4.11 It's late. It's time _____ home.   33
A. we go   B. we must go   C. we should go   D. we went

Conditionals and *wish*

5.1 I'm not tired enough to go to bed yet. I wouldn't sleep if I _____ to bed now.   35
A. go   B. went   C. had gone   D. would go

5.2 If I were you, I _____ that coat. It's much too expensive.   36
A. won't buy   B. don't buy   C. am not going to buy   D. wouldn't buy

5.3 I didn't go out last night. I would have gone out if I _____ so tired.   37
A. wasn't   B. weren't   C. wouldn't have been   D. hadn't been

5.4 I wish I _____ a car. It would make life so much easier.   38, 36
A. have   B. had   C. would have

Passive

6.1 We _____ by a loud noise during the night.   39
A. woke up   B. are woken up   C. were woken up   D. were waking up

6.2 There's somebody walking behind us. I think _____ .   40
A. we are following   B. we are being followed   C. we are followed
D. we are being following

6.3 "Where _____ ?" "In Los Angeles."   41
A. were you born   B. are you born   C. have you been born   D. did you born

6.4 The train _____ arrive at 11:30, but it was an hour late.   42
A. supposed to   B. is supposed to   C. was supposed to

6.5 Where _____ ? Which barber did you go to?   43
A. did you cut your hair   B. have you cut your hair
C. did you have cut your hair   D. did you have your hair cut

Reported Speech

7.1 Hello, Jim. I didn't expect to see you today. Kelly said you _____ sick.   45, 44
A. are   B. were   C. was   D. should be

7.2 Ann _____ and left.   45
A. said good-bye to me   B. said me good-bye   C. told me good-bye

Questions and Auxiliary Verbs

8.1 "How _____ ?" "No one knows."   46
A. happened the accident   B. did happen the accident   C. did the accident happen

8.2 "Do you know where _____?" "No, he didn't say."
A. Tom has gone   B. has Tom gone   C. has gone Tom

47

8.3 The police officer asked us where _____.
A. were we going   B. are we going   C. we are going   D. we were going

47

8.4 "Do you think it's going to rain?" "_____."
A. I hope not   B. I don't hope   C. I don't hope so

48

8.5 "You don't know where Lauren is, _____?" "Sorry, I have no idea."
A. don't you   B. do you   C. is she

49

-ing and the Infinitive

9.1 He tried to avoid _____ my question.
A. to answer   B. answer   C. answering   D. that he answered

50

9.2 I have to go now. I promised _____ late.
A. not being   B. not to be   C. to not be   D. I wouldn't be

51, 38

9.3 Do you want _____ with you, or do you want to go alone?
A. me coming   B. me to come   C. that I come   D. that I will come

52

9.4 I'm absolutely sure I locked the door. I distinctly remember _____ it.
A. locking   B. to lock   C. to have locked

53

9.5 She tried to be serious, but she couldn't help _____.
A. laughing   B. to laugh   C. that she laughed

54

9.6 Ann hates _____, so she doesn't fly very often.
A. flying   B. fly   C. to fly

55

9.7 I'm tired. I'd rather _____ out tonight, if you don't mind.
A. not going   B. not to go   C. don't go   D. not go

56

9.8 "Is it OK if Ben stays here?" "I'd rather _____ with us."
A. he comes   B. him to come   C. he came   D. he would come

56

9.9 Are you looking forward _____ Ann again?
A. seeing   B. to see   C. to seeing

57, 59

9.10 Lisa had to get used _____ on the left when she went to Tokyo.
A. driving   B. to driving   C. to drive

58

9.11 I'm thinking _____ a house. Do you think that's a good idea?
A. to buy   B. of to buy   C. of buying

59, 63

9.12 Did you have any _____ a visa?
A. trouble to get   B. troubles to get   C. troubles getting
D. trouble getting

60

9.13 A friend of mine phoned _____ me to a party.
A. for invite   B. to invite   C. for inviting   D. for to invite

61

9.14 Jim doesn't speak very clearly. _____
A. It is hard to understand him.   B. He is hard to understand.
C. He is hard to understand him.

62

9.15 The sidewalk was icy, so we walked very carefully. We were afraid _____.
A. of falling   B. from falling   C. to fall

63

9.16 I didn't hear you _____ in. You must have been very quiet.
A. come   B. to come   C. came

64

9.17 _____ a hotel, we looked for someplace to have dinner.
A. Finding   B. After finding   C. Having found   D. We found

65

Articles and Nouns

10.1 Call an ambulance. There's been _____ .
A. accident   B. an accident   C. some accident

66

10.2 "Where are you going?" "I'm going to buy _____ ."
A. a bread   B. some bread   C. a loaf of bread

67

10.3 Sandra is _____ . She works at a big hospital.
A. nurse   B. a nurse   C. the nurse

68, 69

10.4 She works six days _____ week.
A. in   B. for   C. a   D. the

69

10.5 There are millions of stars in _____ .
A. space   B. a space   C. the space

70

10.6 Every day _____ begins at 9 and finishes at 3.
A. school   B. a school   C. the school

71

10.7 _____ a problem in most big cities.
A. Crime is   B. The crime is   C. The crimes are

72

10.8 When _____ invented?
A. was telephone   B. were telephones   C. was the telephone
D. were the telephones

73

10.9 We visited _____ .
A. Canada and United States   B. the Canada and the United States
C. Canada and the United States   D. the Canada and United States

74

10.10 Daniel is a student at _____ .
A. the Boston University   B. Boston University

75

10.11 What time _____ on television?
A. is the news   B. are the news   C. is news

76, 67

10.12 It took us a long time to get here. It was _____ trip.
A. three hour   B. a three-hours   C. a three-hour

77

10.13 Where is _____ ?
A. the manager office   B. the manager's office   C. the office of the manager
D. the office of the manager's

78

Pronouns and Determiners

11.1 What time should we _____ tonight?
A. meet   B. meet us   C. meet ourselves

79

11.2 I'm going to a wedding on Saturday. _____ is getting married.
A. A friend of me   B. A friend of mine   C. One my friends

80

11.3 They live on a busy street. _____ a lot of noise from the traffic.
A. It must be   B. There must be   C. There must have   D. It must have

81

11.4 He's lazy. He never does _____ work.
A. some   B. any   C. no

82

11.5 "What would you like to eat?" "I don't care. _____ – whatever you've got."
A. Something   B. Anything   C. Nothing

82, 83

11.6 We couldn't buy anything because _____ of the stores were open.   **83**
A. all   B. no one   C. none   D. nothing

11.7 When we were on vacation, we spent _____ money.   **84**
A. a lot of   B. much   C. plenty

11.8 _____ don't visit this part of town.   **85**
A. The most tourists   B. Most of tourists   C. Most tourists

11.9 I asked two people the way to the station, but _____ of them knew.   **86**
A. none   B. either   C. both   D. neither

11.10 _____ enjoyed the party. It was a lot of fun.   **87**
A. Everybody   B. All   C. All of us   D. Everybody of us

11.11 The bus service is very good. There's a bus _____ ten minutes.   **87, 88**
A. each   B. every   C. all

Relative Clauses

12.1 I don't like stories _____ have unhappy endings.   **89**
A. that   B. they   C. which   D. who

12.2 I didn't believe them at first, but in fact everything _____ was true.   **90**
A. they said   B. that they said   C. what they said

12.3 We saw some people _____ car had broken down.   **91**
A. their   B. which   C. whose   D. that

12.4 Brad told me about his new job, _____ very much.   **92**
A. that he's enjoying   B. which he's enjoying   C. he's enjoying
D. he's enjoying it

12.5 Sheila couldn't come to the party, _____ was a shame.   **93**
A. that   B. it   C. what   D. which

12.6 Some of the people _____ to the party can't come.   **94**
A. inviting   B. invited   C. who invited   D. they were invited

Adjectives and Adverbs

13.1 Jane is _____ with her job because she does the same thing   **95**
every day.
A. boring   B. bored

13.2 The woman was carrying a _____ bag.   **96**
A. black small plastic   B. small and black plastic   C. small black plastic
D. plastic small black

13.3 Maria's English is excellent. She speaks _____ .   **97**
A. perfectly English   B. English perfectly   C. perfect English   D. English perfect

13.4 He _____ to find a job, but he had no luck.   **98**
A. tried hard   B. tried hardly   C. hardly tried

13.5 I haven't seen her for _____ I've forgotten what she looks like.   **99**
A. so long   B. a so long time   C. a such long time   D. such a long time

13.6 Do you have _____ a vacation right now?   **100**
A. money enough to take   B. enough money to take
C. money enough for taking   D. enough money for taking

13.7 The exam was easy – _____ we expected.
A. more easy that   B. more easy than   C. easier than   D. easier as

101

13.8 The more electricity you use, _____ .
A. your bill will be higher   B. will be higher your bill
C. the higher your bill will be

102

13.9 He's a fast runner. I can't run as fast as _____ .
A. he   B. him   C. he can

103

13.10 That movie was really boring. It was _____ I've ever seen.
A. most boring movie   B. the more boring movie   C. the movie more boring
D. the most boring movie

104

13.11 Tom likes walking. _____
A. Every morning he walks to work.   B. He walks to work every morning.
C. He walks every morning to work.

105

13.12 _____ a long time for the bus.
A. Always we have to wait   B. We always have to wait
C. We have always to wait   D. We have to wait always

106

13.13 Ann _____ . She left last month.
A. still doesn't work here   B. doesn't still work here   C. no more works here
D. doesn't work here anymore

107

13.14 _____ she can't drive, she has bought a car.
A. Even   B. Even though   C. Even if   D. Even when

108, 109

Conjunctions and Prepositions

14.1 I couldn't sleep _____ very tired.
A. although I was   B. despite I was   C. despite being   D. in spite of being

109

14.2 You probably won't need it, but I'll give you my phone number _____ to contact me.
A. in case you will need   B. if you will need   C. if you need
D. in case you need

110

14.3 The club is for members only. You _____ you are a member.
A. can play tennis there only if   B. can't play tennis there unless
C. can play tennis there unless

111

14.4 They have been married a long time. They got married _____ they were living in London.
A. when   B. as   C. while

112

14.5 What a beautiful house! It's _____ a palace.
A. as   B. like

113

14.6 They are very kind to me. They treat me _____ their own son.
A. like I am   B. as if I am   C. as if I was   D. as if I were

114

14.7 I'll be in Toronto next week. I hope to see Tom _____ there.
A. while I will be   B. while I am   C. during my visit   D. during I am

115

14.8 Fred is away at the moment. I don't know exactly when he's coming back, but I'm sure he'll be back _____ Monday.
A. by   B. until

116

Prepositions

15.1	I'll be at home _____ Friday morning. You can call me then. A. at B. on C. in	117
15.2	I'm going away _____ the end of January. A. at B. on C. in	118
15.3	When we were in Italy, we spent a few days _____ Venice. A. at B. to C. in	119, 121
15.4	Our apartment is _____ the second floor of the building. A. at B. on C. in	120
15.5	I saw Jack _____ a concert last Saturday. A. at B. on C. in	121
15.6	What time did they _____ the hotel? A. arrive to B. arrive at C. arrive in D. get to E. get in	122
15.7	Tom's away at the moment. He's _____ vacation in France. A. at B. on C. in D. for	123
15.8	We came _____ 6:45 train. A. in the B. on the C. by the D. by	124
15.9	Have you read any books _____ Agatha Christie? A. of B. from C. by	124
15.10	The accident was my fault, so I had to pay for the damage _____ the other car. A. of B. for C. to D. on E. at	125
15.11	I like them very much. They have always been very kind _____ me. A. of B. for C. to D. with	126
15.12	I'm not very good _____ repairing things. A. at B. for C. in D. with	127
15.13	I don't understand this sentence. Can you _____ ? A. explain to me this word B. explain me this word C. explain this word to me	128
15.14	If you're worried about the problem, you should do something _____ it. A. for B. about C. against D. with	129
15.15	"Who is Tom Jackson?" "I have no idea. I've never heard _____ him." A. about B. from C. after D. of	130
15.16	"What time will you get there?" "I don't know. It depends _____ the traffic." A. of B. for C. from D. on	131
15.17	I prefer tea _____ coffee. A. to B. than C. against D. over	132, 56
15.18	They gave me a form and told me to _____ . A. fill out B. fill it out C. fill out it	133

Answer Key to Exercises

In some of the exercises, you have to use your own ideas to write sentences, and sample answers are given in the key. If possible, check your answers with someone who speaks English well.

1.1

2. 'm looking (am looking)
3. 's getting (is getting)
4. 're staying (are staying)
5. 'm coming (am coming)
6. 's starting (is starting)
7. 're making (are making); 'm trying (am trying)
8. 's happening (is happening)

1.2

2. are you looking
3. 's she studying (is she studying)
4. Is anybody listening
5. Is it getting

1.3

3. 's having (is having)
4. 'm not eating (am not eating)
5. 's studying (is studying)
6. 're not / aren't speaking (are not speaking)

1.4

2. 'm training (am training)
3. Are you enjoying
4. 'm not working (am not working)
5. 'm trying (am trying)
6. 'm painting (am painting)
7. Are you doing
8. are helping

1.5

2. 's getting (is getting)
3. is changing
4. is rising *or* is increasing
5. 's getting (is getting)

UNIT 2

2.1

2. drink
3. opens; closes
4. causes
5. live
6. take

7. connects

2.2

2. do the banks close
3. don't use (do not use)
4. do you do
5. takes; does it take
6. play; don't play (do not play)
7. does this word mean

2.3

3. rises
4. make
5. don't eat (do not eat)
6. doesn't believe (does not believe)
7. translates
8. doesn't tell (does not tell)
9. flows

2.4

2. Does; play tennis
3. Which newspaper do you read every day?
4. What does your brother do?
5. How often do you go to the movies?
6. Where does your mother live?
7. What time do you start work?

UNIT 3

3.1

3. is trying
4. are; talking
5. RIGHT
6. 's getting (is getting)
7. RIGHT
8. 'm coming (am coming)
9. 's (is); going

3.2

3. 's waiting (is waiting)
4. Are you listening
5. Do you listen
6. flows
7. is flowing
8. grow; 're not / aren't growing (are not growing)
9. 's improving (is improving)
10. 's staying (is staying); always stays
11. 'm starting (am starting)
12. 'm learning (am learning); is teaching
13. finish; 'm working (am working)

14. live; do your parents live
15. 's looking (is looking); 's staying (is staying)
16. does your father do; 's not / isn't working (is not working)
17. always leaves
18. 's always leaving (is always leaving)

3.3

2. 's always breaking down (is always breaking down)
3. 'm always making (am always making) the same mistake
4. 're always forgetting (are always forgetting) your books

UNIT 4

4.1

2. RIGHT   4. tastes
3. Do; believe   5. think

4.2

2. What are you doing?; I'm thinking. (I am thinking.)
3. Who does this umbrella belong to?
4. Dinner smells good.
5. Is anybody sitting here?
6. I'm having (I am having) dinner.

4.3

2. 'm using (am using)
3. need
4. does he want
5. is he looking
6. believes
7. don't remember (do not remember)
8. 'm thinking (am thinking)
9. think; don't use (do not use)
10. consists

4.4

2. is being
3. 's (is)
4. are you being
5. Is she

UNIT 5

5.1

2. had
3. walked to work
4. took her [about] half an hour

5. She started work
6. She didn't have (did not have)
7. She finished work
8. She was; she got
9. She made
10. She didn't go (did not go)
11. She went to bed
12. She slept

5.2

2. taught
3. sold
4. drank
5. won
6. fell; hurt
7. threw; caught
8. spent; bought; cost

5.3

2. Did you go alone?
3. Was the food good?
4. Did you stay at a hotel?
5. Did you rent a car?
6. Was the weather nice?
7. What did you do in the evenings?

5.4

3. didn't bother (did not bother)
4. went
5. didn't sleep (did not sleep)
6. wasn't (was not)
7. laughed
8. flew
9. didn't cost (did not cost)
10. didn't have (did not have)
11. were

UNIT 6

6.1

Sample answers:
3. I was working.
4. I was watching TV.
5. I was talking on the telephone.

6.2

Sample answers:
2. was taking a shower
3. were driving to work
4. was reading the paper
5. was watching it

6.3

1. didn't see (did not see)
   was looking
2. met
   were going
   was going
   talked

were waiting or waited
3. was riding;
   stepped;
   was going;
   managed;
   didn't hit (did not hit)

6.4

2. were you doing
3. Did you go
4. were you driving; happened
5. took; wasn't looking (was not looking)
6. didn't know (did not know)
7. saw; was trying
8. was walking; heard; was following; started
9. wanted

UNIT 7

7.1

2. 's broken (has broken) her leg
3. Maria's English has improved.
4. Jason has grown a beard.
5. The bus fare has gone up.
6. has dropped
7. 's turned it on (has turned it on)

7.2

2. 've just seen (have just seen) or just saw
3. 's already left (has already left) or already left
4. haven't read (have not read) it yet or didn't read (did not read) it yet
5. 's already seen (has already seen) or already saw
6. 've just gotten (have just gotten) or just got
7. haven't told (have not told) him yet or didn't tell (did not tell) him yet

7.3

2. he's just gone out (he has just gone out) or he just went out
3. I haven't finished (have not finished) yet. or I didn't finish (did not finish) yet.
4. I've already done (I have already done) or I already did
5. Have you found a job yet or Did you find a job yet
6. she's just come back (she has just come back) or she just came back

7.4

3. RIGHT
4. happened
5. wasn't
6. RIGHT

7. Did you see
8. RIGHT
9. bought

UNIT 8

8.1

2. Have you ever been to Mexico?
3. Have you ever run a marathon?
4. Have you ever spoken to a famous person?
5. Have you always lived in this town?
6. 's (is) the most beautiful place you've ever visited (you have ever visited)

8.2

2. haven't seen (have not seen)
3. haven't eaten (have not eaten)
4. I haven't played (have not played)
5. I've had (I have had)
6. I've never read (I have never read) or I haven't read (have not read)
7. I've never been (I have never been) or I haven't been (have not been)
8. 's been (has been) late
9. it's happened (it has happened)
10. I've never seen (I have never seen) her or I haven't seen (have not seen) her

8.3

2. haven't read (have not read) one / a newspaper
3. this year it hasn't made (has not made) one / a profit
4. she hasn't worked (has not worked) hard [at school] this semester
5. it hasn't snowed (has not snowed) [a lot] this winter

8.4

2. you played tennis before; time I've played (I have played) tennis
3. Have you ridden a horse before?; No, this is the first time I've ridden (I have ridden) a horse.
4. Have you been in Los Angeles before?
   No, this is the first time I've been (I have been) in Los Angeles.

UNIT 9

9.1

2. 's been watching (has been watching) TV

3. 've been playing (have been playing) tennis
4. 's been running/jogging (has been running/jogging)

9.2

2. Have you been waiting long?
3. What have you been doing?
4. How long have you been living on Main Street?
5. How long have you been selling computers?

9.3

2. 've been waiting (have been waiting) [for the bus]
3. 've been studying (have been studying) Spanish
4. She's been working (She has been working) there / in Tokyo
5. 've been writing (have been writing) to each other

9.4

2. 've been looking (have been looking)
3. are you looking
4. 've been going (have been going)
5. 've been thinking (have been thinking)
6. 's working (is working)
7. 's been working (has been working)

UNIT 10

10.1

2. 's been traveling (has been traveling) for three months; She's visited (She has visited) six countries so far.
3. He's won (He has won) the national championship four times.; He's been playing (He has been playing) tennis since he was ten.
4. 've made (have made) ten movies since they graduated from college; They've been making (They have been making) movies since they left college.

10.2

2. How long have you been waiting?
3. How many fish have you caught?
4. How many people have you invited?
5. How long have you been teaching?
6. How many books have you written?; How long have you been writing books?

7. How long have you been saving?; How much money have you saved?

10.3

2. 's broken (has broken)
3. Have you been working
4. Have you ever worked
5. 's appeared (has appeared)
6. haven't been waiting (have not been waiting) long
7. 's stopped (has stopped)
8. 've lost (have lost); Have you seen
9. 've been reading (have been reading); haven't finished (have not finished)
10. 've read (have read)

UNIT 11

11.1

3. have been married
4. RIGHT
5. It's been raining (It has been raining)
6. have you been living *or* have you lived
7. has been working *or* has worked
8. RIGHT
9. I haven't worked (have not worked)
10. have you had

11.2

2. How long have you been teaching English?
3. How long have you known Carol?
4. How long has your brother been in Australia?
5. How long have you had that jacket?
6. How long has Scott been working at the airport? *or* How long has Scott worked at the airport?
7. How long have you been taking guitar lessons?
8. Have you always lived in San Francisco?

11.3

3. 's been (has been)
4. 've been waiting (have been waiting)
5. haven't played (have not played)
6. 's been watching (has been watching)
7. haven't been watching (have not been watching) *or* haven't watched (have not watched)

8. 've had (have had)
9. 've been feeling (have been feeling) *or* 've felt (have felt)
10. 's been living (has been living) *or* 's lived (has lived)
11. haven't gone (have not gone)
12. 've always wanted (have always wanted)

UNIT 12

12.1

2. for   6. since
3. since   7. since
4. for   8. for
5. for

12.2

2. How long has she been studying Japanese?
   When did she start studying Japanese?
3. How long have you known him?
   When did you first meet him?
4. How long have they been married?
   When did they get married?

12.3

3. been sick since Sunday
4. been sick for a few days
5. married two years ago
6. had a camera for ten years
7. to France three weeks ago
8. been working in a hotel since June *or* worked in a hotel since June

12.4

2. haven't eaten (have not eaten) in a restaurant for ages
3. haven't seen (have not seen) her for about a month
4. No, I haven't gone/been (have not gone/been) to the movies for a long time.
6. been ages since I ate in a restaurant
7. it's been (it has been) about a month since I saw her
8. No, it's been (it has been) a long time since I went to the movies.

UNIT 13

13.1

3. RIGHT   7. RIGHT
4. were you   8. was
5. graduated   9. wasn't (was not)
6. RIGHT   10. was this book

13.2

2. has been cold recently
3. was cold last week
4. didn't read (did not read) a newspaper yesterday
5. I haven't read (have not read) a newspaper today.
6. Kate's earned (Kate has earned) a lot of money this year.
7. She didn't (did not) earn as much last year.
8. Have you taken a vacation recently?

13.3

2. got; was; went
3. wasn't (was not)
4. worked
5. 's lived (has lived)
6. Did you go; was; was
7. died; never met
8. 've never met (have never met)
9. have you lived; did you live; did you live

13.4

Sample answers:
2. I haven't bought (have not bought) anything today.
3. I didn't watch (did not watch) TV yesterday.
4. I went out with some friends last night.
5. I haven't gone/been (have not gone/been) to the movies recently.
6. I've gone swimming (I have gone swimming) a lot recently.

UNIT 14

14.1

2. It had changed a lot.
3. She'd made (She had made) plans to do something else.
4. I hadn't seen (had not seen) him for five years.
5. The movie had already begun.
6. He hadn't played (had not played) before.
7. She'd just had (She had just had) breakfast.
8. We'd never been (We had never been) there before.

14.2

1. called the police
2. there was; 'd gone (had gone)
3. 'd (had); come back from vacation; looked relaxed

4. got a phone call from Sally; was; 'd written (had written) [to] her; 'd never answered (had never answered)

14.3

2. went
3. had gone
4. broke
5. saw; had broken; stopped

UNIT 15

15.1

2. They'd been playing (They had been playing) soccer.
3. Somebody had been smoking in the room.
4. She'd been dreaming. (She had been dreaming.)
5. He'd been watching (He had been watching) TV.

15.2

2. 'd been waiting (had been waiting); [suddenly] realized [that] I was in the wrong restaurant
3. closed down; had been working
4. had been playing [for] about ten minutes; a man in the audience [suddenly] began shouting

15.3

3. was walking
4. 'd been running (had been running)
5. were eating
6. 'd been eating (had been eating)
7. was looking *or* 'd been looking (had been looking)
8. was waiting; 'd been waiting (had been waiting)
9. 'd had (had had)
10. 'd been traveling (had been traveling)

UNIT 16

16.1

3. don't have (do not have) a ladder *or* haven't got (have not got) a ladder
4. didn't have (did not have) enough time
5. He didn't have (did not have) a map.
6. She doesn't have (does not have) any money. *or* She hasn't got (has not got) any money.

7. They don't have (do not have) a key. *or* They haven't got (have not got) a key.
8. I didn't have (did not have) a camera.

16.2

2. Do you have *or* Have you got
3. Did you have
4. Do you have *or* Have you got
5. did you have
6. Do you have *or* Have you got
7. Did you have

16.3

Sample answers:
Now
2. I have a bicycle. *or* I've got (I have got) a bicycle.
3. I have a job. *or* I've got (I have got) a job.
4. I have a driver's license. *or* I've got (I have got) a driver's license.
10 years ago
2. I didn't have (did not have) a bicycle.
3. I didn't have (did not have) a job.
4. I didn't have (did not have) a driver's license.

16.4

2. had a party
3. have a look
4. Did you have a nice time
5. had a baby
6. had a cold drink
7. Did you have a good flight
8. Are you having trouble

UNIT 17

17.1

2. used to have
3. used to live
4. used to eat
5. used to be
6. used to take
7. used to be
8. did you use to go

17.2

3. He used to go to bed early.
4. He didn't use to go out (did not use to go out) every night.
5. He used to run three miles every morning.
6. He didn't use to spend (did not use to spend) a lot of money.

17.3

(Answers can be in any order.)
2. She used to play the piano, but she hasn't played it for years.

3. She used to be very lazy, but she works very hard these days.
4. She didn't use to like cheese, but she eats lots of cheese now.
5. She used to have a dog, but it died two years ago.
6. She didn't use to drink tea, but she likes it now.
7. She never used to read newspapers, but she reads a newspaper every day now.
8. She used to have lots of friends, but she doesn't see many people these days.
9. She used to be a hotel receptionist, but she works in a bookstore now.

UNIT 18

18.1
2. How long are you staying?
3. When are you going?
4. Are you going alone?
5. Are you traveling by car?
6. Where are you staying?

18.2
2. 'm working (am working) late *or* 'm working (am working) until 9 o'clock
3. I'm going (I am going) to the theater with my mother.
4. I'm meeting (I am meeting) Julia at 8 P.M.

18.3
Sample answers:
2. 'm going (am going) to the park tomorrow morning
3. I'm not doing (I am not doing) anything tomorrow night.
4. I'm playing (I am playing) soccer next Sunday.
5. I'm going (I am going) to the movies this afternoon.

18.4
3. 're having (are having)
4. opens
5. 'm not going (am not going); 'm staying (am staying)
6. Are you doing
7. 're going (are going); begins
8. does this train get
9. 'm going (am going); Are you coming
10. is coming; 's flying (is flying); arrives; 'm meeting (am meeting)

11. 'm not using (am not using)
12. does it end

UNIT 19

19.1
2. What are you going to wear?
3. Where are you going to put it?
4. Who are you going to invite?

19.2
2. I'm going to quit (I am going to quit) soon.
3. I'm not going to take (I am not going to take) it
4. I'm going to complain (I am going to complain).
5. I'm going to call (I am going to call) her tonight.

19.3
2. 's going to be (is going to be) late
3. is going to sink
4. 's going to run out (is going to run out) of gas

19.4
2. were going to play
3. was going to call
4. was going to quit
5. were going to have

UNIT 20

20.1
2. I'll turn
3. I'll go
4. I'll show *or* I'll help *or* I'll teach
5. I'll have *or* I'll take
6. I'll send *or* I'll mail
7. I'll give *or* I'll bring
8. I'll stay *or* I'll wait

20.2
2. I'll go to bed
3. I'll walk
4. I'll play tennis today
5. I don't think I'll go swimming.

20.3
3. I'll meet
4. I'll lend
5. I'm having
6. I won't forget
7. does your train leave
8. won't tell
9. Are you doing
10. Will you come

20.4
2. shall I get
3. I'll do
4. shall we go
5. I won't tell
6. I'll try

UNIT 21

21.1
2. I'm going   5. we are going
3. will get   6. It won't hurt
4. is coming

21.2
2. 'll look (will look)
3. 'll like (will like)
4. 'll get (will get)
5. 'll be (will be)
6. 'll come (will come)
7. 'll be (will be)
8. 'll meet (will meet)

21.3
2. won't   5. 'll (will)   7. 'll (will)
3. 'll (will)   6. won't   8. 'll (will)
4. won't

21.4
Sample answers:
2. I'll be in bed.
3. I'll probably be at work.
4. I guess I'll be at home.
5. I don't know where I'll be.

21.5
2. think it'll rain (it will rain)
3. do you think it'll cost (it will cost)
4. you think they'll get married (they will get married)
5. do you think you'll be back (you will be back)
6. do you think will happen

UNIT 22

22.1
2. I'll lend (I will lend)
3. I'll get (I will get)
4. I'm going to wash (I am going to wash)
5. are you going to paint
6. I'm going to buy (I am going to buy)
7. I'll show (I will show)
8. I'll do (I will do)
9. He's going to take (He is going to take); he's going to start (he is going to start)

22.2

2. I'm going to take (I am going to take); I'll join (I will join)
3. you'll find (you will find)
4. I'm not going to apply (I am not going to apply)
5. You'll wake (You will wake)
6. I'll take (I will take); we'll leave (we will leave); Ann is going to take

UNIT 23

23.1

2. b   3. a; c   4. b; d   5. c; d   6. c

23.2

2. We'll have finished (We will have finished)
3. we'll be playing (we will be playing)
4. I'll be working (I will be working).
5. the meeting will have ended
6. he'll have spent (he will have spent)
7. you'll still be doing (you will still be doing)
8. she'll have traveled (she will have traveled)
9. I'll be staying (I will be staying)
10. Will you be seeing

UNIT 24

24.1

2. goes
3. 'll tell (will tell); come
4. see; won't recognize (will not recognize)
5. 's (is)
6. 'll wait (will wait); 're (are)
7. 'll be (will be); gets
8. is
9. calls; 'm (am)

24.2

2. 'll give (will give) you my address when I've found (I have found) a place to live or . . . when I find a place to live
3. 'll come (I will come) straight home after I've done (I have done) the shopping or . . . after I do the shopping
4. Let's go home before it starts raining.
5. I won't speak (will not speak) to her until she's apologized (she has apologized) to me or . . . until she apologizes to me

24.3

2. you go or you leave
3. you're finished (you are finished) with it or you're finished reading it or you've finished reading (you have finished reading) it
4. you've decided (you have decided) or you decide

24.4

2. If
3. When
4. if
5. If
6. when
7. if
8. if

UNIT 25

25.1

3. can
4. been able to
5. be able to
6. can
7. be able to

25.2

Sample answers:
2. to be able to run fast
3. like to be able to play a musical instrument
4. never been able to get up early

25.3

2. could run
3. can wait
4. couldn't eat (could not eat)
5. can't hear
6. couldn't sleep (could not sleep)

25.4

2. were able to find it
3. I was able to finish it
4. was able to get away

25.5

4. couldn't (could not) or wasn't able to (was not able to)
5. was able to
6. could or was able to
7. was able to
8. could or was able to
9. were able to
10. couldn't (could not) or wasn't able to (was not able to)

UNIT 26

26.1

2. could have fish

3. could give her a book
4. You could call her now.
5. We could go [and see him] on Friday.

26.2

2. could
3. can or could
4. could
5. could
6. can
7. can or could
8. could

26.3

2. could have gone
3. could apply
4. could have gone
5. could come

26.4

2. couldn't have gone out (could not have gone out) for dinner [because he had to work on Friday night]
3. could have played tennis [because he had Monday afternoon off]
4. He couldn't have lent (could not have lent) him $50 [because he ran out of money last week].
5. could have gone to her party [because he didn't do anything on Saturday night]
6. He couldn't have fixed (could not have fixed) her washing machine [because he doesn't know anything about machines].

UNIT 27

27.1

2. must
3. must not
4. must
5. must not
6. must

27.2

3. be
4. have been
5. go or have gone
6. be going
7. have taken or have stolen
8. have been
9. be following

27.3

3. It must have been very expensive.
4. I must have left it in the restaurant last night.
5. The exam must not have been very difficult.

6. She must have been listening to our conversation.
   or She must have listened to our conversation.
7. She must not have understood what I said.
8. I must have forgotten to turn it off.
9. The driver must not have seen the red light.

27.4

3. can't
4. must not
5. can't
6. must not

UNIT 28

28.1

2. She may/might be busy.
3. She may/might be working.
4. She may/might want to be alone.
5. She may/might have been sick yesterday.
6. She may/might have gone home early.
7. She may/might have had to go home early.
8. She may/might have been working yesterday.
9. She may/might not want to see me.
10. She may/might not be working today.
11. She may/might not have been feeling well yesterday.

28.2

2. be
3. have been
4. be waiting
5. have *or* have read

28.3

2. a. She may/might be watching TV in her room.
   b. She may/might have gone out.
3. a. It may/might be in the car.
   b. You may/might have left it in the restaurant last night.
4. a. He may/might have been in the shower.
   b. He may/might not have heard the bell.

28.4

2. might not have been invited
3. couldn't have been invited (could not have been invited)
4. couldn't have been (could not have been) an accident
5. might have been an accident

UNIT 29

29.1

2. may/might buy a Toyota
3. I may/might hang it in the dining room.
4. He may/might come to see us on Saturday.
5. She may/might go to college.

29.2

2. might wake
3. might bite
4. might need
5. might slip
6. might break

29.3

2. might be able to meet/see
3. might have to work
4. might have to go

29.4

2. may/might not go out this evening
3. may/might not like the present I bought for him
4. Sue may/might not be able to meet me/us tonight.

29.5

2. may/might as well go
3. may/might as well eat
4. We may/might as well watch a/the movie on TV

UNIT 30

30.1

2. had to
3. have to
4. have to
5. has to
6. had to
7. had to
8. have to

30.2

2. do you have to go
3. Did you have to wait
4. do you have to be
5. Does he have to travel

30.3

3. have to make
4. had to ask
5. doesn't have to shave (does not have to shave)
6. didn't have to go (did not have to go)
7. has to make
8. don't have to do (do not have to do)

30.4

1. d   2. a   3. e   4. b   5. f   6. c

30.5

3. don't have to
4. mustn't
5. don't have to
6. mustn't
7. doesn't have to
8. mustn't
9. don't have to

UNIT 31

31.1

2. should look for another job
3. shouldn't go (should not go) to bed so late
4. should take a photograph
5. shouldn't use (should not use) her car so much

31.2

2. I don't think you should go out this evening.
3. smoking should be banned in restaurants
4. I don't think the government should raise taxes.

31.3

3. should come
4. should do
5. should have done
6. should have won
7. should be
8. should have arrived

31.4

3. should have reserved a table
4. The store should be open by now. *or* The store should have opened by now / at 8:30.
5. shouldn't be driving (should not be driving) so fast / 50 miles an hour
6. should have come to see me [while you were here / in Dallas]
7. I shouldn't have been driving (should not have been driving) right behind another car.
8. I should have looked where I was going. *or* I should have been looking where I was going.

UNIT 32

32.1

2. I stay a little longer
3. she visit the museum after lunch
4. I see a specialist
5. I not lift anything heavy

6. the tenant pay the rent by Friday at the latest
7. I go away for a few days
8. I not give my children snacks right before mealtime
9. we have dinner early

32.2

3. take/spend   6. sell   9. wear
4. apologize   7. wait   10. be
5. be   8. be

32.3

2. walk to work in the morning
3. [that] he eat more fruit and vegetables
4. suggested [that] he take vitamins

UNIT 33

33.1

2. You'd better put (You had better put) a bandage on it.
3. 'd better make (had better make) a reservation
4. You'd better not go (You had better not go) to work.
5. I'd better pay (I had better pay) my phone bill soon.
6. I'd better not (I had better not) go out.
7. We'd better take (We had better take) a taxi.

33.2

3. 'd better (had   6. 'd better
    better) or should   (had better)
4. should   7. should
5. should   8. should

33.3

1. b. 'd (had); c. close or shut
2. a. did; b. was done; c. thought

33.4

2. took a vacation
3. It's time the train left [the station].
4. It's time I had a party.
5. It's time there were some changes. or It's time some changes were made. or It's time the company made some changes.

UNIT 34

34.1

2. Can/Could I leave a message[, please]? or Can/Could you take a message[, please]?

3. Can/Could you [please] tell me where the post office is? or . . . tell me how to get to the post office? or . . . tell me the way to the post office?
4. Can/Could I [please] try these [pants] on? or Can/Could I try on these pants?
5. Can/Could I [please] have a ride home? or Can/Could I ride home with you? or Can/Could you give me a ride home?

34.2

2. Do you think I could use your phone?
3. Do you think you could check my letter?
4. Do you think I could leave [work] early today?
5. Do you think you could turn the music down? or . . . you could turn down the music?
6. Do you think I could see the apartment today?

34.3

2. Can/Could/Would you show me how to do it? or Do you think you could show me how to do it?
3. Could/Can/May I have a look at your newspaper? or Do you think I could have a look at your newspaper?
4. Would you like to sit down? or Can/May I offer you my seat?
5. Can/Could/Would you slow down? or Do you think you could slow down?
6. Would you like to borrow it?

UNIT 35

35.1

3. 'd take (would take)
4. refused
5. wouldn't get (would not get)
6. closed down
7. pressed
8. 'd be (would be)
9. didn't come (did not come)
10. borrowed
11. walked
12. would understand

35.2

2. would you do if someone offered you a job in Rio de Janeiro or

. . . if you were offered a job in Rio de Janeiro
3. What would you do if you lost your passport?
4. What would you do if there was/were a fire in the building?

35.3

2. took the driver's test, he'd fail (he would fail)
3. If we stayed in a hotel, it would cost too much money.
4. If she applied for the job, she wouldn't get (would not get) it.
5. If we told them the truth, they wouldn't believe (would not believe) us.
6. If we invited Bill to the party, we'd have to invite (we would have to invite) his friends, too.

35.4

Sample answers:
2. my best friend lied to me
3. I'd go (I would go) and see a movie
4. you were invited
5. you could drive to work
6. I opened a window

UNIT 36

36.1

3. 'd help (would help)
4. lived
5. 'd live (would live)
6. would taste
7. were/was
8. wouldn't wait (would not wait); 'd go (would go)
9. didn't go (did not go)
10. weren't (were not); wouldn't be (would not be)

36.2

2. weren't (were not) / wasn't (was not) so expensive, I'd buy (I would buy) it
3. If we could afford it, we'd go out (we would go out) more often.
4. If it weren't (were not) / wasn't (was not) raining, we could have lunch on the patio.
5. If I didn't have to work (did not have to work) late tomorrow, I could meet you for dinner.

36.3

2. I had a key

3. I wish Amanda were/was here.
4. I wish it weren't (were not)/ wasn't (was not) cold.
5. I wish I didn't live (did not live) in a big city.
6. I wish I could go to the party.
7. I wish I didn't have to work (did not have to work) tomorrow.
8. I wish I knew something about cars.
9. I wish I were/was lying on a beautiful sunny beach.

36.4

Sample answers:
1. were/was at home
2. I wish I had more time.
3. I wish I could tell jokes.
4. I wish I were/was taller.

UNIT 37

37.1

2. he'd missed (he had missed); he'd have been (he would have been)
3. I'd have forgotten (I would have forgotten); you hadn't reminded (you had not reminded)
4. I'd had (I had had); I'd have sent (I would have sent)
5. it would have been; the weather had been
6. I were/was
7. I'd been (I had been)

37.2

2. hadn't stopped (had not stopped) so suddenly, the accident wouldn't have happened (would not have happened)
3. 'd known (had known) [that] Matt had to get up early, I'd have woken (I would have woken) him up
4. If Jim hadn't lent (had not lent) me the money, I wouldn't have been able (would not have been able) to buy the car.
5. If Michelle hadn't been wearing (had not been wearing) a seat belt, she'd have been injured (she would have been injured).
6. If you'd had (you had had) [some] breakfast, you wouldn't be (would not be) hungry now.

37.3

2. I wish I'd applied (I had applied) for it / the job.
3. I wish I'd learned (I had learned) to play a musical instrument.

4. I wish I hadn't painted (had not painted) it / the door red.
5. I wish I'd brought (I had brought) my camera.
6. I wish they'd told (they had told) me they were coming.

UNIT 38

38.1

2. 'd enjoy (would enjoy)
3. 'd have enjoyed (would have enjoyed)
4. 'd have called (would have called)
5. 'd be (would be)
6. 'd have stopped (would have stopped)

38.2

2. he'd come (he would come)
3. I wish the baby would stop crying. or I wish the baby would be quiet.
4. would give me a job
5. I wish you'd buy/get (you would buy/get) some new clothes.
6. wouldn't drive (would not drive) so fast
7. I wish you wouldn't always leave (would not always leave) the door open.
8. wouldn't drop (would not drop) [their] litter in the street

38.3

2. RIGHT
3. I wish I had more money.
4. I wish it weren't (were not) / wasn't (was not) so cold today.
5. RIGHT
6. RIGHT
7. I wish everything weren't (were not) / wasn't (was not) so expensive.

38.4

2. would shake
3. 'd (would); forget
4. 'd share (would share)

UNIT 39

39.1

2. is made
3. was damaged
4. is included
5. were invited
6. are shown
7. are held
8. was written; was translated
9. were found

39.2

2. is glass made
3. When was the planet Pluto discovered?
4. What's (What is) silver used for?
5. When was television invented?

39.3

2. covers
3. is covered
4. are locked
5. was mailed; arrived
6. died; were brought up
7. grew up
8. was stolen
9. disappeared
10. did Sue resign
11. was Bill fired
12. is owned
13. called; was injured; wasn't needed (was not needed)
14. were these pictures taken; Did you take

39.4

2. flights were canceled because of fog
3. This road isn't used (is not used) very often.
4. was accused of stealing money
5. are languages learned
6. We were warned not to go out alone.

UNIT 40

40.1

2. can't be broken
3. can be eaten
4. it can't be used
5. it can't be seen
6. it can be carried

40.2

3. be made
4. be woken up
5. be spent
6. have been repaired
7. be carried
8. have been caused

40.3

2. is being used at the moment
3. our conversation was being recorded
4. the game had been canceled
5. A new highway is being built around the city.
6. A new hospital has been built near the airport.

40.4

3. He's been promoted (He has been promoted). *or* He was promoted.
4. Somebody's taken (Somebody has taken) it. *or* Somebody took it.
5. It's being redecorated (It is being redecorated).
6. It had been stolen.
7. It's working (It is working) again; it's been repaired (it has been repaired). *or* it was repaired.
8. Two people were arrested last night.
9. Nobody has seen him since then.
10. Have you ever been mugged?

UNIT 41

41.1

Answers 2–5 should include four of these, in any order:
Leonardo da Vinci was born in 1452.
Galileo was born in 1564.
Beethoven was born in 1770.
Mahatma Gandhi was born in 1869.
Martin Luther King, Jr. was born in 1929.
Elvis Presley was born in 1935.
Diana, Princess of Wales, was born in 1961.
6. was born in ___

41.2

2. was asked some difficult questions at the interview
3. was given a present by her colleagues when she retired
4. told that Michael was sick
5. be paid
6. should have been offered the job
7. been shown what to do

41.3

2. being invited   5. being asked
3. being given   6. being paid
4. being attacked

41.4

2. got stung   6. got stopped
3. get broken   7. get paid
4. get used   8. get damaged
5. got stolen   9. get asked

UNIT 42

42.1

3. are reported to be homeless after the floods

4. alleged to have robbed the store of $3,000 in cash
5. is reported to have been badly damaged by the fire
6. a. is said to be losing a lot of money
   b. is believed to have lost a lot of money last year
   c. is expected to lose money this year

42.2

2. 's supposed to be (is supposed to be) very rich
3. He's supposed to have (He is supposed to have) 12 children.
4. He's supposed to know (He is supposed to know) a lot of famous people.
5. He's supposed to have robbed (He is supposed to have robbed) a bank a long time ago.

42.3

3. 're supposed to be (are supposed to be)
4. 're supposed to start (are supposed to start)
5. 're not / aren't supposed to block (are not supposed to block)
6. was supposed to call
7. weren't supposed to come (were not supposed to come)

UNIT 43

43.1

1. b   2. a   3. a   4. b

43.2

2. have it cleaned.
3. To have it repaired.
4. To have my hair cut.

43.3

2. had it cut
3. had it painted
4. She had them made.

43.4

2. have another key made
3. had your hair cut
4. Do you have a newspaper delivered
5. 're having (are having) air conditioning installed
6. haven't had (have not had) the film developed
7. have it cleaned

43.5

2. had her bag stolen on a train

3. He had his electricity turned off.
4. She had her passport taken away by the police.

UNIT 44

44.1

2. his father wasn't (was not) very well
3. said [that] Amanda and Paul were getting married next month
4. He said [that] Michelle had had a baby.
5. He said [that] he didn't know (did not know) what Eric was doing.
6. He said [that] he'd seen (he had seen) Nicole at a party in June and she'd seemed (she had seemed) fine. *or* He said [that] he saw Nicole at a party in June and she seemed fine.
7. He said [that] he hadn't seen (had not seen) Diane recently.
8. He said [that] he wasn't enjoying (was not enjoying) his job very much.
9. He said [that] I could come and stay at his place if I was ever in Chicago.
10. He said [that] his car had been stolen a few weeks ago. *or* . . . was stolen a few weeks ago.
11. He said [that] he wanted to take a vacation but he couldn't afford (could not afford) it.
12. He said [that] he'd tell (he would tell) Amy [that] he'd seen (he had seen) me. *or* . . . tell Amy [that] he saw me.

44.2

Sample answers:
2. wasn't coming (was not coming)
3. [that] she didn't like (did not like) him
4. didn't know (did not know) many people / anyone
5. I thought you said [that] she'd be (she would be) here this week. *or* . . . [that] she wouldn't be (would not be) here.
6. I thought you said [that] you were staying home.
7. I thought you said [that] you couldn't speak (could not speak) [any] French.
8. I thought you said [that] you'd been (you had been) to the movies last week.

45.1

2. But you said [that] you didn't like (did not like) fish.
3. But you said [that] you couldn't drive (could not drive).
4. But you said [that] Rosa had a very well-paid job.
5. But you said [that] you didn't have (did not have) any brothers or sisters.
6. But you said [that] you'd never been (you had never been) to South America.
7. But you said [that] you were working tomorrow night.
8. But you said [that] Rosa was a friend of yours.

45.2

2. Tell
3. Say
4. said
5. told
6. said
7. tell; said
8. tell; say
9. told

45.3

2. her to [please] slow down
3. her not to worry
4. asked Tom to give me a hand
5. asked me to [please] open my bag
6. told her not to wait for me if I was late
7. asked her to marry him
8. I told him to mind his own business

UNIT 46

46.1

2. do you live now
3. Are you married?
4. How long have you been married?
5. Do you have [any] children?
6. How old are they?
7. What does your wife do?
8. Does she like her job?

46.2

3. gave you the key *or* gave the key to you
4. happened
5. What did Diane tell you?
6. Who does this book belong to?
7. Who lives in that house?
8. What did you fall over?
9. What fell on the floor?
10. What does this word mean?
11. Who did you borrow the money from?

12. What are you worried about?

46.3

2. How is cheese made?
3. When was the computer invented?
4. Why isn't Sue working today?
5. What time are your friends coming?
6. Why was the concert canceled?
7. Where was your mother born?
8. Why didn't you come to the party?
9. How did the accident happen?
10. Why doesn't this machine work?

46.4

2. Don't you like him?
3. Isn't it good?
4. Don't you have any?

UNIT 47

47.1

2. the post office is
3. what this word means
4. whether/if Sue's going out (Sue is going out) tonight
5. where Carol lives
6. where I parked the car
7. whether/if there's (there is) a bank near here
8. what you want
9. why Liz didn't come (did not come) to the party
10. who that woman is
11. whether/if Ann got my letter
12. how far it is to the airport

47.2

1. Amy is
2. when she'll be back (she will be back)
3. whether/if she went out alone

47.3

2. where I'd been (I had been)
3. asked me how long I'd been back (I had been back)
4. He asked me what I was doing now.
5. He asked me where I was living.
6. He asked me why I'd come back (I had come back). *or* . . . why I came back.
7. He asked me whether/if I was glad to be back.
8. He asked me whether/if I planned to stay for awhile.
9. He asked me whether/if I could lend him some money.

UNIT 48

48.1

2. doesn't (does not)
3. was
4. will
5. am; isn't (is not) *or* 'm not (am not); is
6. should
7. won't
8. do
9. could
10. would; could; can't

48.2

3. You do? I don't.
4. You didn't? I did.
5. You haven't? I have.
6. You did? I didn't.

48.3

Sample answers:
3. So did I. *or* You did? I didn't.
4. Neither will I. *or* I won't either. *or* You won't? I will.
5. So do I. *or* You do? I don't.
6. So would I. *or* You would? I wouldn't.
7. Neither can I. *or* I can't either. *or* You can't? I can.

48.4

2. I hope so.
3. I don't think so.
4. I'm afraid not.
5. I'm afraid so.
6. I guess so.
7. I hope not.
8. I think so.

UNIT 49

49.1

3. hasn't she
4. were you
5. does she
6. isn't he
7. has he
8. can't you
9. will he
10. aren't there
11. shall we
12. is it
13. aren't I
14. would you
15. will you
16. should I
17. had he

49.2

2. 's (is) expensive, isn't it
3. was great, wasn't it
4. has a beautiful voice, doesn't she *or* 's got (has got) a beautiful voice, doesn't she

5. doesn't look very good, does it
6. 've had (have had) your hair cut,
   haven't you *or* had your hair cut,
   didn't you
7. isn't (is not) very safe, is it

49.3

2. You couldn't give me a paper bag,
   could you?
3. don't know where Ann is, do you
   or haven't seen Ann, have you
4. you don't have a bicycle pump, do
   you
5. Robert, you haven't seen my keys,
   have you?

UNIT 50

50.1

2. making   6. getting   10. writing
3. listening 7. working   11. being
4. applying   8. using   12. trying
5. washing   9. splashing

50.2

2. driving too fast
3. going swimming
4. breaking the/her CD player
5. waiting a few minutes

50.3

2. traveling during rush hour
3. leaving; tomorrow
4. not having a license
5. turning the radio down
   or turning down the radio
6. not interrupting me all the time

50.4

Sample answers:
2. sitting on the floor
3. having a picnic
4. laughing
5. breaking down

UNIT 51

51.1

2. to help him
3. to carry her bags
4. to meet at 8:00
5. to tell him her name
6. not to tell anyone

51.2

2. to go   6. to use   10. to say
3. to get   7. barking   11. missing
4. waiting 8. to call   12. to find
5. to go   9. having

51.3

2. to be worried about something
3. seem to know a lot of people
4. My English seems to be getting
   better.
5. That car appears to have broken
   down.
6. David tends to forget things.
7. They claim to have solved the
   problem.

51.4

2. how to use   5. what to say
3. what to do   6. whether to go
4. how to ride

UNIT 52

52.1

2. me to lend you some
3. like me to shut it
4. you like me to show you
5. you want me to repeat it

52.2

2. to stay [with them] for a few days
3. him use the/her phone
4. him to be careful
5. her to give him a hand

52.3

2. to rain
3. him do what he wants
4. him look older
5. to know the truth
6. me to call my sister
7. me to apply for the job
8. me not to say anything to the
   police
9. not to believe everything he says
10. you to go places more easily

52.4

2. to go   6. eating
3. to do   7. cry
4. read   8. to study
5. to go

UNIT 53

53.1

2. driving   9. to answer
3. to go   10. breaking
4. to go   11. to pay
5. raining   12. to lock
6. to buy   13. meeting; to see
7. asking   14. to cry *or* crying
8. asking   15. to get

53.2

2. He can remember going to Miami
   when he was eight.
3. He can't remember falling into a
   river.
4. He can remember crying on his
   first day at school.
5. He can't remember saying he
   wanted to be a doctor.
6. He can't remember being bitten by
   a dog.

53.3

1. b. lending
   c. to phone *or* to call
   d. to say *or* to tell her
   e. putting *or* leaving
2. a. saying
   b. to say *or* to tell you
      or to inform you
3. a. to become
   b. working
   c. reading

UNIT 54

54.1

2. turning it the other way
3. tried taking an aspirin
4. try calling him at work

54.2

2. needs to be cut *or* needs cutting
3. It needs to be redecorated.
   or It needs redecorating.
4. They need to be tightened.
   or They need tightening.
5. It needs to be emptied.
   or It needs emptying.

54.3

1. b. knocking
   c. to put
   d. asking
   e. to reach
   f. to concentrate
2. a. to go
   b. to be taken *or* taking
   c. to be washed *or* washing
   d. to iron; ironing *or* to be ironed
3. a. overhearing
   b. get *or* to get
   c. laughing
   d. make *or* to make

UNIT 55

55.1

2. like living in Atlanta

3. didn't like working (did not like working) in a supermarket very much
4. likes teaching biology
5. likes studying medicine
6. doesn't like being (does not like being) famous

55.2

Sample answers:
2. I love to play cards.
   or I love playing cards.
3. I hate to do the ironing.
   or I hate doing the ironing.
4. I enjoy going to museums.
5. I like lying on the beach all day.
   or I like to lie on the beach all day.

55.3

Sample answers:
2. I'd hate (I would hate) to be a dentist.
3. I'd like (I would like) to be a hair stylist.
4. I'd love (I would love) to be an airline pilot.
5. I wouldn't mind (would not mind) being a tour guide.

55.4

2. waiting
3. to go *or* going
4. to write *or* writing
5. working
6. to go
7. to wear *or* wearing
8. to sit
9. living
10. to talk *or* to speak
11. to be *or* being

55.5

2. I'd like (I would like) to have seen the program.
3. I'd hate (I would hate) to have lost my watch.
4. I'd love (I would love) to have met Ann.
5. I wouldn't like (would not like) to have been alone.
6. I'd prefer (I would prefer) to have traveled by train.

UNIT 56

56.1

2. tennis to soccer
3. prefer calling people; writing letters
4. I prefer going to the movies to

watching videos at home.
6. call people rather than write letters
7. I prefer to go to the movies rather than watch videos at home.

56.2

3. I'd prefer to listen to some music.
4. I'd rather go for a swim.
5. I'd prefer to eat at home.
6. I'd rather think about it for a while.
7. I'd rather stand.
8. I'd prefer to go alone.
10. go for a swim than play tennis
11. to eat at home rather than go to a restaurant
12. think about it for a while than decide now

56.3

2. I told her
3. would you rather I did it
4. would you rather I answered it

56.4

2. stayed   4. didn't   6. didn't
3. stay   5. were

UNIT 57

57.1

2. lending you any money
3. remembering names
4. passing the exam
5. being late
6. eating at home, we went to a restaurant
7. doing nothing
8. playing well

57.2

2. by standing on a chair
3. by turning the key
4. by borrowing too much money
5. by driving too fast

57.3

2. paying
3. going
4. saying
5. going
6. using
7. riding *or* sitting *or* being *or* traveling
8. asking *or* telling
9. doing *or* having

57.4

2. looking forward to seeing her again [soon]

3. looking forward to going to the dentist [tomorrow]
4. She's (She is) looking forward to graduating [next summer].
5. I'm (I am) looking forward to playing tennis [tomorrow].

UNIT 58

58.1

1. got used to; 's used to having/ eating (is used to having/eating)
2. wasn't used to working (was not used to working); get used to; 's used to working (is used to working)

58.2

2. 'm used to sleeping (am used to sleeping) on the floor
3. 'm used to working (am used to working) hard
4. I'm not used to going (I am not used to going) to bed late

58.3

2. used to the heat
3. get used to living
4. got used to their new teacher
Sample answer:
5. get used to the food

58.4

2. drink   5. have   7. be
3. eating   *or* own   8. being
4. having   6. go

UNIT 59

59.1

2. doing
3. going *or* coming
4. doing *or* trying
5. buying *or* getting
6. hearing
7. going
8. having *or* carrying *or* using
9. being
10. watching
11. inviting *or* asking

59.2

2. in solving   7. of spending
3. of living   8. from escaping
4. of causing   9. on helping
5. from walking   10. to playing
6. for interrupting

59.3

2. on taking Ann to the station

3. on getting married
4. Sue for coming to see her
5. [to me] for not phoning [me] earlier
6. me of being selfish

UNIT 60

60.1

2. no point in asking him *or* no use asking him
3. in going out
4. calling her now
5. complaining
6. of time to read newspapers *or* of time reading newspapers

60.2

2. fixing
3. visiting
4. It's worth considering. (It is worth considering.)
5. It's worth reading. (It is worth reading.)
6. 're not / aren't worth keeping (are not worth keeping)

60.3

2. trouble/difficulty remembering people's names
3. trouble getting a job
4. difficulty understanding him
5. difficulty getting a ticket [for the concert]

60.4

2. reading   5. watching
3. applying   6. getting
4. writing   7. climbing *or* going

60.5

2. go skiing   4. goes riding
3. went swimming 5. go shopping

UNIT 61

61.1

2. to get some money
3. 'm saving money to go to Canada
4. I went into the hospital to have an operation.
5. I'm wearing two sweaters to keep warm.
6. I called the police to report that my car had been stolen.

61.2

2. to read
3. to walk
4. to drink

5. to put *or* to carry
6. to discuss *or* to talk about
7. to buy *or* to get
8. to talk *or* to speak
9. to wear
10. to help

61.3

2. for   4. to   6. to   8. for; to
3. to   5. for   7. for

61.4

2. warm clothes so that we wouldn't get (would not get) cold
3. spoke very slowly so that I could/would understand what he said
4. arrive early so that we can start the meeting on time
5. She locked the door so that she wouldn't be (would not be) disturbed.
6. I slowed down so that the car behind me could pass.

UNIT 62

62.1

2. easy to use
3. was very difficult to open
4. are impossible to translate
5. isn't safe (is not safe) to stand on
6. car is expensive to maintain

62.2

2. easy mistake to make
3. nice place to live
4. a good game to watch

62.3

2. 's (is) careless of you to make the same mistake again and again
3. It was nice of Don and Jenny to invite me to stay with them.
4. considerate of John to make a lot of noise when I was trying to sleep

62.4

2. 'm (am) glad to hear *or* was glad to hear
3. were surprised to see
4. 'm (am) sorry to hear *or* was sorry to hear

62.5

2. last [person] to arrive
3. the only student/person to pass the exam
4. the second customer/person to complain

5. the first man/person to walk on the moon

UNIT 63

63.1

2. I'm (I am) afraid of losing it.
3. We were afraid to go swimming.
4. We were afraid of missing our train.
5. We were afraid to look.
6. She was afraid of spilling the drinks.
7. a. I was afraid to eat it.
   b. I was afraid of getting sick.

63.2

2. in starting   5. in hearing
3. to read   6. in going
4. in getting

63.3

2. to bother   4. for saying
3. for being   5. to hear

63.4

1. b. to leave   c. to going
   c. from leaving d. to go
2. a. to solve   4. a. to buy
   b. in solving   b. to buy
3. a. of going   c. on buying
   b. to go   d. of buying

UNIT 64

64.1

2. arrive   5. you lock it
3. take it   6. her fall
4. it ring

64.2

2. playing tennis
3. Claire eating
4. Bill playing the guitar
5. smell our dinner burning
6. We saw Linda jogging/running.

64.3

3. tell   8. explode
4. crying   9. run; open; climb
5. riding   10. slam
6. say   11. sleeping
7. crawling

UNIT 65

65.1

2. in an armchair reading a book
3. went out saying she would be back in an hour

4. Linda was in London for two years working as a teacher.
5. Mary walked around the town looking at the sights and taking photographs.

65.2

2. fell asleep watching TV
3. slipped getting off a bus
4. Margaret had an accident driving to work yesterday.
5. Two kids got lost hiking in the woods.

65.3

2. Having bought our tickets, we went into the theater.
3. Having had dinner, they continued their trip.
4. Having done all her shopping, Lucy stopped for a cup of coffee.

65.4

2. Thinking they might be hungry, I offered them something to eat.
3. Being a foreigner, she needs a visa to stay in this country.
4. Not knowing his address, I wasn't able to contact him.
5. Having traveled a lot, Sarah knows a lot about other countries.
6. Not being able to understand English, the man didn't know what I wanted.
7. Having spent nearly all our money, we couldn't afford to stay in a hotel.

UNIT 66

66.1

3. a very nice restaurant
4. RIGHT
5. a toothbrush
6. a bank
7. an insurance company
8. RIGHT
9. RIGHT
10. a gas station
11. a problem
12. an interview for a job
13. a necklace

66.2

3. a key   8. a letter
4. a coat   9. blood
5. sugar   10. a question
6. a cookie   11. a moment
7. electricity   12. a decision

66.3

2. days   6. friends   10. languages
3. meat   7. people   11. countries
4. a line   8. an umbrella 12. space
5. letters 9. patience

UNIT 67

67.1

2. a. a paper
   b. any paper
3. a. a light
   b. Light
4. a. time
   b. a wonderful time
5. advice
6. very good weather
7. bad luck   11. some
8. job   12. doesn't
9. trip   13. Your hair is; it
10. total chaos   14. The damage

67.2

2. information   7. job
3. chairs   8. work
4. furniture   9. permission
5. hair   10. experience
6. progress   11. experiences

67.3

2. some information about places to see [in the city]
3. some advice about which courses to take
4. is the news on [TV]
5. 's (is) a beautiful view
6. horrible weather

UNIT 68

68.1

3. It's a vegetable.
4. It's a game.
5. They're musical instruments.
6. It's a [tall] building.
7. They're planets.
8. It's a flower.
9. They're rivers.
10. They're birds.
12. He was a writer / a playwright.
13. He was a scientist / a physicist.
14. They were American presidents.
15. She was a movie star / an actress.
16. They were singers/musicians.
17. They were painters/artists.

68.2

2. 's (is) a waiter
3. 's (is) a travel agent

4. He's (He is) a pilot.
5. She's (She is) a driving instructor.
6. He's (He is) a plumber.
7. She's (She's) a journalist.
8. He's (He is) an interpreter.

68.3

4. a   9. —   13. a; some
5. an   10. a   14. a; —
6. —   11. a; a   15. —
7. a   12. —   16. a; —
8. Some

UNIT 69

69.1

1. a; The; the
2. an; A; a; The; the; the
3. a; a; The; the; the
4. an; a; a; the; a

69.2

1. b. the   3. a. a   c. the
   c. the   b. the   5. a. the
2. a. a   c. the   b. a
   b. a   4. a. an; The   c. a
   c. the   b. the

69.3

2. the dentist   8. the floor
3. the door   9. the book
4. a mistake   10. a job; a bank
5. the bus station 11. a supermarket;
6. a problem   the corner
7. the post office

69.4

Sample answers:
2. Once or twice a year.
3. Fifty-five miles an hour.
4. Thirty dollars a day.
5. Eight hours a night.
6. Two or three times a week.
7. About an hour a day.

UNIT 70

70.1

2. the; the   5. —; the   8. —; —
3. the; a   6. the; —   9. —; the
4. a; the   7. a; the   10. the; a

70.2

2. the; the   5. —
3. —   6. the
4. The   7. the; the; —

70.3

2. The moon; the earth

3. the highest mountain; the world
4. the same thing
5. a very hot day; the hottest day; the year
6. a good breakfast
7. a foreign country; the language
8. The next train

70.4

2. the movies	5. question 8
3. the sea	6. the gate
4. dinner	7. Gate 21

UNIT 71

71.1

2. to school	5. to work
3. [at] home	6. in bed
4. for school	7. to prison
or for work	

71.2

1. c. school	4. a. prison
d. school	b. the prison
e. school;	c. prison
The school	5. a. bed
f. school	b. home
g. the school	c. work
2. a. college	d. bed
b. college	e. work
c. the college	f. work
3. a. church	6. a. the sea
b. church	b. sea
c. the church	c. the sea

UNIT 72

72.1

Sample answers:
2. I like cats.
3. I hate fast-food restaurants.
4. I don't mind opera.
5. I'm not interested in boxing.

72.2

3. spiders	8. lies
4. meat	9. the hotels
5. the questions	10. The water
6. the people	11. the grass
7. History	12. patience

72.3

3. Apples
4. the apples
5. Women; men
6. The vegetables
7. Life
8. skiing
9. the people

10. people; aggression
11. All the books
12. the beds
13. war
14. The First World War
15. the marriage
16. Most people; marriage; family life; society

UNIT 73

73.1

1. b. the cheetah
   c. the kangaroo
2. a. the swan
   b. the penguin
   c. the owl
3. a. the wheel
   b. the cell phone
   c. the telescope
4. a. the rupee
   b. the euro
   c. *Answers will vary.*

73.2

2. a	4. a	6. the	8. —
3. the	5. the	7. a	9. The

73.3

2. the injured
3. the unemployed
4. the sick
5. the rich; the poor

73.4

2. a German; Germans
3. a Frenchman/Frenchwoman; the French
4. a Russian; Russians
5. a Chinese; the Chinese
6. a Brazilian; Brazilians
7. a Japanese; [the] Japanese
8. *Answers will vary.*

UNIT 74

74.1

2. the	5. the
3. The; the	6. —
4. —	

74.2

3. RIGHT
4. the United States
5. The south; the north
6. RIGHT
7. the Middle East
8. RIGHT
9. the Swiss Alps

10. RIGHT
11. The United Kingdom
12. The Seychelles; the Indian Ocean
13. The Hudson River; the Atlantic Ocean

74.3

2. in South America
3. the Nile
4. Sweden
5. the United States
6. the Rockies
7. the Mediterranean Sea
8. Australia
9. the Pacific Ocean
10. the Indian Ocean
11. the Thames
12. the Mississippi
13. Thailand
14. the Panama Canal
15. the Amazon

UNIT 75

75.1

2. Turner's on Carter Road
3. the Park Hotel on Park Avenue
4. St. Peter's on Forest Avenue
5. the City Museum on Main Street
6. the American Bank on Forest Avenue
7. Lincoln Park on Park Avenue
8. the New China House on Carter Road

75.2

2. The Eiffel Tower
3. The Vatican
4. Buckingham Palace
5. Sunset Boulevard
6. The White House
7. The Acropolis
8. Broadway

75.3

2. Central Park
3. St. James's Park
4. The Ramada Inn; Main Street
5. O'Hare Airport
6. McGill University
7. Harrison's Department Store
8. The Statue of Liberty; New York harbor
9. the Whitney Museum
10. IBM; General Electric
11. The Classic
12. the Great Wall
13. the Independent; the Herald
14. Cambridge University Press

UNIT 76

76.1
3. shorts
4. a means
5. means
6. [some] scissors *or* a pair of scissors
7. a series
8. series
9. species

76.2
2. politics
3. economics
4. physics
5. gymnastics
6. electronics

76.3
2. don't
3. want
4. was
5. aren't
6. wasn't
7. isn't
8. they are
9. are
10. Do
11. is

76.4
2. nice people
3. is not enough
4. buy new pajamas
5. people have
6. RIGHT
7. a police officer / policeman / policewoman
8. Have the police
9. These scissors aren't (are not)

UNIT 77

77.1
2. a computer magazine
3. vacation pictures
4. milk chocolate
5. a factory inspector
6. a Vancouver lawyer
7. exam results
8. a horse race
9. a racehorse
10. the dining room carpet
11. an oil-company scandal
12. a two-part question
13. a seven-year-old girl
14. a five-story building

77.2
2. room number
3. seat belt
4. credit card
5. weather forecast
6. newspaper editor
7. store window

77.3
3. 20-dollar
4. 15-minute
5. 60 minutes
6. two-hour
7. five courses
8. two-year
9. 500-year
10. five days
11. six-mile
12. six miles

UNIT 78

78.1
3. your friend's umbrella
4. OK
5. Charles's daughter
6. Mary and Dan's son
7. OK
8. yesterday's newspaper
9. OK
10. OK
11. Your children's friends
12. Our neighbors' garden
13. OK
14. Bill's hair
15. Catherine's party
16. my father's birthday
17. Mike's parents' car
18. Helen's best friend

78.2
2. a boy's name
3. children's clothes
4. a girls' school
5. a bird's nest
6. a women's magazine

78.3
2. week's storm caused a lot of damage
3. town's only movie theater has closed down
4. Japan's exports to the United States have fallen recently.
5. The region's main industry is tourism.

78.4
2. a year's salary
3. four weeks' pay
4. a minute's rest
5. five hours' sleep

UNIT 79

79.1
2. hurt himself
3. blame herself
4. Put yourself
5. enjoyed themselves
6. burn yourself
7. express myself

79.2
2. me
3. myself
4. us
5. yourself
6. you
7. ourselves
8. themselves
9. them

79.3
2. dried herself
3. concentrate
4. defend yourself
5. meeting
6. relax

79.4
2. themselves
3. each other
4. each other
5. themselves
6. ourselves
7. each other
8. ourselves; each other

79.5
2. it himself
3. mail it myself
4. told me herself *or* herself told me
5. call him yourself

UNIT 80

80.1
2. relative of yours
3. borrowed a book of mine
4. invited some friends of hers to her place
5. We had dinner with a neighbor of ours.
6. I took a trip with two friends of mine.
7. Is that man a friend of yours?
8. I met a friend of Amy's at the party.

80.2
2. my own TV
3. her own money
4. her own business
5. his own private jet
6. his own ideas
7. its own government

80.3
2. your own fault
3. his own ideas
4. your own problems
5. her own decisions

80.4
2. makes her own clothes
3. writes his own songs
4. bake our own bread

80.5
2. by myself
3. by himself
4. by themselves
5. by herself
6. by yourself
7. by ourselves

UNIT 81

81.1

3. Is there; there's (there is)
4. there was; It was
5. It was
6. There was
7. is it
8. It was
9. It's (It is)
10. there wasn't (was not)
11. Is it; it's (it is)
12. there was; There was
13. There wasn't (was not)
14. There was; it wasn't (was not)

81.2

2. 's (is) a lot of salt
3. There was nothing *or* There wasn't (was not) anything
4. There was a lot of violence in the movie.
5. There were a lot of people at the shopping mall.

81.3

2. There might be
3. there will be
4. There's going to be (There is going to be)
5. There used to be
6. there should be
7. there wouldn't be

81.4

2. there was
3. RIGHT
4. There used to be
5. There must have been
6. RIGHT
7. There's sure to be
8. there will be
9. RIGHT
10. there would be; there wasn't

UNIT 82

82.1

2. some   5. some   8. some
3. any   6. any   9. any
4. any; some 7. any   10. any

82.2

2. somebody/someone
3. anybody/anyone
4. anything
5. something
6. somebody/someone; anybody/anyone
7. something; anybody/anyone
8. Anybody/Anyone
9. anybody/anyone
10. anywhere
11. somewhere
12. anywhere
13. anybody/anyone *or* somebody/someone
14. something
15. Anybody/Anyone
16. anybody/anyone; anything

82.3

2. Any day.   6. Any time.
3. Anything.   7. Anybody/Anyone
4. anywhere   8. Any newspaper.
5. Anything. *or* Any kind. *or* Any job.

UNIT 83

83.1

3. no   5. None   7. No   9. any
4. any 6. none   8. any   10. none

83.2

2. Nowhere.
3. None.
4. None.
5. Nobody. / No one.
6. Nothing.
8. 'm not going (am not going) anywhere
9. I don't have (do not have) any.
10. They don't have (do not have) any.
11. I wasn't talking (was not talking) to anybody/anyone.
12. I don't want (do not want) anything.

83.3

2. nobody / no one
3. Nowhere.
4. anything
5. Nothing; anything
6. Nothing
7. anywhere
8. Nobody / No one; anything

83.4

2. no one   4. Anybody   6. Anything
3. anybody   5. Nothing   7. anything

UNIT 84

84.1

3. a lot of salt   7. many / a lot of
4. RIGHT   people
5. RIGHT   8. a lot
6. a lot

84.2

2. plenty of money
3. plenty of room
4. plenty to learn
5. are plenty of hotels
6. plenty of things to wear

84.3

2. little   5. few
3. many   6. little
4. much

84.4

3. a few dollars 6. RIGHT
4. a little time 7. only a few words
5. RIGHT

84.5

2. a little   5. little   7. little
3. a few   6. A little. 8. a few
4. few

UNIT 85

85.1

3. —   5. —   7. of   9. — *or* of
4. of   6. —   8. of   10. —

85.2

3. of my spare time
4. accidents
5. of the buildings
6. of her friends
7. of the population
8. birds
9. of my teammates
10. of her opinions
11. large cities
12. [of] my dinner

85.3

Sample Answers
2. the time / our time
3. my friends
4. [of] the questions
5. the pictures / the photgraphs / the photos
6. [of] the money

85.4

2. All of them   6. None of it
3. none of us   7. Some of them
4. some of it   8. all of it
5. none of them

UNIT 86

86.1

2. Neither   4. Either
3. both   5. Neither

86.2

2. either 5. neither; both
3. both 6. both
4. Neither of

86.3

2. either of them
3. both of them
4. neither of us
5. neither of them

86.4

2. Both Jim and Carol are on vacation.
3. Brian neither smokes nor drinks.
4. was both very boring and very long
5. is either Richard or Robert
6. neither the time nor the money to go on vacation
7. can leave either today or tomorrow

86.5

2. either 5. any 7. neither
3. any 6. either 8. none
4. none

UNIT 87

87.1

3. Everybody/Everyone
4. Everything
5. all
6. everybody/everyone
7. everything
8. All
9. everybody/everyone
10. Everybody/Everyone
11. All
12. everything

87.2

2. whole team played well
3. the whole box [of chocolates]
4. searched the whole house
5. whole family plays tennis
6. worked the whole day
7. rained the whole week
8. worked all day
9. It rained all week.

87.3

2. every four hours
3. every four years
4. every five minutes
5. every six months

87.4

2. every day
3. all day

4. The whole building
5. every time
6. all the time
7. all my luggage

UNIT 88

88.1

3. Each 6. every
4. Every 7. each
5. Each/Every 8. every

88.2

3. Every 9. every
4. Each 10. every
5. every 11. each
6. everyone 12. Everyone
7. every 13. Every
8. each 14. each

88.3

2. had ten dollars each *or* each had ten dollars
3. postcards cost/are 40 cents each *or* postcards each cost 40 cents
4. paid $195 each *or* each paid $195

UNIT 89

89.1

2. who breaks into a house to steal things
3. A customer is someone who buys something from a store.
4. A shoplifter is someone who steals from a store.
5. A coward is someone who is not brave.
6. An atheist is someone who doesn't believe in God.
7. A tenant is someone who pays rent to live in a house or an apartment.

89.2

2. who/that answered the phone told me you were away
3. waitress who/that served us was very impolite and impatient
4. The building that/which was destroyed in the fire has now been rebuilt.
5. people who/that were arrested have now been released
6. The bus that/which goes to the airport runs every half hour.

89.3

2. who/that runs away from home

3. that/which won the race
4. who/that stole my car
5. who/that invented the telephone
6. that/which were on the wall
7. that/which cannot be explained
8. that/which gives you the meanings of words
9. who/that are never on time
10. that/which can support life

UNIT 90

90.1

3. (who) 6. (that) 8. (that)
4. who 7. that 9. that
5. (who)

90.2

2. [that/which] Ann is wearing
3. [that/which] we wanted to visit
4. [that/which] you're going to see
5. [who/that] I invited to the party
6. [that/which] you had to do

90.3

2. [that/which] we were invited to
3. [who/that] I work with
4. [that/which] you told me about
5. [that/which] we went to last night
6. [that/which] I applied for
7. [who/that] you can rely on
8. [who/that] I saw you with

90.4

2. (that) 5. (that) 7. what
3. what 6. (that) 8. (that)
4. that

UNIT 91

91.1

2. whose wife is an English teacher
3. who owns a restaurant
4. whose ambition is to climb Mt. Everest
5. who just got married
6. whose parents used to work in a circus

91.2

2. where we can have a really good meal
3. where I can buy some postcards
4. where we had the car repaired
5. where John is staying
6. where she [had] bought it

91.3

2. where   4. whose   6. whose
3. who   5. where   7. whom

91.4

Sample answers:
2. [that] we got stuck in an elevator
3. [that/why] I didn't write to you
4. [that] you called
5. [that/why] they don't have a car

UNIT 92

92.1

3. which we enjoyed very much
4. I went to see the doctor, who told me to rest for a few days.
5. who/whom I've known (I have known) for a very long time, is one of my closest friends
6. Sheila, whose job involves a lot of traveling, is away from home a lot.
7. new stadium, which can hold 90,000 people, will be opened next month
8. Alaska, where my brother lives, is the largest state in the United States.

92.2

3. , which lasted ten days, is now over
4. the book [that/which] I was looking for
5. , which was once the largest city in the world, is now decreasing
6. the people who/that applied for the job that/which was advertised had the necessary qualifications
7. a picture of her son, who is a police officer

92.3

3. , which is on the second floor of the building,
4. that/which I'm using at the moment
5. , which I wrote down on a piece of paper
6. that/which are very difficult to translate
7. , which is one of millions of stars in the universe,

UNIT 93

93.1

2. of our friends, with whom we went on vacation *or* of our friends, who we went on vacation with

3. , to which only members of the family were invited, took place last Friday *or* , which only members of the family were invited to, took place last Friday
4. Sheila, for whom we'd been waiting (we had been waiting), finally arrived. *or* Sheila, who we'd been waiting (we had been waiting) for, finally arrived.
5. My room, from which you can see the whole lake, has a very large window. *or* My room, which you can see the whole lake from, has a very large window.

93.2

2. a lot of information, most of which was useless
3. There were a lot of people at the party, only a few of whom I had met before.
4. I sent her two letters, neither of which she's received (she has received).
5. Ten people applied for the job, none of whom were suitable.
6. Kate has two cars, one of which she hardly ever uses.
7. Mike won $50,000, half of which he gave to his parents.
8. Julia has two sisters, both of whom are teachers.

93.3

2. have a phone, which makes it difficult to contact her
3. Neil has passed his exams, which is good news.
4. Our flight was delayed, which meant we had to wait four hours at the airport.
5. Ann offered to let me stay at her house, which was very nice of her.
6. The street I live on is very noisy at night, which makes it difficult to sleep.
7. Our car has broken down, which means we can't take our trip tomorrow.

UNIT 94

94.1

2. I didn't talk much to the man sitting next to me on the plane.
3. The taxi taking us to the airport broke down.

4. At the end of the street there is a path leading to the river.
5. A new factory employing 500 people has just opened in town.

94.2

2. made at the meeting were not very practical
3. paintings stolen from the museum haven't been found yet
4. of the man arrested by the police

94.3

3. living   6. blown
4. offering   7. sitting; reading
5. named   8. driving; selling

94.4

3. 's (is) somebody coming
4. There were a lot of people traveling.
5. There was nobody else staying there.
6. There was nothing written on it.
7. There's (There is) a course beginning next Monday.

UNIT 95

95.1

2. a. exhausting   c. depressed
    b. exhausted   4. a. exciting
3. a. depressing   b. exciting
    b. depressed   c. excited

95.2

2. interested
3. exciting
4. embarrassing
5. embarrassed
6. amazed
7. astonishing
8. amused
9. terrifying; shocked
10. bored; boring
11. boring; interesting

95.3

2. bored   7. interested
3. confusing   8. exhausted
4. disgusting   9. excited
5. annoyed   10. amusing
6. boring   11. interesting

UNIT 96

96.1

2. an unusual gold ring
3. a nice new sweater
4. a new green sweater
5. a beautiful old house

6. black leather gloves
7. an old American movie
8. a long thin face
9. big black clouds
10. a lovely sunny day
11. an ugly yellow dress
12. a long wide avenue
13. a little old red car
14. a small black metal box
15. a big fat black cat
16. a charming little old country inn
17. beautiful long black hair
18. an interesting old Japanese painting
19. an enormous red and yellow umbrella *or* an enormous yellow and red umbrella

96.2

2. tastes awful *or* tasted awful
3. feel fine
4. smell nice
5. look wet
6. sounds interesting
   or sounded interesting

96.3

2. happy 5. terrible 7. good
3. happily 6. well 8. slow
4. violent

UNIT 97

97.1

2. badly 5. unexpectedly
3. easily 6. regularly
4. patiently

97.2

2. selfishly 7. badly
3. terribly 8. badly
4. sudden 9. safe
5. colorfully 10. angrily
6. colorful

97.3

2. careful 7. complete
3. continuously 8. perfectly
4. happily 9. nervous
5. fluent 10. financially
6. specially

97.4

2. seriously ill
3. absolutely enormous
4. slightly damaged
5. unusually quiet
6. completely changed
7. unnecessarily long
8. badly planned

UNIT 98

98.1

2. good 5. well 8. well
3. well 6. well 9. good
4. good 7. good 10. well

98.2

2. well known 5. well informed
3. well kept 6. well dressed
4. well balanced 7. well paid

98.3

2. RIGHT 5. RIGHT
3. RIGHT 6. slowly
4. hard

98.4

2. hardly hear 5. hardly said
3. hardly slept 6. hardly changed
4. hardly speak 7. hardly recognized

98.5

2. hardly any
3. hardly anything
4. hardly anybody
5. hardly ever
6. Hardly anybody
7. hardly ever
8. hardly anything; hardly anywhere

UNIT 99

99.1

4. so 8. such 12. so; such
5. so 9. such an 13. so
6. such a 10. such a 14. such a
7. so 11. so 15. such a

99.2

3. so tired [that] I couldn't keep my eyes open
4. We had such a good time on vacation [that] we didn't want to come home.
5. She speaks English so well [that] you would think it was her native language.
6. I've got such a lot to do [that] I don't know where to begin.
7. The music was so loud [that] you could hear it from miles away.
8. I had such a big breakfast [that] I didn't eat anything else for the rest of the day.
9. It was such terrible weather [that] we spent the whole day indoors.

99.3

Sample answers:
2. a. crowded 4. a. exhausting
   b. a busy place b. a hard job
3. a. friendly 5. a. long
   b. a nice person b. a long time

UNIT 100

100.1

2. enough money
3. enough milk
4. warm enough
5. enough room
6. well enough
7. enough time
8. qualified enough
9. big enough
10. enough cups

100.2

2. too busy to talk
3. warm enough to sit
4. too shy to be
5. enough energy to play
6. too far away to hear
7. enough English to read

100.3

2. too hot to drink
3. was too heavy to move
4. isn't warm enough to wear in the winter
5. is too complicated to explain
6. isn't wide enough for three people to sit on
7. was too high to climb over
8. things are too small to see without a microscope

UNIT 101

101.1

2. stronger
3. smaller
4. more expensive
5. more interesting
6. more difficult *or* harder
7. better
8. worse
9. more quietly *or* more softly
10. more often
11. farther/further
12. happier

101.2

3. more serious than
4. thinner

5. bigger
6. more interested
7. more important than
8. simpler *or* more simple
9. more crowded than
10. more peaceful than
11. more easily
12. higher than

101.3

2. longer by train than [it takes/does] by car
3. farther/further than Dave [ran/did]
4. more poorly / worse than Chris [did] on the exam
5. arrived earlier than I expected [them to arrive]
6. run more often / more frequently than the trains [run/do]
7. were busier than usual at work today *or* were busier at work today than we usually are

UNIT 102

102.1

2. much bigger
3. much more complicated than
4. a little happier
5. far more interesting than
6. a little more slowly
7. a lot easier
8. slightly older

102.2

2. any earlier/sooner
3. no higher than
4. any farther/further
5. no worse than

102.3

2. bigger and bigger
3. heavier and heavier
4. more and more nervous
5. worse and worse
6. more and more expensive
7. better and better
8. more and more talkative

102.4

2. the better/more I liked him
3. the more/larger/bigger/greater/ higher your profit [will be]
4. the harder it is to concentrate
5. the more impatient she became

102.5

2. older   3. older/elder   4. older

UNIT 103

103.1

2. as high as yours [is]
3. know as much as I do/know about cars *or* . . . as me about cars
4. feel as tired as [I did/felt] yesterday
5. lived here as long as us
   or . . . as long as we have
6. as nervous as I usually am
   or as nervous as usual

103.2

3. as/so far as I thought
4. go out as/so much as I used to
   or go out as/so often as I used to
5. have longer hair
6. know them as/so well as me
   or know them as/so well as I do
7. as/so many people at this meeting as at the last one

103.3

2. as well as
3. as long as
4. as soon as
5. as often as
6. just as comfortable as
7. just as experienced as
8. just as bad as

103.4

2. is the same color as mine
3. arrived at the same time as you [did]
4. birthday is the same [day] as Tom's [birthday]

103.5

2. than him *or* than he does/knows
3. as me *or* as I do/work
4. than us *or* than we were
5. than her *or* than she is
6. as them *or* as they've been (they have been)

UNIT 104

104.1

2. the cheapest restaurant in
3. the happiest day of
4. 's (is) the most intelligent student in
5. 's (is) the most valuable painting in
6. 's (is) the busiest time of
8. of the richest men in
9. 's (is) one of the oldest houses on
10. 's (is) one of the best colleges in

11. was one of the worst experiences of
12. 's (is) one of the most dangerous criminals in

104.2

3. larger
4. the longest
5. happier
6. the worst
7. the most popular
8. the highest; higher
9. the most enjoyable
10. more comfortable
11. the quickest
12. The oldest *or* The eldest

104.3

2. the funniest joke I've ever heard (I have ever heard)
3. is the best coffee I've ever tasted (I have ever tasted)
4. 's (is) the most patient person I've ever met (I have ever met)
5. 's (is) the farthest/furthest I've ever run (I have ever run)
6. 's (is) the worst mistake I've ever made (I have ever made)
   or was the worst mistake . . .

UNIT 105

105.1

3. Jim doesn't like soccer very much.
4. RIGHT
5. I ate my dinner quickly and went out.
6. Are you going to invite a lot of people to the party?
7. RIGHT
8. Did you go to bed late last night?
9. RIGHT
10. I met a friend of mine on my way home.

105.2

2. We won the game easily.
3. I closed the door quietly.
4. Diane speaks Chinese quite well.
5. Tim watches TV all the time.
6. Please don't ask that question again.
7. Does Ken play soccer every weekend?
8. I borrowed some money from a friend of mine.

105.3

2. go to the bank every Friday
3. did you come home so late

4. drives her car to work every day
5. been to the movies recently
6. write your name at the top of the page
7. remembered her name after a few minutes
8. walked around the town all morning
9. didn't see you at the party on Saturday night
10. found some interesting books in the library
11. took the children to the zoo yesterday
12. are building a new hotel across from the park

UNIT 106

106.1
3. I usually have
4. RIGHT
5. Steve hardly ever gets
6. I also went
7. Jane always has to hurry
8. We were all; RIGHT
9. RIGHT

106.2
2. We were all on vacation.
3. We were all staying at the same hotel.
4. We all enjoyed ourselves.
5. Catherine is always very generous.
6. I don't usually have to work on Saturdays.
7. Do you always watch TV in the evenings?
8. is also studying Japanese
9. That hotel is probably very expensive.
10. It probably costs a lot to stay there.

106.3
2. usually take
3. 'm (am) usually
4. 's probably gone (has probably gone)
5. were both born
6. can also sing
7. always sleeps
8. 've never spoken (have never spoken)
9. can only read *or* can read only
10. 'll probably be leaving (will probably be leaving)
11. probably won't be

12. 's hardly ever (is hardly ever)
13. 're still living (are still living)
14. would never have met
15. always am

UNIT 107

107.1
3. doesn't write (does not write) poems anymore
4. He still wants to be a teacher.
5. He isn't (is not) interested in politics anymore. *or* He's (He is) not interested in politics anymore.
6. He's (He is) still single.
7. He doesn't go fishing (does not go fishing) anymore.
8. He doesn't have a beard anymore.
10. He no longer writes poems.
11. He's (He is) no longer interested in politics.
12. He no longer goes fishing.

107.2
2. hasn't left (has not left) yet
3. haven't finished (have not finished) yet
4. They haven't woken up (have not woken up) yet.
5. I haven't decided (have not decided) yet.
6. It hasn't taken off (has not taken off) yet.

107.3
5. I don't want to go out yet.
6. she doesn't work there anymore
7. I still have a lot of friends there.
8. We've already met. *or* We've met already.
9. Do you still live in the same house
10. have you already eaten *or* have you eaten already
11. He isn't here yet.
12. he still isn't here
13. are you already a member *or* are you a member already
14. I can still remember it very clearly
15. These pants don't fit me anymore.

UNIT 108

108.1
2. even Amanda

3. not even Julie
4. even Amanda
5. even Sarah
6. not even Amanda

108.2
2. She even has to work on Sundays.
3. even painted the floor
4. could even hear the noise from the next street
6. can't even remember her name
7. There isn't even a movie theater.
8. He didn't even tell his wife [where he was going].

108.3
2. even older   5. even worse
3. even better   6. even less
4. even more difficult

108.4
2. if   6. Even
3. even if   7. Even though
4. even   8. even if
5. even though

UNIT 109

109.1
2. Although I had never seen her before
3. although it was pretty cold
4. although we don't like them very much
5. Although I didn't speak the language
6. Although the heat was on
7. although I'd met her twice before
8. although we've known each other for a long time

109.2
2. a. In spite of
   b. Although
3. a. because
   b. although
4. a. because of
   b. in spite of
5. a. although
   b. because of
Sample answers:
6. a. he didn't study very hard
   b. he studied very hard
7. a. I was hungry
   b. being hungry

109.3
2. having very little money, they are happy

3. Although my foot was injured, I managed to walk to the nearest town. or I managed to walk to the nearest town although my foot was injured.
4. Despite living on the same street, we hardly ever see each other. or Despite the fact [that] we live on the same street, we hardly ever see each other. or We hardly ever see each other despite living on the same street. or We hardly ever see each other despite the fact [that] we live on the same street.
5. Even though I had an umbrella, I got very wet in the rain. or I got very wet in the rain even though I had an umbrella.

109.4
2. It's a little windy though.
3. We ate it though.
4. don't like her husband though

UNIT 110

110.1
2. she gets lost
3. take an umbrella in case it rains
4. She's going to take her camera in case she wants to take some pictures.
5. She's going to take some water in case she gets thirsty.
6. She's going to take a towel in case she wants to go for a swim.

110.2
1. in case you need to contact me
2. good-bye now in case I don't see you again before you go
3. check the list in case we've forgotten something

110.3
2. my parents in case they were worried about me
3. wrote to Jane again in case she hadn't gotten my first letter
4. gave them my address in case they come to New York [one day]

110.4
3. If   7. if
4. if   8. in case
5. in case   9. in case
6. if

UNIT 111

111.1
2. unless you listen carefully
3. never speak to her again unless she apologizes to me
4. He won't be able to understand you unless you speak very slowly. or Unless you speak very slowly, he won't be able to understand you.
5. I'm going to look for another job unless the company offers me more money. or Unless the company offers me more money, I'm going to look for another job.

111.2
2. to the party unless you go, too
3. The dog won't attack (will not attack) you unless you move suddenly.
4. He won't speak (will not speak) to you unless you ask him a question.
5. The doctor won't see (will not see) you today unless it's an emergency.

111.3
2. unless   7. provided
3. providing   8. Unless
4. as long as   9. unless
5. unless   10. as long as
6. unless

111.4
Sample answers:
2. it's humid
3. it's not too humid
4. she has time
5. it isn't raining
6. I'm in a hurry
7. you have something else to do
8. you pay it back
9. you take risks

UNIT 112

112.1
2. We all smiled as we posed for the photograph.
3. I burned myself as I was taking a hot dish out of the oven.
4. The crowd cheered as the two teams ran onto the field.
5. A dog ran out in front of the car as we were driving along the road.

112.2
2. when   4. When   6. when
3. as/when   5. as/when

112.3
3. because
4. at the same time as
5. at the same time as
6. because
7. because
9. Since I was tired, I went to bed early.
10. We decided to go out to eat since we had no food at home.
11. Since we don't use the car very often, we've decided to sell it.

112.4
Sample answers:
1. you were getting into your car
2. we started playing tennis
3. I had to walk home
4. somebody walked in front of the camera

UNIT 113

113.1
3. like   7. As/Like   11. like
4. like   8. as   12. like
5. as/like   9. like   13. like
6. like   10. as   14. as

113.2
2. as a tour guide
3. like blocks of ice
4. like a beginner
5. like a church
6. as a birthday present
7. like winter
8. like a child

113.3
2. as   7. as/like   12. as
3. like   8. as   13. Like
4. like   9. as   14. as
5. as/like   10. like   15. as
6. like   11. like

UNIT 114

114.1
2. as if/like she had hurt her leg
3. as if/like he meant what he was saying
4. as if/like he hadn't eaten for a week
5. as if/like she was enjoying it
6. as if/like she didn't want to come

114.2
2. look as if you've seen (you have seen) a ghost

3. You sound as if you're enjoying
   (you are enjoying) it. *or* . . . as if
   you've been enjoying (you have
   been enjoying) it. *or* . . . as if you
   enjoy it.
4. I feel as if I've run (I have run) a
   marathon

114.3

2. looks like it's going to rain
3. It sounds like they're having an
   argument.
4. It looks like there's been an
   accident.
5. It looks like we'll have to walk.
6. It sounds like you had a good
   time.

114.4

2. as if I were/was
3. as if she were/was
4. as if it were/was

UNIT 115

115.1

3. during   7. for   11. for
4. for   8. for   12. for
5. during   9. during   13. during
6. for   10. for   14. for

115.2

3. while   7. during   11. during
4. While   8. During   12. while
5. During   9. while   13. during
6. while   10. while   14. while

115.3

Sample answers:
3. I was playing baseball
4. I make a phone call
5. the class
6. my interview
7. the car is moving
8. dinner
9. the game
10. we were playing soccer

UNIT 116

116.1

2. by 10:30
3. by Saturday whether you can
   come to the party
4. make sure that you're here by
   2:00
5. If we leave now, we should arrive
   by lunchtime.

116.2

3. by   7. until   10. until
4. until   8. by   11. By
5. until; by   9. by   12. by
6. by

116.3

Sample answers:
3. until I come back
4. by 5:00
5. by next Friday
6. until midnight

116.4

2. By the time I got to the station
3. By the time the police arrived
4. By the time the guards discovered
   what had happened
5. By the time I finished my work

UNIT 117

117.1

2. on Sundays
3. at night
4. in the evening
5. on July 21, 1969
6. at the same time
7. in the 1920s
8. in about 20 minutes
9. at the moment
10. in the Middle Ages
11. in 11 seconds

117.2

2. on   8. on   14. in
3. in   9. on   15. on; in
4. on   10. On; at   16. at
5. in   11. at   17. on
6. in   12. at; in   18. in
7. at   13. on; in

117.3

2. a   4. a   6. b   8. BOTH
3. b   5. BOTH   7. b   9. b

UNIT 118

118.1

2. on time   5. in time   8. in time
3. in time   6. on time   9. on time
4. on time   7. in time

118.2

2. at the end of the month
3. at the end of the course
4. at the end of the race
5. at the end of the interview

118.3

2. In the end she resigned.
3. In the end I gave up.
4. In the end we didn't go.

118.4

2. In   4. in   6. at   8. at
3. at; at   5. in   7. in   9. in

UNIT 119

119.1

2. at the traffic light
3. on the man's / his arm
4. a. on the door
   b. in the door
5. at the table
6. in Paris
7. a. at the front desk
   b. on the [front] desk
8. on the beach *or* at the beach

119.2

2. on my guitar
3. at the next gas station
4. in your coffee
5. on that tree
6. in the mountains
7. on the island
8. at the window

119.3

2. on; in   6. on   9. on
3. at   7. at   10. in
4. on   8. in   11. on
5. in

UNIT 120

120.1

2. On the second floor.
3. On the corner. *or* At the corner.
4. In the corner.
5. At the end of the line.
6. in a/the mirror
7. At the top of the stairs.
8. In the last row.
9. a. On the left.
   b. On the right.
10. On a farm.

120.2

2. in the front row
3. At the end of the street
4. on the west coast
5. in the back of the class
   or at the back of the class
6. on the back of this card

120.3

2. on *or* at   5. at   8. in
3. in   6. on   9. on
4. on; on   7. in; on   10. on

UNIT 121

121.1

2. on a train
3. at a conference
4. in the hospital
5. at the hairdresser['s]
6. on her bicycle
7. in New York
8. at the Ford Theater

121.2

2. in bed   6. in the hospital
3. in prison   7. at the airport
4. in school   8. on the plane
5. at the gym

121.3

2. at   6. at *or* in; in   10. in
3. on   7. in   11. at
4. in   8. at; at; in   12. in; at
5. at   9. at

UNIT 122

122.1

3. at   10. in; to; in
4. to   11. to
5. to   12. into
6. into *or* to   13. to
7. —; to   14. at
8. to; in   15. to
9. to

122.2

Sample answers:
2. I've been (I have been) to Thailand once.
3. I've never been (I have never been) to London.
4. I've been (I have been) to Mexico a few times.

122.3

2. in   4. at   6. —
3. —   5. to

122.4

2. got on the bus
3. I got out of my/the car.
4. I got off the train.
5. I got into/in the taxi.
6. I got off the plane.

UNIT 123

123.1

2. on strike   6. on purpose
3. on a tour   7. on a diet
4. on vacation   8. on business
5. on television   9. on the whole

123.2

2. in pencil   5. in the shade
3. in love   6. in my opinion
4. in capital letters   7. in cash

123.3

2. on   7. for   11. In; on   15. on
3. on   8. on   12. on   16. at
4. at   9. at   13. on   17. on
5. in   10. on   14. at   18. in
6. on

UNIT 124

124.1

2. by mistake   5. by satellite
3. by hand   6. by chance
4. by check

124.2

2. on   5. by; on   7. by
3. by   6. in   8. on
4. on

124.3

Sample answers:
3. "Yesterday" is a song by Paul McCartney.
4. *The Old Man and the Sea* is a novel by Ernest Hemingway.
5. *Guernica* is a painting by Pablo Picasso.

124.4

2. with   5. with   8. by
3. by   6. by; in   9. by; with; on
4. by   7. on   10. by

124.5

2. by 10 cents   4. by five minutes
3. by 2 votes

UNIT 125

125.1

2. to the problem
3. with her brother
4. in prices
5. to your question
6. for a new road
7. in the number of people without jobs

8. for shoes like these anymore
9. between your job and mine

125.2

2. invitation to
3. contact with
4. key to
5. cause of
6. reply to
7. connection between
8. photographs of
9. reason for
10. damage to

125.3

2. of   7. toward   11. to
3. to   8. with   12. for; in
4. for   9. in   13. to
5. of   10. for   14. with
6. in *or* to

UNIT 126

126.1

2. nice of
3. was generous of him
4. That's (That is) very kind of
5. That wasn't (was not) very polite of him.
6. That's (That is) a little childish of them.

126.2

2. kind to
3. sorry for
4. annoyed with
5. annoyed about
6. impressed with/by
7. bored with
8. astonished at/by

126.3

2. of   12. about; at
3. to; to   13. at/with; for
4. of   14. about
5. with   15. about
6. to   16. at/by
7. with   17. with/by
8. at/by   18. about
9. with   19. about
10. about   20. for
11. about

UNIT 127

127.1

2. of furniture
3. at tennis
4. of sports

5. to a Russian [man]
6. of time
7. from/than yours
8. of Robert

127.2

2. similar to
3. afraid of
4. interested in
5. responsible for
6. proud of
7. different from/than

127.3

2. for	8. of	13. of
3. of	9. with	14. of
4. of	10. of	15. to
5. in	11. of	16. on
6. to	12. in	17. of
7. of; of		

127.4

Sample sentences:
2. I'm hopeless at telling jokes.
3. I'm very good at mathematics.
4. I'm pretty good at remembering names.

UNIT 128

128.1

2. explain; to	6. throw; at
3. glanced at	7. throw; to
4. invited to	8. speaking to
5. listen to	9. point; at

128.2

2. at	5. to	8. to
3. at	6. to	9. at
4. to	7. at	10. at

128.3

3. this question to me
4. you explain the system to me
5. Can you explain to me how this machine works?
6. Can you explain to me what your problem is?

128.4

3. to	5. —	7. to
4. to	6. to	8. —

UNIT 129

129.1

2. for	6. about	10. for
3. for	7. —	11. about
4. to	8. about	12. for
5. for	9. —	

129.2

2. waiting for	6. do; about
3. talk about	7. taken care of
4. asked; for	8. left; for
5. applied for	

129.3

2. for	5. for	7. about
3. about	6. of	8. —
4. of		

129.4

2. looking for	5. look for
3. looked after	6. looks after
4. looking for	

UNIT 130

130.1

2. about
3. to; about
4. about
5. of
6. about; about; about; about
7. of
8. about
9. of *or* about

130.2

2. complaining about
3. think about
4. warn; about
5. heard of
6. dream of
7. reminded; about
8. remind; of

130.3

2. hear about	5. hear from
3. heard from	6. hear about
4. heard of	7. heard of

130.4

2. think about
3. think of
4. think of
5. thinking about *or* thinking of
6. think of
7. thinking about
8. thought about
9. think; of

UNIT 131

131.1

2. for the misunderstanding
3. on winning the tournament
4. from [his] enemies *or* against [his] enemies

5. of 11 players
6. on bread and eggs
7. for everything
8. for everything
9. for the economic crisis
10. violent crime on television
11. is to blame for the economic crisis
12. television is to blame for the increase in violent crime

131.2

2. paid for	5. live on
3. accused of	6. congratulated; on
4. depends on	7. apologize to

131.3

2. from	6. for	10. —
3. on	7. —	11. from
4. of	8. on	12. of
5. for	9. on	

UNIT 132

132.1

2. small towns to big cities
3. with all the information I needed
4. $60 on a pair of shoes

132.2

2. happened to	6. fill; with
3. drove into	7. Concentrate on
4. divided into	8. succeeded in
5. believe in	

132.3

2. to	11. into	
3. on	12. to	
4. in	13. into	
5. to	14. on	
6. in	15. from; into	
7. with	16. to; on	
8. into	17. into	
9. in	18. with	
10. on		

132.4

Sample answers:
2. on books
3. into a wall
4. to volleyball
5. into many languages

UNIT 133

133.1

2. show up	5. dropped out
3. moving in	6. dozed off
4. closed down	7. clears up

133.2

2. back at
3. out of
4. along with
5. up at
6. forward to
7. away with

133.3

2. cross it out
3. made it up

4. give them back
5. see her off
6. gave them away
7. show you around
8. turned it down

133.4

3. them up

4. off the television
   or the television off
5. him down
6. on a jacket *or* a jacket on
7. out your cigarette
   or your cigarette out
8. it out
9. up a word *or* a word up

Answer Key to Additional Exercises

1

3. 'm getting (am getting)
4. do you do
5. was the car going
6. calls; didn't call (did not call)
7. were thinking; decided
8. 's happening (is happening)
9. doesn't rain (does not rain)
10. rang; were having
11. went; was studying; didn't want (did not want); didn't stay (did not stay)
12. told; didn't believe (did not believe); thought; was joking

2

2. didn't go
3. is wearing
4. is being
5. wasn't reading
6. didn't have
7. is beginning
8. found
9. wasn't
10. you've been
11. I've been doing
12. did she go
13. I've been playing
14. do you come
15. since I saw her
16. for 20 years

3

3. are you going
4. Do you watch
5. have you lived *or* have you been living
6. Did you have
7. Have you seen
8. was she wearing
9. Have you been waiting/here
10. does it take
11. Have you finished *or* Are you finished
12. Have you [ever] been

4

2. 've known (have known) each other
3. I've ever had (I have ever had)
4. He left
5. I've worn (I have worn) it
6. [I was] playing
7. been/gone [swimming] for
8. since I've gone (I have gone) *or* since I've been (I have been)
9. did you buy/get

5

1. got; was already waiting; had arrived

2. was lying; wasn't watching (was not watching); 'd fallen (had fallen); was snoring; turned; woke
3. 'd just gone (had just gone); was reading; heard; got; didn't see (did not see); went
4. missed; was standing; realized; 'd left (had left); had; got
5. met; was walking; 'd been (had been); 'd been playing (had been playing) *or* 'd played (had played); were going; invited; 'd arranged (had arranged); didn't have (did not have)

6

2. Somebody has taken it.
3. They'd only known (They had only known) each other a few weeks.
4. It's been raining (It has been raining) all day. *or* It's rained (It has rained) all day.
5. I'd been dreaming (I had been dreaming).
6. I'd had (I had had) a big breakfast.
7. They've been going (They have been going) there for years.
8. I've had (I have had) it since I got up.
9. He's been training (He has been training) very hard for it.

7

1. I haven't seen (have not seen)
2. You look *or* You're looking (You are looking)
3. are you going
4. are you meeting
5. I'm going (I am going)
6. Do you often go
7. are you going
8. I'm meeting (I am meeting)
9. has been *or* was *or* is
10. I've been waiting (I have been waiting)
11. has just started *or* just started
12. 's she doing (is she doing)
13. Does she like
14. she thinks
15. Are you working
16. spoke
17. you were working
18. went

19. I started *or* I'd started (I had started)
20. I lost
21. you haven't had (you have not had)
22. I've had (I have had)
23. have you seen
24. has he been
25. I saw
26. he went
27. He'd been (He had been)
28. he decided
29. He was really looking forward
30. is he doing
31. I haven't heard (have not heard)
32. he left

8

1. invented
2. it's gone (it has gone) *or* it went
3. had gone
4. did you do; Did you go
5. have you had
6. it was raining
7. She's been teaching (She has been teaching)
8. I saw; was; I'd seen (I had seen); I remembered; he was
9. Have you heard; She was; died; She wrote; Have you read
10. does this word mean; I've never seen (I have never seen)
11. Did you get; it had already begun
12. knocked; was; he'd gone (he had gone); he didn't want (he did not want)
13. She'd never used (She had never used); she didn't know (did not know)
14. went; She needed; she'd been sitting (she had been sitting)

9

3. used to drive
4. was driving
5. were working
6. used to have
7. was taking
8. was playing
9. used to play
10. was wearing

10

2. I'm going to the dentist.
3. we're going to rent (we are going to rent) a car *or* we're renting (we are renting) a car
4. I'll take care (I will take care) of the children.

5. I'm going to have (I am going to have) lunch with Sue *or* I'm having (I am having) lunch with Sue
6. are you going to have
7. I'll turn on (I will turn on) the light.
8. I'm going to turn on (I am going to turn on) the light. *or* I'm turning on (I am turning on) the light.

11

2. I'll go (I will go)
3. shall/should we meet
4. begins
5. I'll meet (I will meet)
6. I'm seeing (I am seeing)
7. Shall/Should I ask
8. I'll see (I will see)
9. are going
10. does the movie begin
11. Are you meeting
12. I'll be (I will be)

12

1. (2) Are you going to take
   (3) it starts *or* it's starting (it is starting)
   (4) you'll enjoy (you will enjoy)
   (5) it'll be (it will be) *or* it's going to be (it is going to be)
2. (1) you're going (you are going) *or* you're going to go (you are going to go)
   (2) We're going (We are going) *or* We're going to go (We are going to go)
   (3) you have *or* you'll have (you will have)
   (4) I'll send (I will send)
   (5) I'll get (I will get)
   (6) I get
3. (1) I'm having (I am having) *or* I'm going to have (I am going to have)
   (2) are coming *or* will be coming
   (3) they'll have left (they will have left)
   (4) they're (they are)
   (5) I won't be
   (6) you know
   (7) I'll call (I will call)
4. (1) shall/should we meet *or* are we going to meet
   (2) I'll be waiting (I will be waiting)
   (3) you arrive
   (4) I'll be sitting (I will be sitting)
   (5) I'll be wearing (I will be wearing)
   (6) Is Agent 307 coming *or* Is Agent 307 going to come *or* Will Agent 307 be coming

   (7) Shall/Should I bring
   (8) I'll explain (I will explain)
   (9) I see
   (10) I'll try (I will try)

13

1. I'll have (I will have)
2. Are you going
3. It's going to land (It is going to land)
4. it's (it is)
5. I'll miss (I will miss) *or* I'm going to miss (I am going to miss); you go
6. does it end
7. I'm going (I am going) *or* I'm going to go (I am going to go); is getting
8. I'll tell (I will tell); I'm (I am); I won't be (I will not be)
9. I'm going to have (I am going to have) *or* I'm having (I am having)
10. she apologizes
11. we'll be living (we will be living)
12. you finish

14

3. He must have forgotten.
4. You shouldn't have left (should not have left) so early.
5. It can't be changed (cannot be changed) now.
6. She may be watching television.
7. She must have been waiting for somebody.
8. He couldn't have done (could not have done) it.
9. You should've been (should have been) here earlier.
10. I would've helped (would have helped) you.
11. You should've been warned (should have been warned).
12. He might not have been feeling very well. *or* He might not have felt very well.

15

3. could rain *or* might rain
4. might have gone *or* could've gone (could have gone)
5. couldn't go (could not go)
6. couldn't have seen (could not have seen)
7. should get
8. wouldn't recognize (would not recognize) *or* might not recognize
9. must have heard
10. should have turned

16

4. rings
5. were
6. 's (is)
7. were *or* was
8. had been
9. had
10. hadn't had (had not had)
11. 'd driven (had driven)
12. didn't read (did not read)

17

2. came to see us now
3. wouldn't have disturbed (would not have disturbed) you
4. you hadn't provoked (had not provoked) the dog, it wouldn't have attacked (would not have attacked) you
5. 'd be upset (would be upset); I told them what happened
6. wouldn't have gotten (would not have gotten) wet; I'd had (I had had) an umbrella
7. hadn't been (had not been) [so] nervous, he wouldn't have failed (would not have failed) [his driver's test]

18

Sample answers:
1. I wasn't (was not) / weren't (were not) feeling so tired
2. I hadn't had (had not had) so much to do
3. I would've forgotten (would have forgotten) Jessica's birthday
4. you hadn't taken (had not taken) so long to get ready
5. I would've gone (would have gone) to the concert
6. you were in trouble
7. there was/were no traffic
8. people would go out more

19

3. I knew
4. I'd taken (I had taken)
5. Ann were *or* Ann was
6. they'd hurry up (they would hurry up)
7. we didn't have (did not have)
8. we'd had (we had had)
9. it weren't (were not) *or* it wasn't (was not)
10. I could
11. I hadn't said (had not said)
12. you'd slow down (you would slow down)

13. we hadn't gone (had not gone)
14. you wouldn't go (would not go)

20

3. was canceled
4. has been repaired
5. is being restored
6. 's believed (is believed)
7. 'd be fired (would be fired)
8. might have been thrown
9. was taught
10. being arrested
11. Have you ever been arrested?
12. are reported; have been injured

21

3. sold
4. 's been sold (has been sold)
5. are made
6. might be stolen
7. must have been stolen
8. must have taken
9. can be solved
10. should have left
11. is delayed
12. is being built; is expected

22

1. Fire at City Hall
   (2) was discovered
   (3) was injured
   (4) be rescued
   (5) are believed to have been destroyed
   (6) is not known
2. Convenience Store Robbery
   (1) was forced
   (2) being threatened
   (3) had been stolen
   (4) was later found
   (5) had been abandoned
   (6) has been arrested
   (7) is still being questioned
3. Road Delays
   (1) is being resurfaced
   (2) are being asked *or* are asked *or* have been asked
   (3) is expected
   (4) will be closed
   (5) will be rerouted
4. Accident
   (1) was taken
      (2) was allowed
      (3) was blocked
      (4) be rerouted
      (5) have been killed

23

3. changing
4. to change
5. change
6. being
7. saying
8. to call
9. drinking
10. to be
11. to see
12. to be
13. living; to move
14. to be; playing
15. being stopped; stealing; driving
16. work; pressing

24

3. He tends to forget things.
4. Would you mind helping me?
5. Everybody seems to have gone out.
6. We're thinking (We are thinking) of moving.
7. I was afraid to touch it.
8. He's (He is) afraid of being robbed.
9. It's not (It is not) worth seeing.
10. I'm not used to (I am not used to) walking so far.
11. She seems to be enjoying herself.
12. He insisted on showing them to me.
13. I'd rather someone else did it.

25

3. reading newspapers
4. not go out tonight
5. walking
6. me to call you tonight
7. anyone/anybody seeing me *or* being seen
8. of being a liar
9. to seeing them again
10. to do
11. to have gone out with you
12. not taking your advice *or* not having taken your advice

26

2. —; a; a
3. —; —; the
4. —; —; —
5. an; —; the; —; —

6. an; the; —; an; the
7. the; the; The; —; the; the
8. The; a; —; The; —; —; —; —

27

2. If
3. when
4. if
5. when
6. if
7. if
8. unless
9. if
10. as long as
11. in case
12. in case
13. if
14. even if
15. Although
16. Although
17. When
18. when

28

2. on
3. at; on
4. on
5. on
6. at
7. In
8. at
9. during *or* in
10. on; since
11. for
12. at
13. at; until
14. by

29

2. by
3. at
4. on
5. on; in
6. to; at
7. on
8. on
9. to; to
10. in; at
11. in; on
12. to; in
13. on; by
14. at
15. on
16. in; on
17. on
18. in; by
19. On; by
20. on; on

30

2. at
3. to
4. to
5. in
6. with
7. of
8. to
9. of
10. at *or* by
11. of
12. about

31

2. after
3. —
4. about
5. to
6. —; for
7. into
8. of
9. to
10. on
11. of
12. of
13. at *or* about
14. on

Answer Key to Study Guide

Present and Past

1.1	A	1.4	B/C
1.2	B	1.5	C
1.3	C	1.6	A

Present Perfect and Past

2.1	B/C	2.8	D
2.2	C	2.9	A
2.3	A	2.10	A
2.4	C	2.11	A
2.5	A	2.12	C
2.6	B	2.13	B
2.7	A	2.14	C

Future

3.1	B	3.4	B
3.2	C	3.5	C
3.3	A/C	3.6	A

Modals

4.1	A/B	4.7	B
4.2	A/C	4.8	B
4.3	C	4.9	A
4.4	B	4.10	A
4.5	A/B/D	4.11	D
4.6	B		

Conditionals and *wish*

5.1	B	5.3	D
5.2	D	5.4	B

Passive

6.1	C	6.4	C
6.2	B	6.5	D
6.3	A		

Reported Speech

7.1	B	7.2	A

Questions and Auxiliary Verbs

8.1	C	8.4	A
8.2	A	8.5	B
8.3	D		

-ing and the Infinitive

9.1	C	9.10	B
9.2	B/D	9.11	C
9.3	B	9.12	D
9.4	A	9.13	B
9.5	A	9.14	A/B
9.6	A/C	9.15	A
9.7	D	9.16	A
9.8	C	9.17	B/C
9.9	C		

Articles and Nouns

10.1	B	10.8	C
10.2	B/C	10.9	C
10.3	B	10.10	B
10.4	C	10.11	A
10.5	A	10.12	C
10.6	A	10.13	B
10.7	A		

Pronouns and Determiners

11.1	A	11.7	A
11.2	B	11.8	C
11.3	B	11.9	D
11.4	B	11.10	A/C
11.5	B	11.11	B
11.6	C		

Relative Clauses

12.1	A/C	12.4	B
12.2	A/B	12.5	D
12.3	C	12.6	B

Adjectives and Adverbs

13.1	B	13.8	C
13.2	C	13.9	B/C
13.3	B/C	13.10	D
13.4	A	13.11	A/B
13.5	A/D	13.12	B
13.6	B	13.13	D
13.7	B/C	13.14	B

Conjunctions and Prepositions

14.1	A/C/D	14.5	B
14.2	D	14.6	C/D
14.3	A/B	14.7	B/C
14.4	A/C	14.8	A

Prepositions

15.1	B	15.10	C
15.2	A	15.11	C
15.3	C	15.12	A
15.4	B	15.13	C
15.5	A	15.14	B
15.6	B/D	15.15	D
15.7	B	15.16	D
15.8	B	15.17	A
15.9	C	15.18	B

Index

The numbers in the index are *unit* numbers, not page numbers.